# This book comes with access to more content online.

Quiz yourself with practice questions.

Register your book or ebook at
**www.dummies.com/go/getaccess.**

Select your product, and then follow the prompts to validate your purchase.

You'll receive an email with your PIN and instructions.

# PMP® Exam Prep

by Crystal J. Richards, PMP, PMI-ACP, CSM

**PMP® Exam Prep For Dummies®**

Published by: **John Wiley & Sons, Inc.**, 111 River Street, Hoboken, NJ 07030-5774, www.wiley.com

Copyright © 2025 by John Wiley & Sons, Inc. All rights reserved, including rights for text and data mining and training of artificial technologies or similar technologies.

Media and software compilation copyright © 2025 by John Wiley & Sons, Inc. All rights reserved, including rights for text and data mining and training of artificial technologies or similar technologies.

Published simultaneously in Canada

No part of this publication may be reproduced, stored in a retrieval system or transmitted in any form or by any means, electronic, mechanical, photocopying, recording, scanning or otherwise, except as permitted under Sections 107 or 108 of the 1976 United States Copyright Act, without the prior written permission of the Publisher. Requests to the Publisher for permission should be addressed to the Permissions Department, John Wiley & Sons, Inc., 111 River Street, Hoboken, NJ 07030, (201) 748-6011, fax (201) 748-6008, or online at http://www.wiley.com/go/permissions.

**Trademarks:** Wiley, For Dummies, the Dummies Man logo, Dummies.com, Making Everything Easier, and related trade dress are trademarks or registered trademarks of John Wiley & Sons, Inc. and may not be used without written permission. All other trademarks are the property of their respective owners. John Wiley & Sons, Inc. is not associated with any product or vendor mentioned in this book.

LIMIT OF LIABILITY/DISCLAIMER OF WARRANTY: THE PUBLISHER AND THE AUTHOR MAKE NO REPRESENTATIONS OR WARRANTIES WITH RESPECT TO THE ACCURACY OR COMPLETENESS OF THE CONTENTS OF THIS WORK AND SPECIFICALLY DISCLAIM ALL WARRANTIES, INCLUDING WITHOUT LIMITATION WARRANTIES OF FITNESS FOR A PARTICULAR PURPOSE. NO WARRANTY MAY BE CREATED OR EXTENDED BY SALES OR PROMOTIONAL MATERIALS. THE ADVICE AND STRATEGIES CONTAINED HEREIN MAY NOT BE SUITABLE FOR EVERY SITUATION. THIS WORK IS SOLD WITH THE UNDERSTANDING THAT THE PUBLISHER IS NOT ENGAGED IN RENDERING LEGAL, ACCOUNTING, OR OTHER PROFESSIONAL SERVICES. IF PROFESSIONAL ASSISTANCE IS REQUIRED, THE SERVICES OF A COMPETENT PROFESSIONAL PERSON SHOULD BE SOUGHT. NEITHER THE PUBLISHER NOR THE AUTHOR SHALL BE LIABLE FOR DAMAGES ARISING HEREFROM. THE FACT THAT AN ORGANIZATION OR WEBSITE IS REFERRED TO IN THIS WORK AS A CITATION AND/OR A POTENTIAL SOURCE OF FURTHER INFORMATION DOES NOT MEAN THAT THE AUTHOR OR THE PUBLISHER ENDORSES THE INFORMATION THE ORGANIZATION OR WEBSITE MAY PROVIDE OR RECOMMENDATIONS IT MAY MAKE. FURTHER, READERS SHOULD BE AWARE THAT INTERNET WEBSITES LISTED IN THIS WORK MAY HAVE CHANGED OR DISAPPEARED BETWEEN WHEN THIS WORK WAS WRITTEN AND WHEN IT IS READ.

For general information on our other products and services, please contact our Customer Care Department within the U.S. at 877-762-2974, outside the U.S. at 317-572-3993, or fax 317-572-4002. For technical support, please visit https://hub.wiley.com/community/support/dummies.

Wiley publishes in a variety of print and electronic formats and by print-on-demand. Some material included with standard print versions of this book may not be included in e-books or in print-on-demand. If this book refers to media that is not included in the version you purchased, you may download this material at http://booksupport.wiley.com. For more information about Wiley products, visit www.wiley.com.

Library of Congress Control Number is available from the publisher.

ISBN 978-1-394-30049-5 (pbk); ISBN 978-1-394-30051-8 (ebk); ISBN 978-1-394-30050-1 (ebk)

# Contents at a Glance

Introduction ................................................................. 1

## Part 1: Starting Your PMP Journey .......................... 5
- CHAPTER 1: Welcome to Your PMP Certification Journey ...................... 7
- CHAPTER 2: Get Ready For the PMP Exam! ................................. 15
- CHAPTER 3: Getting into the Right PMI Mindset ........................... 29
- CHAPTER 4: Maintaining Your PMP Credential ............................. 33
- CHAPTER 5: Taking a Pre-Assessment ..................................... 41

## Part 2: What Is Project Management Really? .............. 51
- CHAPTER 6: An Overview of Projects ..................................... 53
- CHAPTER 7: Project Management Key Concepts ............................ 59

## Part 3: The Environment in Which Projects Operate ....... 85
- CHAPTER 8: Project, Program, Portfolio, and Operations Management ...... 87
- CHAPTER 9: Organizational Influences ................................... 97
- CHAPTER 10: Roles and Functions That Drive Project Delivery ........... 103

## Part 4: Managing Your Projects from Conception to Completion .................................... 111
- CHAPTER 11: Project Success Starts with the Team ...................... 113
- CHAPTER 12: Initiating Your Project ................................... 149
- CHAPTER 13: Planning Your Project Roadmap ............................. 171
- CHAPTER 14: Elevating Your Project Roadmap ............................ 207
- CHAPTER 15: Integration of Plans and Processes ........................ 245
- CHAPTER 16: Turning Your Plan into Action ............................. 259
- CHAPTER 17: Keeping Your Project on Track ............................. 287
- CHAPTER 18: Closing the Project or Phase .............................. 317

## Part 5: Agile and Hybrid Approaches ..................... 337
- CHAPTER 19: The Fundamentals of Agile Project Management .............. 339
- CHAPTER 20: Agile Teams: Key Roles and Responsibilities ............... 353
- CHAPTER 21: Key Agile Practices ....................................... 359

## Part 6: The Part of Tens ................................ 371
- CHAPTER 22: Ten Tips for PMP Exam Success ............................. 373
- CHAPTER 23: More Than Ten Common Acronyms ............................. 379
- CHAPTER 24: Ten Assumptions of the PMP Exam ........................... 381

Index ..................................................................... 387

# Table of Contents

**INTRODUCTION** .................................................... 1
    About This Book. ............................................... 2
    Foolish Assumptions. ........................................... 2
    Icons Used in This Book ........................................ 3
    Beyond the Book. .............................................. 3
    Where to Go from Here ........................................ 4

**PART 1: STARTING YOUR PMP JOURNEY** .................... 5

**CHAPTER 1: Welcome to Your PMP Certification Journey** ........ 7
    PMP: Recognizing the Global Standard ........................... 7
    Introducing the Project Management Institute. ................... 8
    Professional Skill Sets: Excelling with the PMI Talent Triangle ........ 9
        Power Skills. ............................................... 9
        Ways of Working ......................................... 10
        Business Acumen ........................................ 10
    Exploring Process Groups, Knowledge Areas,
    and Project Management Processes ............................ 11
        Taking a granular look: 49 project management processes ...... 11
        Looking at Process Groups from start to finish ................ 12
        Gaining specialization through Knowledge Areas .............. 13

**CHAPTER 2: Get Ready For the PMP Exam!** ....................... 15
    Do You Have What It Takes? .................................... 16
        Meeting education level and project management
        experience requirements. .................................. 16
        Obtaining 35 contact hours of PM education .................. 17
        Demonstrating professional competence. ..................... 17
        Meeting industry demand ................................. 17
        Strengthening the profession .............................. 17
    License and Registration, Please. ............................... 18
        Contact hours of project management education .............. 19
        Application submission and payment, pretty please. ........... 21
    Getting Familiar with PMP Exam Domains ....................... 21
        People (42 percent of the exam): Leading and building teams ... 22
        Process (50 percent of the exam): Seeing a project
        through to completion .................................... 22
        Business Environment (8 percent of the exam):
        Ensuring compliance and delivering value ................... 22
        Some Guidance on the *PMBOK Guide*. ....................... 23

Getting Ready for the PMP Examination: The Basics . . . . . . . . . . . . . . . 24
  The fee . . . . . . . . . . . . . . . . . . . . . . . . . . . . . . . . . . . . . . . . . . . . . . . . . . . 24
  Questions, time, and breaks . . . . . . . . . . . . . . . . . . . . . . . . . . . . . . . . 24
  Results and diagnostic information . . . . . . . . . . . . . . . . . . . . . . . . . . 25
  The mysterious passing score . . . . . . . . . . . . . . . . . . . . . . . . . . . . . . 25
  Preparation: Boot camp or self-paced course? . . . . . . . . . . . . . . . . . 25
  Practice exams, practice exams, practice exams . . . . . . . . . . . . . . . 26
  Where to take the exam: On a warm couch or in a
  cold testing center? . . . . . . . . . . . . . . . . . . . . . . . . . . . . . . . . . . . . . . . . 27

**CHAPTER 3: Getting into the Right PMI Mindset** . . . . . . . . . . . . . . . . . . . 29
  Discovering the Dos and Don'ts . . . . . . . . . . . . . . . . . . . . . . . . . . . . . . . . . 30
  Spotting the Scenario . . . . . . . . . . . . . . . . . . . . . . . . . . . . . . . . . . . . . . . . . 31
  Understanding the ABCs of PMI . . . . . . . . . . . . . . . . . . . . . . . . . . . . . . . . 32

**CHAPTER 4: Maintaining Your PMP Credential** . . . . . . . . . . . . . . . . . . . . 33
  Keeping Your PMP Credential Once You've Earned It . . . . . . . . . . . . . . 34
  Getting Those PDUs . . . . . . . . . . . . . . . . . . . . . . . . . . . . . . . . . . . . . . . . . . 35
    Meeting the Education requirement . . . . . . . . . . . . . . . . . . . . . . . . . 35
    Meeting the Giving Back minimum . . . . . . . . . . . . . . . . . . . . . . . . . . 36
    Paying the renewal fee . . . . . . . . . . . . . . . . . . . . . . . . . . . . . . . . . . . . 37
  Earning (and Keeping) Your Credentials . . . . . . . . . . . . . . . . . . . . . . . . . 37
    Executing a winning plan . . . . . . . . . . . . . . . . . . . . . . . . . . . . . . . . . . 37
    Having no plan . . . . . . . . . . . . . . . . . . . . . . . . . . . . . . . . . . . . . . . . . . . 38
  Taking Action If Your Certification Cycle Lapses . . . . . . . . . . . . . . . . . . . 39

**CHAPTER 5: Taking a Pre-Assessment** . . . . . . . . . . . . . . . . . . . . . . . . . . . . . 41
  Questions . . . . . . . . . . . . . . . . . . . . . . . . . . . . . . . . . . . . . . . . . . . . . . . . . . . 41
  Answer Key . . . . . . . . . . . . . . . . . . . . . . . . . . . . . . . . . . . . . . . . . . . . . . . . . 47
  How Did You Do? . . . . . . . . . . . . . . . . . . . . . . . . . . . . . . . . . . . . . . . . . . . . 49

## PART 2: WHAT IS PROJECT MANAGEMENT REALLY? . . . . . . 51

**CHAPTER 6: An Overview of Projects** . . . . . . . . . . . . . . . . . . . . . . . . . . . . . . 53
  What Are Projects? . . . . . . . . . . . . . . . . . . . . . . . . . . . . . . . . . . . . . . . . . . . 54
  Why Do We Have Projects? . . . . . . . . . . . . . . . . . . . . . . . . . . . . . . . . . . . . 55
    Driving change . . . . . . . . . . . . . . . . . . . . . . . . . . . . . . . . . . . . . . . . . . . 55
    Optimizing business value creation . . . . . . . . . . . . . . . . . . . . . . . . . 55
    Complying with regulations and requirements . . . . . . . . . . . . . . . 55
    Ensuring stakeholder satisfaction . . . . . . . . . . . . . . . . . . . . . . . . . . . 56
    Making product, process, or service improvements . . . . . . . . . . . 56
    Initiating strategic changes . . . . . . . . . . . . . . . . . . . . . . . . . . . . . . . . 56
  Where Do Projects Happen? . . . . . . . . . . . . . . . . . . . . . . . . . . . . . . . . . . . 56

**CHAPTER 7: Project Management Key Concepts** .................. 59
    Defining Project Management ................................... 60
        Exploring the continuum of project management ............. 60
        Using the predictive approach: You know, you know .......... 61
        Taking the adaptive approach: You don't know
        what you don't know ........................................ 61
        Adopting the hybrid approach: A little bit of this, a little bit
        of that .................................................... 62
        Defining terms: Exploring methodology, development
        approach, and project life cycle ............................. 62
    Finding a Reason for the Project Management Season ............. 63
    Shifting from Outputs to Outcomes .............................. 65
        Taking a systems view of value .............................. 66
        Creating value through projects ............................. 66
        Focusing on the organization's view of value delivery .......... 67
        Unpacking organizational structure and its impact
        on project value delivery ................................... 68
    Center of the Universe: The Project Manager ..................... 70
        Uncovering the many responsibilities of a project manager ..... 70
        Project manager by many names ............................ 71
        Applying project management principles ..................... 72
    Comparing Different PMs: Product Management versus
    Project Management ........................................... 74
        Progressing through a product life cycle ..................... 75
        Defining roles: Product manager versus project manager ...... 76
        Breaking down the work: Projects, products, and programs ..... 77
        Dividing a project into phases ............................... 79
    Exploring Additional Foundational Concepts ...................... 81
        Applying progressive elaboration ............................ 81
        Rolling with rolling wave planning ........................... 82
        Meeting the project needs through tailoring .................. 83

## PART 3: THE ENVIRONMENT IN WHICH PROJECTS OPERATE ............... 85

**CHAPTER 8: Project, Program, Portfolio, and Operations Management** ............................. 87
    Organizing the Way You Manage Projects ........................ 88
        Projects ................................................... 89
        Programs .................................................. 89
        Portfolios .................................................. 90
    Looking at Operations Management ............................. 90
    Defining the Role of Organizational and Project Governance ....... 91
        Organizational governance .................................. 91
        Project governance ......................................... 92

        Creating a Project Management Office .......................92
        Test Your Knowledge: Supportive, Controlling, and
        Directive PMOs ..........................................93
        Deciding How Much Governance Is Needed....................94
            Example 1: Small, internal IT upgrade project...............94
            Example 2: Implementation of a new EHR system in the NICU ...95
            Example 3: Hospital-wide expansion of telemedicine services ...95
        Answer Key: Supportive, Controlling, and Directive PMOs .........95

**CHAPTER 9: Organizational Influences** ........................... 97
        OPAs: Knowing Your Internal Policies and Procedures ...........98
        EEFs: Gaining Awareness of the Environment ..................99
        Test Your Knowledge: OPA or EEF...........................100
        Answer Key: OPA or EEF..................................101

**CHAPTER 10: Roles and Functions That Drive Project Delivery** ................................. 103
        The Project Manager.....................................104
        The Sponsor............................................104
        The Product Owner......................................105
        The Customer and End User ..............................105
        The Project Team........................................106
            Project management team ............................107
            SMEs ............................................108
            Business partners ..................................108
            Functional and operations managers....................108
        The Program Manager ...................................108
        The Portfolio Manager ...................................109
        Stakeholders and Key Stakeholders.........................109

## PART 4: MANAGING YOUR PROJECTS FROM CONCEPTION TO COMPLETION ........................ 111

**CHAPTER 11: Project Success Starts with the Team**............... 113
        Determining Resource Needs to Meet Project Needs ............114
        Planning for the People, the Equipment, and the Tools (Oh My!) ...115
            Human resource planning.............................116
            Physical resource planning ...........................116
        Estimating Resource Requirements.........................117
        Acquiring Resources.....................................117
        Gaining Project Success through Teamwork...................121
            Looking at team roles and responsibilities ................121
            Comparing management to leadership..................122
            Establishing team norms .............................124
            Grasping decision-making dynamics ....................125

Addressing gaps and encouraging professional
development ............................................125
Exercise: Mad Libs for a challenging project ..................126
Working with diverse and global teams......................127
Fostering team development and culture ....................128
Outlining the stages of team development:
The Tuckman Ladder .....................................129
Exercise: Tuckman Ladder stages of team development .......130
Creating motivation for high-performing teams...............132
Using recognition and rewards .............................133
Applying motivational theories .............................134
Developing Interpersonal Skills....................................136
Critical thinking .........................................136
Motivation...............................................137
Emotional intelligence....................................137
Influencing .............................................137
Conflict management .....................................137
Active listening..........................................138
Negotiating..............................................138
Team building ...........................................138
Coaching................................................138
Cultural awareness .......................................139
Political awareness .......................................139
When conflict occurs......................................140
Exercise: Conflict management scenarios ....................143
Understanding Teams in the Adaptive Environment................143
Adapting Your Leadership Style .................................145
Outlining the characteristics of strong leaderaship ............145
Determining the right leadership approach .................146
Achieving a High-Performing Team: The Ultimate Goal ..........147
Answer Keys..................................................147

CHAPTER 12: **Initiating Your Project** .................................149
Setting the Stage: The Five Process Groups .....................150
Starting with Business Value ..................................150
The Role of the Business Case: Telling the Project's Origin Story....151
Evaluating and Realizing Benefits...............................152
Prioritizing Projects for Strategic Impact .......................153
Test Your Knowledge: Benefit Measurement Methods............154
The Project Charter: Creating a High-Level Blueprint for Success ...155
The Human Element: Analyzing and Engaging Stakeholders .......156
Identifying stakeholders: Casting a wide net..................157
Understanding stakeholders: Decoding motivations
and expectations.........................................158
Analyzing stakeholders: Mapping influence and interest .......158

        Prioritizing stakeholders: Knowing who matters most . . . . . . . . .161
        Engaging stakeholders: Building meaningful connections . . . . . .162
        Monitoring stakeholder engagement: Keeping a
        finger on the pulse . . . . . . . . . . . . . . . . . . . . . . . . . . . . . . . . . . . .164
    Test Your Knowledge: Mapping Stakeholder Engagement . . . . . . . . .165
    Using Project Charters and Engaging Stakeholders in
    Adaptive Projects. . . . . . . . . . . . . . . . . . . . . . . . . . . . . . . . . . . . . . . . .166
        Adaptive charters: Less concrete, more directional. . . . . . . . . . . .166
        Using dynamic tools and techniques to engage
        dynamic stakeholders. . . . . . . . . . . . . . . . . . . . . . . . . . . . . . . . . .167
    Answer Keys . . . . . . . . . . . . . . . . . . . . . . . . . . . . . . . . . . . . . . . . . . . . .168

## CHAPTER 13: Planning Your Project Roadmap . . . . . . . . . . . . . . . . . . . . .171

    Getting Familiar with the Planning Process Group. . . . . . . . . . . . . . .172
    Develop Project Management Plan . . . . . . . . . . . . . . . . . . . . . . . . . .174
        Differentiating between predictive and adaptive projects . . . . . .176
        Triple constraints planning: scope, schedule, and cost . . . . . . . . .176
    Plan Scope Management . . . . . . . . . . . . . . . . . . . . . . . . . . . . . . . . . .177
        Understanding project scope and product scope . . . . . . . . . . . .177
        Planning the scope of work . . . . . . . . . . . . . . . . . . . . . . . . . . . . . .178
        Collecting requirements . . . . . . . . . . . . . . . . . . . . . . . . . . . . . . . . .179
        Defining scope . . . . . . . . . . . . . . . . . . . . . . . . . . . . . . . . . . . . . . . .182
        Creating a work breakdown structure . . . . . . . . . . . . . . . . . . . . . .183
        Managing scope in the adaptive environment . . . . . . . . . . . . . . .185
        Staying within the boundaries of scope . . . . . . . . . . . . . . . . . . . .187
    Plan Schedule Management . . . . . . . . . . . . . . . . . . . . . . . . . . . . . . .188
        Developing the Schedule Management Plan. . . . . . . . . . . . . . . . .188
        Defining activities . . . . . . . . . . . . . . . . . . . . . . . . . . . . . . . . . . . . .189
        Identifying activity dependencies . . . . . . . . . . . . . . . . . . . . . . . . .190
        Determining the sequence of activities . . . . . . . . . . . . . . . . . . . .191
        Accounting for leads and lags . . . . . . . . . . . . . . . . . . . . . . . . . . . .192
        Estimating activity durations . . . . . . . . . . . . . . . . . . . . . . . . . . . . .193
        Conducting reserve analysis . . . . . . . . . . . . . . . . . . . . . . . . . . . . .195
    Develop Schedule . . . . . . . . . . . . . . . . . . . . . . . . . . . . . . . . . . . . . . . .196
        Schedule network analysis. . . . . . . . . . . . . . . . . . . . . . . . . . . . . . .196
        Using the critical path method . . . . . . . . . . . . . . . . . . . . . . . . . . .196
        Addressing resource overallocation: Resource
        optimization techniques. . . . . . . . . . . . . . . . . . . . . . . . . . . . . . . . .198
        Reducing the timeline: Schedule compression techniques. . . . . .199
        Evaluating the alternatives: What-if scenario analysis . . . . . . . . .199
        Looking at the probability: Simulations . . . . . . . . . . . . . . . . . . . . .200
        Using a project management information system. . . . . . . . . . . .200
        Managing a schedule in the adaptive environment. . . . . . . . . . .201

Plan Cost Management . . . . . . . . . . . . . . . . . . . . . . . . . . . . . . . . . . . .202
    Estimating costs. . . . . . . . . . . . . . . . . . . . . . . . . . . . . . . . . . . . . . . .202
    Using a guesstimate range. . . . . . . . . . . . . . . . . . . . . . . . . . . . . . . .203
    Estimating costs with familiar tools and techniques . . . . . . . . . .204
    Determining the budget. . . . . . . . . . . . . . . . . . . . . . . . . . . . . . . . . .204
    Managing costs in adaptive projects . . . . . . . . . . . . . . . . . . . . . . .205

## CHAPTER 14: Elevating Your Project Roadmap . . . . . . . . . . . . . . . . . . .207

Planning Process Group. . . . . . . . . . . . . . . . . . . . . . . . . . . . . . . . . . . .208
Plan Quality Management . . . . . . . . . . . . . . . . . . . . . . . . . . . . . . . . . .209
    Examining the three processes of quality management. . . . . . .210
    Looking at the Quality Management Plan . . . . . . . . . . . . . . . . . .211
    Applying quality management in adaptive projects. . . . . . . . . . .215
Plan Communications Management . . . . . . . . . . . . . . . . . . . . . . . . .215
    Communications tools and techniques . . . . . . . . . . . . . . . . . . . .216
    Communication models. . . . . . . . . . . . . . . . . . . . . . . . . . . . . . . . .218
    Communication methods. . . . . . . . . . . . . . . . . . . . . . . . . . . . . . . .219
    Creating the Communications Management Plan . . . . . . . . . . . .220
    Communication matrix: A supplement to the
    Communications Management Plan . . . . . . . . . . . . . . . . . . . . . . .220
    Additional communication concepts . . . . . . . . . . . . . . . . . . . . . .221
    Managing communications in adaptive projects . . . . . . . . . . . . .223
    Agile ceremonies: Fostering transparency, accountability,
    and decision-making. . . . . . . . . . . . . . . . . . . . . . . . . . . . . . . . . . .224
Planning for Risks . . . . . . . . . . . . . . . . . . . . . . . . . . . . . . . . . . . . . . . . .225
    Ensuring robust risk planning happens. . . . . . . . . . . . . . . . . . . . .225
    Performing qualitative risk analysis . . . . . . . . . . . . . . . . . . . . . . .228
    Performing quantitative risk analysis. . . . . . . . . . . . . . . . . . . . . .230
    Planning risk responses . . . . . . . . . . . . . . . . . . . . . . . . . . . . . . . .232
    Applying risk management in adaptive projects. . . . . . . . . . . . . .234
Plan Procurement Management. . . . . . . . . . . . . . . . . . . . . . . . . . . . .234
    Mastering the plan procurement management process. . . . . . .234
    Understanding procurement essential terms. . . . . . . . . . . . . . . .235
    Deciding to make or buy . . . . . . . . . . . . . . . . . . . . . . . . . . . . . . . .235
    Creating a Procurement Management Plan . . . . . . . . . . . . . . . . .236
    Getting ready to procure . . . . . . . . . . . . . . . . . . . . . . . . . . . . . . .236
    Interpreting contract types . . . . . . . . . . . . . . . . . . . . . . . . . . . . .238
    Ensuring procurement integration. . . . . . . . . . . . . . . . . . . . . . . .240
    Looking at procurement management in adaptive projects . . . .241
Addressing the People Factor in Planning. . . . . . . . . . . . . . . . . . . . .242
    Planning for the project resource needs . . . . . . . . . . . . . . . . . . .242
    Aligning stakeholder expectations . . . . . . . . . . . . . . . . . . . . . . . .243

**CHAPTER 15: Integration of Plans and Processes**................245
- Planning: The Final Steps............................246
- Integrating Project Management Activities..................246
- The Project Manager: The Expert Project Integrator............247
- Changes are Possible: Creating a Change Control Plan..........248
- Maintaining Control with the Configuration Management Plan....249
  - Comparing change control and configuration management....249
  - Test your knowledge: Change Control or Configuration Management?........................250
- Developing a Comprehensive Project Management Plan.........250
  - Approving the Project Management Plan.................253
  - Using project documents to stay on track...............253
- Developing an Agile Project Management Plan...............256
  - Iteration planning.................................256
  - Addressing Agile project changes.....................257
- Answer Key: Change Control or Configuration Management?......258

**CHAPTER 16: Turning Your Plan into Action**....................259
- Executing Process Group..............................260
- Directing and Managing Project Work.....................261
  - Tracking and resolving issues.......................261
  - Implementing approved changes......................263
  - Generating work performance insights.................263
- Managing Project Knowledge...........................264
  - Differentiating levels of knowledge..................264
  - Differentiating between explicit and tacit knowledge..........265
  - Using knowledge-sharing tools and techniques............266
  - Managing project artifacts..........................267
- Managing Quality....................................269
- Managing Risks.....................................270
  - Quantifying risks.................................272
  - Additional risk management considerations..............273
  - Managing risks in the adaptive environment.............274
- Managing Procurements and Vendor Relationships.............275
  - Selecting the vendor..............................275
  - Integrating the vendor.............................277
- Managing People Performance and Expectations..............278
- Project Execution in the Adaptive Environment..............279
  - Visualizing the flow of work through kanban boards.........282
  - Tracking progress with burn charts....................282
  - Assessing team capacity with velocity charts.............283
  - Identifying bottlenecks with cumulative flow diagrams.......284
  - Decision-making in Agile teams......................285

## CHAPTER 17: Keeping Your Project on Track ... 287

- Getting Familiar with the Monitoring and Controlling Process Group ... 288
- Monitor and Control Project Work ... 289
- Perform Integrated Change Control ... 289
  - Detailing the different types of change requests ... 291
  - Outlining the workflow of the change control process ... 292
  - Keeping key project documents current and consistent ... 292
- Validate Scope ... 294
- Control Scope ... 294
- Control Schedule ... 295
- Control Costs ... 296
  - Assessing project performance: Earned value management ... 297
  - Forecasting overall project financial health ... 300
- Test Your Knowledge: What's the Situation at Week 7? ... 302
- Control Quality ... 303
- Control Resources ... 307
- Monitor Communications ... 307
- Monitor Risks ... 308
- Control Procurements ... 310
  - Types of contract changes ... 310
  - Closing procurements ... 311
- Monitor Stakeholder Engagement ... 312
- Monitoring and Controlling in the Adaptive Environment ... 313
- Answer Key: What's the Situation at Week 7? ... 315

## CHAPTER 18: Closing the Project or Phase ... 317

- The Closing Process Group ... 318
- Uncovering Why Projects End ... 318
  - Realizing the project's objectives have been achieved ... 319
  - Seeing that the objectives will not or cannot be met ... 319
  - Cutting the project funds ... 319
  - Discovering that the project is not needed ... 319
  - Identifying that the human or physical resources are no longer available ... 319
  - Terminating the project for legal cause or convenience ... 320
- Addressing Project Closure: Close Project or Phase Process ... 320
  - Tackling essential tasks for smooth project closure ... 321
  - Supporting project closure efforts with project artifacts ... 323
  - Supporting project closure with key meetings ... 323
  - Bringing projects to a close in the Agile environment ... 324
- Reflecting on Project Achievements: Documenting the Journey ... 325
- Capturing Insights: Lessons Learned ... 326
- Referencing the Business Case and Benefits Management Plan ... 327

Test Your Knowledge: Closing the Project ................... 328
Sustaining Project Outcomes .............................. 329
    Applying change management as a strategy ............ 329
    Using change management frameworks ................ 330
    Applying change management models .................. 333
Delivering Value ........................................... 334
Answer Key: Closing the Project ............................ 335

## PART 5: AGILE AND HYBRID APPROACHES ............ 337

### CHAPTER 19: The Fundamentals of Agile Project Management ........................................ 339

Realizing that History Matters ............................. 340
Examining the Values and Principles of the Agile Manifesto ....... 341
    The four values ....................................... 342
    The Twelve Principles ................................ 342
    Exercise: Agile Manifesto principles scenario matching ..... 344
Delivering Value: The Agile Development Life Cycle ............ 345
Implementing Common Agile Frameworks ..................... 347
    Scrum framework ..................................... 348
    Extreme Programming ................................ 348
    Kanban Method ....................................... 349
    But wait, there's more: Additional Agile methods ......... 349
    Deciding which framework to use ....................... 350
Comparing the Triangle of Constraints in Predictive
and Agile Projects ........................................ 350
Answer Key: Agile Manifesto Principles ..................... 351

### CHAPTER 20: Agile Teams: Key Roles and Responsibilities ....... 353

Getting an Overview of Agile Teams ......................... 354
Building Better Products with Cross-Functional Team Members ... 355
Representing the Voice of the Customer: Product Owner ........ 356
Using Skilled Facilitation via the Team Facilitator ............. 356
Focusing on Servant Leadership ............................ 357
Benefitting from an Agile Coach ............................ 358

### CHAPTER 21: Key Agile Practices .............................. 359

Facilitating Agile Ceremonies .............................. 360
    Planning dynamically: Iteration planning ................ 360
    Gathering the team for insight: The daily stand-up ........ 361
    Engaging the stakeholders: Iteration review ............. 361
    Reflecting on the outcomes: Iteration retrospective ....... 362
    Refining the backlog: An unofficial Agile event ........... 362

    Using Agile Artifacts .................................................363
        Envisioning the Agile journey: The product roadmap .........363
        Maintaining a master list of requirements: The
        product backlog..............................................364
        Planning the team's list of to-dos: The iteration backlog.......366
        Bringing the vision to life: The product increment............366
        Gaining a competitive advantage with an MVP...............367
    Exercise: Convert Scenarios into User Stories.....................368
    Answer Key: Convert Scenarios into User Stories..................369

## PART 6: THE PART OF TENS .....................................371

### CHAPTER 22: Ten Tips for PMP Exam Success .....................373
    Pick an Exam Date..........................................373
    Familiarize Yourself with the Exam Content Outline ..............374
    Create a Study Plan..........................................374
    Take Practice Exams .........................................374
    Adopt Good Study Habits......................................375
    Take Good Notes...........................................375
    Find the Right Testing Environment ............................376
    Stay Healthy and Focused ....................................376
    Stay Motivated with a Study Buddy or Study Groups .............377
    Plan for PMP Success ........................................377

### CHAPTER 23: More Than Ten Common Acronyms..................379

### CHAPTER 24: Ten Assumptions of the PMP Exam ................381
    Organizational Structure .....................................382
    Best Practices..............................................382
    Proactive Project Managers....................................382
    Conflict Resolution .........................................383
    Procurement .............................................383
    Organizational Context.......................................383
    Historical Information.......................................384
    Absolute Statements.........................................384
    Change Control ............................................384
    Agile Environment..........................................385

## INDEX ........................................................387

# Introduction

*If you're always trying to be normal, you will never know how amazing you can be.*

—MAYA ANGELOU

Hi there! I'm Crystal Richards and *I am a misfit project manager*. (Misfit, noun: a person who is different from other people and who does not seem to belong in a particular group or situation.)

In my professional career, I noticed that I was a bit of an oddball. My background is not in traditional IT project management, fancy software development projects, or construction project management. I worked in healthcare, improving patient flow, patient registration processes, and employee training efforts.

I often felt underrepresented and overlooked with some of these textbooks and exam prep materials that talked endlessly about IT and construction project management when my world revolved around leading business process improvement projects. The current library of project management resources were hard to follow and, quite frankly, downright boring to read. This realization that my voice was missing inspired me to embark on a journey to write a book that would bridge the gap and provide a different perspective — a perspective that is long overdue. That's why I wrote this book.

I know, I know. There are countless project management books, training materials, and exam preparation guides out there in these project management streets. However, it became apparent to me that there was something missing — an authentic voice that resonated with my unique experiences and perspectives. And I imagine you feel the same way.

Misfit project managers unite!

This book speaks to the unique project managers like you and me, learning in a way that speaks in a common-sense, practical, break-it-down approach. By sharing my insights, experiences, and knowledge, I hope to contribute to a more comprehensive and inclusive body of project management literature.

# About This Book

I think this book rocks, but I'm biased. My goal is that this book becomes your essential guide to set you up for success on the Project Management Professional (PMP) Exam and beyond. I provide a comprehensive yet accessible deep-dive into the principles and best practices of project management, combined with actionable tips and strategies that are designed to prepare you for the rigors of the PMP Exam and for managing real-world projects. I use my real-world experience to teach you the foundations of project management and Agile project management. I show you how to bring all these concepts together, and I explain how they align to the Project Management Institute's (PMI) Exam Content Outline (ECO) and PMI Talent Triangle. This book includes

- » Concrete examples to solidify concepts
- » Stories and examples from healthcare, home renovation projects, and web development to add clarity and interest.
- » A dash of humor. After all, managing projects can be stressful, so why not find humor along the way?

If you're an aspiring project management professional preparing for your PMP Exam, or an experienced professional seeking to sharpen your skills with the current best practice strategies, this book is designed to be your go-to resource. Not only does it prepare you for the exam, but it also equips you with the necessary tools to thrive in the project management world.

# Foolish Assumptions

Were you an accidental project manager? I was! But what makes you and me super cool is that we are unique within our organizations given our talents and penchant for project management. Here are some assumptions about why you probably picked up this book:

- » Maybe you're the only project manager or PM-thinking person in your organization.
- » You're dabbling in project management in pursuit of career growth or a career change.
- » You're tired of "Googling" your way to an answer for your projects and you just wish you had a resource that didn't make you feel like you were incompetent.

Sound familiar? That's why I wrote this book. With your three-plus years of project management experience (depending on your educational level and a requirement of the exam, which is covered in Chapter 2), and your desire to ace this lengthy examination, you want a resource that will say it plainly. I get you.

## Icons Used in This Book

Throughout this book, I use icons in the left margin that call attention to important information that's particularly worth noting:

This icon indicates an important tip for the PMP Exam. Think of this information as the "so what" while reading a particular section or topic.

This icon serves as a reminder of an important concept that you should commit to memory.

Danger, Will Robinson! This icon highlights pitfalls you may encounter as you prep for the PMP Exam.

## Beyond the Book

In addition to what you're reading right now, this book comes with a free access-anywhere Cheat Sheet that includes tips and advice to help you prepare for the PMP Exam. To get this Cheat Sheet, simply go to www.dummies.com and type **PMP Exam Prep For Dummies Cheat Sheet** in the Search box.

You can also work on an online practice quiz. To gain access to this online resource, all you have to do is register. Just follow these simple steps:

1. **Go to www.dummies.com/go/getaccess.**
2. **Create a new account or log in to an existing account.**

    If you create a new account you'll receive an email confirmation. Click through to finish creating a new account.

    *Note:* If you do not receive a confirmation email after creating your account, please check your spam folder before contacting us through our Technical Support website at http://support.wiley.com or by phone at 877-762-2974.

3. **After you've logged into your new or existing account, select "Dummies" under the "Select the brand for your product" header.**

4. **Select your title from the drop-down list. Choose "PMP Exam Prep For Dummies."**

5. **Answer a validation question about the product, and then click "Redeem."**

REMEMBER

You must choose the correct title and edition from the drop-down list. Select the option that says **"PMP Exam Prep For Dummies."**

Now you're ready to go! You can come back to the practice material as often as you want — simply log on with the username and password you created during your initial login.

Your registration is good for one year from the day you redeem your product.

# Where to Go from Here

I wrote this book in a way to let you skip around as needed, but if this is your first deep-dive into the PMP Exam content, here are some key first steps: Step 1: Start with Chapter 3. This chapter sets the foundation, helping you develop the right mindset for PMP Exam preparation. Step 2: After reading Chapter 3, take the pre-assessment in Chapter 5. Your results serve as your guide to the chapters you should review in detail.

Of course, reading the book from the beginning is perfectly fine, especially for those of you who prefer a linear approach to tackling this content. So please feel free to read from front to back. Or if you're more of a free-spirited reader, skip around as you see fit.

# 1
# Starting Your PMP Journey

### IN THIS PART . . .

Get familiar with PMI and what it represents.

Discover the requirements of the PMP Exam.

Prepare yourself to study for and take the PMP Exam.

Explore how to keep your PMP credentials.

Try some practice questions to assess your readiness for the PMP Exam.

> **IN THIS CHAPTER**
> » Recognizing the role and purpose of the Project Management Institute
> » Discovering the PMI Talent Triangle
> » Exploring the project management framework

Chapter **1**

# Welcome to Your PMP Certification Journey

Congratulations on taking the first step in your PMP journey! This chapter is your welcome mat to the world of project management — what I like to call "Planet PMI." Here, you'll gain insight into the global standard of project management certification and find out what makes the PMP credential so highly regarded. You'll take a closer look at the organization behind it all — the Project Management Institute (PMI) — and unpack the essential skills and competencies every project manager needs to excel, as outlined in the PMI Talent Triangle. To help you hit the ground running, I'll also introduce some foundational terminology to familiarize you with the language of project management.

Let's dive in!

## PMP: Recognizing the Global Standard

When it comes to project management certification, the Project Management Professional (PMP) credential says, "Mamma, I made it!" in regard to project management excellence. For professionals with project management experience, the PMP certification is the ultimate badge of honor. It signifies a mastery of project management concepts, techniques, and best practices, distinguishing individuals as competent project management specialists.

The journey toward PMP certification is not an easy one, as it requires a substantial amount of project leadership experience. However, it's precisely the challenges and dedication required that make achieving this certification such a remarkable feat. As a trainer, being part of the PMP certification process fills me with immense pride. Witnessing individuals invest countless hours honing their skills and demonstrating their expertise is a testament to their unwavering determination.

REMEMBER

Here are a few reasons why the PMP designation matters:

- It is a globally recognized credential.
- It includes benefits such as industry recognition, professional development, increased job prospects, and higher earning potential.
- It requires that a project manager meet certain work and education requirements and then pass a rigorous, closed-book, 180-question exam.
- It reports 32-percent higher compensation than non-credentialed project managers.

This means that you have greater potential for job opportunities, networking, promotions, industries, and compensation as a result. Mamma, I made it!

As you prepare to take the PMP Exam, you may wonder why the requirements to sit for the exam are so stringent. This chapter aims to shed light on the rationale behind these requirements and their significance in maintaining the integrity and value of the PMP certification.

# Introducing the Project Management Institute

You may wonder who makes this all happen with the PMP credential. That would be the Project Management Institute (PMI). PMI is the leading professional association for project management, with over 700,000 PMI members worldwide, offering eight certifications that recognize knowledge and competency, and more than 1,200,000 PMP certification holders worldwide. The PMP certification recognizes project managers who have proven they have the skills to manage projects successfully. The PMP certification was introduced by PMI in 1984, and ever since then, the PMP certification has become the gold standard for project management professionals worldwide.

So there.

PMI has established stringent requirements for candidates to uphold the credibility and value of the PMP certification. These requirements are designed to ensure that individuals who hold the PMP credential possess a standardized level of knowledge, experience, and competence. By maintaining consistent standards, the PMP certification becomes a reliable indicator of a project manager's capabilities across industries and geographical boundaries.

# Professional Skill Sets: Excelling with the PMI Talent Triangle

Another essential aspect of preparing for the PMP journey is understanding the PMI Talent Triangle. The PMI Talent Triangle is a framework introduced by PMI to highlight the key skills and competencies that project managers should possess for success in their roles. These skills are not just about the key competencies of skilled project managers; they also reflect the key domains of the PMP Exam: People, Process, and Business Environment.

The PMI Talent Triangle represents the ideal set of skills project professionals must develop and sharpen to be successful and work smarter in today's evolving world of project management. Each side of the Triangle reflects the skills project professionals should possess to be successful in their projects. For an illustration of the PMI Talent Triangle, see Figure 1-1.

For further insight on each element of the PMI Talent Triangle, let's take a look at each one and how they're demonstrated in practice.

## Power Skills

Power Skills, formerly Leadership, pertain to interpersonal skills, collaborative leadership, communication, an innovative mindset, for-purpose orientation, and empathy. Power Skills in practice include the following:

>> Clearly communicating the goals and expectations of the project

>> Clearly and effectively communicating between team members, stakeholders, and clients

>> Delegating tasks effectively, providing feedback, and motivating team members to work towards the project's goals.

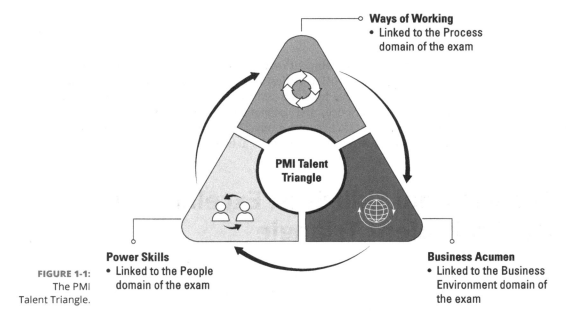

FIGURE 1-1: The PMI Talent Triangle.

## Ways of Working

Ways of Working, formerly Technical Project Management, focus on project managers learning different ways to manage their projects, whether they are predictive, Agile, design thinking, or other new practices still to be developed. Ways of Working in practice include the following:

» Knowing the right tools and techniques to use, given the project context and environment

» Structuring a project team with the right skills to execute to the project plan

## Business Acumen

Business Acumen, formerly Strategic and Business Management, provides an understanding of the macro- and micro-influences across an organization or industry in order to make effective decisions while understanding how the project aligns with the big picture of broader organizational strategy and global trends. Business Acumen in practice involves the following:

» Understanding the business, the industry, and how projects align specifically with the organization's strategic objectives

- Understanding the organization's strategic objectives, market positioning, and financial goals
- Understanding the organization's culture, structure, and processes to develop change management strategies that are effective and sustainable

For more information about the PMI Talent Triangle, visit the PMI webpage: https://www.pmi.org/certifications/certification-resources/maintain/talent-triangle

# Exploring Process Groups, Knowledge Areas, and Project Management Processes

The current PMP Exam is structured around the Exam Content Outline (ECO), which references multiple resources beyond the *PMBOK Guide*. Therefore, the *PMBOK Guide* is not the sole source of exam content. (For detailed information, refer to the PMI Exam Content Outline webpage: https://www.pmi.org/certifications/project-management-pmp.)

However, for years, success on the PMP Exam hinged on being familiar with the three key areas: Process Groups, Knowledge Areas, and the project management processes. While this level of detail is no longer required, many instructors, like myself, still find the framework uber-helpful in providing structure to explain the enormity of the best practice details of project management.

That said, let's walk through a brief overview of those topics.

## Taking a granular look: 49 project management processes

The project life cycle is managed by following a series of steps called project management processes. There are 49 of these processes, and this study guide will walk you through the majority of them. Each process includes three key components:

- **Input:** What you need to get the process started
- **Tools and techniques:** The methods, tools, or systems used to move the process forward
- **Output:** The result or deliverable produced by the process

Do you need to memorize all the project management processes by name? Good news — you don't! While the processes are mentioned in this exam prep guide for context, the current PMP Exam does not require you to commit all 49 project management processes to memory, unlike the old days. You're off the hook! You'll find out about each one as you continue. Keep reading!

Project management processes are used globally and are applicable across all industries.

## Looking at Process Groups from start to finish

Process Groups provide a way to categorize the 49 project management processes to achieve specific objectives (such as processes to start the project, processes to execute the project, and so on). There are five Process Groups encompassing the entire project management life cycle, and each Process Group consists of specific processes and activities that help manage a project from initiation to closure. Here are the five Process Groups.

- » **Initiating:** This is where it all starts — setting the project's initial scope and objectives, getting authorization, and laying the groundwork for success.
- » **Planning:** Think of this as creating your roadmap. It's all about preparing detailed plans and documentation to guide every aspect of the project, covering all knowledge areas.
- » **Executing:** This is where the action happens. You coordinate people and resources to bring the project plan to life and work toward the objectives.
- » **Monitoring and controlling:** Here, you're keeping an eye on things — measuring performance, spotting variances, and taking corrective actions to stay on track.
- » **Closing:** At this point, you're wrapping it all up by finalizing activities, ensuring deliverables are complete, and getting formal acceptance to close the project.

The five Process Groups follow a logical sequence that reflects how you will likely encounter the processes in real-world projects.

The Process Groups aren't the same as project phases, but it's common for people to use their names when referring to project phases in the real world. While that's not technically wrong in practice, it would definitely be the wrong answer on the exam. For the PMP, it's important to understand that Process Groups are a framework for organizing project management processes, not the actual phases of a project. Keep this distinction in mind as you prepare for the exam!

## IS THERE A GLOSSARY?

I ran out of pages to include a glossary section in this study guide. (Paper is expensive these days.) But never fear! While there is no glossary section in this book, terms are defined throughout this resource. Refer to the index for additional reference to the terms. You're guaranteed to find the term someplace in the book with its corresponding definition.

PMI members can access a comprehensive list of the PMI lexicon on their website: https://www.pmi.org/standards/lexicon. PMI membership has its benefits!

Based on years of teaching this content, this exam prep guide is designed around the Process Group framework to help students confidently grasp and organize the material.

## Gaining specialization through Knowledge Areas

A Knowledge Area represents a group of processes related to a specific aspect of project management. Many projects depend on these Knowledge Areas and subject matter experts to provide valuable insights, ensuring all facets of the project are addressed. Here are the ten Knowledge Areas.

- » **Integration management:** Coordination of project elements for unified execution
- » **Scope management:** Defining and controlling what is included in the project
- » **Schedule management:** Planning and managing project timelines
- » **Cost management:** Estimating, budgeting, and controlling project costs
- » **Quality management:** Ensuring deliverables meet required standards
- » **Resource management:** Identifying, acquiring, and managing project resources
- » **Communications management:** Effective dissemination of project information
- » **Risk management:** Identifying and managing project risks
- » **Procurement management:** Managing contracts and external vendor relationships
- » **Stakeholder management:** Engaging and satisfying project stakeholders

I often tell students that a project manager's knowledge is a mile wide but only an inch deep. This means you know enough to be dangerous — but also enough to know you're not the expert in everything. Your job is to use that broad knowledge to ask the right questions and tap into the expertise of those who can dig deeper. While the experts focus on the technical details, you focus on managing and coordinating the overall project efforts.

A Knowledge Area that project managers must thoroughly understand and take full responsibility for is Project Integration Management.

**IN THIS CHAPTER**

» Finding out about the requirements to sit for the exam

» Applying for the exam

» Focusing on the exam content outline — including the domains

» Discovering what's in the *PMBOK Guide*

» Taking the exam in person versus online

# Chapter 2
# Get Ready For the PMP Exam!

In this chapter, you will explore the qualifications required to sit for the PMP Exam and the best strategies for preparation. These include options for self-paced study, boot camps, and the importance of taking practice exams. Additionally, I will cover some key things you need to know when applying for the exam. Once you are ready to take the exam, I will discuss the choice between taking it at home or at a testing center. Finally, I will cover the PMP Exam domains.

Over the last few years, there has been a surge of interest in the project management field. Many social media "experts" (I use *experts* lightly) have indicated that transitioning into project management is a no-brainer and that you already possess transferable skills. While that may be true, the Project Management Institute (PMI) has established stringent criteria to determine if you qualify for the exam. I would encourage you to read this chapter to ensure you have the qualifications you need to be ready for this rigorous exam.

# Do You Have What It Takes?

To sit for the PMP Exam, you need more than just the desire to take the exam. PMI has rigorous standards and requirements that you must meet to qualify. PMI has established rigorous requirements for candidates to uphold the credibility and value of the PMP certification. These requirements are designed to ensure that individuals with the PMP credential possess standardized knowledge, experience, and competence levels. Maintaining consistent standards makes the PMP certification a reliable indicator of a project manager's capabilities across industries and geographical boundaries.

## Meeting education level and project management experience requirements

PMI has set educational levels and project management experience requirements for PMP aspirants. Here's a breakdown of the requirements to sit for the exam based on your education level.

If you have a four-year degree, you need the following:

- 36 months of experience leading projects within the past eight years, and
- 35 hours of project management education/training or hold the Certified Associate in Project Management (CAPM) certification.

If you have a high school diploma or associate degree, you need the following:

- 60 months of experience leading projects within the past eight years, and
- 35 hours of project management education/training or CAPM certification.

If you have a bachelor's or postgraduate degree from a GAC-accredited program (bachelor's or master's degree, or global equivalent), you need the following:

- 24 months of experience leading projects within the past eight years

REMEMBER

The PMI Global Accreditation Center for Project Management Education Programs (GAC) is the world's leading specialized accrediting body for project management and related degree programs, accrediting programs at the bachelor's, postgraduate, and doctorate levels. Established in 2001, they offer over 170 degree programs. For more information, visit `https://www.pmi.org/global-accreditation-center/`.

## Obtaining 35 contact hours of PM education

In addition to the previously mentioned project management experience, applicants must have a minimum of **35 contact hours of formal project management education,** unless they hold an active Certified Associate in Project Management (CAPM) certification. If you are an active CAPM holder, you do not need to provide documentation of the 35 contact hours, as your project management education requirement is waived. GAC core project management coursework is pre-approved to fulfill the 35-contact hours requirement.

The basis of the credential requirements is to ensure that PMP credential-holders display the character and values covered in the following sections.

## Demonstrating professional competence

The PMP Exam tests candidates' understanding of the project management best practices and their ability to apply project management concepts in real-world scenarios. The rigorous eligibility criteria, including education and experience requirements, ensure that candidates have gained sufficient practical exposure to project management. This helps validate your ability to handle complex projects, lead teams, mitigate risks, and deliver successful outcomes.

## Meeting industry demand

As the demand for skilled project managers continues to grow, employers and organizations rely on the PMP certification as a reliable indicator of a candidate's project management expertise. The stringent requirements to sit for the PMP Exam contribute to the certification's reputation as a trusted credential, enabling employers to make informed decisions in hiring or promoting project management professionals.

## Strengthening the profession

The PMP certification plays a pivotal role in advancing the project management profession. By setting high standards, PMI encourages project managers to continuously enhance their skills, stay updated with evolving practices, and contribute to the overall growth and development of the discipline. The stringent requirements act as a driving force, pushing professionals to strive for excellence and contribute to the advancement of project management knowledge.

> ## THE PMI CODE OF ETHICS AND PROFESSIONAL CONDUCT
>
> PMI has established a Code of Ethics and Professional Conduct that extends to all PMI members, volunteers, certification holders, and certification applicants.
>
> PMI members have determined that *honesty, responsibility, respect,* and *fairness* are the values that drive ethical conduct for the project management profession. PMI's Code of Ethics and Professional Conduct applies those values to the real-life practice of project management.
>
> Per PMI, "ethics is about making the best possible decisions concerning people, resources, and the environment...[and] the best possible outcome is the most ethical one." Ethical choices diminish risk, advance positive results, increase trust, contribute to long-term success, and build reputations.
>
> While the topic of ethics is not specifically tested on the exam, you may encounter some questions with an ethical situation that you need to assess to select the most correct PMI answer.
>
> For more information, refer to the PMI webpage Ethics Guidelines and retrieve a copy of the PMI Code of Ethics and Professional Conduct: `https://www.pmi.org/about/ethics/guidelines`.

REMEMBER

In order to help you garner the coveted positions and earn 32 percent more than non-PMP credential holders, the stringent requirements for the PMP Exam are essential for maintaining the integrity, value, and reputation of the certification. The requirements ensure that project management professionals possess the necessary knowledge, experience, and competence to meet the challenges of today's complex projects. By achieving the PMP certification, you join a community of highly skilled professionals committed to excellence in project management.

Welcome to the cool kids' club.

# License and Registration, Please

Okay, applying for the PMP Exam is not that intimidating, but it *is* a process. PMP aspirants need to submit their work experience in the experience verification section of the online application. This work experience needs to demonstrate that you led and/or directed a project.

Admittedly, documenting your project management experience can seem daunting. However, I assure you that it's not that cumbersome. Here are some key points about your project management experience that I've shared with the 2,500-plus students I've taught to date:

» Your job title does not have to be "project manager," but your role on the project has to be where you led and/or managed the project. In my 20 years as a project manager, I've never had the official title of project manager, but I assure you I have managed projects.

» PMI also states in the PMP Exam Content Outline, that your experience does not necessarily have to be paid work but it does need to be in a professional setting. Think, volunteering with a local professional chapter or for a non-profit organization.

» PMI also indicates that activities such as overseeing school projects or planning personal events would not qualify. That means you cannot count planning your wedding or the European family trip as a project, although I would agree, those are massive projects.

TIP

Great news! If you're a U.S. military veteran and you're eligible for Montgomery GI Bill or Post-9/11 GI Bill benefits, the GI Bill offers financial assistance for PMP certification as well as supplemental education and training. Eligible service members and veterans can use the GI Bill to pay up to $2,000 in fees for certification exams. For additional information or help regarding your eligibility, contact VA 888-GIBILL-1 (888-442-4551). If you are eligible, the following link has specific information on the process and contains the Application for Reimbursement of Licensing or Certification Test Fees (Form 22-0803): www.va.gov/education/about-gi-bill-benefits/how-to-use-benefits/test-fees.

Your project management experience needs to incorporate non-overlapping projects (see Figure 2-1) over the course of 36 months (or 24 or 60 months depending on your educational background). Also, keep in mind that your work experience is tracked in months, not the number of projects. If you managed four projects in 9 months, you will only have the 9 months counted toward the total 36 months (or 60 months) that are necessary, rather than four projects times 9 months, which, coincidentally, equates to 36 months. It doesn't work that way.

## Contact hours of project management education

PMI also requires that you have completed 35 contact hours of project management education. The coursework needs to be completed by the time you submit your application.

CHAPTER 2 Get Ready For the PMP Exam! 19

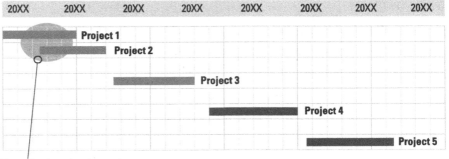

FIGURE 2-1: Overlapping projects.

Example of overlapping projects

© John Wiley & Sons, Inc.

TIP

One hour of classroom instruction equals one contact hour. For instance, if you completed a university course that met for three hours per week for 16 weeks, you can record 48 contact hours (although you only need to record 35 contact hours). If only a portion of the course touched on project management, then you would only record the appropriate hours to be applied toward the total.

Per the current PMI Exam Content Outline, you can fulfill the education requirements by successfully completing courses, workshops, and training sessions offered by various education providers. These providers can include the following:

- PMI Authorized Training Partners (ATPs)
- PMI chapters
- Employer-sponsored programs
- Training companies or consultants, such as a training school
- Distance-learning companies, provided they include an end-of-course assessment, such as a practice exam
- University or college academic and continuing-education programs

WARNING

Reading this book alone will not meet the education requirements you need. You will need to supplement the valuable information in this book with a course from one of the aforementioned providers. For more details, refer to PMI's Exam Content Outline, available on their website at pmi.org.

You are not limited to just one type of education provider. You can absolutely accrue the necessary contact hours from more than one source. The Exam Content Outline specifies that education will not be satisfied by merely attending PMI chapter meetings or engaging in self-directed study alone, such as reading books or watching instructional videos that do not include an end-of-course assessment.

### Application submission and payment, pretty please

The process time to review and approve your application may take up to five business days. This timeline does not apply if your application has been selected for audit.

Once your application has been approved, your PMI account will be updated with information on the next steps for payment ("Congratulations, your application has been approved. You are now invited to pay. . ." or something to that effect).

Make your payment to PMI directly based on your membership level. PMI does give you the opportunity to become a member at the time of payment for the exam, and the exam fee will be prorated accordingly.

TIP

Many people expect PMI to email them about updates regarding their PMP application or access code to schedule an exam. The truth is, PMI does not. Rather, if during the time of your application you receive an email from PMI, it's usually to inform you that your application has been selected for audit or your application has been rejected. With this in mind, you should set up a PMI account and get used to checking it on a regular basis.

Once payment is made, it takes PMI a couple of hours to provide an authorization access code that will be populated within your PMI account. Check your account often.

## Getting Familiar with PMP Exam Domains

You may have noticed that I've mentioned the Exam Content Outline several times in this chapter, but you might still be wondering what it's all about. The Exam Content Outline is your decoder ring. . .kind of. Think of the PMP Exam Content Outline as your ultimate study guide, detailing everything you need to focus on to ace the exam. It's like a roadmap, helping you navigate both the technical and leadership aspects of project management with confidence.

Not only does the outline break down the structure and content of the PMP Exam, but it also covers the certification process and requirements — topics I've already tackled in this chapter. It's designed to give you a balanced approach, ensuring you're well prepared on all fronts.

REMEMBER

The PMP exam is not just a test; it's a reflection of the ever-evolving nature of project management. PMI recognizes that the roles and responsibilities of project managers continuously evolve with the changing business landscape. To ensure that the PMP exam remains relevant and aligned with the demands of the profession, PMI conducts a rigorous review called a Role Delineation Study (RDS) every three to five years. The RDS aims to assess whether the exam's contents accurately represent the current realities of the field.

The PMP exam is divided into three domains: People, Process, and Business Environment.

## People (42 percent of the exam): Leading and building teams

Project management is ultimately about people — inspiring, guiding, and collaborating with individuals to achieve project goals. This domain emphasizes your ability to effectively lead and manage teams, foster a positive project culture, and engage stakeholders. Mastering this domain will enhance your skills in communication, negotiation, conflict resolution, and team dynamics.

## Process (50 percent of the exam): Seeing a project through to completion

The process domain forms the core of project management, encompassing the Knowledge Areas defined in the *PMBOK Guide* and other reference materials. It emphasizes your understanding of project management processes, from initiating and planning through executing, monitoring, controlling, and ultimately closing a project. You'll delve into the intricacies of project scope, schedule, cost, quality, risk, procurement, and more, ensuring that projects are executed efficiently and deliver value to stakeholders.

## Business Environment (8 percent of the exam): Ensuring compliance and delivering value

Successful project managers grasp the big picture and align their projects within the larger organizational context. This domain focuses on your understanding of the business environment, including compliance requirements, legal and ethical considerations, and the ability to deliver value to the organization and its customers. By comprehending core business strategies, you'll make informed decisions that contribute to the long-term success of your projects.

To become a truly successful project manager, you must possess the ability to navigate all three domains effectively. By blending your interpersonal skills with a deep understanding of project management processes and a keen awareness of the business environment, you'll be poised for success — or at least not pulling your hair out.

This book will guide you through each domain, providing in-depth explanations, practical examples, and invaluable tips for exam success.

## Some Guidance on the *PMBOK Guide*

*A Guide to the Project Management Body of Knowledge (PMBOK Guide)* is PMI's flagship publication and also a fundamental resource for effective project management in any industry. The *PMBOK Guide* holds a significant position as PMI's premier publication, serving as a fundamental resource for project management practices across industries. Although the *PMBOK Guide* was originally considered the sole authoritative source for the Project Management Professional (PMP) exam, the landscape has evolved, and the exam now incorporates multiple reference materials.

While the *PMBOK Guide* remains an essential resource for project management practitioners, it is crucial to acknowledge that it is no longer the exclusive resource for the PMP Exam. PMI recognized the need to align the certification with industry practices and diverse perspectives, leading to the incorporation of additional reference materials into the exam content.

The inclusion of multiple materials in the PMP Exam allows candidates to demonstrate a broader understanding of project management concepts, methodologies, and approaches. By drawing from various sources, the exam aims to assess an individual's ability to apply their knowledge in real-world scenarios, making the certification more comprehensive and reflective of the challenges faced by project managers today.

Therefore, aspiring PMP candidates should recognize the importance of the *PMBOK Guide* as a vital foundation for project management knowledge. However, they should also acknowledge the significance of studying and referencing other relevant materials to develop a well-rounded understanding of project management principles and practices.

# Getting Ready for the PMP Examination: The Basics

The PMP Exam is brutal — there's no sugarcoating it. For many, it's been a long time since they've taken a 3-plus hour exam that demands such intense focus and mental effort. Now that I've acknowledged that, let's delve into the details to get you well prepared.

## The fee

The current exam fee in the United States is US$425 as a PMI member and US$675 as a non-member. Take my advice and become a PMI member; there are long-term savings. You can cancel or reschedule your exam by contacting Pearson VUE by telephone at least 24 hours in advance of your scheduled exam or online at least 48 hours in advance. The fee to reschedule is US$70.

TIP

The PMP Exam fees vary based on your region. If you are taking the exam outside of the United States, the fee will be reflected in your PMI account based on your location when it's time to pay for the exam. Contact the PMI customer service team directly for more information.

## Questions, time, and breaks

The PMP Exam consists of 180 questions, of which 5 are experimental questions. These experimental questions do not affect your score and are used to test the validity of future exam questions. All questions are randomly placed throughout the examination.

TIP

The majority of exam question types are multiple-choice questions. However, PMI has incorporated new exam item types to include drag-and-drop questions, hot-area questions, and limited fill-in-the-blank questions. For a list of current item types included in the exam, you can refer to the PMI website for exam updates: https://www.pmi.org/certifications/project-management-pmp/pmp-exam-preparation.

The total time allocated for the exam is 230 minutes (three hours and fifty minutes). Why not just four hours? Who knows. While some individuals may finish sooner, most PMP candidates have reported needing the full 230 minutes.

The PMP Exam now includes two 10-minute breaks. The first break occurs after you have completed and reviewed questions 1 to 60. The second break happens after you have finished and reviewed questions 61 to 120. Please note that once you start your break after reviewing your answers, you cannot return to the previous section's questions. After each break, you will have the remaining allotted time to complete the remaining sections. In total, you have 230 minutes to answer 180 questions.

The examination is preceded by a tutorial and followed by a survey, both of which are optional and take 5 to 15 minutes to complete. The time used to complete the tutorial and survey is not included in the examination time of 230 minutes.

## Results and diagnostic information

In addition to the overall pass/fail status, you will get important diagnostic information on your performance in each domain. This guidance is helpful for both passing and failing candidates. Please note that any score provided at the end of your testing session is preliminary until PMI officially confirms the results.

Candidates who take a center-based examination will receive a copy of their preliminary test results at the test center on the day of the exam. All candidates can access their exam report on the online certification system no later than 10 business days after their examination date. You will receive an email notification when your exam report is available online.

## The mysterious passing score

So what's considered a passing score? Nobody knows. PMI does not disclose what's considered a passing score.

The passing score for all PMI exams is determined through psychometric analysis. PMI uses subject matter experts — project professionals from around the world and various disciplines — to determine the number of questions you must answer correctly to pass the exam.

The rule of thumb: score 75 percent or better on your practice exams (see the later section about taking practice exams) and you should do fine on the real exam.

## Preparation: Boot camp or self-paced course?

When it comes to preparing for the exam, many PMP candidates often ask whether they should pursue self-paced study or consider the pricier boot camp options. The answer depends on how you learn best. Many self-paced study options are available, including online learning platforms and massive open online courses (MOOCs). If you are self-disciplined, can stick to a schedule, and need a budget-friendly option, self-paced study might be the best choice for you.

On the other hand, boot camps offer an intensive, structured learning experience designed to get results quickly. These programs are typically strenuous and aim to prepare you to take the exam within four to six weeks after completion. Personally, I prefer boot camps if I have the budget or if my employer covers the cost. The focused setting of a boot camp allows you to concentrate solely on the content without distractions, and the investment motivates you to achieve your goal. However, the choice is entirely up to you.

To best prepare for the PMP Exam, it's essential to understand your learning style. Some individuals thrive in boot camps, benefiting from intensive, short-term preparation, while others prefer a longer, more gradual study approach. Additionally, some learners gain more from group discussions, whereas others find reading alone more effective. Understand your strengths and preferences, and choose the method that works best for you.

## Practice exams, practice exams, practice exams

Regardless of which route you take to achieve your education hours (boot camp versus self-paced course), I cannot overemphasize the value and importance of taking practice exams as the key to your success with the PMP Exam. Practice exams help you understand what it's like to take a timed exam, experience the pressure, and see how you perform in a time-constrained environment. Many students who are unsuccessful with the exam often report having taken few or no practice exams (say what, now?). Familiarizing yourself with the types of questions, observing how you react under pressure, and identifying your pain points are invaluable, sometimes even more so than reading a book. However, please keep reading my book.

When students practice answering questions, even incorrectly, before learning the content, their future learning is enhanced. Research has shown that pre-testing improves post-test results more than spending the same amount of time studying. So there.

Taking practice exams is a helpful way to get familiar with the types of questions and topics you need to know for the PMP Exam. Be sure to take advantage of the online practice exam questions included with this book (see the introduction for more information).

**REMEMBER**

Keep in mind that the practice questions are just that — practice. They are not the exact questions you will encounter on the real exam. Think of the practice questions as a diagnostic tool to test your knowledge of the PMP Exam content and to help you get into the PMI mindset.

Often, boot camp training providers include access to a test bank of practice questions, which may be worth the investment.

## Where to take the exam: On a warm couch or in a cold testing center?

Well, you can't take the exam on your couch, typically, but some people prefer the convenience of taking the exam at home versus driving to the nearest testing center. The PMP Exam is administered via computer-based testing at local Pearson VUE testing centers worldwide or via their OnVUE online proctoring. Once your application has been approved, PMI will provide you with an authorization code and instructions to register directly on the Pearson VUE website (https://home.pearsonvue.com/pmi).

The decision to take the PMP Exam online or in person is really up to you. If you are like me and you like to read the exam questions aloud, your eyes wander off the screen (daydreamer, anyone?), or you put your hands on your face, then you should take the exam in person at a testing center. Oh, and if your cat, dog, parakeet, or kids like to bust into your room or scratch your door, definitely take the exam at a Pearson VUE testing center.

Still, some people prefer the online option to avoid traffic and enjoy the comfort of wearing their fuzzy slippers.

**TIP**

One factor in deciding whether to take the exam online or in person is the availability of time slots. Currently, the waiting period for an in-person exam is about four to six weeks. Eek! In contrast, online exam slots may be available within 20 to 30 minutes. No kidding.

### Choosing a testing center

Many people have recommended taking the exam at a testing center for the following reasons:

- » No setup preparation — just show up at the testing center and be ready
- » Reliability of their internet connection

CHAPTER 2 **Get Ready For the PMP Exam!** 27

- Distraction-free testing environment
- Security protocols being in place
- Face-to-face exam proctors rather than an online proctor watching your every move on camera — and I mean watching your *every* move.

**WARNING**

Pearson VUE is the only authorized testing center for the PMP Exam. Fraudulent proxy test services sometimes attempt to contact PMP candidates. These are scams. PMI encourages candidates (and PMI members) to report exam fraud (or cheating) by emailing examsecurity@pmi.org with a screenshot or picture of the message so that they can investigate.

If you fail to show up for your exam or you're more than 15 minutes late for your exam appointment, you forfeit your entire exam fee!

### Choosing to take the exam online

Taking the exam online does not limit you to your home. You can take it in a hotel room, at your office, or even at your grandmother's house. Just ensure you follow the security protocols and provide photographic evidence that you have no unauthorized items like books, bags, phones, or cheat notes near your computer station. Taking the exam at the office is my favorite "online" option. Just make sure to lock the door and put up a sign saying, "Exam in Progress — DO NOT DISTURB," so your colleagues don't accidentally interrupt you with, "Hey, I didn't know you were coming in today." Exam terminated.

**WARNING**

Online testing comes with much stricter security measures. If the offsite proctor suspects a violation of the security rules, they may terminate your exam and you will have effectively failed the exam.

**IN THIS CHAPTER**

» Discovering key exam dos and don'ts

» Preparing the right way

» Gaining insight into the PMI lexicon and common acronyms on the exam

Chapter **3**

# Getting into the Right PMI Mindset

This chapter will underscore the pivotal role of the right mindset in exam preparedness. By understanding the key dos and don'ts of the exam, mastering the scenario-based exam questions, and implementing the key logistical tips, you'll be in control and empowered during the real exam experience.

Many PMP aspirants think the exam is about rote memorization and formulas. That thought process is far from the truth. While there are indeed terms you need to know and memorize for the exam, the exam is about applying your knowledge and skills as a project manager to determine the best practice approach. It's about having the PMI mindset.

I like to call it "Planet PMI."

Think of it as a unique place, Planet PMI, with its set of rules and customs and a language of its own. To ensure a smooth journey, it's crucial to familiarize yourself with these rules and customs, just like absorbing the local language when visiting a new place. This understanding will prevent you from getting into trouble and ensure that you have a good time.

The ultimate goal is for you to pass the exam and look back on this journey as a fulfilling learning experience, feeling reassured and confident in your project management knowledge and skills.

# Discovering the Dos and Don'ts

To open this chapter, I want to talk about the dos and don'ts. I like to get the *don'ts* out of the way first.

Let me guess: you're looking at your desk stacked with multiple project management books that you plan to read, a stack of flashcards, your pretty collection of book tabs, and your multitude of many-colored highlighters. Trust me, I've been there. You may be surprised by the list of don'ts that make you clear your desk of all the clutter, leaving you feeling lighter and more organized. Here is a list of don'ts in your preparation for the exam:

- **Don't rely on flashcards alone.** Flashcards are good, but they should supplement your studies and not be the only way you prepare for the exam.
- **Don't waste your time on memorizing and stressing about formulas.** Performing math calculations is not the main focus of the exam, and you would be doing yourself a disservice if you spent too much time on mastering a bunch of calculations.
- **Don't assume that your ten-plus years of experience alone will prepare you for the exam.** You still need to study and know the "PMI way" of managing projects.
- **Don't assume that reading books is enough to prepare you for the exam.** PMP aspirants need to take practice exams to be well prepared for the time pressure and use of test-taking techniques.

Was that an eye-opening list? I hope so! Now you won't be wasting valuable time on ineffective strategies. Instead, put your focus on tried and true strategies. Here are the key *dos* that I recommend:

- **Do take practice exams!** (You'll see this advice appear quite frequently.)
- **Do use the results of practice exams to see where you have gaps in your knowledge.**
- **Do refer to sections of your study guides (like this book) to drill down and truly understand the content so you'll see why the answer is the answer.**
- **Do consider creating cheat sheet notes (in the exam prep world, we like to call them "brain dumps") of your problem areas.**

# Spotting the Scenario

If you didn't get the memo, the PMP Exam is almost entirely a *scenario-based exam*. This means that for each exam question, you will be presented with a scenario for which you will need to dissect and determine the best answer (might I add, the *best PMI answer*) based on the information provided in the scenario. This is why rote memorization is not the key to your success with the exam. Not only will you need to know the content, but your reading comprehension will also need to be sharpened so you can read between the lines as to what's relevant information versus what's red herring information.

TIP

A *red herring* in an exam question is a misleading statement or piece of information in the question that distracts students from reaching the correct answer. Red herrings are intended to divert attention from the main question at hand. It's important to stay focused and not let these distractions affect your ability to comprehend and discern the facts being tested.

Many PMP aspirants have reported that the scenarios are what take up their time on the exam and what make the exam so exhausting, because of the need to process so much information.

Here's the pro tip for tackling these scenario-based questions: read the call of the question first. This means you should focus your attention on the last statement of the scenario, typically the one that ends with a question mark. The popular questions that the PMP Exam presents include the following:

- What should the project manager do?
- What should you do next?
- What's the first thing you should do?
- How should you handle this situation?

Focusing on these questions will help you determine how to best answer them. At this point, you will typically need more information. So, add to your strategy the following items:

1. Read the last two sentences of the scenario. Typically that's enough information to see what you can eliminate from the answer options.
2. Go straight to the answer options. Generally speaking, most question types will be multiple choice with A, B, C, D options. It's possible you can eliminate two answer options that do not pertain to the call of the question.

3. Now go back to the beginning of the scenario-based question to read through all of the information to determine what key facts of the scenario are relevant to the call of the question.

At the time of this writing, the current PMP Exam allows you to highlight words and phrases, such as the call of the question. This feature is awesome. Why? Because highlighting the key words, phrases, and even sentences allows you to be reminded of the key items you need to keep at the forefront of your mind when answering the question.

Another cool feature of the PMP Exam is that you can actually cross out answer options so you only focus on the remaining choices. This strategy allows you to reduce the chance of returning to an item and selecting an option you had already eliminated.

## Understanding the ABCs of PMI

It's important to know the PMI lexicon. A *lexicon* is the vocabulary of a language or subject, and this is so appropriate for the language of *Planet PMI*. Many PMP aspirants have found that their biggest hang-up in preparing for the exam is knowing and using PMP vocabulary such as the following: *acceptance criteria, servant leadership, T-shaped,* and more. What do they mean? Don't worry, you'll find out about that in Chapter 14.

And if discovering new terminology is not overwhelming enough, the exam is notorious for including acronyms — lots and lots of acronyms. Do any of the following make sense to you: EVM, EMV, OPM, ETC, EAC, BAC, CPM? Are you still with me? I'm not saying all of this to scare you away from your pursuit of passing the PMP Exam. I promise! Consider yourself warned and now well prepared with the right PMI mindset. I promise, you will be saying under your breath during your preparation, "Crystal warned me about this."

Lucky for you, Chapter 23 contains a list of the common acronyms on the exam. You're welcome.

**IN THIS CHAPTER**

» Gaining insight into what it takes to maintain your PMP credential.

» Executing strategies to earn Professional Development Units

» Avoiding the common mistakes that lead to an expired credential

» Avoiding Suspended Status

Chapter **4**

# Maintaining Your PMP Credential

This chapter provides tips and guidance on maintaining your PMP credential. Once you pass the PMP Exam, you never, ever have to retake it, even when the exam goes through its update process. However, there's a caveat: you must maintain your continuing education credits with the Project Management Institute (PMI), plus pay a recertification fee to maintain your hard-earned credential.

Perhaps you're thinking, *I haven't even passed the exam yet, so why even think about this now?* That's because after ten years of teaching PMP boot camp courses to over 2,500 students, it amazes me when I get frantic messages from past students and general connections that they are in need of all 60 Professional Development Units (PDUs), or worse yet, they let their certification lapse. What's even more gut wrenching is that they contact me *after* their suspension period has passed, where PMI allows you to complete the required PDUs during that timeframe to meet your credential requirements and renew your certification.

Yikes!

I want to emphasize that this chapter is deliberately positioned at the beginning of the book to ensure it remains at the forefront of your mind after you sit for the exam. You can absolutely skip this chapter. But go ahead and do yourself a favor and flag it for review after you pass the exam. I'd rather you not accidentally overlook this topic, especially if it appears at the end, after you've covered all the necessary material during your preparation for the exam. You worked too hard to earn your PMP to lose it.

# Keeping Your PMP Credential Once You've Earned It

Once you pass the PMP Exam, you are a certified PMP. Yay you! Now let's keep that hard-earned credential.

One of the most valuable resources to bookmark and/or save on your hard drive is PMI's *Continuing Certification Requirements (CCR) Handbook*, which outlines the requirements for maintaining your credential. Per the *CCR Handbook*, all PMI certification holders must earn PDUs to actively maintain their PMI certifications. PDUs can be earned through a variety of ways that focus on one of two areas.

- **Education**: Training opportunities that enhance your skills in one or more of the domains of the PMI Talent Triangle.
- **Giving back to the profession**: Activities where you share your knowledge and skills as a way to contribute to the profession.

While there are different requirements to maintain the various PMI credentials, the requirements to maintain the PMP certification are as follows:

- **Three-year certification cycle.** This means you need to earn the required PDUs within a three-year timeframe.
- **60 required PDUs.** That's the equivalent of 60 hours of learning and giving back within a three-year timeframe.
- **Education minimum of 35 PDUs.**
- **Giving Back maximum of 25 PDUs.**

If you did the math, between the Education minimum and the Giving Back maximum, that equates to 60 PDUs. Easy!

Or one would think it was easy.

# Getting Those PDUs

It may help to first decode PDUs. *Professional Development Units,* or PDUs, are the measuring units to quantify your approved learning and professional development activities. PDUs are one-hour blocks of time that you spend learning, teaching others, or volunteering. One (1) PDU equates to one contact hour of learning, teaching, reading, or volunteering your time related to the PMI Talent Triangle domains.

TIP

The PMI Talent Triangle consists of three domains:

» Ways of Working (formerly Technical Project Management)

» Power Skills (formerly Leadership)

» Strategic Business Acumen (formerly Strategic and Business Management)

## Meeting the Education requirement

In terms of the Education PDUs, Table 4-1 gives a breakdown according to the *CCR Handbook.*

**TABLE 4-1 PMP: Education Minimum 35 PDUs**

| Ways of Working PDUs Required | Power Skills PDUs Required | Strategic Business Acumen PDUs Required | Remaining PDUs (Any area of the Talent Triangle) |
|---|---|---|---|
| 8 | 8 | 8 | 11 |

Educational PDUs include participating in webinars, workshops, or training relevant to project management. This also includes training for other PM-related certifications such as Agile or Six Sigma certifications.

Per the *CCR Handbook,* PMI lists the various ways in which you can earn Education PDUs:

» Courses or training such as instructor-led formal education courses or classes held in person or online

» Organization meetings that include activities and local events related to the profession

- » Online or digital media such as self-paced learning conducted online or through varied forms of digital media, such as podcasts
- » Self-directed reading that is relevant to the certification you hold
- » Informal learning

For a detailed description of each activity, examples, and associated reporting policies, refer to the PMI *CCR Handbook* (https://www.pmi.org/-/media/pmi/documents/public/pdf/certifications/ccr-certification-requirements-handbook.pdf).

## Meeting the Giving Back minimum

The Giving Back category is an optional way to earn PDUs. It's not required; however, your total PDUs toward the Giving Back category cannot exceed 25 PDUs for the PMP credential. Under the Giving Back to the Profession category, PMI allows a "free bingo space" opportunity to count eight (8) PDUs for working as a project manager.

Earning PDUs through the Giving Back category includes sharing your knowledge through blogging, presentations, or mentoring, to name a few examples.

The Giving Back category is way cool, right? Are you thinking, *What's the catch?* Giving back is a way for you to share your knowledge and apply your skills toward mentoring junior project managers, volunteering your time at a nonprofit organization, or volunteering your project management skills with your local professional association, such as a local PMI chapter. PMI doesn't want you to hoard your knowledge. Their philosophy reflects a great quote from Maya Angelou: "When you get, give. When you learn, teach."

TIP

Over 300 volunteer-led PMI chapters exist worldwide. There is no limit to the number of chapters you can join — I'm a member of four chapters, including an international chapter. However, for more intentional networking, you get the best results when you join a local chapter in your area.

The various ways you can earn Giving Back PDUs include the following:

- » Work as a practitioner in your certified role
- » Create content
- » Give a presentation on topics relevant to the profession
- » Share knowledge to help others learn and grow
- » Provide volunteer services to non-employer or non-client organizations

The PMI *CCR Handbook* contains a detailed description of each activity, examples, and associated reporting policies related to the Giving Back category.

## Paying the renewal fee

In addition to earning 60 PDUs during your three-year certification cycle, you also pay a fee at the time of certification renewal. At the time of this writing, PMI members pay a renewal fee of US$60 and non-members pay a renewal fee of US$150. The certification is valid for three years and must be renewed before it expires.

# Earning (and Keeping) Your Credentials

Hopefully you are encouraged to see that so many options are available to maintain your PMP credential. You're probably thinking, *Wow, I can't wait to earn my PMP certification and keep learning and growing!* If you have that mindset, let's break down the winning plan of maintaining your credential and earning PDUs.

## Executing a winning plan

Recognizing that achieving the PMP credential is only the beginning of your PMP journey will set you up for creating a winning plan to project-manage your professional development. Create a plan that combines elements of live events, online courses, and readings that keep your professional development interesting and diverse. Your plan could incorporate courses and readings on the topics you struggled with during your studies or on topics that really interested you. Also consider breaking down the PDU requirements into chunks:

- 60 PDUs every three years is 20 PDUs per year.
- That's 5 PDUs per quarter.
- That's 1 to 2 PDUs per month.

Imagine this scenario: you picked up a highly recommended business strategy book that's approximately an eight-hour read, equating to 8 PDUs. And then there's the one-hour webinar, hosted by PMI, about using a project management tool. Another PDU. Don't forget about the interesting course about being a better delegator that you saw on a course platform such as LinkedIn Learning or Udemy.

Boom. Another PDU. And if you noticed, each example highlights the domains of the PMI Talent Triangle: Strategic Business Acumen, Ways of Working, and Power Skills, respectively.

## Having no plan

Some individuals treat earning PDUs like they're doing taxes or watching paint dry. Typically, these are the individuals who have no plan and expect the PDUs to just fall in their lap. These folks are scrambling to "find" the required PDUs within weeks (not months, mind you) of their certification cycle. They watch hours of free webinars and/or purchase PDU-eligible webinars in bulk from a training company.

Talk about watching paint dry.

While this is *a strategy*, it is not the preferred method of truly growing and developing one's skills as a project professional.

TIP

Activities you complete before you earn a PMI certification are not eligible as PDUs. PMI also stipulates that you cannot claim participation in the same course or activity more than once. If you earn more than the required PDUs in your CCR cycle, you may apply a portion of the PDUs to your next cycle. Only PDUs earned in the final year (12 months) of your certification cycle can be applied to a future cycle.

Let's look at two case studies to illustrate this point.

### Case study 1: Quinn

Let's take Quinn. Quinn is a project manager who has over 15 years of project management experience. She works in the IT sector and so the PMP was a requirement for her job. Like many busy professionals with many family obligations, Quinn let her PMP credential lapse. Quinn didn't have a plan to maintain her credential. She just felt that since there were so many ways to earn PDUs, she would take advantage of them when the opportunity came up. As such, everything else took priority over Quinn's professional development. Here's a laundry list of the common mistakes she made:

>> Quinn kept putting it off, saying, "I have plenty of time."

>> Quinn started a webinar, but never finished it because something else took priority.

>> Quinn didn't discuss her goals with her manager to garner the support she needed to take the necessary time away from work for professional development opportunities.

>> Quinn didn't set up a plan for making sure that professional development was a high priority for her.

### Case study 2: Jonah

Now let's look at Jonah. Jonah is a digital project manager with 10 years of experience. After six months of preparation, he declared he was never going to retake this exam if he could help it. Jonah put together a plan. He was intentional, and thought about some of his problem areas in preparing for the exam. He made a list of courses that he wanted to take to enhance his understanding of those problem areas. One of his pain points was quality management, so he registered for a Lean Six Sigma class a month after passing the PMP Exam. Jonah spoke with his boss, who supported his goals of additional training and certifications — which was good for the company to have a trained project manager and be able to compete for contracts with certified personnel. In summary, Jonah did the following to make sure he was in a good position to keep current with his certification:

>> Jonah created a plan.

>> Jonah spoke with his manager to support his plan.

>> Jonah made professional development a priority.

What's the difference between Quinn and Jonah? Planning. Being intentional. Making your professional development a priority.

Don't be like Quinn. Be like Jonah.

WARNING

Letting your PMP certification lapse can have serious implications for your professional growth and career advancement. It means losing the recognition of your project management expertise and the competitive edge it brings. Employers often prioritize certified professionals for key project management roles.

# Taking Action If Your Certification Cycle Lapses

If your certification cycle lapses, PMI will put your credential on "Suspended Status." This means if you do not satisfy the CCR program requirements within your current cycle dates, you will be placed on Suspended Status. The good news is that this suspension period lasts one year (12 months). The bad news is that during this time, you cannot refer to yourself as a certification holder or use the certification designation.

During the suspension period, you will be required to earn the necessary PDUs and complete the renewal process. The date of your next CCR cycle will not change after you are reinstated to Active Status from Suspended Status.

If you do not earn the necessary PDUs or do not complete the renewal process within the suspension period, you will lose your certification and go into an Expired Status. *Expired Status* means your certification has expired, and you are no longer a certified PMP. To become active, you will need to reapply to sit for the exam, pay the associated fees, and retake the PMP Exam. All. Over. Again.

IN THIS CHAPTER

» Tackling some practice questions

» Reviewing the answers

Chapter **5**

# Taking a Pre-Assessment

Before you dive into the PMP Exam content, this chapter gives you a quick pre-assessment to gauge your current knowledge. Taking this quiz isn't about getting a perfect score. Instead, see it as a starting point to identify what you already know and where you need to focus your efforts. Take your time and have fun with it. At the end of each answer explanation is a cross-reference to the chapter where you can find more information on the topic.

## Questions

**1.** You are managing a project to implement a new customer relationship management (CRM) system. After months of work, the project has reached the closure phase. During this phase, you notice a few key tasks remain unfinished, including final acceptance of deliverables, archiving project documents, and gathering lessons learned from the team and stakeholders. Which of the following actions should you prioritize to ensure proper project closure?

   **a.** Develop a new risk register to capture any remaining project risks.

   **b.** Conduct a lessons learned meeting with the project team and stakeholders to document insights for future projects.

   **c.** Verify that all deliverables meet the acceptance criteria and obtain formal stakeholder sign-off.

d. Create a follow-up plan to reassign project team members to new tasks after the project ends.

2. You are managing a project to roll out a new accounting system for a company. The project sponsor has set a firm deadline for the project completion. After analyzing the project schedule, you find that the project has a float of −5 days. What does negative float mean?

   a. The project can start 5 days later than planned without delaying the sponsor's deadline.

   b. The project is not meeting the sponsor's deadline by 5 days.

   c. The project must be completed 5 days earlier than planned to meet the sponsor's deadline.

   d. The project has a buffer of 5 days to accommodate risks and uncertainties.

3. You are managing a project to implement a new customer relationship management (CRM) system. The project has a wide range of stakeholders, including senior management, sales teams, software developers, and external consultants. What project artifact are you developing to ensure effective engagement with and involvement of all stakeholders throughout the project?

   a. Resource Management Plan

   b. Stakeholder Engagement Plan

   c. Stakeholder Register

   d. Communications Management Plan

4. You are managing a project to implement a new IT infrastructure for a company with operations in multiple countries. During the project, a geopolitical event results in trade sanctions between two countries where your key suppliers are based. How should you handle the situation?

   a. Evaluate the geopolitical event to determine its impact on the project.

   b. Ignore the geopolitical event and proceed with the project as planned.

   c. Stop the project completely and wait for the geopolitical situation to stabilize.

   d. Continue with the project and commit to watching 24/7 news outlets.

5. As a project manager, you are working in a Directive PMO. What is the primary function of this type of PMO?

   a. To provide guidance and support for project managers

   b. To oversee project performance and ensure consistency

c. To manage and execute projects directly

   d. To develop and implement project management standards and methodologies

6. You are managing a hybrid team working on a new software project. During a sprint review meeting, one of your developers, Alex, feels his contributions are being overlooked and accuses another team member, Priya, of taking credit for his work. Priya disputes this, and the conversation becomes tense. You need to address the conflict and keep the team focused on their objectives. Which strategy is most appropriate to resolve this issue?

   a. Avoid the conflict by postponing the discussion to the next sprint planning meeting.

   b. Use a collaborative approach to facilitate a discussion between Alex and Priya, ensuring both perspectives are heard.

   c. Enforce your authority and make a unilateral decision about who contributed more to avoid further delays.

   d. Encourage the team to use osmotic communication tools to discuss the issue asynchronously.

7. Your team is developing a fitness app. The stakeholders want a fully finished product by the deadline, but the development team prefers delivering smaller, functional pieces over time to gather early user feedback. As the project manager, you must balance delivering value quickly and managing conflicting expectations. Which development approach should you recommend?

   a. Predictive

   b. Incremental

   c. Iterative

   d. Agile

8. During a sprint, your Agile team is working in a shared space. While testing a feature, a developer, Sam, overhears a conversation between two developers about a change in the acceptance criteria for a user story. Sam immediately realizes the change impacts her current work and makes the necessary adjustments to ensure the deliverable meets the updated criteria. This quick response prevents the team from missing the sprint goal. What does this situation best describe?

   a. Synchronous communication

   b. Scheduled communication

   c. Osmotic communication

   d. Formal communication

**9.** Your team is working on a software upgrade project. During a critical design phase, a senior developer makes an unapproved change to the system's architecture, arguing it improves performance. However, the testing lead discovers the change conflicts with the baseline design, potentially causing delays. The developer insists the change is necessary, while the testing lead demands a rollback to the approved baseline. As the project manager, you need to address the conflict and determine which project artifact governs the process for evaluating and documenting this situation. Which project artifact should you reference to resolve this conflict?

   **a.** Change control plan

   **b.** Team ground rules

   **c.** Team charter

   **d.** Gold plating

**10.** Members of an Agile team have taken on tasks outside their primary area of expertise to ensure project progress. For example, a software developer with deep technical expertise also collaborates on user interface design, while a tester contributes to creating user stories. This flexibility helps the team adapt to changing requirements and maintain momentum despite resource constraints. Which concept best describes the team members in this scenario?

   **a.** Co-dependent teams

   **b.** T-shaped people

   **c.** I-shaped people

   **d.** Agile specialists

**11.** A product owner is working with their team to develop a new feature. Which of the following values from The Agile Manifesto does the product owner most closely embody by involving the team in the decision-making process?

   **a.** Working software over comprehensive documentation

   **b.** Customer collaboration over contract negotiation

   **c.** Responding to change over following a plan

   **d.** Individuals and interactions over processes and tools

**12.** Your project is in the execution phase, and you've been actively engaging stakeholders based on their needs and expectations. However, you've noticed a decline in engagement from a key stakeholder who initially showed strong interest. What should you do to address this situation?

   **a.** Reduce communication with the stakeholder to avoid further disengagement.

b. Initiate a one-on-one meeting to understand their concerns.

   c. Assign a team member to handle all interactions with the stakeholder.

   d. Focus on engaging other stakeholders instead.

13. You're leading a project team that is building an app for a health system that has the potential to improve patient satisfaction. What is the definition of a stakeholder in a project?

    a. Any individual or group who can affect or be affected by the project.

    b. A team member responsible for project execution.

    c. The patients receiving the care.

    d. A person who provides funding for the project.

14. You are managing a team responsible for launching a new customer onboarding process at a financial institution. The initiative involves implementing a software solution and training staff to improve customer experience. However, after the software is deployed and training is complete, the operations manager expects your team to continue monitoring the process and resolving issues indefinitely. As the project manager, what should you say?

    a. It is operations because the project team must monitor and maintain the new process over time.

    b. It is operations because the initiative involves delivering unique outputs within a defined timeline.

    c. It is a project because the initiative involves delivering unique outputs within a defined timeline.

    d. It is project because the new process contributes to the organization's ongoing business objectives.

15. Your project team has just successfully completed a complex project ahead of schedule. To recognize their exceptional performance, you decide to give them an extra day off to celebrate their accomplishment. Which type of motivation does this reward primarily represent?

    a. Extrinsic motivation

    b. Intrinsic motivation

    c. McClelland's Achievement Motivation

    d. Maslow's esteem needs

**16.** You are the project manager for a software development project. Your team is geographically dispersed, with members in different time zones. You need to ensure that project information is accessible to all team members in real time to facilitate collaboration. Which of the following tools or techniques would be most suitable for this situation?

   **a.** Weekly status meetings

   **b.** Shared cloud-based document repository

   **c.** Monthly progress reports

   **d.** Team-building workshops

**17.** Your project is facing potential risks, and you need to determine how to convey this information to your stakeholders as well as what actions to take to address these risks before they become major issues on the project. To which document would you record individual risks?

   **a.** Risk report

   **b.** Risk audit

   **c.** Risk register

   **d.** Issue log

**18.** You are leading a project to develop a new inventory management system. You are collecting requirements and using various tools and techniques to gather requirements from stakeholders, including interviews, focus groups, and surveys. Which of the following is not a tool or technique for gathering requirements?

   **a.** Prototyping

   **b.** Observations

   **c.** Storyboards

   **d.** Monte Carlo simulation

**19.** Your Agile team is tasked with developing a budgeting app. The product owner has proposed an initial release that includes the ability to track expenses, categorize spending, and generate simple monthly reports. The goal is to quickly deliver a functional product to users and gather feedback before investing in advanced features like predictive analytics or AI-driven recommendations. A senior stakeholder, however, insists on including these advanced features up front to ensure the product stands out in the market. What is the product owner's proposed approach called?

   **a.** Minimum Marketable Features (MMF)

   **b.** Incremental release

c. Prototype

d. Minimum Viable Product (MVP)

20. You are managing a project where team members express concerns about a lack of resources and unclear priorities. Instead of dictating solutions, you dedicate time to removing roadblocks, clarifying objectives, and ensuring the team has the tools and support they need to succeed. You also encourage open communication, asking the team for feedback on how you can better support their efforts. Which leadership style does this situation best illustrate?

a. Transformative leadership

b. Servant leadership

c. Intentional leadership

d. New Age leadership

# Answer Key

1. Answer: **c.** In the project closure phase, the top priority is to confirm that all deliverables meet the agreed-upon acceptance criteria and obtain formal sign-off from stakeholders. This ensures the project's objectives have been achieved and the deliverables are ready to transition to the receiving organization. **Refer to Chapter 18.**

2. Answer: **b.** The project is not meeting the sponsor's deadline by 5 days. Negative project float means that the critical path is longer than the externally imposed deadline, indicating that the project is currently scheduled to finish 5 days later than the sponsor's deadline. Project float is the only type of float that can be a negative number. **Refer to Chapter 13.**

3. Answer: **b.** The Stakeholder Engagement Plan includes stakeholder analysis, engagement strategies, and communication requirements to ensure effective stakeholder engagement and involvement throughout the project. **Refer to Chapter 12.**

4. Answer: **a.** The geopolitical event could significantly impact the project. The best approach is to evaluate how these changes affect the project in terms of risk, cost, and viability. Ignoring the geopolitical event (Option b) or stopping the project completely (Option c) without further evaluation would be risky. Option d is the same thing as Option b. **Refer to Chapter 9.**

5. Answer: **c.** A Directive PMO is responsible for managing and executing projects directly. The primary function of a Directive PMO is to assume full control of projects and manage them from start to finish. **Refer to Chapter 8.**

6. **Answer: b.** A collaborative approach fosters open communication and mutual understanding, aligning with Agile principles of teamwork and transparency. Avoiding the conflict (Option a) could escalate tensions, while enforcing authority (Option c) risks damaging trust. Osmotic communication tools (Option d) are excellent for passive information flow but are not suitable for resolving interpersonal disputes. **Refer to Chapter 11.**

7. **Answer: d.** Agile combines iterative and incremental approaches, enabling quick delivery of value while adapting to feedback. It is ideal for balancing the need for flexibility with the stakeholders' expectations. **Refer to Chapter 7.**

8. **Answer: c.** This situation exemplifies osmotic communication, where team members absorb information naturally by overhearing conversations in a shared space, enabling them to act quickly and collaboratively. **Refer to Chapter 14.**

9. **Answer: a.** The change control plan provides the framework for evaluating and managing changes to the project, including assessing the impact on scope, schedule, and quality. In this scenario, it helps ensure the unapproved change is formally reviewed and either approved or rejected. As the project manager, addressing the developer's and tester's concerns through a formal change control process helps resolve the conflict while maintaining project governance. **Refer to Chapter 15.**

10. **Answer: b.** T-shaped people are individuals with deep expertise in one area (the vertical stroke of the "T") and a willingness to contribute in other areas (the horizontal stroke). This combination of specialization and adaptability is key to the scenario described. **Refer to Chapter 20.**

11. **Answer: d.** The value, "Individuals and interactions over processes and tools," emphasizes the importance of collaboration and communication within the team, including involving team members in decision-making processes. **Refer to Chapter 19.**

12. **Answer: b.** To address the decline in engagement from the key stakeholder, you should initiate a one-on-one meeting to understand their concerns, gather feedback, and reconfirm their expectations, allowing you to take corrective actions and re-engage them effectively. **Refer to Chapter 17.**

13. **Answer: a.** A stakeholder is anyone who has an interest in the project or can influence its outcome. This includes not only the project team, but also external parties such as customers, vendors, regulatory bodies, and even the local community. The correct answer reflects the comprehensive definition of stakeholders. **Refer to Chapter 10.**

14. **Answer: c.** Projects are temporary endeavors with a clear start and finish, aimed at creating a unique product, service, or result — such as deploying a new onboarding process. After the software is deployed and training is

complete, the project is considered closed. Operations involve ongoing, repetitive activities to sustain business functions, such as monitoring and maintaining the onboarding process. While the operations manager may expect ongoing involvement, the project team's responsibilities should end after the handover to operations is completed. **Refer to Chapter 6.**

15. Answer: **a.** Extrinsic motivation refers to motivation that comes from external rewards or recognition, such as an extra day off. **Refer to Chapter 11.**

16. Answer: **b.** In a geographically dispersed team, a shared cloud-based document repository is the most effective tool for real-time access to project information. It allows team members to collaborate and access documents, regardless of their location and time zone. **Refer to Chapter 16.**

17. Answer: **c.** The risk register documents individual risks. The risk report documents overall risk exposure. A risk audit is a meeting about the overall risk management process. The issue log tracks and manages issues, not risks. **Refer to Chapter 14.**

18. Answer: **d.** Monte Carlo analysis is a tool and technique used for risk planning. The other tools — prototyping, observations, and storyboarding (a form of prototyping) — are used for gathering detailed information from stakeholders about their requirements and expectations. **Refer to Chapter 13.**

19. Answer: **d.** The product owner's approach aligns with the MVP concept, which involves delivering only the essential features needed to provide value and validate the product idea through user feedback. MMF (a) is incorrect because it focuses on making the product competitive in the market, which may include additional features beyond the MVP. **Refer to Chapter 21.**

20. Answer: **b.** This scenario exemplifies servant leadership, which focuses on supporting the team by addressing their needs, removing obstacles, and fostering a collaborative environment. **Refer to Chapter 20.**

# How Did You Do?

Don't stress about your score. After all, this quiz is just a starting point. Use this pre-assessment as an opportunity to identify areas to focus on. Jot down any missed questions and watch for those topics as you move through the book. Your goal is progress, not perfection.

# What Is Project Management Really?

**IN THIS PART . . .**

Uncover the key characteristics of projects.

Develop a foundational understanding of the key concepts in project management.

**IN THIS CHAPTER**

» Defining the key characteristics of a project and how they differ from operations

» Uncovering why projects happen

» Finding out what industries and sectors need project management

# Chapter 6
# An Overview of Projects

From the smallest start-ups to the globe's largest multinational corporations, projects are shaping our world. They are changing the way we communicate, live, work, and play. They are influencing governments, touching lives, and leading to advancements that, just a generation ago, we couldn't have even imagined. These projects are making headlines, bringing on innovation, and triggering shifts in society.

While newsworthy, high-profile projects are happening across the world, let's not forget the quieter, equally important projects happening right in our backyards. It's not always about making the news; sometimes, it's about making a difference.

Maybe your community is like mine, bustling with projects aimed at boosting workforce development opportunities for the unemployed and the underemployed. Perhaps your local library is getting its wheels on, implementing a mobile library project to bring the world of books to doorsteps. There could be an entrepreneur down the street, opening up a shiny, new brick-and-mortar store in the town center, a testament to dreams taking flight through dedicated project management.

Moreover, urban sprawl is giving rise to new community development projects. These ventures aim to accommodate sustainable and inclusive growth, tackling housing issues and city planning challenges while promoting quality of life and community engagement. Urban sprawl is transforming empty landscapes into bustling new communities, a result of countless hours of planning, designing, and building — a massive project management effort in itself.

So, you see, projects that make the headlines are not the only ones making a difference. Projects happen everywhere and they touch everyone.

In this chapter, you will gain a better understanding of what project management is all about, have a solid definition of a project, gain a better understanding of why projects exist, and recognize where they happen.

# What Are Projects?

It's important to be clear on the distinction between projects and operations — a potential exam question. Projects and operations, while seemingly similar, hold distinct roles within an organization. Let's dive into my world of healthcare administration. A hospital setting provides an excellent real-life illustration to delve into this difference.

REMEMBER

Projects are temporary initiatives that have a start and an end, creating a unique product, service, or result. Projects fulfill objectives by producing deliverables that result in desired outcomes.

For instance, imagine that a hospital decides to create a new neonatal intensive care unit (NICU). This initiative is a project. It starts with the initial planning phase, and ends when the NICU is ready and functional, offering specialized care for newborn babies.

In this case, the unique *product* is the fully equipped NICU, the *service* is enhanced neonatal care, and the *result* is an improved ability of the hospital to care for newborns' health needs. The *objective* of this project might be to reduce the mortality rate of premature infants, and the *deliverables* are the various milestones completed along the way, such as finishing the construction work, installing the medical equipment, and training the staff. Each of these milestones contributes to the desired outcome, which is a fully operational NICU.

Now, let's consider operations. These are the ongoing, routine activities that keep the hospital running smoothly day after day. They don't have an end point; they're part of the hospital's "business as usual." For example, performing routine patient check-ups, administering daily medications, maintaining medical records — these are all operations.

Occasionally, projects and operations do overlap. Using the previous example, once the NICU project is complete and the unit is running, it transitions into an operational department. The daily care of infants in the unit becomes a routine operational activity, even as it started as a part of a unique project.

**REMEMBER** Understanding the difference between projects and operations is important in project management. It helps managers allocate resources effectively, keep track of progress, and ensure that the organization meets its objectives while maintaining daily functions efficiently.

# Why Do We Have Projects?

Projects entail a wide range of activities and objectives, depending on the specific circumstances and goals of the organization. Let's explore some common elements and reasons why projects are initiated.

## Driving change

One common reason for initiating a project is to drive change within an organization or department. This could involve implementing new technologies, improving business processes, or adopting new strategies to stay competitive in the market. Change is essential for organizations to adapt and grow in a rapidly evolving business environment. And let's be real: there is always some executive with some new idea that they read about in the latest issue of *Forbes* magazine.

## Optimizing business value creation

Projects often aim to create or enhance business value. This can involve developing new products or services that generate revenue or improve customer satisfaction. Projects may also focus on optimizing existing processes to increase efficiency, reduce costs, or improve quality. The goal is to deliver tangible benefits that contribute to the success of the organization. Who doesn't want to increase or add value to their organization? Sometimes the brand-new idea from said executive is motivated by the desire to increase value, whether it be for the customer or the shareholders (not to be confused with stakeholders).

## Complying with regulations and requirements

Projects may be necessary to ensure compliance with changing regulatory, legal, or social requirements. This is without a doubt my life in the healthcare industry. Organizations must stay up to date with laws and regulations (hello, Healthcare.gov) that govern their industry and adapt their operations accordingly. Projects can help organizations implement the necessary changes to meet these requirements and avoid potential penalties or reputational damage.

### Ensuring stakeholder satisfaction

Projects may be initiated to satisfy the demands and expectations of stakeholders. Stakeholders can include customers, clients, employees, shareholders, and the community at large. For example, a project might focus on improving customer service, addressing specific stakeholder concerns, or meeting sustainability goals to enhance the organization's reputation. Happy customers, happy project.

### Making product, process, or service improvements

Projects are often undertaken to create, improve, or fix products, processes, or services. This could involve developing a new version of a software application, enhancing manufacturing processes to increase productivity, or redesigning a service delivery model to enhance the customer experience. Projects enable organizations to adapt and respond to changing market demands or address performance issues.

### Initiating strategic changes

Projects can be driven by a strategic change in the focus of the business or the need to upgrade technological capabilities. For instance, a company may undertake a project to enter a new market, diversify its product offerings, or implement emerging technologies to gain a competitive advantage. These strategic initiatives require careful planning and execution to ensure successful outcomes.

It's important to note that the specific nature and objectives of projects can vary greatly across industries and organizations. The examples previously provided are meant to illustrate common reasons why projects occur, but so many other possibilities exist as to why projects are initiated.

## Where Do Projects Happen?

As you've probably gathered by now, projects are not limited to any specific industry or sector. They can be found across various fields and organizations, each with their own unique requirements and objectives. Let's take a look at some industries where projects can take place.

> » **Information technology:** In the rapidly evolving world of technology, information technology (IT) projects are prevalent. These projects can involve

developing software applications, implementing cybersecurity measures, upgrading hardware infrastructure, migrating to new platforms, or integrating artificial intelligence (AI) as a part of the workflow. IT projects aim to enhance operational efficiency, improve data security, and meet the evolving technological needs of organizations.

» **Construction:** The construction industry is inherently project-based, as it involves the creation of physical structures. Construction projects can include building residential or commercial properties, developing infrastructure such as roads or bridges, or renovating and maintaining existing structures. Projects in construction focus on managing resources, adhering to safety standards, and delivering projects on time and within budget. One of my favorite (albeit short-lived) TV shows is *Impossible Builds*, where you get to watch the most amazing construction projects in the world. You should check it out!

» **Healthcare and public health:** This is my jam! Because I built my career in the healthcare industry, and this is where I got my start in project management. The healthcare industry often undertakes projects to implement new technologies, improve patient care processes, or upgrade medical equipment and facilities. These projects aim to enhance the quality of healthcare services, streamline administrative tasks, and ensure compliance with regulatory requirements such as electronic health records (EHR) implementation. And let's not forget the massive project implementation of a COVID-19 vaccine in 2020 and 2021. Let's face it, there will *always* be a need for projects in this field as you touch lives from cradle to grave. Crass to say, I know, but it is the truth.

» **Retail:** In the retail sector, projects are initiated to optimize store layouts, improve customer experiences, or introduce new product lines. Retail projects can involve redesigning store layouts, implementing new point-of-sale (POS) systems, launching e-commerce platforms, or conducting marketing campaigns to attract customers. Think about today's world of brick-and-mortar shopping malls and online stores.

» **Marketing:** Marketing projects focus on developing and executing strategies to promote products or services effectively. These projects may involve market research, branding initiatives, advertising campaigns, social media management, or launching new marketing channels. Marketing projects aim to increase brand visibility, engage target audiences, and drive sales.

» **Urban planning:** Urban planning projects are essential for shaping the development of cities and communities. These projects can involve redesigning public spaces, improving transportation infrastructure, implementing sustainable initiatives, or revitalizing neighborhoods. Urban planning projects aim to create livable, accessible, and environmentally friendly urban environments. Look around your community and you will probably see these types of projects in your neighborhood.

- **Private sector:** Projects occur in various private-sector organizations across industries such as finance, manufacturing, and telecommunications. These projects can involve implementing new business processes, expanding operations into new markets, adopting new technologies, or launching new products and services.

- **Government:** Projects are also common in government organizations at the local, state, and national levels. Government projects can include infrastructure development, policy implementations, public health initiatives, social welfare programs, or large-scale public events. These projects aim to serve the public interest and address the needs of citizens.

It's worth noting that projects can be found in numerous other industries not listed here. If you're thinking it, yes, projects happen in that space, too (nonprofits, education, and on the battlefield). The prevalence of projects across industries highlights the need for skilled project managers to effectively plan, execute, and deliver successful outcomes.

## IN THIS CHAPTER

» Defining project management and the continuum of approaches

» Making sense of value and value delivery

» Differentiating between product management and project management

» Examine how organizational structures shape project management execution

» Looking at additional key concepts: tailoring, project manager responsibilities, and project life cycle

Chapter **7**

# Project Management Key Concepts

This chapter aims to ensure a foundational understanding of the key concepts in project management. You'll need to understand key terminology that I often reference throughout the book. These concepts are fundamental to your understanding of not only good project management practices, but also the content that may appear on the exam.

Throughout your PMP Exam prep journey, you will encounter terms that sound very foreign. Others might sound familiar, but perhaps you've defined them a little bit differently. You should dig deep into this chapter to understand these key concepts, as it's important for you to know what and how PMI defines these terms, how they are used in the exam context, and how you can better refine your project management work. And quite frankly, it's good to know these terms when you prepare for an interview and want to ensure that you speak the same language.

# Defining Project Management

Per the *PMBOK Guide*, project management is defined as follows:

> The application of knowledge, skills, tools, and techniques to project activities to meet the project requirements.

Project management is a fusion of intuition and precision. The *precision* aspect involves following steps, procedures, and processes and implementing a system to manage work efficiently. On the other hand, the *intuition* of project management is about utilizing skills such as active listening, influencing, and interpersonal skills. This unique balance is what makes project management so intriguing (at least to me). What's more, the systematic approach to managing projects can take on various forms, from predictive to Agile, and even a hybrid approach that falls somewhere in between, showcasing the flexibility and adaptability of the field.

## Exploring the continuum of project management

The continuum of project management refers to the range of approaches that can be used to manage projects, from predictive to adaptive and hybrid.

On one end of the continuum is predictive project management, also known as the *waterfall approach*. This approach involves a linear sequence of project phases, with each phase completed before proceeding to the next phase.

On the other end of the continuum is adaptive project management, frequently referred to as *Agile*. This involves an iterative and incremental approach to project delivery, where requirements and solutions evolve.

In your exam preparation, you may see *development approach* referred to as *project management approach*, or project life cycle. Maddening, isn't it? Refer to the section, **"Defining terms: Exploring methodology, development approach, and project life cycle"** later in the chapter, for more insight.

In between these two extremes of the project management continuum, you have the hybrid approach that combines predictive and adaptive elements. Many organizations that are not quite ready for full-scale Agile development often rely on the hybrid approach to achieve their project goals.

You will also find out about the iterative and incremental development approaches in your exam preparation. These approaches are key characteristics of adaptive project management and can also be incorporated into hybrid approaches to balance predictability with flexibility. It's a lot, I know.

For more context, take a look at Figure 7-1, which illustrates the continuum of project management approaches.

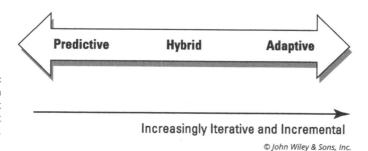

FIGURE 7-1: Continuum of project management approaches.

## Using the predictive approach: You know, you know

The predictive approach assumes that the project can be fully planned up front and that changes can be managed through a formal change control process. This approach is best suited for projects with well-defined objectives and stable requirements. With this approach, project scope, time, and costs are determined early in the project. A plan is created, which is the driver of all the project efforts. Changes to the project are carefully managed.

TIP

This approach is also referred to as traditional, plan-driven, and waterfall.

## Taking the adaptive approach: You don't know what you don't know

The adaptive approach assumes that change is inevitable and that projects must be flexible enough to adapt to changing requirements. This involves an iterative and incremental approach to project delivery, where requirements and solutions evolve through the collaborative effort of self-organizing and cross-functional teams. With the adaptive approach, the scope is *outlined* and agreed upon before the start of product development.

TIP

This approach may also be referred to as change-driven or Agile. In truth, many people default to saying "Agile." For exam preparation purposes, the adaptive approach includes Agile, iterative, and incremental approaches; Agile is the extreme version of the adaptive approach.

> ## AGILE WITH A CAPITAL 'A' OR SMALL 'A'?
>
> Have you been wondering why sometimes you see *Agile* spelled with both a capital 'A' and a lowercase 'a'? Here's the distinction.
>
> **Agile (noun):** Uppercase 'A' Agile is something you do. It's the methodology, relating to or denoting a method of project management. For example, "In organization X, Agile is practiced by our teams."
>
> **agile (adjective):** Lowercase 'a' is what you are. You are able to move quickly and easily, to think, understand, and respond quickly. For example, "In our organization, we are able to be agile with some of our projects."
>
> Over the last decade, there has been a shift to using the lowercase *agile* to denote the methodology as well as to indicate your position within an organization ("We are agile"). In fact, the latest editions of the *PMBOK Guide* have chosen to use lowercase 'a' when mentioning *agile* unless, of course, it is part of a formal document or proper title, such as the Agile Manifesto.
>
> This author has decided to use uppercase A. (It just looks better.)

## Adopting the hybrid approach: A little bit of this, a little bit of that

The hybrid approach is a combination of predictive and adaptive life cycles. This approach has become quite popular as organizations see the benefits of Agile but are not ready to go all in. Hybrid leverages the tools and techniques of both predictive and adaptive approaches, where well-known or fixed requirements follow a predictive development approach, but you may have evolving requirements that follow an adaptive life cycle. The hybrid approach also often uses iterative and incremental development approaches.

## Defining terms: Exploring methodology, development approach, and project life cycle

In your studies, you may encounter the terms *methodology*, *development approach*, and *project life cycle*, which can be confusing.

» **A methodology** refers to a set of principles, tools, and practices that are used to guide project management activities. Methodologies provide a framework for project management and typically include processes and procedures for planning, executing, monitoring, and controlling project activities. This may be something that is defined by your organization, such as through your Project Management Office (PMO).

» **A development approach** refers to the overall strategy used to deliver a project, which can be either predictive or adaptive. A *predictive approach* assumes that the project can be fully planned up front and that changes can be managed through a formal change control process. An *adaptive approach*, on the other hand, assumes that change is inevitable and that projects must be flexible enough to adapt to changing requirements. A *hybrid approach* assumes that you are incorporating predictive and adaptive techniques.

» **A project life cycle** refers to the phases or stages that a project goes through from initiation to closure. Each life cycle phase typically has specific objectives, deliverables, and stakeholders.

While the continuum of project management describes a range of approaches, methodologies provide a specific set of principles and practices to guide project management activities. The development approach refers to the overall strategy used to deliver a project, and the project life cycle refers to the phases or stages that a project goes through from initiation to closure.

By the way, even PMI concedes that these are confusing terms. If you have the *PMBOK Guide* Seventh Edition handy, check out page 33 of Section 2, where they provide definitions. Also, be sure to check out their sidebar, titled "What's in a name?" on page 49 of Section 2. In this sidebar, they indicate that many project professionals use the terms *development approach* and *project life cycle* interchangeably. Go figure.

TIP

For the exam, you'll be fine if you are familiar with the terms and understand the context of the questions and the answer options.

# Finding a Reason for the Project Management Season

Contrary to popular belief, the decision to choose one project management approach over another should be intentional rather than haphazard. Should be. You may have heard people implementing the Agile approach at an organization, for instance, because it's the "flavor of the month." But you're not going to fall into that trap. As a trusted advisor and trained project professional, you will help the organization decide on the best approach with intention, based on whether you foresee frequent changes in scope or a need for one deliverable. To illustrate, let's look at the visual in Figure 7-2, the continuum of life cycles.

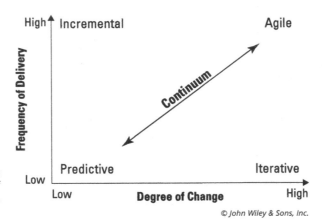

**FIGURE 7-2:** The continuum of life cycles.

Let's take a closer look at each life cycle in detail, examining their key characteristics, advantages, and best-use scenarios.

- **Predictive:** The frequency of output delivery is low, meaning that you will have one deliverable, and the degree of change is low because you have developed a plan that will be followed. The predictive approach assumes that requirements are known and uncertainty is low. This allows teams to segment work into a sequence of predictable activities.

- **Iterative:** The frequency of output delivery is low, meaning that you will have one deliverable; however, the degree of change is high. The benefit of this life cycle is that it allows for feedback on partially completed or unfinished deliverables to improve and modify the work. The focus is on the correctness of the solution.

- **Incremental:** The frequency of output delivery is high, meaning that you will have multiple deliveries and deliverables, yet the degree of change is low. The focus is on providing deliverables that can be used immediately by the customer. In short, the goal is speed.

- **Agile:** Outputs are delivered frequently, meaning that there will be multiple deliveries and deliverables. The degree of change is high with Agile. Agile leverages the aspects of iterative and incremental life cycles. Project teams iterate to create finished product increments based on stakeholder feedback.

### IS IT ADAPTIVE OR AGILE?

The *adaptive life cycle* is a broad term that refers to a type of project management approach where the project is designed to adapt and respond to changes as they occur. It emphasizes flexibility and iterative progress, allowing the project to evolve as new information and feedback are received. An adaptive life cycle is commonly used in projects where requirements are not clearly defined from the outset and are expected to change over time. Adaptive life cycles are also referred to as Agile or change-driven life cycles.

*Agile,* a specific subset of adaptive life cycles, is characterized by a set of principles and practices that promote iterative development and collaboration. This collaborative aspect of Agile is a key strength, as it fosters a sense of teamwork and shared responsibility. Agile is often implemented through frameworks like Scrum, Kanban, or Extreme Programming (XP), and it focuses on delivering small, incremental improvements frequently, usually in the form of sprints.

When preparing for the exam, remember that Agile is an example of an adaptive life cycle but not the only one. Adaptive life cycles are the overarching concept, while Agile refers to specific methods and practices within that concept. To help differentiate between the two, focus on the context in which the terms are used; adaptive life cycles are more about the overall approach, while Agile is about the specific frameworks and practices used to implement that approach.

A lot goes into thinking about the right approach and life cycle for your project. From the frequency of deliverables to the project needs to the delivery of value, you really want to be intentional and strategic about your approach to managing projects. For instance, selecting the adaptive approach should take more thought than, "Let's do Agile; I hear it's way cooler than waterfall project management!" Oh, I have heard this declaration before. You want to make the right decisions based on the outcomes and benefits that your stakeholders will gain.

# Shifting from Outputs to Outcomes

Over the last couple of years, PMI has shifted the focus of the project profession. Today's focus is more on a systems view of value delivery and recognizing that project management is more than just producing outputs. The focus is on how those outputs can drive outcomes that deliver value to stakeholders and end users. Furthermore, an organization's viewpoint on value delivery can have a significant impact on your project management approach, whether it is predictive, adaptive, or hybrid.

## Taking a systems view of value

Projects are a part of a system for value delivery within organizations. Think of it this way: all of the strategic business activities that occur in an organization that are focused on building, sustaining, and/or advancing that organization make up a system for value delivery. This can consist of the portfolios, programs, products, and operations within the organization.

The components of a value delivery system create deliverables that will, in turn, produce outcomes. Outcomes create benefits. Benefits, in turn, create value.

## Creating value through projects

Value is something of worth, importance, or usefulness. And value can be perceived by stakeholders in different ways. Value can mean one thing for your customers, something different to the organization, and something totally different to society. Projects produce value in a variety of ways, including the following:

- **Increased revenue:** Projects that help increase revenue are valuable to businesses. For instance, a project focusing on developing a new product or service can increase the company's revenue. Another example is a project that improves customer experience, leading to increased sales and repeat business.

- **Cost savings:** Projects that help reduce costs can also produce value. For example, a project that focuses on optimizing supply chain operations can reduce the cost of raw materials and transportation, leading to lower production costs. Another example is a project that implements energy-efficient practices, reducing energy costs.

- **Improved efficiency:** Projects focusing on improving efficiency can add value by increasing productivity and reducing waste. For example, a project that implements lean manufacturing techniques can improve production efficiency and decrease waste. Another example is a project that streamlines business processes, reducing the time and effort required to complete tasks.

- **Competitive advantage:** Projects that give an organization a competitive advantage can produce value. For instance, a project that develops a new technology or process that competitors do not have can give a company a competitive edge. Another example is a project that improves brand recognition, leading to increased market share.

» **Enhancing customer experience:** Projects can improve the customer experience by developing new products or services, improving existing offerings, or creating more engaging user interfaces.

» **Mitigating risk:** Projects can reduce risk by implementing robust security measures, ensuring compliance with regulatory requirements, or developing contingency plans to minimize the impact of unforeseen events.

» **Fostering innovation:** Projects can produce value by encouraging innovation within an organization, leading to new ideas and breakthroughs that can improve products, services, or processes.

» **Promoting sustainability:** Projects can improve community relations and promote social responsibility. For example, developing sustainable supply chains that support local communities can create jobs and stimulate economic development.

» **Increasing social value:** Projects can produce social value by addressing social, environmental, or humanitarian issues and contributing to society's well-being.

When thought out well and planned well, projects have a way of creating value and impacting an organization and the end users the organization serves in all sorts of ways.

## Focusing on the organization's view of value delivery

While projects undoubtedly create and add value to society, the organization itself has its own perspective of value.

From a larger scale, the organizational viewpoint of value delivery involves the organization's internal environment, such as the following:

» Policies

» Procedures

» Methodologies

» Frameworks

» Governance

Specifically, a governance system works alongside the value delivery system to enable smooth workflows, manage issues, and support decision-making. An example of a governance framework is having a Project Management Office (PMO) in place (I discuss the role of the Project Management Office in Chapter 9).

A *value delivery system* is a collection of strategic business activities aimed at building, sustaining, and/or advancing an organization.

Within organizations, a plethora of roles and functions are drivers of value delivery. These roles include the following:

- **Project manager:** Provides project oversight and coordination and is responsible for achieving the project objectives
- **Functional manager:** Provides management oversight for a functional or business unit (for example department manager)
- **Sponsor:** Provides resources and direction
- **Sponsor/product owner:** Presents objectives and feedback
- **Scrum Master:** Facilitates and supports
- **Project team:** Performs work and contributes insights
- **Subject matter experts (SMEs):** Apply expertise
- **Product owner/customer:** Provides business direction and insight
- **Project governance/PMO:** Maintains governance

Project management is more than just producing outputs and deliverables. It's about producing outcomes and delivering value — it's about making an impact. What you've discovered so far is that projects exist within a larger organization and that an organization's viewpoint on value delivery can have a significant impact on how you manage projects.

In the next section, I dive into one additional concept on value delivery and how organizations can influence your authority and collaboration efforts with stakeholders.

## Unpacking organizational structure and its impact on project value delivery

Organizational structure pertains to how a company or organization is arranged to achieve its goals and objectives. It includes hierarchy, roles, responsibilities, and communication channels within the organization. Three key types of organizational structures may appear on the exam.

- **Functional structure:** In a functional structure, employees are grouped by their specialized skills or functions, such as marketing, finance, or operations and report to a functional manager. This structure can provide a high level of expertise and specialization, which can be beneficial for complex projects that require specific skills. However, it can also create silos and hinder communication and collaboration between departments, which can lead to delays and reduced project delivery value. In this structure, typically, the project manager's authority is low, their role is part-time, and resource availability is part-time. The functional manager is responsible for managing the budget.

- **Project-oriented structure:** In a project-oriented structure (sometimes referred to as *projectized*), employees are organized around specific projects, and project managers have full authority over project resources. This structure can provide a high level of flexibility and responsiveness to changing project needs, which can increase project delivery value. However, it can also create inefficiencies and duplication of effort when resources are dedicated to multiple projects simultaneously. With project-oriented structures, the project manager's authority is high and they tend to be full-time on the project. Resource availability tends to be full-time on the project, as well. The project manager is responsible for managing the budget.

- **Matrix structure:** In a matrix structure, employees are assigned to both functional teams and project teams. This structure can provide a balance of functional expertise and project-specific focus, which can lead to increased project delivery value. However, it can also create confusion over roles and responsibilities and result in conflicts between functional and project managers. There are three types of matrix structures: *weak matrix, balanced matrix,* and *strong matrix*.

TIP

A great way to discern among the structures is that in the functional and project-oriented structures, employees report to one manager (either the functional manager or the project manager). With a matrix structure, think two managers — staff are reporting to both the project manager and the functional manager.

Organizational structures can significantly impact project delivery value. They influence the project in various ways, from the selection of the methodology to how you acquire resources and procure materials to how much authority a project manager has on a project.

TIP

For exam preparation purposes, assume that, at minimum, a strong matrix is in place. This means that as you answer questions from the perspective of a project manager, you *assume* that you have a high level of control and management over your projects, you have high authority, and you directly manage the project team. Oh, happy day.

# Center of the Universe: The Project Manager

Project managers are the driving force behind a project's success, taking ownership of the entire process from start to finish. They play a vital role in ensuring that the project is delivered on time, within budget, and to the highest standards. This multifaceted role requires a combination of technical expertise, communication skills, and strong organizational abilities.

## Uncovering the many responsibilities of a project manager

Project managers are the unsung heroes who thrive amidst the chaos of projects from start to finish. They navigate the complexities of communication, data analysis, and quality assurance to deliver projects on time, within budget, and to the satisfaction of all stakeholders. They are the ones who need to have their finger on the pulse of the project, understanding what's happening, who to engage with for each element, and whether it's progressing on time and within budget. Their unique set of skills, adaptive thinking, and ability to handle the moving parts make them invaluable in the world of project management. They are able to balance technical expertise with interpersonal skills.

TIP

Assume all of these project manager attributes as you answer questions on the exam. Trust me on this.

### Accountability

The project manager is accountable for every aspect of the project. They need to stay informed about the project's progress, understand each element, and know who to collaborate with at every stage. Project managers constantly assess timelines and budgets to ensure the project stays on track.

The responsibilities of a project manager are no walk in the park!

## Communication

As a project manager, you need to be a good communicator (I can't stress this enough). Effective communication is at the core of a project manager's responsibilities. So many project managers crash and burn at their jobs; despite being technically competent, they are inept communicators. As the project manager, *you are* the central point of contact for everyone involved in the project. This means being able to communicate effectively with team members, stakeholders, clients, and executives. Your responsibilities can entail anything from providing regular updates on the project's status to communicating both upwards to your supervisors or executives and downwards to the team members. It is your responsibility to provide clear and concise communication to ensure that everyone understands their tasks and responsibilities, fostering collaboration and synergy.

## Data

Project managers also delve into the world of data. They extract and analyze relevant information to complete the various reports required for each project. By leveraging data, project managers can identify potential risks, track progress, and make informed adjustments to ensure the project's success.

## Meetings

Project managers spend a significant amount of time in meetings. This reminds me of a famous meme on the internet where a message reads, "I just survived another meeting that could have been an email." But I digress.

Why meetings? Because, like it or not, part of communicating with your team members and stakeholders is about bringing team members up to speed and ensuring that everyone is aligned. You will facilitate discussions, resolve conflicts, and provide guidance to keep the project moving forward smoothly.

## Quality assurance

Project managers also play a critical role in quality assurance. They review and approve the finished deliverables at various stages, ensuring that the project's objectives and quality standards are met.

# Project manager by many names

When I talk about being a project manager, it's important to recognize that project management skills are not exclusive to a specific title or profession. In fact, you may be a project manager under a different name. Several different names and titles are used for project managers, depending on the industry, organization, and context. Here are some common alternatives:

- Project coordinator
- Team lead
- Scrum Master
- Delivery manager
- Engagement manager
- Implementation manager
- Consultant
- Analyst
- Executive assistant
- Customer success manager / lead
- Account manager
- Editor
- Operations manager (can include project management responsibilities)
- Business analyst (can include project management responsibilities)
- Change manager
- Business owner
- Entrepreneur

You may already be practicing project management in your everyday life without even realizing it. Let's say, for instance, you are a board member of a cancer foundation. Let's explore an example to demonstrate how you are indeed a project manager in this role.

## Applying project management principles

Imagine your cancer foundation has set a goal to launch a fundraising campaign to support research and provide assistance to cancer patients. As a board member, you will play a crucial role in overseeing and coordinating various aspects of this project.

The following sections show how you can apply project management principles.

### Defining objectives

You would work with the foundation's team to clearly define the fundraising campaign's objectives. This includes identifying the target fundraising amount, the timeline for the campaign, and the specific projects or initiatives that will benefit from the funds raised.

### Ensuring stakeholder management

As a board member, you would engage with various stakeholders, such as donors, volunteers, medical professionals, and community members. You would communicate the campaign's goals, build relationships, and ensure their support and participation in the project.

### Planning and budgeting

You would collaborate with the team to develop a comprehensive project plan, including a timeline, milestones, and a budget. This plan would outline specific tasks, responsibilities, and resources required for the campaign's success.

### Evaluating risks

Identifying and managing risks is crucial in any project. In this case, you would assess potential risks to the fundraising campaign, such as donor fatigue, competition from other causes, or unforeseen challenges. By anticipating and addressing these risks proactively, you can increase the chances of achieving your fundraising goals.

### Monitoring and evaluating

Throughout the campaign, you would monitor the progress, track fundraising efforts, and evaluate the outcomes. This includes analyzing donation patterns, measuring the campaign's impact, and making necessary adjustments to improve results.

### Aligning team coordination

As a board member, you would work closely with the foundation's team, including staff, volunteers, and other board members. You would facilitate communication, provide guidance and support, and ensure that everyone is aligned with the campaign's objectives.

By recognizing your role as a project manager within the context of the cancer foundation, you can appreciate the skills and knowledge you already possess. This is what this book sets out to do: show you that you have the skills and aptitude to be the best project manager you can be, building upon your existing abilities and introducing the best-practice strategies and tools that will enable you to handle more complex projects and expand your project management expertise.

The rest of this book will continue to dive deeper into specific strategies, techniques, and tools to help you excel in managing more complex projects in various professional settings. I'll put names to strategies and tools that you probably already use, teach you some new ones to handle more complex projects, and round out your knowledge so your skills are transferable and current! And, of course, I'll provide you with the information you need to confidently pass the PMP Exam.

# Comparing Different PMs: Product Management versus Project Management

Projects are often undertaken to create, improve, or update products, processes, or services. Presumably, the project outputs are delivering outcomes, and those outcomes are delivering value to your stakeholders. These projects, temporary in nature with well-defined objectives and timelines, represent a critical aspect of project management. However, in the broader spectrum of organizational strategy, there exists another important discipline: **product management**. Product management, with its comprehensive approach to the entire life cycle of a product, goes beyond the specific project delivery focus of project management.

Product management is the integration of people, data, processes, and business systems to create, maintain, and develop a product or service throughout its life cycle. It is the process of overseeing the development, marketing, and distribution of a product. It involves understanding customer needs, defining product requirements, and working with teams of designers, engineers, and marketers to bring the product to market. The focus is on creating, maintaining, and developing a product throughout its life cycle.

Product management and project management are related in that they both involve managing resources and working toward a specific goal. Product management is more focused on the big picture of developing a product, while project management is more focused on the day-to-day tasks required to complete a project. Table 7-1 shows a comparison of product management versus project management.

**TABLE 7-1** **Product Management versus Project Management**

| Product Management | Project Management |
|---|---|
| Long term | Short term |
| Products are customer-focused and benefits-driven | Projects have defined objectives |
| Product teams engage in continuous development | Success is measured by meeting the constraints (cost, scope, time, quality) |
| Stable teams | Temporary teams |
| "Inception to retirement" accountability | "Deliver value" accountability |

Perhaps you have encountered the term *product management* in your research of project management or your job search for related project management roles. Hopefully this comparison chart provides a bit more clarity between the terms. Regardless of your role as a product manager or project manager, it's good for you to understand the differences and similarities.

## Progressing through a product life cycle

A product life cycle is a series of phases that represent a product's evolution, from introduction through growth, maturity, and retirement (or decline). Refer to Figure 7-3, which illustrates the product life cycle.

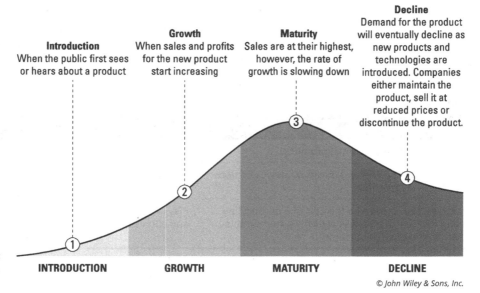

**FIGURE 7-3:** Product life cycle.

© John Wiley & Sons, Inc.

Here's how to think about the product life cycle as it relates to the healthcare industry.

1. **Introduction:** A medical device is launched and introduced to the market. The device is initially only available in select hospitals and clinics.

2. **Growth:** The device is adopted by more hospitals and clinics, and its popularity increases. The company begins to ramp up production to meet the increasing demand.

3. **Maturity:** The device becomes a standard treatment option for the condition it was designed to treat. Sales may begin to level off as the market becomes saturated.

4. **Decline:** As newer and more advanced medical devices enter the market, demand for the original device starts to decline. The company may begin to phase out the device or offer it at only select hospitals.

In the context of project management, products and projects are closely related, but they are not the same thing. If you recall, a *project* is a temporary endeavor with a defined beginning and end that is undertaken to create a unique product, service, or result. A *product*, on the other hand, is a tangible or intangible item produced through a project.

## Defining roles: Product manager versus project manager

It's worth noting the difference between a product manager and a project manager. Product and project management are related in that they involve managing resources and working toward a specific goal. It may help to see the side-by-side comparison shown in Table 7-2.

**TABLE 7-2 Comparison of Product Manager and Project Manager**

| Product Manager | Project Manager |
| --- | --- |
| Drives the development of products. | Oversees previously approved and developed plans. |
| Prioritizes initiatives and makes strategic decisions about what gets built. | Manages schedules and resources to get things done. |
| Sometimes considered the CEO of a product line and focuses on business objectives, measurable goals, and positive outcomes. | Plays an essential part in defining the project plan and successfully executing according to that plan. |

REMEMBER

Product managers focus on the overall product strategy, while project managers focus on the successful completion of a specific project. It's very possible you may encounter an exam question that tests your understanding of the differences.

## Breaking down the work: Projects, products, and programs

Projects, products, and programs are integral components that define how organizations innovate, create value, and execute strategies, respectively. *Projects* represent focused initiatives with defined goals, *products* encapsulate the tangible or intangible outcomes of those initiatives, and *programs* coordinate interconnected projects to achieve overarching objectives. Understanding the distinctions and interplay among these elements is fundamental to effective project management and strategic success. Here's a breakdown of each term:

Projects:

- Duration is short-term, temporary.
- The scope is defined by objectives; scope is iterated (progressively elaborated) throughout the life cycle.
- Success is measured by product and project quality, timelines, budget, customer satisfaction, and achievement of intended outcomes.
- Funding is largely determined up front, based on initial estimates; updates are based on actual performance and change requests.

Products:

- Duration is longer-term.
- Scope of work entails products that are customer-focused and benefits-driven.
- Success is measured by the ability to deliver intended benefits and ongoing viability for continued funding.
- Product teams engage in continuous development via funding, development blocks, and reviews of value delivery.

Programs:

- » Duration is longer-term.
- » The scope of programs is on producing aggregate benefits delivered through multiple components.
- » Success is measured by the realization of intended benefits and the efficiency and effectiveness of delivering those benefits.
- » Funding is up front and ongoing; funding is updated, with results showing how benefits are being delivered.

Per PMI, programs are not large projects. Very large projects may often be referred to as megaprojects. The guiding principle is that megaprojects cost US$1 billion or more, affect 1 million or more people, and run for years.

Let's revisit the product life cycle incorporating all of the concepts of projects, products, and programs.

In the context of project management, products and projects are closely related, but they are not the same thing. A *project* is a temporary endeavor with a defined beginning and end that is undertaken to create a unique product, service, or result. A *product*, on the other hand, is a tangible or intangible item that is produced through a project.

In other words, a project is a means to an end, while a product is the end itself. The project is the process of creating the product, and the product is the outcome of the project.

As you can see in Figure 7-4, there can be significant overlap between products and projects.

For example, a company may create a new product by launching a project within a program to create, develop, and manufacture it. Similarly, that same company may have another program and projects within that program to improve an existing product, which may involve making revisions to the product design, updating production processes, or enhancing product features. There could also be a project to retire a product that is no longer in demand.

The *PMBOK Guide* offers this helpful summary: Product management often initiates programs or projects ("hey, we want to incorporate this new medical device in our hospital"), which can start at any point during the product life cycle. Programs and projects focus on enhancing features, functions, or capabilities to deliver value to end users (that is, the patients) or the organization. In some cases, a program can take on the full product life cycle to manage benefits and ensure ongoing value for the organization.

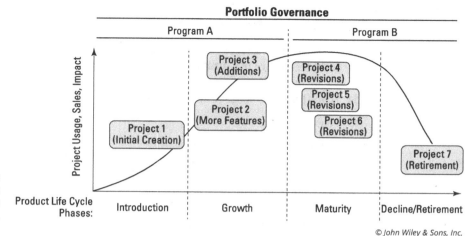

FIGURE 7-4: How products and projects overlap.

© John Wiley & Sons, Inc.

The value delivery system can consist of various components, including portfolios, programs, projects, and products. This section discussed product management and its connection to project management. It explained how project management is divided into different components, starting from a high-level strategic perspective (portfolios and programs) to more detailed components (projects and products). So, let's finally explore one more aspect of breaking down project work, which is to divide the work into phases.

## Dividing a project into phases

Sometimes, it's challenging to see the value of a project because it is just way too big. One way to break down your work is into phases or stages. Breaking down your work into phases allows you to better manage the project work and ultimately better manage the outcomes of your projects.

TIP

Predictive projects use the term *phase* to break down the work into smaller component parts. In the adaptive/Agile environment, *iterations* or *sprints* are used to indicate this.

Phases consist of segments of work that allow for easier management, planning, and control. Typically, this means creating a collection of logically related project activities, each of which may result in one or more deliverables. A project life cycle describes the series of phases that a project passes through from initiation to closing. It includes various deliverables that aid in monitoring the progress and identifying if the project is delayed before it becomes a problem. That way, action can be taken to correct the course of the project. Each phase may produce at least one deliverable at the end of the phase (a feasibility report). Project phases are determined by the project itself and/or the industry you are in.

## Determining types of phases

Phases come in all shapes, sizes, and naming conventions. Attributes of a phase may include, but are not limited to, the following:

- Name (Phase A, Phase B, Phase 1, Phase 2)
- Feasibility
- Number (three phases, five phases)
- Duration (one week, one month, one quarter)
- Resource requirements
- Entrance criteria
- Exit criteria

Figure 7-5 shows a few examples of project phases and their naming conventions.

**FIGURE 7-5:** Project phases.

© John Wiley & Sons, Inc.

## Reviewing progress through phase gates

A *phase gate* is a review to check the desired outcomes or exit criteria for the phase and is often held at the end of each phase before moving on to the next phase. Phase gates may also be referred to as *phase review, stage gate, kill point, phase entrance,* or *phase exit.* During a phase gate, the key stakeholders review how the project is developing and determine whether it's on track, in need of adjustment, or experiencing significant problems and needing to be delayed or terminated as a result. This decision could be made based on delays to the project, the potential of going over budget, or results that aren't meeting the objectives of the project.

TIP

Yep, you read that right. There is a term called "kill point" in project management. It's a review point at the end of a project phase to make the decision to continue, modify, or terminate (kill) the project. Not a term used too much in the healthcare industry.

# Exploring Additional Foundational Concepts

Incorporating phases is a way to subdivide your project work for ease of management and control. But that takes planning. And as you know, projects rarely go exactly according to plan, and new information always affects how you move forward. This is where the concepts of progressive elaboration and rolling wave planning come into play. These are both iterative and continuous planning processes that allow you to adapt to new information and changes as they arise.

By using progressive elaboration and rolling wave planning to continuously improve and refine project plans over time, project managers can ensure that their projects are executed within the context of a larger project life cycle and development approach. This can help to ensure that the project stays on track, delivers the expected value to stakeholders, and meets the requirements of the chosen development approach.

Additionally, deciding which activities and artifacts to incorporate in your project and determining which deliverables to produce fall into the realm of tailoring, an important consideration of your project management work.

## Applying progressive elaboration

*Progressive elaboration* is the process of continuously improving and refining project plans as more information becomes available. In other words, it's an iterative process where the project plan is developed over time rather than all at once at the beginning. This allows for more accurate planning and reduces the risk of unexpected issues arising later in the project. Through progressive elaboration, you can adjust the project plan to account for unforeseen issues and ensure the project stays on track. For example, the cancer foundation's fundraising campaign starts with a high-level plan for its year-long campaign, outlining broad goals and key milestones. As they begin executing the campaign, they progressively develop more detailed plans for each phase.

Continuing with the cancer foundation example I've used throughout this chapter, initially, the foundation starts with a high-level plan for launching a new awareness campaign. As the project moves forward, they gather more details, such as specific target audiences, preferred communication channels, and feedback from initial implementation. These details are progressively added to the project plan, refining the campaign's strategies and tactics over time.

Progressive elaboration is also the process of continuously refining and elaborating on a project's scope and details as more information becomes available. This means that as a project progresses through its phases, the level of detail and understanding of the project increases, allowing for more informed decision-making and adjustments to the project plan.

## Rolling with rolling wave planning

*Rolling wave planning* is a form of progressive elaboration where the project activities are developed in waves, with each wave building upon the previous one, as shown in Figure 7-6. This allows for more detailed planning of near-term activities while still allowing flexibility for later stages of the project.

Here's another example using the cancer foundation: For the cancer foundation's awareness campaign, the team creates a detailed plan for the first three months, focusing on immediate activities like initial outreach and creating promotional materials. The activities planned for six months later, such as nationwide events or large-scale partnerships, are kept at a high-level outline. As the campaign progresses, detailed planning for these future activities is done closer to their execution time, based on the outcomes and feedback from the initial phase.

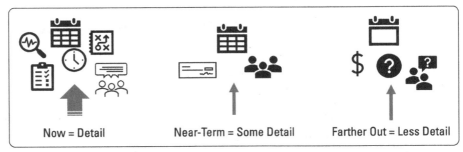

**FIGURE 7-6:** Iterative planning through rolling wave planning.

© *John Wiley & Sons, Inc.*

**TIP**

Be sure you are clear on the difference between progressive elaboration and rolling wave planning. The PMP Exam is known to test you on these two concepts. You will, at least, see these concepts on practice exams.

While progressive elaboration and rolling wave planning help to refine the project plan over time, they are part of a larger framework that includes the entire project life cycle and the development approach used to manage it.

# Meeting the project needs through tailoring

*Tailoring* is an essential concept in project management that enables project managers to customize the project work, such as use of principles and practices, to fit the unique needs of the project. Imagine if you tried to incorporate *all* of the elements of project management, meaning all the documents and all the tools and techniques — it would probably do you more harm than good.

However, tailoring is not about removing processes, but rather about selecting the right processes and adapting them to meet project needs. It is essential to strike a balance between tailoring too much and too little. Tailoring too much may result in losing the benefits of standardization, while tailoring too little may result in inefficiencies and inadequate project outcomes. By tailoring a project, you are being more thoughtful about the best tools, techniques, and artifacts to incorporate so that you can best utilize project resources, increase efficiency, and ultimately achieve project success.

Unlike previous editions of the *PMBOK Guide,* the Seventh Edition has a dedicated chapter on tailoring. The exam will include at least one question related to this concept.

Tailoring occurs on projects because every project is unique. Different projects require different project management approaches to meet their specific needs, constraints, and requirements. A tailored project management approach can help ensure that a project is delivered successfully on time, within budget, and to the satisfaction of stakeholders.

Tailoring is necessary on projects to ensure that the project management approach is appropriate, effective, efficient, and responsive to the project's unique characteristics, organizational culture, stakeholder expectations, resource constraints, and environmental factors.

# 3 The Environment in Which Projects Operate

**IN THIS PART . . .**

Delve into the interplay of projects, programs, portfolios, and operations management.

Monitor organizational influences throughout a project life cycle.

Coordinate the roles of the people who drive project delivery.

> **IN THIS CHAPTER**
>
> » Reviewing the purpose and goals of projects, programs, and portfolios
>
> » Getting to know the concept of organizational project management (OPM)
>
> » Examining the interplay of operations management with the OPM framework
>
> » Evaluating the impact of organizational and project governance
>
> » Defining the role and functions of a Project Management Office

Chapter **8**

# Project, Program, Portfolio, and Operations Management

This chapter focuses on the interplay of projects, programs, portfolios, and operations management. There are instances where projects are standalone or operating within the boundaries of a program and/or portfolio. Within an organization, you also need to recognize that projects often rely on operational resources to fulfill the task and meet the project's objectives.

Depending on the type of organization in which your projects operate, these concepts may be blended, and you may be unable to discern the distinction. However, for mature organizations, distinctions are important. For the exam, you need to understand the difference.

Chapter 7 provides an overview of projects. This chapter offers a deeper understanding of projects and how they interrelate with additional aspects of project management.

# Organizing the Way You Manage Projects

A key concept you will need to know for the exam is organizational project management (OPM). This represents the strategy execution framework utilizing portfolio, program, project management, and operations management. Working together, these components make up the system for value delivery and are aligned with the organization's strategic goals. A great deal of coordination is required to ensure that the projects and programs in the portfolio are successful. Organizational project management enables organizations to consistently and predictably deliver on strategic objectives.

TIP

Assume the OPM framework is in place when answering PMP Exam questions.

The purpose of OPM is to make sure that organizations implement practices and processes that align projects, programs, and portfolios with strategic goals. Organizations must also recognize that business operations play an important role in supporting the vision, objectives, and deliverables of projects and programs. At the portfolio level, this is where value decisions are made. The program and project levels deliver results, while operations focuses on business value realization. Having a governance structure at the organizational and project levels can ensure structure and coordination to achieve success in all efforts. If your organization is starting out in implementing project management practices, consider this chapter as a foundation for the future. If you are in a mature organization, this chapter can serve as a refresher on improving existing processes. PMP aspirants need to assume that an OPM framework is in place and that the interplay of projects, programs, portfolios, and operations is in full effect when answering exam questions. Figure 8-1 shows the hierarchy of portfolios, programs, projects, and operations.

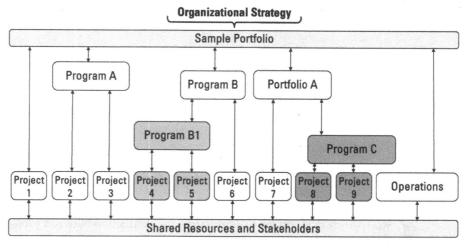

**FIGURE 8-1:** The relationship among portfolios, programs, projects, and operations.

© John Wiley & Sons, Inc.

## Projects

Projects are temporary endeavors with a beginning and an end. They fulfill objectives by producing deliverables that result in desired outcomes. Projects can include the creation of a unique product, service, or result. Finally, projects are managed by a project manager. Let's take a look at an example of a project.

> A hospital initiates a project to implement a new electronic health record (EHR) system in the Neonatal Intensive Care Unit (NICU). This involves selecting a vendor, training staff, and ensuring the system integrates with the existing hospital infrastructure. The goal is to improve patient record-keeping and communication among healthcare providers in the NICU.

## Programs

Programs are made up of related projects, subsidiary programs, and program activities. Programs are managed in a coordinated way to achieve benefits that would not be possible if managed individually with a focus on interdependencies. Because programs often rely on the same resources, such as personnel, equipment, and supplies, program management focuses on coordinating and harmonizing all of those resources so that programs complement each other rather than compete with each other. A program manager manages programs. Here's an example of a program.

> The hospital establishes a program focused on enhancing overall pediatric care. This program includes multiple projects, such as the implementation of NICU EHR, hiring of specialized pediatric staff, and expansion of pediatric outpatient services. The program aims to improve care quality, patient outcomes, and operational efficiency across various pediatric departments.

CHAPTER 8 **Project, Program, Portfolio, and Operations Management** 89

## Portfolios

Portfolios comprise projects, programs, subsidiary portfolios, and operations that are managed in a coordinated way to achieve strategic objectives. A portfolio manager manages portfolios. Let's see what a portfolio may look like.

> The hospital's leadership manages a portfolio of initiatives that span different areas of hospital operations, such as clinical excellence, patient safety, and infrastructure upgrades. The portfolio includes the pediatric care program, a hospital-wide initiative for improving patient satisfaction, and a construction project for a new cardiac wing. The goal is to align these projects and programs with the hospital's strategic objectives.

A great reminder to summarize the distinction between projects, programs, and portfolios:

- » Program and project management emphasize executing programs and projects in the "right" way.
- » Portfolio management emphasizes selecting and prioritizing the "right" programs and projects.

Project managers need to be aware of the many moving parts within an organization. A project can operate as a standalone initiative or within a program or portfolio. Furthermore, an OPM can add structure and governance to best ensure that the projects are aligned with the organization's strategy. OPM allows organizations to integrate project management practices into their overall strategic planning and decision-making processes. Organizations can improve project success rates, enhance efficiency, and achieve their strategic goals and objectives by adopting a systematic and consistent approach to project management.

# Looking at Operations Management

Chapter 6 covers the distinction between operations and projects. To recap, projects are temporary initiatives with a start and an end, creating a unique product, service, or result. Operations can directly support or influence portfolios, programs, projects, and other functions such as human resources, IT, and finance. Let's go back to the hospital example:

> In the NICU, operations involve the day-to-day management of ongoing activities, such as ensuring adequate staffing levels for each shift, maintaining equipment like incubators and monitors, and providing continuous patient care. Operations

focus on sustaining essential services, such as managing patient admissions, overseeing nursing schedules, and ensuring that the EHR system (once implemented) runs smoothly without interruptions. Unlike projects, operations are ongoing and focus on maintaining and improving the hospital's core functions.

In a nutshell,

> » **Operational work** is ongoing work to support the business and systems of the organization.
>
> » **Project work** ends when the project (or phase) is closed and project deliverables are transferred to business operations.

Operations management is outside the scope of project management efforts. However, projects can intersect with operations at multiple points, especially if the project outputs lead to significant changes to business operations. A project's outputs are typically transitioned to operations for implementation by transferring project resources or knowledge. For instance, if the project involves upgrading an IT system, the final upgrade, training materials, standard operating procedures, and so on will be transitioned to the operational team for use in everyday business operations.

# Defining the Role of Organizational and Project Governance

Having an OPM may add structure and governance to help organizations better coordinate the moving parts of projects, programs, portfolios, and operations. Let's dig a little deeper in the next section to understand the difference between organizational and project governance.

## Organizational governance

*Organizational governance* refers to the overarching structure, policies, and procedures that guide the entire organization's strategic direction, decision-making, and accountability. It ensures that the organization's operations align with its mission, values, and long-term goals. This governance is typically established at the executive level and applies to all areas of the organization.

Here is an example of organizational governance:

> The hospital's board of directors sets the strategic direction for the entire organization, focusing on improving patient care, financial stability, and regulatory compliance. They establish policies that dictate how funds are allocated across departments, set long-term healthcare goals, and ensure that all hospital operations comply with legal and ethical standards. For instance, the board decides to allocate more resources to expand the hospital's pediatric services as part of their five-year strategic plan.

### Project governance

*Project governance* focuses specifically on the framework, processes, and decision-making structures that guide a particular project or group of projects. It ensures that the project aligns with organizational objectives and is delivered successfully by providing oversight, risk management, and performance monitoring specific to that project.

Here is an example of project governance:

> The hospital launches a project to implement a new electronic health record (EHR) system in the Neonatal Intensive Care Unit (NICU). Project governance involves creating a steering committee to oversee the project's progress, setting up reporting mechanisms, and assigning a project manager responsible for risk management, budgeting, and meeting deadlines. The steering committee ensures the project stays on track, aligns with hospital goals, and meets the specific needs of the NICU.

TIP

PMI uses the terms *governance board*, *project board*, and *steering committee* interchangeably.

## Creating a Project Management Office

A *Project Management Office*, or *PMO*, is a natural liaison among an organization's portfolios, programs, projects, and organizational measurement systems (that is, a balanced scorecard). PMO is not a typo and is not to be confused with OPM.

While the OPM is a framework for coordinating and managing projects, programs, portfolios, and operations, a PMO is a management structure that standardizes the project-related governance processes. The PMO executes the OPM framework. This includes facilitating the sharing of resources, methodologies, tools, and techniques. The PMO is a key decision-maker and stakeholder responsible for making recommendations, leading knowledge transfer, terminating projects, and taking other actions as necessary. The specific form, function, and structure depends on the needs of the organization, which may include the following:

- **Supportive:** Provides policies, methodologies, templates, and lessons learned, and serves a consultative role; *low degree of control.*
- **Controlling:** Provides support, guidance, and training, and ensures compliance with organizational practices; *moderate degree of control.*
- **Directive:** Directly manages projects; project managers are assigned and report to the PMO; *high degree of control.*

Some organizations define PMO as a *Program* Management Office or *Portfolio* Management Office. And some organizations have the 'O' stand for *Organization*. For the exam, the default term is *Project Management Office*, or simply *PMO*. The exam loves to use abbreviations.

# Test Your Knowledge: Supportive, Controlling, and Directive PMOs

**Instructions**: Read each of the following scenarios and determine whether the PMO described is *Supportive*, *Controlling*, or *Directive*. Note that there may be more than one answer for some scenarios. You'll find the answer at the end of the chapter.

**Scenario 1:** The PMO is tasked with ensuring that high-priority projects meet deadlines and quality standards. It monitors these projects closely, provides resources when needed, and steps in to make decisions in case of major risks or issues. For lower-priority projects, the PMO offers support and tools, but project managers are largely autonomous.

**Scenario 2:** The PMO provides templates, best practices, and training to project managers across the organization but does not enforce their usage. Project managers are free to adopt the resources if they find them helpful.

**Scenario 3:** The PMO requires that project managers submit monthly reports and follow standardized project documentation practices. However, the project teams can still choose their project management tools, and there's some flexibility in how they run their projects. The PMO conducts periodic reviews but allows for minor deviations without requiring pre-approval.

**Scenario 4:** The PMO directly assigns project managers to high-priority projects and holds full authority over decision-making and resource allocation. Project managers report directly to the PMO, and the PMO controls every aspect of project execution.

**Scenario 5:** The PMO offers guidance, mentoring, and support to project managers. While it suggests best practices, all projects must adhere to a formal risk management process, and deviations require PMO approval. The PMO conducts periodic reviews to ensure compliance.

# Deciding How Much Governance Is Needed

In most organizations, some level of governance structure is already in place, established by a PMO or aligned with organizational policies. Specifically, governance is most often involved in the phase gate review to approve deliverables and/or to approve the continuation or termination of a project. The level of governance depends on the project's strategic importance and on constraints or oversight requirements.

The following are three examples of varying levels of governance in the hospital case study.

## Example 1: Small, internal IT upgrade project

**Project:** Upgrading the hospital's internal Wi-Fi network in non-patient-facing areas.

**Governance level:** Low

Governance in this case might be minimal, involving only a small, internal IT team. The project manager may provide occasional status updates to the IT department, and there's little oversight from senior leadership because the project has limited impact on the hospital's strategic goals or patient care. There are fewer external constraints or regulatory requirements, and the project scope is contained within internal operations.

## Example 2: Implementation of a new EHR system in the NICU

**Project:** Roll out a new electronic health record (EHR) system for the NICU.

**Governance level:** Moderate

The project directly impacts patient care, making it strategically important to the hospital's clinical operations. Governance here involves a project steering committee including IT, clinical staff, and hospital administration representatives. There are frequent status reports, risk assessments, and performance reviews to ensure the project stays on schedule and meets regulatory requirements for data security and patient privacy. The level of governance is moderate due to the potential impact on clinical outcomes, but it's contained to one department.

## Example 3: Hospital-wide expansion of telemedicine services

**Project:** A hospital-wide initiative to expand telemedicine services across all departments, allowing for remote patient consultations.

**Governance level:** High

This project is critical to the hospital's long-term strategy of expanding patient access and aligning with modern healthcare trends. Given its high strategic importance, a comprehensive governance structure is established. Senior executives, department heads, legal advisors, and external stakeholders (for example, regulatory bodies) are involved. The project is subject to stringent oversight, frequent audits, and reports to the board of directors. Significant regulatory requirements regarding telemedicine, patient data protection, and billing require close compliance monitoring.

# Answer Key: Supportive, Controlling, and Directive PMOs

1. **Controlling** or **Directive:** The PMO takes a Directive approach for high-priority projects by stepping in to make decisions. For lower-priority projects, it acts more like a Controlling PMO by monitoring and supporting but allowing autonomy.

2. **Supportive:** The PMO provides resources without mandating their use, showing that it is Supportive in nature.

3. **Controlling** or **Supportive:** The PMO enforces some standardized documentation and reviews, which aligns with a Controlling PMO. However, the flexibility in tool usage and minor deviations also shows traits of a Supportive PMO, so either answer can be correct depending on your interpretation.

4. **Directive:** The PMO controls project manager assignments, decisions, and resource allocation, indicating a Directive PMO.

5. **Controlling:** The PMO requires adherence to a formal risk management process and conducts reviews, showcasing a Controlling PMO.

**IN THIS CHAPTER**

» Defining OPAs and EEFs in project management contexts

» Analyzing how OPAs and EEFs influence decision-making and project outcomes

» Evaluating the impact of different OPAs and EEFs on project success

# Chapter 9
# Organizational Influences

Projects do not operate in a bubble, and you need to understand what factors can enhance or constrain your project. Many PMP aspirants often state that it feels like the concepts of project management best practices assume that projects operate in a vacuum. That declaration cannot be farther from the truth. What you will see in this chapter is that many factors that are internal to the organization as well as environmental factors — both internal and external — need to be acknowledged and monitored throughout the project life cycle.

You need to be aware of the internal policies, procedures, methodologies, and governance that impact your projects, and you need to have insight into the external influences of the economy, competitive landscape, and legislative constraints that can change their direction. These factors are called organizational process assets (OPAs) and enterprise environmental factors (EEFs); this chapter focuses on both of these concepts.

# OPAs: Knowing Your Internal Policies and Procedures

Given that projects operate within the boundaries of organizations, it would make sense to recognize that organizations have internal policies and practices that have been established to set the norms for how things are to operate. These practices and policies, known as organizational process assets (OPAs), are internal to the organization and arise from the organization itself. These include unique process assets developed and maintained by the organization: the plans, processes, procedures, policies, and organizational knowledge repositories, including historical information and lessons learned.

These processes, policies, and procedures are typically created through an authoritative entity within the organization. For example, your Human Resources (HR) department has established HR policies and practices, such as paid time off or inclement weather policies. Your IT department may establish policies and procedures related to accessing software or even installing software onto your company laptops. In turn, your Project Management Office (PMO) may establish OPAs related to project management procedures, use of tools, and access to project templates.

There are two categories of OPAs: 1) Processes, Policies, and Procedures; and 2) Organizational Knowledge Repositories. Table 9-1 lists the common examples of OPAs in each category. As you can imagine, these assets can significantly influence the management and direction of a project.

**TABLE 9-1**    **Categories of OPAs**

| Processes, Policies, and Procedures | Organizational Knowledge Repositories |
|---|---|
| Facility access guidelines | Configuration management knowledge repositories |
| Data protection policies | Financial data repositories |
| Cost and scheduling policies | Lessons learned repositories |
| Resource management policies and guidelines | Files from previous projects |
| Templates | |
| Guidelines on change management and configuration management | |

# EEFs: Gaining Awareness of the Environment

There is a saying: "Know your environment to navigate it successfully." This underscores the importance of being aware of the context and/or surroundings in which you're operating — especially the environment in which your projects operate. This includes physical space, organizational culture, and social customs.

Project managers need to understand this to make informed decisions and take effective actions. All of this describes another project influence called enterprise environmental factors (EEFs). Similar to organizational process assets, they provide context within which to plan the project. EEFs may be internal or external to the organization and are generally outside the control of the project team. EEFs can influence, constrain, or direct the project.

REMEMBER

This bears repeating: EEFs encompass both the external and internal environmental constraints of a project. Many PMP aspirants overlook the internal influences that also qualify as EEFs.

See Table 9-2 for a list of the common internal and external EEFs that can impact a project.

**TABLE 9-2 Common Internal and External EEFs**

| Internal EEFs | External EEFs |
| --- | --- |
| Organizational culture, structure, and governance | Marketplace conditions |
| Geographic distribution of facilities and resources | Social and cultural influences and issues |
| Infrastructure | Regulatory environment |
| IT / software | Commercial databases |
| Resource availability | Academic research |
| Employee capability | Industry standards |
|  | Physical environment |

The key difference between OPAs and EEFs is that OPAs are the internal tangible assets you can get your hands on: policies, procedures, templates, and access to databases housing internal data and historical information. EEFs, on the other hand, are the environmental factors that you have to deal with: software systems, organizational culture, market conditions, and weather. Think of EEFs as the world you live in; you just have to recognize how these environmental conditions can impact your projects.

Project managers should consider OPAs and EEFs as a part of their routine management of a project. They are considered inputs into getting your project started and even getting a process started within your project. In turn, OPAs and updates to EEFs may be an "output" of your project work.

You can't ignore the internal environment that makes your projects subject to policies and procedures, nor can you turn a blind eye to the external environment of organizational culture, economic and marketplace conditions, and the physical environment. In particular with EEFs, the tip I often provide is to think of EEFs as the world you work in: This is the way it is; this is how we've always done things. EEFs are out of your control and can come up at any time during the course of your projects. This is why the concepts of progressive elaboration and rolling wave planning (see Chapter 7) are essential to your project management work. See how things are coming together?

# Test Your Knowledge: OPA or EEF

In the following exercise, determine whether the situation describes an OPA or EEF. The answers are revealed immediately after, so no peaking.

| Scenario | OPA or EEF? |
|---|---|
| 1. Your project must be adjusted due to a federal holiday that affects the availability of key stakeholders. | |
| 2. The project manager must consider the organization's established change control procedures when planning for potential scope changes. | |
| 3. Unexpected inclement weather causes delays in the delivery of materials to your project site. | |
| 4. The project team refers to a company's standard procedure for managing projects during federal holidays. | |
| 5. Due to a recent economic downturn, the project budget has been cut, forcing the team to reassess resource allocation. | |
| 6. The team has to adapt to a new project management software recently adopted by the organization, which changes how project tasks are signed and tracked. | |
| 7. The project's timeline is influenced by the organization's standard working hours and holiday schedule. | |

# Answer Key: OPA or EEF

1. **EEF:** Federal holiday impacting stakeholder availability.
2. **OPA:** Established change control procedures within the organization.
3. **EEF:** Inclement weather causing delivery delays.
4. **OPA:** Company standard procedure on managing projects during holidays.
5. **EEF:** Economic downturn impacting project resources, including budget.
6. **EEF:** New project management software adoption. (Remember, EEFs are internal.)
7. **EEF:** This was tricky! This pertains to the organization's working hours and holiday schedule. It is what it is.

## STAYING AHEAD AND COMPLIANT IN A DYNAMIC BUSINESS ENVIRONMENT

Understanding OPAs and EEFs helps you see how internal and external factors shape project execution. But beyond these foundational elements, project managers need to stay tuned into the bigger picture — the broader business environment — especially when it comes to compliance.

Compliance isn't just about following the rules for the sake of it. It's what keeps your project out of legal hot water, aligned with industry expectations, and running with integrity. It ensures that you're meeting the right laws, regulations, and standards, reducing legal risks and reinforcing ethical business practices.

Compliance requirements come from many sources: industry standards, government regulations, company policies, and contractual obligations. That's why it's critical to confirm those requirements early. Talk to your stakeholders, review key documents like regulatory guidelines and internal policies, and clarify what applies to your project.

Some common compliance categories include the following:

- **Regulatory:** Health and safety laws, environmental regulations, financial oversight
- **Contractual:** Service level agreements, intellectual property rights, non-disclosure agreements

*(continued)*

*(continued)*

- **Quality:** International Organization for Standardization (ISO) standards, product safety requirements, process audits
- **Data Privacy & Security:** General Data Protection Regulation (GDPR), Health Insurance Portability and Accountability Act (HIPAA), cybersecurity standards
- **Ethical:** Anti-corruption policies, fair labor practices
- **Operational:** Standard operating procedures, risk management policies, supply chain compliance

Overlooking compliance can lead to schedule delays, financial penalties, and even project failure. The best approach? Stay proactive. Document compliance requirements from the start and weave them into your project management plan.

IN THIS CHAPTER

» Identifying the key roles and responsibilities within a project delivery framework

» Defining the different roles that contribute to the success of project delivery

» Comparing the functions of a project manager with those of a program manager and portfolio manager

# Chapter 10
# Roles and Functions That Drive Project Delivery

This chapter is a precursor to Chapter 12, which covers stakeholders. With this in mind, it's important to set the stage here about a critical fact within projects and project management: People make or break projects. And people drive project delivery because they are fulfilling certain roles and/or functions within the organization and within the project context itself. This chapter outlines the major project roles and provides a great reference point about the various stakeholders.

REMEMBER

It's critical to know all of the functions and roles of a project so you are aware of the key stakeholders who can make or break your project.

# The Project Manager

People in the project manager role help the project team to achieve the project objectives. How this is accomplished varies from organization to organization. This person can be responsible for leading efforts in the following areas:

- Planning
- Monitoring and controlling
- Evaluation and analysis
- Monitoring and improving the performance of the project team

The project manager role, due to its collaborative nature, can also include consulting with executive leaders and department heads to better coordinate activities that will advance the project objectives. The project manager can support portfolios and programs within which the project is initiated by providing strategic guidance, aligning project objectives with overall business goals, and ensuring effective communication and coordination among different projects.

REMEMBER

Keep in mind that the project manager role can have other names, such as project coordinator, project lead, or project facilitator, and can be tailored to meet the organization's needs.

# The Sponsor

The project sponsor plays a critical role in every project, whether predictive or adaptive. The sponsor formally authorizes the project's start and is generally accountable for developing and maintaining the project *business case*, the document that justifies the project. The sponsor is not just the initiator, but also a crucial factor in the project's success. They are typically the brainchild behind the project's goals and outcomes, and their unwavering support is essential for the project's success. As such, they should be fully committed to the project.

The sponsor also provides financial resources for the project and, ideally, protects it from unnecessary changes. As such, they have the authority to approve specific project changes.

The sponsor should have significant authority in the organization. They should have the authority to make decisions and the influence to remove roadblocks that may hinder the project's progress. This authority and political capital are essential for the sponsor to support the project effectively.

Not all sponsors are equal. Some accidental sponsors attend a meeting and grunt, providing no feedback and no clear direction, and expecting the project manager to take care of the project with no additional resources. Lucky for you, on the PMP Exam, you can assume that you have an actively participating project sponsor who supports the project manager, ensures the project has the right resources, values the project manager's opinion, and welcomes your recommendations. Lucky you.

# The Product Owner

The product owner plays a unique and essential role in Agile and hybrid projects. They are responsible for delivering on the product value, guiding the direction of the product, and working with Agile teams on a daily basis. Their feedback and direction on the key features and functionality are instrumental in delivering a successful product.

On Agile projects, the product owner holds significant decision-making authority. They are often referred to as the *customer representative* or *sponsor representative*, titles that highlight their authority. This empowerment stems from their responsibility to deliver business benefits within a firm budget and timeline.

The product owner's role is not just about making decisions, but also about collaboration. They work closely with stakeholders, customers, and teams to define the direction of the product, ensuring that everyone's needs and expectations are considered.

Similar in nature to the sponsor, strong product ownership is a critical success factor, especially for Agile teams. The product owner's role is not just about setting direction, but also about preventing wasteful work. By being attentive to the highest-value needs of the customer, they ensure that Agile teams do not create features that are not valuable nor appreciated by the customer.

# The Customer and End User

While many people will argue that the most important role of a project is the sponsor or even the project manager, it's important to understand that neither one can be effective without a clear grasp of the project requirements, outcomes, and expectations. This vital information comes from customers and end users, making their roles pivotal in the project's success. For the purposes of your studies, the customer and end user are not always the same.

>> **Customer:** An individual or group who has requested or is funding the project.

>> **End user:** An individual or group who will directly experience the use of the project deliverable.

TIP

While the use of the terms *customer* and *end user* can be confusing, it's important to remember that in the context of project management, *customer* refers to someone internal to the organization and actively involved in the project. This could even be the sponsor in some cases. The words *customer* and *sponsor* are often used interchangeably, especially when it comes to formally signing off on and approving accepted deliverables. On the other hand, the end user is typically an individual or group external to the organization who will directly experience the project deliverable.

# The Project Team

The *project team* refers to the group of individuals who work together to accomplish the project's deliverables. These team members are selected based on their skills, expertise, and roles required to complete the project successfully. The project team can include various stakeholders, employees, contractors, and consultants with different skill sets and responsibilities. They collaborate under the project manager's guidance to perform the tasks and activities outlined in the project plan, and their collective efforts contribute to achieving the project's objectives. Here are some key considerations about the makeup of project teams:

>> They can be full-time or part-time for the duration of the project.

>> They may be needed for only a portion of the project.

>> Work can be co-located or virtual.

>> They may need specialists providing unique skills or generalists possessing broad skill sets.

The project team is the group of individuals working on the ground to execute the project and deliver the desired outcomes. The team includes the project manager and some other roles.

In high-change project environments, such as adaptive and Agile projects, cross-functional teams are desired as a way to gain insights and reap the benefits of a mix of perspectives, skills, and knowledge. These teams are independent and self-organizing, and are able to fluidly assume leadership as needed to achieve the team's objectives. This independence and self-organizing nature is important in allowing team members to take charge and lead when necessary, which is critical in adaptive and Agile environments.

The following sections cover the subset roles of the project team.

## Project management team

On large projects, the project manager is entrusted with a significant amount of project management work. To ensure the project's success, the project manager may select team members to assist in performing some of the project management work and provide leadership support to manage the team. Ideally, the project manager selects key members of the project team to support the project manager in planning and managing the project. They are the leadership arm of the project team, working in close collaboration with the project manager to specify project requirements, define the scope of work, develop project plans, monitor progress, and provide guidance and support to the rest of the project team members. This collaborative effort is vital in aligning the project with organizational goals, ensuring that the project stays on track, and addressing any challenges that arise during project execution. The project management team works closely with the sponsor, with each member contributing their unique skills and expertise to the team.

The project sponsor is *not* part of the project management team, but rather, works closely with the project management team on communications and decision-making. As the project manager, you should be selective about who from your team communicates with the sponsor. Imagine if you had a team of 50 people consisting of junior staff, external vendors, and subcontractors. Would you want any and all of them to reach out to the sponsor? Chances are, your answer is no. Instead, only a select few, one or two additional people on the project team, should be empowered to communicate with the sponsor.

### SMEs

People exist within an organization who have particular skills, institutional knowledge, and expertise in a specific subject matter for a project. Subject matter experts (or SMEs, often pronounced "smee") provide advice and guidance, supporting many other projects within the organization. SMEs can contribute to the learning process of the team by sharing their knowledge and experience, thereby enhancing the team's skills and understanding of the project. SMEs can be internal or external to the organization. Given their specific subject matter knowledge, SMEs may only be required during certain times of the project duration.

### Business partners

On a project, outside suppliers may sometimes be needed to provide the personnel, supplies, or equipment to complete the project's tasks. The role of the business partner can come in the form of vendors, suppliers, or contractors who provide a service or can meet a need if the necessary resources are not available within the organization. A need for such a resource typically triggers a conversation with the organization's procurement team.

### Functional and operations managers

Projects are an integral part of the larger organization, and their resource needs often depend on the collaborative and coordinated efforts of functional and operations managers. A *functional manager* oversees a functional or business unit, such as an IT manager or HR director. On the other hand, an *operations manager* ensures the efficiency of business processes. Both roles, which are responsible for the human and physical resources in a department, work closely with the project manager to meet the project's needs. Depending on the organizational structure, the project manager may report to a functional manager, who could then have total control over the project. In other cases, the functional manager may share control with the project manager or have no control over the project.

## The Program Manager

A program manager is tasked with managing related projects to achieve results that would be challenging to achieve separately. They act as the "harmonizer" of these projects, ensuring that the program benefits are delivered as expected by coordinating the activities of the program's components.

The program manager provides oversight to adjust projects to benefit the program, and ensures that projects support the strategic goals of the organization. They monitor the progress of program components to ensure the overall goals, schedules, budget, and benefits of the program will be met.

Project managers interact with program managers when a project is within a program, and the program managers guide and support individual project managers' efforts.

## The Portfolio Manager

A portfolio manager is responsible for the executive level of governance of the projects, programs, and operational work that make up a portfolio. They are responsible for managing projects or programs that are largely unrelated. Their focus is to ensure that selected projects provide value to the larger organization and to make sure that the organization is getting the best return on investment.

Portfolio managers continuously monitor changes in the broader internal and external environments, as well as strategic changes. They aggregate resources, performance results, and risk of the portfolio, ensuring adaptability in the face of change. Project managers interact with portfolio managers when a project is within a portfolio.

## Stakeholders and Key Stakeholders

A stakeholder is anyone who will be impacted by the project or can influence it. The project manager and stakeholders determine their project roles. If you are thinking, "Aren't the roles you just discussed stakeholders, too?" the answer is yes.

Stakeholders can directly or indirectly influence a project, its performance, or its outcome in either a positive or negative way. The previously mentioned roles embody this potential impact. Stakeholders also encompass a broad range of individuals or entities who have an interest in or are impacted by a project. They can be internal or external to an organization and hold various degrees of influence and power. Awareness of this potential impact and preparing for it can result in successful project management.

REMEMBER

Stakeholders typically include project sponsors, customers, end users, employees, suppliers, regulatory bodies, and the community affected by the project.

Are all stakeholders equal? The short answer is no. Not every stakeholder carries equal weight in terms of your interaction with them and their involvement in the project. Many of the PMI textbooks mention key stakeholders, yet there is no specific definition. It is assumed that there's the world of the larger community of stakeholders, and then there are key stakeholders. But how do you define who is a key stakeholder? That is in the eye of the beholder.

Generally, a *key stakeholder* is someone or some entity that will be continuously involved in the project, and they are the ones who provide frequent feedback. In short, their opinions matter. Is that someone who's a senior leader? Possibly. Does that mean you disregard anyone who is a frontline manager? Not necessarily. This is where your power skills and business acumen as a project manager come into play. You need to make that determination and use expert judgment to decide whether a person or entity involved in the project needs to be considered a key stakeholder.

# 4
# Managing Your Projects from Conception to Completion

**IN THIS PART...**

Build and motivate a capable team.

Get your project off the ground.

Develop a project roadmap.

Expand and improve your roadmap.

Discover project integration management.

Effectively execute your project.

Monitor and control your project.

Bring your project to a successful close.

**IN THIS CHAPTER**

» Developing a Resource Management Plan and estimating and acquiring project resources

» Establishing team norms using a team charter and ground rules

» Defining the stages of team development and the Tuckman Ladder

» Motivating team members using various strategies

» Recognizing the key elements of leading teams in the adaptive (Agile) environment

Chapter **11**

# Project Success Starts with the Team

In Chapter 10, I discuss how the project team refers to the group of individuals who work together to accomplish the project's deliverables. Ideally, these team members are selected based on their skills, expertise, and roles required to complete the project successfully. For your understanding in the context of the exam, the project team includes the project manager as well as various stakeholders, employees, contractors, and consultants with different skill sets and responsibilities. They collaborate under the project manager's guidance to perform the task and activities outlined in an overarching plan (called the Project Management Plan), and their collective efforts contribute to achieving the project's objectives.

In this chapter, you will explore key aspects of building a team, such as defining team roles and responsibilities, establishing team objectives and goals, team building techniques, working with diverse and global teams, effective communication, addressing conflict, recognizing and motivating team members, training and developing staff, empowering the team and monitoring team performance. That is no easy feat!

As you prepare for the PMP Exam and your future role as a project manager, you must understand that a project's success hinges not only on assembling the right people but also on acquiring and allocating the necessary resources. As the project manager, your task goes beyond identifying team members. You must also thoroughly assess and plan for all the resources required to execute your project efficiently. This comprehensive evaluation will empower you to make informed decisions, anticipate potential bottlenecks, and minimize risks before they jeopardize your project's progress.

For the purposes of PMP Exam preparation, assume that you will need to bring together a team of talented professionals — rarely will you work on a project alone. As such, your ability to assemble, lead, and empower a capable project team will significantly impact your project's outcome. Your responsibility as the project manager is to foster a supportive and collaborative environment that nurtures innovation, productivity, and commitment from the team.

# Determining Resource Needs to Meet Project Needs

Here's a scenario that happens all too often on projects:

Senior Leader: "Hey, that new guy, Thomas, is available for your project. Why don't you bring him on?"

Savvy Project Manager: "Thomas, the new guy that started two days ago and was hired as a junior consultant? That's an interesting suggestion, but I need someone to fulfill the role as a senior analyst."

Senior Leader: "Junior consultant, senior analyst, what's the difference? You need a body on this project and we can't delay this project anymore."

Savvy Project Manager: "I understand, but bringing on a person with the wrong skills will not accelerate the project schedule. In fact, it may even delay the project because of the time spent training this person and fixing their mistakes."

Senior Leader: "You're a great teacher. I'm sure you'll figure it out."

*The Savvy Project Manager looks in disbelief as the Senior Leader walks away in triumph.*

Despite popular belief, there are better ways to go about building a team than just *bringing a body onto the project* when trying to meet the needs of the project goals.

REMEMBER

Project managers must carefully determine the skills, abilities, attitudes, and availability of the people they bring onto a project. The project manager is also considering the need for physical resources such as equipment and materials, which require trained people to use the equipment properly.

Let's take a look at key steps that project managers undertake to determine personnel needs for project success.

# Planning for the People, the Equipment, and the Tools (Oh My!)

A key *project artifact* that guides the project manager in effective resource planning is the *Resource Management Plan.* This plan serves as a comprehensive guide that outlines how resources will be identified, acquired, utilized, and managed throughout the project's life cycle. Its purpose is to ensure that the right resources are available at the right time in the right quantities and with the necessary skill sets and expertise to successfully execute the project. The Resource Management Plan is primarily used in predictive project environments, and there are two parts to the Resource Management Plan: human resources and physical resources. I'll detail those elements later in this chapter.

REMEMBER

On large-scale projects, there may be too much project management work for one person to plan and perform. The project manager may select team members to assist in performing some of the project management work and provide leadership to manage the team. This group is called the project management team, and they are a subset of the project team that includes the project manager. The project management team can be instrumental in assisting the project manager in the planning efforts. Refer to Chapter 10 for more about the project management team.

TIP

Project artifacts are documents, files, or any tangible byproducts produced during the course of a project. They serve as documentation or evidence of the project's progress and are used to communicate, execute, and manage the project throughout its life cycle.

## Human resource planning

The Resource Management Plan includes information on human resources. This part documents the human resource requirements: who, when, how many, what skills, what level of experience, and how long they'll be on the project. It indicates the roles and responsibilities of the project personnel. The human resource information also documents the project's organizational charts. And it provides a process for acquiring human resources, whether they're internal to the organization or procured as external resources (think, subcontractors and vendors), as well as providing training, team development, and recognition plans. This portion of the plan also provides a process for project team management, often guided by having a team charter, ground rules, and communication processes. It provides information around being in compliance with corporate policies and safety policies, and it also provides information on how to release the human resource needs, such as end of project reviews, and team celebrations.

## Physical resource planning

The Resource Management Plan also contains guidance on how to address physical resource needs by identifying the physical resource requirements: the what, when, quantity, type, quality, grade, and duration on the project. It provides a process for acquiring those physical resources, whether they're internal to the organization or they need to be procured. It provides guidance around inventory management and also provides guidance on releasing those physical resources.

TIP

While this chapter focuses primarily on human resources, resources also include physical resources. If you encounter a generic reference to "resources," assume that it includes both human and physical resources, unless otherwise specified. I provide additional details on physical resources and procurements in Chapter 17.

As you develop a Resource Management Plan, the plan may incorporate estimating methods to help you complete the process for estimating resource requirements.

# Estimating Resource Requirements

The process of *estimating resource requirements* involves identifying and determining the types and quantities of resources needed to complete a project successfully. Resources can include personnel, equipment, materials, facilities, and any other inputs that are necessary to execute the project tasks. You need to consider the following:

- » Types of resources (people, equipment, materials, supplies, software, working space)
- » Specific skills (junior consultant, senior analyst, coder, administrative, and so on)
- » Quantities (for example, 2 junior consultants, 1 senior engineer, 4 coders, and so on)
- » Availability of each resource for the duration of the project
- » Available resources in-house versus outsourced as a subcontractor or supplier

And like any good project manager, you should leave room for making adjustments to your estimates as resource availability might change, or you may need new skills or resources. You may also want to consider alternative resources that can get the job done efficiently.

Accurate resource estimation is ideal for successful project execution and helps you avoid delays, cost overruns, and resource shortages. By going through the estimating resource requirements process, you'll have a clear plan for the number of resources required and will be able to allocate them effectively to ensure the project's successful completion. And this process is something you will revisit throughout the project life cycle.

If you think estimating resource requirements is a lot to think about, you also need to make sure that they're available so that you can acquire them into your project in a timely manner.

# Acquiring Resources

So, you have excitedly identified and estimated the resources that you need to get the work done. Great! Now you actually have to acquire those resources and make sure that they are available and motivated to get the work done. Acquiring resources involves identifying, procuring, and allocating the necessary resources to support the project activities. Let's put this concept into perspective with some scenarios.

Let's first tackle acquiring human resources for your project. Imagine you're managing a software development project. To acquire the necessary human resources, you identify the roles required, such as programmers, testers, and designers. You then procure these resources by hiring new team members, by reallocating existing team members from other projects, or by working with your procurement team to find external human resources to fulfill the needed roles.

Let's not forget about the physical resources such as materials, equipment, supplies, tools, and even cubicle space. In a software development project, physical resources include computers, servers, software licenses, cloud storage, testing devices, and development tools. You identify the necessary quantities and specifications; determine if they are available in-house and/or procure them from vendors or service providers; and ensure they are allocated to the development team (the people) efficiently.

A set of tools and techniques exist that help the project manager to effectively identify and acquire the right resources for the project. These tools and techniques include the following:

>> **Preassignment:** This is a resource management technique where specific individuals are assigned to a project team before the project officially starts. This means that team members are selected and allocated to the project based on their expertise, skills, and availability even before the project work begins. Preassignment can be beneficial when certain critical resources are required for the project, and their availability needs to be ensured from the outset.

>> **Negotiations:** In resource management, negotiations refer to the process of discussing and finalizing the terms and conditions for obtaining and utilizing resources. This could involve negotiations with various stakeholders, vendors, and other teams within the organization, or even negotiating with the individual. Think about that coveted staff member *everyone* wants on their project. You need to be a great negotiator with their boss or another project manager to get that person on your project.

- **Resource calendars:** A tool used in resource management to track and manage the availability and allocation of resources over time. These calendars provide a visual representation of when specific resources are planned to be utilized, helping project managers avoid resource conflicts, overbooking, or underutilization. Resource calendars can include information about team member schedules, equipment availability, and other resource-related constraints. This is helpful when you are trying to reconcile vacation schedules and work with resources that are assigned to more than one project. Yes, that happens.

- **Virtual teams:** These are project teams that consist of members who are geographically dispersed and work together remotely, often using digital communication and collaboration tools. In resource management, virtual teams pose unique challenges, as team members may live in different time zones and have diverse cultural backgrounds. Effective resource management for virtual teams involves ensuring clear communication, setting up appropriate collaboration tools, and understanding and accommodating individual team members' work preferences and constraints.

- **Breakdown structures:** These provide a visual hierarchical breakdown of your resources or work. An *organizational breakdown structure*, or OBS, shows assignments of project responsibilities to divisions or departments within the organization — think the marketing department or the engineering department. *Resource breakdown structure*, or RBS, breaks the work down by types and quantities of resources that are needed for your project. And a *work breakdown structure*, or WBS, ensures that each work package has an assigned owner.

These concepts are all important aspects of resource management, and understanding and applying them effectively can significantly contribute to the success of a project.

TIP

The Resource Management Plan also includes guidance on releasing resources in a controlled manner to help optimize resource utilization and minimize unnecessary costs. Release of the team and resources will be addressed in the discussion of project closure and procurement closure.

By carefully planning, procuring, and allocating resources, project managers ensure that the right resources are available at the right time.

# VIRTUAL TEAMS ARE PREVALENT IN THE REAL WORLD AND IN THE PMP EXAM

Virtual teams are project teams in which members are geographically dispersed and collaborate primarily through technology-mediated communication, such as video conferencing, instant messaging, email, and online collaboration tools. As a way to ensure team members have a sense of connectedness, project managers may implement *virtual co-location,* which is the practice of simulating the benefits of a co-located team. Here are some reasons why virtual co-location can be effective when managing projects with virtual teams.

- **Communication and collaboration:** In co-located teams, face-to-face interactions facilitate spontaneous communication, easy access to information, and quick decision-making. Virtual co-location aims to replicate these benefits through video conferencing and other collaborative tools, promoting real-time communication and reducing the delays caused by time zone differences.
- **Team cohesion and trust:** Building trust and strong team cohesion is challenging in virtual teams, where team members might not have met each other in person. Virtual co-location encourages regular virtual meetings and informal interactions, fostering trust, camaraderie, and a sense of belonging among team members.
- **Alignment and goal clarity:** Co-located teams often benefit from a shared understanding of project goals and objectives due to their physical proximity. Virtual co-location emphasizes the importance of clear communication and frequent updates to ensure all team members remain aligned and focused on project objectives.
- **Knowledge sharing and learning:** Co-located teams can learn from each other organically, but virtual teams may lack these opportunities. Virtual co-location encourages knowledge sharing through virtual workshops, webinars, and collaborative platforms, enabling team members to learn from each other's expertise.

Understanding virtual teams and the need for virtual co-location is essential for the PMP Exam for a few reasons:

- **Real-world relevance:** Given the increasing prevalence of virtual teams in projects, questions related to virtual co-location may appear to assess the candidate's understanding of how to manage such teams effectively.
- **Resource management is a key topic:** As a PMP aspirant, you must be well-versed in resource management, including strategies for managing resources in various team setups, including virtual teams.
- **Situational questions:** The PMP Exam often includes situational questions that require candidates to analyze a scenario and select the best course of action. Virtual teams may be featured in these scenarios,.

# Gaining Project Success through Teamwork

As the project manager, you will establish both a culture and environment that bring together a diverse group of individuals and help them to evolve into a high-performing team. One of the most important responsibilities of a project manager is assembling and managing a high-performing team that can deliver successful outcomes.

Some project teams will employ a variety of skill and personality assessments to better understand the skills, interests, and personalities of the team members, such as the following:

- SWOT analysis (to assess the strengths, weaknesses, opportunities, and threats of the team skills and dynamics)
- Myers-Briggs Type Indicator
- DISC personality assessment tool (dominance, influence, steadiness, and conscientiousness)
- Big Five Personality Model (OCEAN: openness, conscientiousness, extraversion, agreeableness, and neuroticism)

Personality assessments are valuable tools for gaining a better understanding of the project team members. They provide insights into individual thinking styles, helping the project manager determine which roles or tasks may be the best fit for each person. The tools are meant to help the project managers ensure that everyone has the opportunity to excel.

## Looking at team roles and responsibilities

An important tool used to define roles within the team and align team skills with project objectives is the use of a *responsibility assignment matrix* (RAM). A RAM cross-references team members with the activities or sets of work — that is, work packages — they are to accomplish. A variation of the RAM is the *RACI chart*, which defines role assignments on a responsibility matrix using R for the responsible person, A for the accountable person, C for the person you consult, and I for keep informed (think of them as the FYI — maybe they need to know something that impacts their work stream).

TIP

A key takeaway regarding the RACI chart is that you can have more than one person who's responsible, consulted, or informed, but you only have one person who's accountable — the buck stops with them. Refer to Figure 11-1 for an example of a RACI chart.

| Task Name | RACI Matrix | | | | | |
|---|---|---|---|---|---|---|
| | Name | | | | | |
| | Ronnie | Bobby | Ricky | Mike | Ralph | Johnny |
| Market Research | R | C | C | A | I | |
| Advertising | R | A | C | I | I | |
| Storyboarding | A | R | | C | I | C |
| Funding | | C | R | I | A | I |
| Design | | R | A | C | I | C |
| Production | | | A | R | I | |
| Distribution | C | | C | | R | A |
| R - Responsible   A - Accountable   C - Consulted   I - Informed | | | | | | |

FIGURE 11-1:
An example of a RACI chart.

© John Wiley & Sons, Inc.

The RAM and RACI charts can be effective tools to clearly define the roles and responsibilities of each team member, as well as to define the roles of subject matter experts, vendors, and other key resources of the project. Clarity in roles minimizes confusion and promotes accountability. This can also aid the project manager in determining if there are any gaps and how to address those gaps through training, coaching, or mentoring.

## Comparing management to leadership

At the core of effective project execution is the understanding of the differences between management and leadership, as well as how these concepts relate to using *power skills* to lead diverse teams, tackle complex challenges, and achieve organizational goals. While the terms *management* and *leadership* are often used interchangeably, they represent distinct yet complementary roles in advancing projects.

Management encompasses the skills, techniques, and processes employed to ensure efficient utilization of resources, adherence to timelines, and attainment of predetermined goals. Management focuses on efficiently organizing resources, coordinating tasks, and achieving set objectives within a project or organizational context. And these skills are essential for overseeing day-to-day operations, ensuring effective utilization of resources, and maintaining project schedules and budgets. Management is task oriented, focused on processes and resources. It emphasizes being efficient and executing the work. It also ensures compliance with established procedures and relies on authority and formal power.

Leadership, on the other hand, revolves around inspiring, motivating, and guiding individuals and teams toward a shared vision. Leadership is more people oriented. It's about sharing the vision and inspiring team members and stakeholders. It emphasizes innovation and strategic thinking. Leadership encourages risk taking, promotes change, and relies on influence and personal power. Table 11-1 shows a side-by-side comparison of the two.

**TABLE 11-1 Comparing Management and Leadership**

| Management | Leadership |
|---|---|
| Focuses on tasks, processes, and resources | Focuses on people, vision, and inspiration |
| Emphasizes efficiency and execution | Emphasizes innovation and strategic thinking |
| Ensures compliance with established procedures | Encourages risk taking and promotes change |
| Relies on authority and formal power | Relies on influence and personal power |

While this side-by-side comparison captures some general distinctions, it's important to note that management and leadership are not mutually exclusive. Effective project managers often need to embody elements of both management and leadership to achieve project success. The key lies in striking the right balance, leveraging the appropriate skills and approaches based on the organizational culture, the specific needs of the project, and the individuals involved.

Project managers often tap into *power skills*, which refer to the interpersonal and intrapersonal capabilities that enable individuals to exert influence, build relationships, communicate effectively, and navigate the complexities of human dynamics within a project setting. These power skills are integral to both management and leadership as they enable project managers to inspire their teams, foster collaboration, make informed decisions, and adapt to changing circumstances. Project managers who are able to strike the right balance between managing and leading are able to effectively manage project constraints, but also to lead teams, inspire innovation, and foster a culture of collaboration, thereby propelling their projects toward success.

REMEMBER

Power skills are one of the domains of the PMI Talent Triangle. The PMI Talent Triangle represents the ideal sets of skills that project professionals must develop and sharpen to be successful and work smarter in today's evolving world of project management. Refer to Chapter 1 for details of the PMI Talent Triangle.

## MANAGEMENT AND LEADERSHIP SKILLS IN THE REAL WORLD

Leadership skills manifest in various ways during the life cycle of your projects. Here are some examples of how leadership skills can be demonstrated:

- A project leader establishes a clear and compelling vision for the project, articulating the desired outcome, and inspiring team members with a sense of purpose and direction. They communicate the vision effectively, ensuring that all stakeholders understand and align with the project's overarching goals.

- A project leader communicates openly and transparently, inspiring and motivating team members to perform at their best. They share the project's significance, recognize individual contributions, and create a positive work environment that encourages enthusiasm, commitment, and a shared sense of ownership.

- A project leader sets a positive example through their own actions and behaviors. They demonstrate integrity, professionalism, and a strong work ethic, inspiring team members to follow suit. They're reliable, accountable, and dedicated, earning the respect and trust of the team.

These examples illustrate how leadership skills can impact team motivation, collaboration, and the overall success of the project. Effective project leaders leverage these skills to guide their teams, foster innovation, and create an environment that brings out the best in every individual team member.

## Establishing team norms

The project team's culture may be established deliberately by developing project team norms in the form of a team charter. The *team charter* is a working agreement developed by the members of the project team. It describes the approach the team will take regarding communications, decision-making, and conflict resolution. The team may establish *ground rules* to help eliminate conflicts or problems. Specifically, ground rules represent the behaviors and actions of the project team members. They establish clear agreement on how team members will treat each other and behave as a part of the team. They help guide the behavior to a level that the group finds acceptable. Ground rules can cover anything from how meetings will run, to how the team will handle the conflict and how they'll make decisions. Teams may establish ground rules, in particular, to help minimize conflicts or problems.

While it may seem like the differences between the team charter and the ground rules are very minor, these differences matter in the case of the PMP Exam. The team charter is a *project artifact* that documents the values, vision, expectations (such as ground rules), guidelines, decision-making criteria, and processes for the team. Ground rules are a tool used to inform team members of acceptable behavior — so that no one has to second-guess good behavior or bad behavior. An example of ground rules can include how you conduct yourselves in a meeting with stakeholders or how you conduct yourselves during times of interpersonal conflict (such as no shouting or name calling — sometimes it's necessary to spell it out).

## Grasping decision-making dynamics

Ground rules also lay the foundation for how a team makes decisions. Throughout the project, the team will face choices, from selecting estimating techniques and tools to something as simple as ordering lunch for those long working sessions. Establishing decision-making norms up front ensures smoother collaboration. One popular approach is to employ voting as it factors in diverse input but also gives everyone an equal voice, making it a go-to method for many project teams.

Here are three common voting techniques:

- **Unanimity:** Everyone agrees (rare, but it can happen).
- **Majority:** The choice that receives more than half the total votes (over 50 percent).
- **Plurality:** The option with the most votes wins, even if it's less than a majority.

Teams may also use techniques like *multicriteria decision analysis*, weighing options based on key factors, or the more top-down *autocratic decision-making*, where one person makes the decision for the group. Whatever the method, the key is aligning the team to ensure decisions stick — and avoiding chaos down the line.

## Addressing gaps and encouraging professional development

Project managers are frequently tapping into power skills to mentor and coach project team members and offering opportunities for growth and skill development. It's important to understand the difference between training, coaching, and mentoring for real-world application and for the PMP Exam.

- **Training** is a structured and systematic approach to sharing knowledge and developing specific skills. It involves providing team members with the necessary information, tools, and techniques to perform their roles effectively. Training is often conducted through workshops, courses, or online learning platforms. In the context of project management, training might cover topics like project planning, risk management, communication, and other project-related skills. Training typically involves a structured instructor-student relationship, where knowledge is transferred from the trainer to the trainees. The trainer is usually an expert or subject matter specialist. Training typically has a specific duration with a defined curriculum.

» **Mentoring** is a relationship-based approach where a more experienced person, known as the mentor, provides guidance, support, and advice to a less experienced team member, known as the mentee. The mentor draws on their expertise and shares their knowledge to help the mentee grow and develop professionally. In project management, a mentor might assist a less experienced project manager in handling complex projects, making strategic decisions, or navigating challenging situations. The mentor has significant experience and knowledge in the mentee's field. Mentoring supports personal and professional development, sharing experiences and wisdom. It can be an ongoing relationship, lasting as long as both parties find it beneficial.

» **Coaching** is a process that focuses on improving an individual's performance by helping them set and achieve specific goals. In project management, a coach may help team members develop their project management skills, improve their collaboration, or overcome specific challenges they face during the project. Coaching is goal-oriented, helping the coachee reach specific objectives, and can be short-term or long-term, depending on the coachee's goals.

REMEMBER

Training, mentoring, and coaching are distinct approaches to developing a project team. While training provides structured knowledge and skills, mentoring offers personalized guidance based on the mentor's experience, and coaching focuses on helping individuals achieve specific goals. Understanding these differences is vital for project managers to effectively support and nurture their project teams.

## Exercise: Mad Libs for a challenging project

Fill in the blanks with the words *training*, *coaching*, or *mentoring* to complete the story. Each word can be used more than once! The answers are at the end of the chapter.

> Taylor was recently assigned as the project manager for a high-stakes software implementation project. Although excited, Taylor quickly realized the team would need a mix of professional development activities to stay on track and meet the ambitious deadlines.

The project began with the need for (1)_____ to familiarize the team with the new project management tools and methodologies required to run the project smoothly. This structured learning ensured that everyone had the same baseline knowledge and could follow the processes.

As the project moved into execution, several team members struggled to manage their workloads efficiently. Taylor provided (2)_____ to these individuals, offering real-time feedback and practical advice on how to improve performance. These sessions focused on helping them apply new skills in the context of their daily tasks.

However, some challenges went beyond technical skills. Taylor sought (3)_____ from a more experienced project manager, who shared lessons learned from similar projects. This guidance was invaluable, helping Taylor navigate difficult stakeholder relationships and manage team dynamics.

As the deadline approached and pressure increased, the blend of (4)_____ to build foundational skills, (5)_____ to fine-tune performance, and (6)_____ to gain insight and perspective proved essential. Thanks to this balanced approach, the project was completed successfully, leaving both the team and stakeholders satisfied.

## Working with diverse and global teams

Every project team comprises individuals with diverse backgrounds — whether in terms of gender, language, ability, nationality, or life philosophy. Recognizing and valuing these differences creates an environment where unique perspectives thrive, and varied approaches lead to better problem-solving. Effective leaders go beyond merely acknowledging differences but take steps to establish an inclusive environment and encourage meaningful connections with team members from diverse groups.

REMEMBER

Creating a *psychologically safe* workplace is essential, particularly when working with diverse and global teams, a concept deeply aligned with Agile practices. In such environments, team members feel empowered to share ideas and concerns without fear of ridicule or retaliation, promoting transparency and openness. This is particularly important in project settings, where different motivations, working styles, and experiences — ranging from cultural backgrounds to job roles — can influence performance. Project managers play an important role in cultivating this safety by fostering trust and ensuring that all voices are heard and valued.

Furthermore, projects often serve stakeholders with varying expectations and requirements. By integrating varied perspectives into project leadership and processes, teams are better positioned to deliver outputs that resonate with a wide range of users, ensuring fair access and satisfaction.

**TIP** On the PMP Exam, expect questions that will test your understanding of working with global teams and creating environments where teams thrive and project outputs address diverse end-user needs.

## Fostering team development and culture

There are some common aspects of project team development that are relevant for most project teams. They include the following:

- Having a clear vision and well-defined objectives is essential. This involves creating a shared understanding among team members about the project's purpose, goals, and desired outcomes. It sets the direction and provides a sense of purpose to guide the team's efforts.

- Defining how the team will collaborate, communicate, and make decisions. It includes setting up workflows, communication channels, and decision-making processes to ensure smooth project execution. Efficient operations lead to improved project performance.

- Continuous improvement and development. It focuses on enhancing team members' skills, competencies, and knowledge over time. Encouraging professional development, training, and learning opportunities helps the team adapt to changing project requirements and stay competitive.

- Defining the roles and responsibilities of each team member within the project. It's essential to establish clear job descriptions, expectations, and the authority of team members. Clarity in roles minimizes confusion and promotes accountability, which can also aid the project manager in determining if there are any gaps and how to address those gaps through training, coaching, or mentoring.

- Providing support, coaching, and mentorship to team members. Project managers and experienced team members may offer guidance to less-experienced colleagues. This aspect is vital for skill development, knowledge transfer, and ensuring that the team can perform effectively.

These common aspects of team development play an important role in building a strong and effective project team and encouraging a positive project *team culture*. Team culture refers to the shared values, beliefs, attitudes, and norms that develop within a project team as they work together over time. Project team culture is the unique identity and atmosphere that characterizes a particular project team. Each project team develops its own team culture. The project manager is key in establishing and maintaining a safe and respectful environment and positive team culture. As such, the project manager should model behaviors such as transparency, integrity, respect, support, courage, and celebration of successes. As the project leader, you should demonstrate the behaviors you want to see in your own project team members.

# Outlining the stages of team development: The Tuckman Ladder

A positive team culture does not happen overnight. Teams will go through stages of team development with the goal of achieving a high level of performance. The *Tuckman Ladder*, also known as the Tuckman Stages or Tuckman's Group Development Model, is a widely recognized framework in project management for understanding the stages of team development. It was developed by Bruce Tuckman in 1965, and has five stages: forming, storming, norming, performing, and adjourning.

- **Forming:** In this stage, team members come together for the first time and there's a sense of uncertainty and politeness among them. They may not yet know each other's working styles, strengths, and weaknesses, and the team is just starting to understand the project's goals and objectives. Communication is often formal and cautious. For example, imagine a newly formed project team assigned to develop a new mobile app. In this stage, team members may introduce themselves, discuss the project scope, and start understanding their roles and responsibilities.

- **Storming:** In this stage, team members begin to voice their ideas, opinions, and differences more openly. Conflict and disagreements may arise as individuals start advocating for their preferred approaches or solutions. This stage can be challenging as it requires navigating through different viewpoints. For example, during the storming stage, the mobile app project team might face disagreements on which programming language to use or the design approach. Some team members may argue for a more user-friendly interface, while others may prioritize technical performance.

- **Norming:** In this stage, the team starts resolving their differences and establishing common ground. Team members recognize the value of each other's contributions and begin to cooperate more effectively. Common processes and communication channels are established, fostering a sense of unity. Going back to the mobile app project team, after resolving the conflicts during the storming stage, they agree on using a specific programming language that aligns with both user-friendliness and performance. They develop a shared understanding of the project's timeline and milestones.

- **Performing:** This stage is characterized by increased collaboration, productivity, and synergy. The team operates efficiently as a cohesive unit. They understand each other's strengths and weaknesses, and are capable of making decisions collectively. The focus is on achieving project goals and delivering high-quality results. In the performing stage, the mobile app project team works seamlessly together. They regularly communicate updates, collaborate on features, and address challenges proactively. The app development progresses smoothly, meeting timelines and quality standards. This is the stage you want your teams to be.

» **Adjourning (or mourning):** This stage is about the project's closure. As the project comes to an end, the team disbands and members transition to new assignments or projects. There might be a mix of emotions, including satisfaction from project completion and some sadness about the team disbanding. Going back to the mobile app team, after successfully launching the mobile app, the project team holds a retrospective meeting to reflect on the project's successes and areas for improvement. The team members bid farewell and move on to their next projects.

REMEMBER

It's important to note that while the Tuckman Ladder provides a useful framework, teams can revisit earlier stages if there are changes in the team composition or project requirements. Effective project managers should be aware of these stages, and take approaches and actions to facilitate team growth and development throughout the project life cycle.

Here are a few key PMP Exam tips as it relates to the Tuckman Ladder:

» New teams go through the stages of the Tuckman Ladder.

» Teams that have worked together in the past may experience a shorter version or skip early stages.

» A new team member takes the team back to the forming stage — even the loss of a team member takes the team back to forming.

Pay attention to the context of the question to determine which stage the team is in. Rarely does the PMP Exam specify the stage — you need to figure it out by reading between the lines.

## Exercise: Tuckman Ladder stages of team development

Following are five scenarios describing team dynamics at different stages of development. Your task is to identify the Tuckman stage depicted in each scenario and write your answer in the right column.

| Scenario | Tuckman Stage |
| --- | --- |
| 1. The team has developed a rhythm, with members supporting one another and focusing on their tasks. Processes are running smoothly, communication is clear, and everyone understands their role without needing constant supervision. | |

| Scenario | Tuckman Stage |
|---|---|
| 2. There's a deep sense of trust, and members proactively resolve problems on their own. They are committed to achieving the project goals and consistently deliver high-quality work. | |
| 3. With the project nearing completion, the team wraps up tasks and celebrates their success. Members reflect on their accomplishments and begin to part ways, transitioning to other assignments or projects. | |
| 4. Tensions arise as some members express disagreements about the project approach. Conflicts over responsibilities and workflows surface, with team members testing boundaries and trying to assert themselves. The project manager steps in to mediate disputes. | |
| 5. The project team has just been assembled. Members are polite and cautious, trying to understand their roles and responsibilities. Conversations are light, and the team leader takes charge to set goals and assign tasks. | |

## TEAM DEVELOPMENT IN AGILE: SHU-HA-RI

The concept of *Shu-Ha-Ri* holds immense importance in the context of team development for Agile teams. The Shu-Ha-Ri model is a concept borrowed from the Japanese martial art Aikido, and it has been adapted and applied to Agile team development. It describes the stages of learning and mastery that individuals and teams go through as they progress in their understanding and application of Agile principles and practices.

The Shu-Ha-Ri model outlines three stages:

- **Shu** means to obey. In the Shu stage, team members are beginners and novices in Agile practices. They follow the prescribed rules, processes, and guidelines of Agile frameworks such as Scrum or Kanban without much deviation. They focus on understanding and mastering the fundamental principles and mechanics of Agile. The emphasis is on learning and establishing a common foundation for the team.

- **Ha** is the stage where team members have gained a solid understanding of Agile practices and principles. They start to question and experiment with the established rules and guidelines. At this stage, team members actively seek to improve their processes and practices, tailoring them to better fit their specific context and needs. The team might adopt advanced Agile techniques and explore new ways of working that go beyond the basics they learned in the Shu stage.

*(continued)*

*(continued)*

- **Ri** means to transcend. In this stage, the team has reached a level of deep mastery and expertise in Agile. At this point, the team members have internalized Agile values and principles and can apply them intuitively without being bound by any specific frameworks or guidelines. The Ri stage represents the highest level of Agile maturity and continuous improvement.

The *retrospective meeting* is integral to the Shu-Ha-Ri concept, as it provides a dedicated time and space for the team to assess their progress and make informed decisions about their Agile practices. Through the retrospective, the team gains valuable insights into their growth and identifies areas of strength and pinpoints opportunities for further development.

## Creating motivation for high-performing teams

Motivating project team members is a part of the job of being an effective project manager. A motivated team is more likely to be engaged, productive, and committed to achieving project goals. As a project manager, you play a significant role in fostering motivation within the team.

Motivation refers to the internal process that drives and sustains a person's behavior toward achieving a goal or fulfilling a need. It is the combination of forces within an individual that directs their efforts, energy, and persistence toward specific actions or outcomes. Motivation can be influenced by various factors, including personal desires, values, beliefs, external rewards, and the environment.

Project managers need to understand what motivates project team members and work with them in a way that keeps them motivated and committed to the project.

People are not motivated by just one thing, but most people have a dominant motivator. As such, project managers need to tailor their motivation methods based on individual preferences. This helps to elicit the best individual and project team performance.

People perform better when they are motivated, and as you can imagine, people are motivated by different things. There are two primary aspects of motivating project team members: intrinsic motivation and extrinsic motivation.

>> **Intrinsic motivation** refers to the internal drive and enjoyment that individuals experience when they engage in tasks they find interesting, challenging, or

meaningful. It involves personal satisfaction, a sense of achievement, and the desire to grow and learn. When team members are intrinsically motivated, they are more likely to be proactive, innovative, and willing to take ownership of their responsibilities.

>> **Extrinsic motivation** involves external factors that influence a person's behavior and performance. This could include rewards, recognition, bonuses, or other tangible benefits offered by the project manager or the organization. Extrinsic motivators are external incentives that drive individuals to work harder or achieve specific outcomes to gain the rewards associated with their performance.

Both intrinsic and extrinsic motivation can be employed to drive positive behavior and performance. However, it is essential to balance those motivational factors effectively to maintain long-term engagement and dedication among the team members.

## Using recognition and rewards

The project manager appraises performance and provides recognition and rewards in response to the work of the team or individual team members. While these two concepts (recognition and rewards) sound similar, they have specific purposes.

>> **Recognition** refers to acknowledging and appreciating the efforts, contributions, or achievements of an individual or a team. It involves giving praise and positive feedback, or expressing gratitude for the hard work and dedication shown. A key characteristic of recognition is that it's a non-monetary recognition that doesn't involve financial incentives or material gifts. It is more about acknowledging and valuing the individual's efforts and accomplishments. It recognizes someone's achievements, which can boost their self-esteem and *intrinsic motivation*. It reinforces a sense of accomplishment and encourages individuals to continue performing at their best. Recognition can be public, such as during team meetings or company-wide announcements, or private, such as a one-on-one appreciation conversation between a manager and an employee. For example, the team leader might recognize a team member's exceptional problem-solving skills by publicly praising them during a team meeting. This recognition can motivate the team member to continue being resourceful and proactive in addressing project challenges.

>> **Rewards** are tangible or monetary items or benefits given to an individual or a team in response to achieving specific goals or demonstrating exceptional performance. Rewards are usually external incentives that aim to encourage

and reinforce desired behaviors. They can include bonuses, gift cards, promotions, additional time off, or other tangible benefits that have a monetary value. They encourage individuals to strive for specific targets to obtain the reward. Rewards are typically given upon meeting predetermined criteria or achieving specific milestones. For example, a project manager could offer a financial bonus to the team if they successfully complete the project ahead of schedule and under budget. This reward serves as an *extrinsic motivator* to encourage the team to work efficiently and deliver results.

Recognition is about acknowledging and appreciating the individual's efforts and accomplishments, often through praise and positive feedback, without involving monetary incentives. Rewards are consumable or monetary incentives given in response to achieving specific goals or exceptional performance, aiming to motivate individuals through external benefits.

Both recognition and rewards can be powerful tools to motivate and engage team members, but they serve different purposes in the overall motivation strategy. Typically, guidance on recognizing and rewarding team members is documented within the Resource Management Plan. The guiding principle is that the project manager's primary focus is to recognize and reward the team over individuals.

### Applying motivational theories

Understanding what motivates project team members helps in tailoring the right strategies to use to recognize or reward individuals. This understanding, facilitated by motivation theories, can lead to improved team engagement and performance. These theories aim to explain the underlying factors that drive human behavior and performance in the workplace. Here are four prominent motivation theories:

- » **Maslow's Hierarchy of Needs:** Proposed by Abraham Maslow, this theory suggests that human needs can be arranged in a hierarchical order ranging from basic physiological needs at the bottom to higher-order psychological needs at the top, as shown in Figure 11-2. As individuals satisfy their lower-level needs, they become motivated to fulfill higher-level needs. The five levels of needs are physiological, safety, belongingness and love, esteem, and self-actualization.

   PMP aspirants should memorize the levels of needs in the described order. The PMP Exam has been known to test your knowledge of the correct order of the hierarchy of needs.

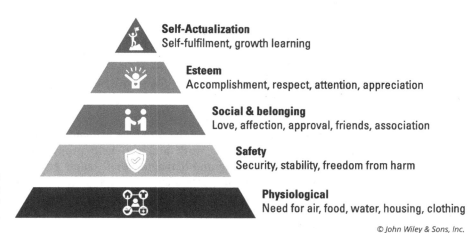

FIGURE 11-2: Maslow's Hierarchy of Needs.

» **McClelland's Theory of Needs:** Developed by David McClelland, this theory focuses on three fundamental needs that drive human behavior — achievement, affiliation, and power. According to this theory, individuals have varying degrees of these needs, and they are motivated by different factors, depending on their dominant need. Achievement is about the drive to excel, succeed, and accomplish challenging tasks. Affiliation is the need to establish positive relationships, socialize, and be a part of a group. Power is the desire to influence, lead, and control others.

» **Herzberg's Two-Factor Theory:** Proposed by Frederick Herzberg, this theory introduces the concept of hygiene factors and motivators. Hygiene factors are essential for preventing dissatisfaction in the workplace, such as job security and working conditions, while motivators, such as recognition and challenging work, are the factors that lead to job satisfaction and increased motivation. Examples of hygiene factors include salary, job security, working conditions, and company policies. Hygiene factors are those elements that when lacking, can lead to job dissatisfaction. However, their very presence does not necessarily lead to motivation. Addressing hygiene factors can prevent dissatisfaction, but to truly motivate their staff, organizations need to provide opportunities for growth and intrinsic rewards. Motivators are those factors that directly contribute to job satisfaction and intrinsic motivation. They include recognition, opportunities for growth, responsibility, and achievement.

» **Motivational Theories of X, Y, and Z:** Theory X and Theory Y were developed by Douglas McGregor. Theory X assumes that employees are inherently lazy. They dislike work and need strict supervision. This theory is associated with more traditional authoritarian management styles. Theory Y believes that employees are intrinsically motivated. They take responsibility and seek challenges in their work. This theory supports a more participative and empowering management approach. Theory Z, developed by William Ouchi, is a management approach that combines the best aspects of Japanese and American management practices, emphasizing long-term employment, employee involvement, and group decision-making.

Each of these motivation theories provides valuable insights into what drives individuals to perform at work and can help project managers tailor their approaches to motivating and managing their teams effectively. Understanding these concepts allows project managers to design effective strategies to inspire and engage their teams.

TIP

It's essential to recognize that each team member is unique and may respond differently to various motivational strategies. Some may thrive with public recognition and praise, while others may value financial incentives or additional time off. A comprehensive approach that combines recognition and appropriate rewards tailored to individual preferences can maximize team motivation and productivity.

# Developing Interpersonal Skills

Project managers play a key role in guiding teams, helping them overcome obstacles, and keeping them motivated. While technical expertise is important, it is the mastery of leadership skills that sets exceptional project managers apart. This section focuses on the skills of critical thinking, motivation, emotional intelligence, influencing, conflict management, active listening, negotiating, team building, coaching, cultural awareness, political awareness, and conflict resolution. Each of these skills is essential for project managers to excel in their roles and drive project success.

REMEMBER

Interpersonal skills are sometimes referenced as power skills or leadership skills. These terms are used interchangeably on the PMP Exam.

## Critical thinking

Critical thinking is the ability to objectively analyze and evaluate information. Its impact on teams is that it enhances problem-solving, helps identify risks, enables effective decision-making, and leads to improved team performance. For instance, perhaps you're managing a complex project with tight deadlines. Critical thinking helps you to assess risks, identify alternative options, and make informed decisions. Or, perhaps a project team is faced with a major design flaw in a critical component. The team needs to assess the impact, identify alternatives, and make a decision on the best course of action.

## Motivation

Motivation is the ability to inspire and energize individuals and teams toward achieving project goals. The impact on teams is that they're more engaged, more productive, and more committed to the project goals. They produce higher-quality work and achieve timely project delivery. From the stakeholders' perspective, increased productivity is something that they see from the team, and they also are witnessing successful project outcomes, which instills confidence in the project manager's leadership. Consider a situation where a project is falling behind schedule and team members are demotivated. The project manager needs to find ways to reignite enthusiasm and commitment among the team or the team is facing a challenging phase in the project. Motivation helps to boost team morale, provide encouragement, and maintain productivity.

## Emotional intelligence

Emotional intelligence involves understanding and managing emotions both in oneself and in others. The impact on the team is that it fosters positive team dynamics. High emotional intelligence leads to effectively resolving conflicts, and it provides a supportive work environment, thereby promoting collaboration and trust among team members. For instance, a team member may be struggling with personal issues that are impacting their performance. Emotional intelligence can help the project manager be more empathetic, offer support, and find solutions that consider the individual's well-being.

## Influencing

Influencing is the skill of persuading others to support your ideas, decisions, or initiatives. In terms of impact on teams, it helps the project manager gain team buy-in. It aligns stakeholders' expectations and it drives decision-making, leading to improved cooperation and goal achievement. You may use these skills when you need to gain stakeholder buy-in for critical project change. Influencing helps you effectively communicate the benefits and address concerns to gain support.

## Conflict management

Conflict management is the ability to handle disagreements and conflicts in a constructive way. As it relates to your team, it can foster a positive team environment, encourage open communication, and promote collaboration, which boosts team productivity and cohesion. There may be a situation where two team members have conflicting opinions that are hindering progress. Conflict management helps you facilitate open dialogue, find common ground, and potentially reach a resolution.

## Active listening

Active listening is the skill of fully engaging and understanding what others are saying. The impact on your team is that it creates an inclusive and respectful environment. It can have the benefit of strengthening relationships and it helps to improve understanding, resulting in clearer communication and reduced misunderstandings. For project stakeholders, active listening sets the tone where stakeholders feel heard and valued, leading to stronger engagement, improved trust, and higher stakeholder satisfaction with the project management process. For example, a team member may share concerns about project requirements. Active listening helps you attentively listen, clarify doubts, and ensure alignment between expectations and deliverables.

## Negotiating

Negotiating involves reaching mutually beneficial agreements by finding common ground. The impact on teams is that it enables project managers to resolve conflicts, manage expectations, and secure necessary resources, resulting in improved team collaboration and overall project success. Effective negotiation outcomes lead to favorable agreements, minimize disputes, and increase stakeholder support and satisfaction. Many project managers have found themselves in the situation where they need to negotiate resource allocation with another project manager. Good negotiating skills enable you to find win-win solutions while balancing priorities.

## Team building

Team building involves fostering collaboration, trust, and synergy within a project team. The impact on the team is that it enhances collaboration, trust, and synergy within the team, leading to increased productivity, creative ideas, and overall project success. As for stakeholders, team building instills confidence in the project manager's leadership. It ensures smooth project execution, and it has the ability to enhance stakeholder satisfaction. A typical scenario is where the project manager is leading a newly formed team with diverse backgrounds. Team building helps to establish a positive team culture, encourage cooperation, and leverage individual strengths.

## Coaching

Coaching is the process of guiding and developing team members to reach their full potential. The impact on a team is that it fosters continuous learning and skill development and growth, resulting in increased team performance and job satisfaction. Perhaps a team member lacks the necessary skills for a specific task.

Coaching enables you to provide guidance, offer training opportunities, and empower individuals to excel.

## Cultural awareness

Cultural awareness involves understanding and respecting diverse cultural perspectives within a project environment. For the team, it promotes inclusivity, understanding, and collaboration among team members, leading to improved team dynamics, creativity, and innovation. Consider a project team that consists of members from different cultural backgrounds. Cultural awareness helps you appreciate differences, promote inclusivity, and minimize misunderstandings.

## Political awareness

Political awareness, also known as office politics, refers to understanding and navigating the informal power dynamics and relationships within your organization. The impact on teams is that you can manage relationships, resolve conflicts, and navigate organizational hierarchies, which can lead to better teamwork, reduced power struggles, and improved collaboration. For instance, your project requires collaboration with various stakeholders who have conflicting agendas. Political awareness helps you navigate the power dynamics, build alliances, and influence decision-making effectively.

These core leadership skills can enhance your project management capabilities, as well as have a positive impact on your team's morale and performance. Effective leadership is not about exerting authority, but rather inspiring and empowering others to achieve their full potential. It involves building relationships, fostering collaboration, and adapting to different circumstances.

TIP

You may be wondering, "Do I need to know all of these interpersonal skills for the PMP Exam?" The answer is yes. Knowing and applying core leadership skills in the context of the PMP Exam will be important for demonstrating your ability to handle real-world project challenges and effectively engage your team and key stakeholders. And hopefully, you will notice the common theme that you want to keep the stakeholders satisfied and that typically the best PMI answer hinges on achieving the satisfaction of your stakeholders. These skills go beyond theoretical knowledge and highlight your practical understanding of the people-centric domain of project management, which is integral to the PMP certification exam.

These interpersonal leadership skills represent a diverse range of abilities that are fundamental to effective leadership and good project management. Each skill is a building block, contributing to your ability to lead, inspire, and motivate your teams toward achieving project goals.

# When conflict occurs

Unless you live under a rock, you understand that conflict happens on projects. In fact, PMP aspirants should expect to encounter quite a few exam scenarios that are peppered with some kind of conflict situation.

*But not all conflicts are bad.*

Conflict is a part of team culture. When teams work in a psychologically safe environment, team members are comfortable with exchanging ideas and sharing different perspectives and points of view.

*Ineffective conflict management is bad.*

Ineffective or nonexistent conflict management can lead to destructive behavior, animosity, poor performance, and reduced productivity, all of which are disruptive to teams and threaten the successful completion of a project. Conversely, effective conflict management can lead to improved understanding, performance, and productivity. When conflict is handled well, team members and stakeholders can candidly challenge and disrupt the status quo with new ideas that may actually present opportunities.

Ideally, all team members and stakeholders are responsible for managing conflict. There may be appropriate instances where the project manager needs to provide direction on handling a conflict situation. In the Agile environment, the servant leader assists in the removal of impediments or sources of conflict. In Agile projects, the team lead facilitates conflict resolution sessions, or the team is empowered to resolve conflicts on their own.

For the PMP Exam, unless the question says otherwise, the first instance of conflict should be handled at the individual level (among the disputing parties, such as team members) before the project manager steps in to intervene.

The typical causes of conflict include the following:

>> Competition for resources

>> Differences in objectives, values, and perceptions

>> Disagreements about role requirements, work activities, and individual approaches

>> Communication breakdowns

These common causes of conflict are a normal part of most human interactions that occur in the workplace. By recognizing the issues rather than focusing on the individual or personality differences, teams can effectively address conflicts with sound resolutions.

Having a team charter outlining conflict resolution strategies and the ground rules on good (and bad) behavior when dealing with conflicts can help teams effectively navigate the conflict as well. This is where interpersonal skills such as critical thinking, emotional intelligence, influencing, and negotiations play a critical role in effectively managing conflicts.

## Conflict management approaches

There are five basic approaches to handling conflict. The approach to managing conflict can depend on the importance of the conflict, the sense of urgency to resolve the conflict in a timely manner, the positions of the conflicting parties, and the motivation to resolve the conflicts in the short term or the long term. The five approaches are as follows:

- » **Withdraw/Avoid.** Parties retreat or postpone a decision on a problem (lose-lose).

- » **Smooth/Accommodate.** Individuals make concessions, emphasizing agreement rather than differences. This is used when reaching the overall goal is more important than the disagreement. Parties want to maintain harmony in the relationship.

- » **Force/Direct.** Pushing one's viewpoint at the expense of another (win-lose). This is used when there is not enough time to collaborate or problem-solve.

- » **Compromise/Reconcile.** Solutions bring some degree of satisfaction to both parties, but not all parties are fully satisfied. This approach shows a willingness to give and take.

- » **Collaborate/Problem-Solve.** Involves incorporating multiple viewpoints about the conflict. Parties openly discuss differences and arrive at a consensus (win-win).

TIP

Whenever possible, resolve conflict in favor of the customer or the sponsor. You're still following good project management practices (or selecting the best answer option) that also ensures the resolution keeps your key stakeholders satisfied.

When presented with two good answer options to a question (is it A or B?!), the best answer is typically the one that demonstrates collaboration and problem-solving. Forcing is usually not the ideal solution, unless the scenario indicates otherwise. Of course, answers depend on the situations described.

## Conflict management in the adaptive environment

Speed B. Leas developed a framework to assess the seriousness of conflicts and understand how they can escalate. This model is widely used for managing project teams, particularly in adaptive environments. It offers insights into the nature of disagreements, the appropriate moments for intervention, and when escalation may be necessary for resolution beyond observation. There are five levels of conflict within the Leas model:

- » **Level 1 — Problem to solve:** This involves differences that are identified and discussed among team members in a collaborative manner. The conflict is task-focused rather than personal, making it easier to resolve through discussion and problem-solving.

- » **Level 2 — Disagreement:** Issues become entangled with personalities, leading to distrust and strained interactions. At this stage, disagreements start to feel personal, making it harder to define the actual problem.

- » **Level 3 — Contest:** Participants adopt a win/lose mindset, taking sides, and engaging in distorted communication and personal attacks. The goal shifts from resolving the issue to protecting oneself and winning the argument. Some participants may feel invigorated, while others feel threatened, fueling the conflict.

- » **Level 4 — Fight/flight:** Participants aim to hurt or remove their opponents rather than resolve the issue. Intervention is necessary to manage the situation.

- » **Level 5 — Intractable situation / World War:** Participants lose the ability to understand the core issues objectively. Actions become destructive, focusing on harming reputations, positions, or well-being. Relationships are often damaged beyond repair.

Conflict behaviors can overlap between levels, and shifts between stages are common. Levels 1 through 3 offer opportunities for positive outcomes with appropriate conflict resolution strategies. Levels 4 and 5 often require formal intervention. The Leas framework encourages the use of interpersonal skills and conflict management strategies, particularly in the earlier stages, to de-escalate issues before they become unmanageable.

## Exercise: Conflict management scenarios

Instructions: Indicate which conflict management technique was employed in each scenario *(withdraw/avoid, smooth/accommodate, force/direct, compromise/reconcile, or collaborate/problem solve)*. The answers are at the end of the chapter.

| Conflict Scenario | Technique |
|---|---|
| 1. Emily wants to expedite the project's completion, while David emphasizes the need for thorough testing. They work together to create a revised schedule that accommodates both objectives. | |
| 2. A conflict arises between two project team leads, Sarah and Mark, over the division of responsibilities. They decide to temporarily assign roles based on individual strengths and skills until a more permanent solution can be found. | |
| 3. A disagreement emerges among team members, Jane and Mike, about the project's communication plan. Jane insists on regular status meetings, while Mike prefers email updates. They decide to alternate between status meetings and email updates to accommodate both preferences. | |
| 4. During a project meeting, a heated argument arises between two stakeholders, Mike and Lisa, regarding budget allocation. To avoid further conflict, they both agree to postpone the discussion and gather more data before making a decision. | |

# Understanding Teams in the Adaptive Environment

Throughout this book, we discuss the application of project management techniques in the Agile environment, so it's important to understand team dynamics on Agile projects.

Resource planning in the Agile environment differs from traditional project management approaches. In Agile, the focus is on adaptability, flexibility, and collaboration.

>> Resource planning is not done up front for the entire project but is instead carried out incrementally throughout the project's life cycle.

>> Agile projects are typically executed by cross-functional teams consisting of individuals with diverse skills and expertise. These teams work collaboratively and have the necessary skills to handle various aspects of the project.

» Capacity planning involves understanding the team's availability in terms of hours per sprint. The team considers factors like vacations, holidays, and other commitments to determine their capacity.

» Resource allocation in Agile is dynamic and occurs at the beginning of each sprint. The team collaboratively decides which tasks they will work on, taking into account their capacity and the priorities defined by the product owner. Agile resource planning allows adaptation and changes in the project scope and priorities. If the team faces unexpected challenges or if the product owner reprioritizes tasks, the team can adjust their resource allocation accordingly, thus providing flexibility along the way.

» At the heart of the Agile methodology lies the concept of self-organizing, cross-functional teams working collaboratively to deliver value in incremental iterations. These Agile teams form the backbone of successful project execution, fostering innovation, efficiency, and continuous improvement.

Unlike traditional project management where rigid hierarchies and top-down decision-making prevail, Agile teams operate with a sense of autonomy and ownership. They are empowered to make decisions, manage their workloads, and continuously learn and evolve.

In the adaptive environment, the Agile team lead (Scrum Master, Agile project manager, team facilitator) often demonstrates what's called *servant leadership*. This focuses on understanding and addressing the needs and development of project team members. This is where they share power and put the needs of the team first. Servant leadership allows teams to self-organize where the focus is on removing obstacles, being a diversion shield, and providing encouragement and development opportunities for the Agile team members.

Agile teams can also work virtually, although it is not ideal. To facilitate virtual co-location and improve communications among dispersed teams, Agile teams may create a *fishbowl window* (set up a long-lived video conferencing link for the entire work day) or *remote pairing* (use video conferencing tools to share screens, including voice and video links).

Whether working in an Agile environment or using traditional project management techniques, project managers should focus on a mix of strategies and actions that foster the growth and performance of their team members. For Agile teams, it's ideal to keep the team stable to minimize the need to go through the stages of team development — such as forming, storming, and norming — during every sprint. Yipes!

# Adapting Your Leadership Style

Project management leadership is the art of influencing and motivating individuals and teams to achieve project goals effectively and efficiently. Leadership skills are necessary for creating and sustaining high-performing teams. However, your leadership style may change depending on the context of the environment and the changing needs of your project.

## Outlining the characteristics of strong leadership

Effective leadership plays a pivotal role in shaping the team's culture, setting its direction, and guiding the team toward success. Strong leadership does the following:

- Provides the team with a clear vision of the project's goals and objectives. This shared understanding of the project's direction aligns the team's efforts and enhances overall performance.
- Inspires and motivates their team members. Strong leaders recognize individual strengths, encourage personal growth, and create an environment where team members feel valued and appreciated.
- Fosters open lines of communication, encourages feedback, listens to concerns, and addresses issues promptly.
- Ensures that conflicts are handled constructively and promotes positive resolution.
- Empowers teams to make decisions and take ownership of their work. Empowered team members are more invested in their work, and tend to take initiative, leading to higher performance.
- Demonstrates adaptability and resilience by guiding the team through challenges and uncertainties. A strong leader remains adaptable and resilient in the face of changing circumstances and inspires the team to do the same.
- Acknowledges achievements and celebrates successes, which in turn boosts team morale, and fosters a culture of positivity and comradery. Recognized team members are more likely to feel motivated and continue performing at their best.
- Invests in the growth of their team members by providing opportunities for skill development, training, and career advancement.

Leadership skills are the foundation upon which high-performing teams are built. Given the dynamic nature of projects and working with different personalities, project managers need to tailor their leadership styles to specific situations, as that is essential for effective project management.

Building a strong team is an ongoing process. As a project manager, your role is to support and guide the team, ensuring they have the resources, information, and motivation they need to excel. Project managers who feel they don't have time for team building and developing their teams typically are also not using good project management practices. In the end, a well-built team can turn challenges into opportunities and lead the project to success.

By exhibiting the leadership qualities listed earlier in this section, a project manager creates a positive work environment, encourages teamwork, and maximizes the team's potential to achieve exceptional results. A high-performing team in turn leads to successful project outcomes and contributes to the overall success of the organization.

## Determining the right leadership approach

On some projects, leadership could be assigned to one person. This is called *centralized management and leadership.* On other projects, project management and leadership activities may be shared among the project management team, and perhaps the project team members themselves. This is called *distributed management and leadership.*

Different project teams and team dynamics may require varying approaches to leadership to ensure high performance and success. Your experience with the project and the type of project can certainly define your leadership style. More experienced teams may be more self-managed, and require less of the project manager's time and attention around leadership efforts. Think about the maturity of your project team members. The experience and skill level of team members also impacts your leadership approach. For a team of seasoned professionals with a high level of expertise, a more hands-off approach, or delegating your tasks, can be effective as they require less guidance. Conversely, for less experienced or junior team members, a more supportive and *coaching leadership style* may be needed to help them to develop and grow.

Be aware of the organizational governance structure. The governance structures within an organization can influence how much autonomy a project leader has, and how decisions are made.

- » In a highly hierarchical organization with rigid governance, a more *authoritative leadership style* might be necessary to ensure adherence to protocols and procedures.

- » In contrast, in a decentralized organization with a focus on empowerment, a more *servant leadership style* can foster innovation and collaboration, and also factor in having distributed teams.

Leadership becomes particularly challenging in distributed project teams where team members are geographically dispersed. In such cases, leaders must adopt a more inclusive and virtual leadership style. Effective communication becomes even more critical to bridge the physical distance and maintain team cohesion. Utilizing technology and tools to facilitate collaboration and stay connected becomes important.

# Achieving a High-Performing Team: The Ultimate Goal

A high-performing team is a cohesive unit with open communications, shared understanding, trust and shared ownership. They collaborate effectively, embrace adaptability and resilience, feel empowered and receive recognition for their contributions. As a project manager, investing time and effort and nurturing these factors within your team will significantly contribute to achieving project goals and create a positive rewarding work environment.

# Answer Keys

**Mad Libs: The Challenging Project:** 1. Training. 2. Coaching. 3. Mentoring. 4. Training. 5. Coaching. 6. Mentoring.

**Tuckman Ladder Stages of Team Development:** 1. Norming. 2. Performing. 3. Adjourning. 4. Storming. 5. Forming.

**Conflict Management**

1. **Collaborating.** Collaborating involves actively engaging in discussions to find a mutually acceptable solution. In this scenario, Emily and David collaborate to create a balanced project timeline.

2. **Smoothing.** Smoothing involves emphasizing common ground and minimizing differences. Here, Sarah and Mark smooth the situation by temporarily assigning roles to avoid further conflict.
3. **Compromising:** Compromising involves finding a middle ground. Jane and Mike compromise by alternating between status meetings and email updates, addressing their differing communication preferences.
4. **Withdraw.** Mike and Lisa postponed the discussion.

**IN THIS CHAPTER**

» Discovering the five Process Groups

» Analyzing the concept of business value

» Presenting a business case and Benefits Management Plan

» Creating project charters and stakeholder engagement strategies

Chapter **12**

# Initiating Your Project

This chapter delves into the "why" behind your project — why it exists, its alignment with organizational strategy, and its expected outcomes. Understanding this "why" is not just a philosophical exercise; it's necessary for creating clarity, building alignment, and securing buy-in from stakeholders. Projects that lack this clarity often suffer from scope creep, misaligned goals, or lack of stakeholder support.

This chapter is your guide to avoiding that fate. It focuses on building the "blueprint" of your project — the foundational practices and tools that ensure a strong start. I'll walk you through the steps to initiate your project, from understanding its purpose to documenting the high-level scope and securing the necessary buy-in.

You'll also explore the essential documents and key players that connect your project to the broader organizational strategy. Initiating your project involves establishing its initial scope and objectives, securing authorization, and getting the key players involved to establish the foundation of a successful project.

# Setting the Stage: The Five Process Groups

Every project, regardless of size or industry, progresses through five Process Groups: Initiating, Planning, Executing, Monitoring and Controlling, and Closing. These groups provide a structured approach to managing a project from start to finish, thus ensuring consistency and alignment with organizational goals.

This chapter focuses on the activities of the Initiating Process Group, where the foundation for the project is laid. Initiating your project is where you define the project at a high level, secure authorization to proceed, and align stakeholders on the project's purpose and expected outcomes.

The specific processes that fall under this Process Group include

- Develop Project Charter
- Identify Stakeholders

Think of the Initiating Process Group as the compass for your project. It sets the direction, clarifies the destination, and ensures everyone involved understands the "why" behind the work. Without this initial alignment and formalization, projects risk veering off course or failing to deliver value.

# Starting with Business Value

The foundation of any project lies in its ability to deliver business value. At its core, a project is initiated to address a need, seize an opportunity, or solve a problem that aligns with an organization's strategic goals. Whether the benefits are financial, operational, or reputational, the ultimate purpose of a project is to contribute measurable value to the organization and its stakeholders.

*Business value* encompasses both tangible and intangible benefits. *Tangible benefits* such as increased revenue, reduced costs, or acquired assets can be directly measured. *Intangible benefits* include enhanced customer satisfaction, improved employee morale, or a strengthened brand image. Projects often deliver a combination of these benefits, emphasizing the importance of understanding value beyond purely financial terms.

The concept of business value is also contextual, varying by stakeholder. Here are some examples:

- **Shareholder value:** For publicly traded companies, this is often measured by equity capitalization — calculated as the number of outstanding shares multiplied by the current share price.
- **Customer value:** This reflects the utility or satisfaction customers derive from a product or service.
- **Employee knowledge:** Intellectual capital and employee expertise are increasingly recognized as significant contributors to organizational value.
- **Channel partner value:** These benefits are derived from strategic partnerships that can bolster revenue and operational efficiencies.

Channel partner value is an odd concept. To simplify, it refers to the benefits a company gains by working with partners who sell, distribute, or promote its products or services. These partners bring value through their market reach, expertise, and ability to connect with customers in ways the organization may not be able to on its own. Now that's value!

# The Role of the Business Case: Telling the Project's Origin Story

A *business case* is an important document at the onset of a project to justify the investment. It lays out the rationale for the project, articulating how it aligns with organizational objectives and detailing the expected benefits. A well-crafted business case begins with a *needs assessment*, which evaluates the organization's current challenges, opportunities, and strategic goals. Based on this assessment, recommendations are proposed, including the following:

- Constraints, assumptions, and risks
- Potential solutions
- Success criteria
- An implementation approach

The business case may also include *project selection techniques* to prioritize initiatives. These techniques often weigh the costs and benefits, helping decision makers determine the project's viability and alignment with organizational strategy.

In short, the business case justifies the need for the project by detailing the business problem or opportunity it addresses. It is an important document that supports the decision to initiate the project, ensuring it aligns with the organization's strategic goals.

# Evaluating and Realizing Benefits

With the business case providing a clear justification for the project, the next step is to focus on how the project will deliver value. This is where the Benefits Management Plan comes into play. While the business case outlines *why* the project is being undertaken, the Benefits Management Plan focuses on *how* the project's intended outcomes will be realized and sustained over time. It serves as a bridge between the strategic goals of the organization and the tangible results of the project, defining the metrics for success, identifying who will own the benefits, and outlining the timeline for their realization. Key components of the Benefits Management Plan include the following:

- **Target benefits:** The plan specifies the tangible and intangible outcomes expected from the project.
- **Benefit metrics:** It defines how success will be measured.
- **Realization timeline:** It outlines when benefits are expected, from short-term wins to long-term gains.
- **Benefit owner:** It identifies who is responsible for achieving each benefit.
- **Risk assessment:** It highlights risks that could impact benefit realization and suggests mitigation strategies.
- **Monitoring and reporting:** It describes how progress will be tracked and communicated.

The Benefits Management Plan explains how the project's benefits will be identified, quantified, managed, and tracked to ensure that the project delivers the expected value to the organization and stakeholders.

# Prioritizing Projects for Strategic Impact

For many organizations, selecting which projects to pursue often comes down to determining value versus feasibility. While every project proposal may promise exciting outcomes, constraints such as time, budget, and available resources mean that not all projects can be implemented. To make these tough decisions, organizations employ various project selection methods.

- » **Mathematical model techniques (constrained optimization):** Large, complex projects requiring intricate calculations often rely on constrained optimization methods. These mathematical models identify the best projects to pursue while adhering to specific constraints. Examples include linear programming, integer programming, and multi-objective optimization. While these techniques can be intimidating, here's the good news for exam prep: all you need to remember is that constrained optimization is a mathematical approach used for large-scale project selection.

- » **Benefit measurement methods (comparative approach):** For most organizations, however, benefit measurement methods are the go-to tools for evaluating and comparing projects. These methods take a comparative approach, focusing on the cost versus benefits of each proposed project. Projects are evaluated side by side to determine which initiatives offer the greatest value to the organization.

Benefits are typically evaluated using *business-based* and *financial-based measurement methods*. Business-based methods focus on non-financial metrics, such as the following:

- » **Payback period:** How long it will take for a project to recover its initial investment. Shorter durations are often more favorable.

- » **Opportunity cost:** Opportunity given up by selecting one project over another.

REMEMBER

For these measurement methods, *the smaller the better.*

Common financial-based benefit measurement methods include the following:

- » **Cost-Benefit Analysis:** A straightforward comparison of expected costs and anticipated benefits. Typically the calculation is referred to as benefit cost ratio (BCR).

- » **Net Present Value (NPV):** The value of future cash inflows and outflows discounted to their present value. A higher NPV indicates greater financial benefit.

- **Internal Rate of Return (IRR):** The discount rate at which a project's NPV equals zero. It's an indicator of a project's profitability. The project with the highest and positive IRR should be selected; a project with a negative IRR should always be rejected.

- **Return on Investment (ROI):** A percentage showing the net benefit divided by the project's cost. Positive ROI indicates a worthwhile investment.

REMEMBER

For these measurement methods, *the bigger the better*.

While these methods vary in complexity, they share a common goal: to help organizations make informed decisions about how to allocate resources effectively. As a project manager, you must understand these methods — even if you're not the one performing the calculations — because they provide the foundation for why certain projects get the green light while others do not.

Initiating a project begins with a clear understanding of its purpose and expected contributions to business value. By grounding the project in well-defined benefits, supported by robust analysis and documentation, organizations can ensure that their investments yield meaningful and measurable outcomes. As a project manager, your role is to deliver on the project's objectives, and to safeguard the organization's investment.

# Test Your Knowledge: Benefit Measurement Methods

Instructions: For each row, put a checkmark (✔) next to the project that you would select, either Project A or Project B. Refer to the previous section, "Prioritizing Projects for Strategic Impact," for a refresher about these measurements.

|  | Project A | ✔ | Project B | ✔ |
|---|---|---|---|---|
| 1. Net Present Value | $77,000 |  | $59,000 |  |
| 2. Internal Rate of Return | 12 percent |  | 18 percent |  |
| 3. Payback Period | 10 months |  | 12 months |  |
| 4. Benefit-Cost Ratio | 2.25 |  | 1.5 |  |

Overall, which project should you choose?

# The Project Charter: Creating a High-Level Blueprint for Success

The project charter's creation is fundamentally supported by the business case and Benefits Management Plan. These documents provide the necessary justification, strategic alignment, and framework for benefit realization, ensuring the project is well founded and poised to deliver significant value to the organization. Here are the key components of the project charter:

- **Authorization:** Officially approves the project, providing the project manager with authority to use resources.
- **Sponsor**: Names the individual or organization (for example PMO) who authorizes the project and their authority levels.
- **Assignment of project manager:** Names the project manager and their authority on the project.
- **Purpose:** Explains the business need or problem being addressed and how it aligns with strategic goals.
- **High-level description:** Provides an overview of the project's objectives, scope, and deliverables.
- **High-level risks:** Identifies potential constraints, assumptions, and uncertainties.
- **Summary milestone schedule:** Outlines significant points on the project and their expected timelines.
- **Summary budget:** Offers a preliminary financial framework.
- **Stakeholder list:** Highlights key stakeholders, their roles, and their influence on the project.

The project charter is the starting point for detailed planning. It ensures that the project is grounded in strategic alignment, stakeholder support, and organizational priorities. For PMP aspirants, understanding the purpose, composition, and significance of the project charter is essential, as it forms the foundation for project planning and execution, and is a key topic in the PMP Exam framework.

The project charter serves as the official authorization for the project, granted by the sponsor, and defines the project's goal, purpose, composition, and approach. Think of it as the *who*, *what*, and *why* of the project, written to align all stakeholders around the key objectives and to provide the project manager with the authority to use organizational resources.

Another important document created as a result of initiating the project is the *assumption log*, a companion tool for tracking known uncertainties and constraints.

# The Human Element: Analyzing and Engaging Stakeholders

The value behind the project charter is that it clarifies the project objectives. Most especially, it helps stakeholders understand the project's objectives and expected outcomes, aligning their expectations and ensuring everyone is working toward a common goal. The charter identifies key stakeholders involved in the project, enabling project managers to focus on engaging relevant individuals or groups. The charter establishes decision-making authority, outlining roles and responsibilities, which helps project managers involve stakeholders appropriately and ensure effective communication and engagement. Effective stakeholder engagement is essential for gaining buy-in, setting realistic expectations, and building the relationships necessary to move the project forward. This involves identifying who the stakeholders are and understanding their interests, concerns, and level of influence.

Stakeholder engagement involves actively collaborating with stakeholders throughout a project's life cycle. It goes beyond mere communication and includes seeking input and feedback and incorporating stakeholder perspectives into the decision-making process.

The *PMBOK Guide*, Seventh Edition outlines six steps to engage stakeholders effectively. To help you remember each step, here's a creative mnemonic:

**I** Understand **All P**rojects **E**xperience **M**ayhem, which stands for

>> **I**dentify
>> **U**nderstand
>> **A**nalyze
>> **P**rioritize
>> **E**ngage
>> **M**onitor your stakeholders

While there is a general "order" to these steps, it's important to understand that they are fluid and may need to be revisited multiple times as needed.

## Identifying stakeholders: Casting a wide net

The initial stakeholders are often those who identify the problem or need that the project aims to address. Documents such as the business case and Benefits Management Plan can provide additional insight into potential stakeholders. However, missed stakeholders are often discovered later, and their input or requests may lead to changes that could delay the project. Additionally, as the project evolves, changes may introduce new stakeholders who will need to be engaged and managed effectively.

The typical tools and techniques used to identify stakeholders include the following:

- » **Expert judgment:** A technique that project managers use to obtain additional guidance from individuals who are more experienced in various areas needed to be understood for the project. It also can refer to the project manager's own expertise, or expert judgment in project management or other matters. Expert judgment in this instance can include an understanding of the politics and power structures in the organization.
- » **Questionnaires and surveys:** Stakeholders, team members, and subject matter experts may be asked to identify other potential stakeholders.
- » **Brainstorming and brain writing:**
  - *Brainstorming* involves a group of people interacting and working together to identify additional stakeholders.
  - *Brain writing* is a refinement of brainstorming that allows individuals time to consider the question(s) individually before gathering as a group.

Stakeholder identification should occur as early in the project as possible and is an ongoing process. Identifying project stakeholders involves pinpointing and understanding all individuals, groups, or entities that have an interest in or can be affected by the project.

The result of stakeholder identification is the initial creation of the *stakeholder register*, which serves as a rough draft at this stage. As you progress through the steps of stakeholder analysis, you'll see how the stakeholder register is continuously updated with more detailed and comprehensive information.

## Understanding stakeholders: Decoding motivations and expectations

The importance of identifying project stakeholders lies in understanding their interests, needs, and influence, and actively involving them throughout the project. This enables project managers to manage expectations, gain support, manage risk, and ensure project success by aligning project goals with stakeholder requirements and fostering effective collaboration. The project team continuously seeks to understand stakeholders' feelings, emotions, beliefs, and values as well as find out about their aspirations, goals, and motives. Per the *PMBOK Guide*, these elements can lead to helping the project team identify additional threats and opportunities that can impact the project outcomes.

## Analyzing stakeholders: Mapping influence and interest

Analyzing stakeholders provides valuable insights for the project team to understand the dynamics and potential impacts of stakeholder motivations, actions, and behaviors. It is important to consider stakeholder interactions, as alliances or conflicts can significantly influence project outcomes. However, the project team should make every effort to maintain the confidentiality of this analysis. Sharing this information outside the context of the analysis may lead to misinterpretation and potentially harm stakeholder relationships. (Can you imagine if Bob saw in writing that he is considered a "difficult stakeholder"?)

By treating the stakeholder analysis as confidential, the project team ensures the trust and integrity necessary to manage stakeholder interactions effectively. The project team needs to analyze aspects of each stakeholder's position and perspective on the project. Analysis may consider several elements, such as power, impact, attitude, beliefs, and expectations. They need to also analyze the degree of influence, proximity to the project, interest in the project, and other aspects surrounding stakeholder interaction.

### Key tools of stakeholder analysis

Analyzing stakeholders provides valuable insights for the project team to understand the dynamics and potential impacts of stakeholder motivations, actions, and behaviors. There are several tools that provide a visual representation of stakeholders' influence and interest, enabling project managers to effectively manage stakeholder relationships, prioritize engagement efforts, mitigate risks, and align project activities with stakeholder expectations.

## DIRECTION OF INFLUENCE

The *direction of influence* refers to the flow of influence or power between stakeholders and the project. It helps project managers understand how stakeholders can impact the project and vice versa. There are four primary directions of influence:

- **Upward influence** involves stakeholders who have higher levels of authority or control over the project. They might include senior management, investors, or regulatory bodies. Their decisions and actions can significantly affect the project.

- **Downward influence** includes the stakeholders who may be lower in the organizational hierarchy or have less control over the project but are still affected by its outcomes. For example, team members or subcontractors fall into this category.

- **Sideward influence** relates to stakeholders who are at a similar level within the organization or project and can impact each other. They can involve team members, departments, or groups within an organization who may have competing interests.

- **Outward influence** pertains to stakeholders who are external to the organization, but have a stake in the project. These could be clients, customers, suppliers, or even local communities. Their demands or expectations can shape the project's direction.

## THE POWER INTEREST GRID

The *Power Interest Grid* is a two-dimensional tool used to categorize stakeholders based on their level of power or influence over the project and their level of interest or involvement. The grid typically consists of four quadrants: high power-high interest, high power-low interest, low power-high interest, and low power-low interest. The Power Interest Grid helps project managers prioritize their stakeholder engagement efforts by identifying key stakeholders who require the most attention and influence over the project's success. It assists in determining the appropriate level and type of communication, involvement, and relationship-building activities for different stakeholder groups. The Power Interest Grid helps project managers allocate resources and ensures that the project team invests adequate time and effort in engaging stakeholders who have the highest potential to impact the project positively or negatively. This tool aids in building stronger relationships with key stakeholders, and increases the chances of achieving stakeholder support. See Figure 12-1 for an example.

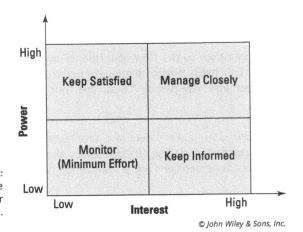

FIGURE 12-1: An example of a Power Interest Grid.

© John Wiley & Sons, Inc.

TIP

Variations of the Power Interest Grid include the Power Influence Grid and Interest Influence Grid. Which one you choose for your projects is entirely up to you — and your expert judgment.

## Stakeholder Cube

The *Stakeholder Cube* provides a comprehensive view of stakeholders by considering their power, interest, and attitude. This is a refinement of the 2D Power Interest Grid models by combining grid elements into a three-dimensional model that can be useful with the development of communication strategies. Project managers may choose to use a Stakeholder Cube over the stakeholder Power Interest Grid in certain situations because the Stakeholder Cube provides a more comprehensive and nuanced view of stakeholders, particularly in complex projects or environments where they need to consider multiple dimensions of stakeholder relationships.

## Salience Model

The *Salience Model* describes classes of stakeholders based on assessments of their power (level of authority or ability to influence the outcomes of the project), urgency (need for immediate attention, either time-constrained or relating to the stakeholders' high stakes in the outcome), and legitimacy (whether their involvement is appropriate). By understanding stakeholder salience, project managers can allocate appropriate resources, manage stakeholder relationships effectively, and address their needs and concerns in a prioritized manner. See Figure 12-2 for a visual representation of the Salience Model.

A stakeholder who falls within all three categories is a *definitive (or core) stakeholder*.

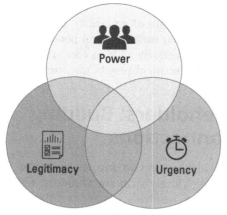

FIGURE 12-2:
The Salience Model.

© John Wiley & Sons, Inc.

## Prioritizing stakeholders: Knowing who matters most

There's no such thing as too many stakeholders, but not all stakeholders carry the same weight, nor do they warrant equal time and attention. Prioritizing stakeholders helps project managers allocate their limited resources more effectively, such as time, budget, and personnel. By identifying and prioritizing stakeholders based on their influence, impact, and interest in the project, project managers can focus their efforts and resources on stakeholders with the greatest potential to affect the project's outcomes.

Prioritization allows project managers to tailor their engagement and communication strategies to different stakeholder groups. Prioritizing stakeholders helps project managers manage their diverse and often conflicting expectations. Stakeholders with higher priority receive more attention and focus, enabling project managers to align their expectations with project objectives and constraints. This discernment is especially important when working with large stakeholder communities—you cannot be all things to all of the stakeholders.

Prioritizing stakeholders allows project managers to identify influential stakeholders who can shape project outcomes or provide crucial support. Engaging these stakeholders early and addressing their needs and concerns increases the likelihood of securing their support and assistance throughout the project. And prioritizing stakeholders helps project managers identify potential risks and manage their impact.

REMEMBER

Stakeholders with higher priority are often closely involved in project activities and decisions. By recognizing their influence and potential risks associated with them, project managers can proactively address concerns, manage conflicts, and mitigate risks, ensuring a more resilient project environment.

## Engaging stakeholders: Building meaningful connections

Stakeholder engagement involves active involvement and collaboration with them. This includes working closely with stakeholders, eliciting their requirements, managing expectations, resolving issues, negotiating, continuing to prioritize them, problem-solving, making decisions together, and, of course, communicating with them.

This entails tailoring your engagement strategies to match stakeholder needs and power dynamics. Engaging your stakeholders enlists a variety of tools and techniques and the creation of key project artifacts.

### Stakeholder engagement assessment matrix

The *stakeholder engagement assessment matrix* is a tool that helps project managers evaluate the current level of stakeholder engagement and identify areas for improvement. It assesses stakeholders based on their current engagement level, desired engagement level, and the actions required to bridge the gap. The matrix provides a visual representation of stakeholder engagement progress and enables project managers to monitor and measure stakeholder engagement effectiveness. The matrix facilitates a systematic approach to continuously improve stakeholder engagement throughout the project.

Figure 12-3 represents an example of a stakeholder engagement assessment matrix where C represents the current engagement level of each stakeholder, and D indicates the level that the project team has determined where they want the stakeholder to be to ensure successful project outcomes.

The typical categories of the stakeholder engagement assessment matrix are Unaware, Resistant, Neutral, Supportive, and Leading.

The gap between the current and desired levels will direct the project team as to the level of necessary communications and engagement with each stakeholder.

TIP

While you can have different categories listed for this matrix, the categories you should be familiar with for the purposes of the PMP Exam are Unaware, Resistant, Neutral, Supportive, and Leading.

162  PART 4 **Managing Your Projects from Conception to Completion**

**FIGURE 12-3:**
An example of a stakeholder engagement assessment matrix.

| Level Of Engagement | People Or Groups | | | | |
|---|---|---|---|---|---|
| | Stakeholder A | Stakeholder B | Stakeholder C | Stakeholder D | Stakeholder E |
| Leading | | | | | D |
| Supportive | | D | C D | D | |
| Neutral | D | | | C | C |
| Resistant | | C | | | |
| Unaware | C | | | | |

© John Wiley & Sons, Inc.

**TIP**

You may encounter an exam question that describes this tool, and you'll need to identify it as the stakeholder engagement assessment matrix.

## Stakeholder Engagement Plan

Stakeholder analysis helps to identify and understand the interests, influence, and impact of various stakeholders on the project. To ensure a thorough and proactive approach, this analysis often includes the creation of a *Stakeholder Engagement Plan*, which outlines strategies for assessing and managing stakeholder expectations and involvement throughout the project's duration.

The Stakeholder Engagement Plan is a strategic document that outlines how stakeholders will be engaged during the entire project. It identifies engagement strategies, communication channels, frequency of interactions, and methods for involving stakeholders and decision-making processes. This plan ensures that stakeholder engagement is intentional and proactive, rather than ad hoc or reactive. It helps project managers establish a systematic approach to engage stakeholders, leading to better communication, alignment, and collaboration.

The plan enables project managers to identify different stakeholder groups and develop tailored and customized engagement strategies based on their needs, interests, and influence. It also ensures that engagement efforts are targeted and effective. By including stakeholder engagement strategies in the plan, project managers can address potential risks, manage expectations, and mitigate conflicts or resistance that may arise from inadequate stakeholder involvement.

**TIP**

The Stakeholder Engagement Plan is a subcomponent plan of the Project Management Plan, which is described in greater detail in Chapter 13.

**CHAPTER 12 Initiating Your Project** 163

### Issue log

The *issue log,* an effective project artifact for stakeholder engagement, helps project managers to track and address stakeholder concerns and issues promptly. The issue log is a record of identified issues, concerns, or conflicts throughout the project. It captures details such as the issue description, impact, assigned responsibility, and resolution status. It ensures that stakeholder issues are acknowledged, managed, and resolved in a timely manner, and by actively managing and resolving issues, project managers maintain stakeholder satisfaction, build trust, and foster positive stakeholder relationships.

Collectively, the tools, techniques, and project artifacts that you read about in this chapter all contribute to successful stakeholder engagement by providing structure, clarity, and guidance in managing stakeholder relationships and communications. They help project managers effectively identify stakeholders, understand their needs and expectations, manage issues, and ensure stakeholders are well informed and actively involved in the project. Refer to Chapter 16 for additional details about the issue log.

## Monitoring stakeholder engagement: Keeping a finger on the pulse

The purpose of monitoring stakeholders is to actively track and assess the engagement, satisfaction, and changing dynamics of stakeholders throughout a project's life cycle. It involves systematically observing and analyzing stakeholders' attitudes, interests, concerns, and interactions to ensure their needs are addressed and their expectations are managed effectively. You'll frequently refer to the stakeholder engagement assessment matrix, Power Interest Grid, and other tools to support your monitoring efforts. And, of course, you'll revisit the stakeholder register.

Specifically, the stakeholder register, which started as a rough draft, should now be a dynamic document reflecting all the updates and insights gathered throughout the process.

REMEMBER

To reiterate the steps of analyzing and engaging stakeholders:

**I U**nderstand **A**ll **P**rojects **E**xperience **M**ayhem.

- » **I**dentify
- » **U**nderstand

- **A**nalyze
- **P**rioritize
- **E**ngage
- **M**onitor your stakeholders

As mentioned before, while these steps follow a general "order," they are not rigid. It's important to remember that engaging your stakeholders is a fluid process, and you may need to revisit certain steps more than once to adapt to changing circumstances and the changing perspectives of your stakeholders.

# Test Your Knowledge: Mapping Stakeholder Engagement

**Scenario:** *You are managing a project to launch a new website for a company. Key stakeholders include the marketing manager, IT specialist, CEO, and an external consultant.*

**Stakeholder details:** The list of stakeholders and their current attitude or involvement are as follows.

- **Marketing manager:** Acknowledges the project's importance and sees its potential benefits but has expressed concerns about the team's capacity to manage the additional workload. Ideally, the marketing manager will actively champion the project within their team, helping to secure their buy-in and providing feedback on marketing-specific requirements.

- **IT specialist:** Vocal about potential risks, particularly regarding the system's compatibility with existing infrastructure. While they have technical expertise, their focus on challenges has slowed progress. It would be great if you could get the IT specialist to shift toward a collaborative role, contributing solutions and advising on integration strategies to ensure smooth implementation.

- **CEO:** Expressed a high level of enthusiasm for the project and is eager to see it succeed, setting a positive tone for other stakeholders. The project would benefit greatly if this engagement was maintained while leveraging their influence to remove barriers and secure resources as needed.

- **External consultant:** Has been fulfilling their obligations but has not yet demonstrated a deeper understanding of the project's context or objectives. It would be ideal if the consultant took a proactive approach, offering insights and recommendations that align with the company's goals and timeline.

**Instructions:** Based on the descriptions, in the following table, place a **C** where you think their current engagement levels are, and a **D** to indicate the desired level of engagement. For instance, if you think the description for the marketing manager's current engagement level is Neutral, you would place a 'C' in the Neutral column in the Marketing Manager row.

You can find answers at the end of the chapter.

| Stakeholder | Unaware | Resistant | Neutral | Supportive | Leading |
|---|---|---|---|---|---|
| Marketing Manager | | | | | |
| IT Specialist | | | | | |
| CEO | | | | | |
| External Consultant | | | | | |

# Using Project Charters and Engaging Stakeholders in Adaptive Projects

In adaptive or Agile environments, project initiation requires a different mindset. These projects are inherently dynamic — requirements are changing, stakeholders evolve, and the path to success is often discovered through iterative learning rather than predetermined planning. This fluid nature of adaptive projects calls for a flexible approach to both developing project charters and engaging stakeholders with an emphasis on collaboration, adaptability, and continuous alignment with organizational goals.

## Adaptive charters: Less concrete, more directional

Project charters in the Agile environment typically differ from those of traditional projects. Traditional project charters tend to offer more detail on the scope, timeline, budget, and deliverables. By contrast, Agile charters are shorter, less detailed, and more focused on how the project will be managed, rather than defining exactly what will be built. Agile charters emphasize collaboration, team roles, and high-level goals, recognizing that requirements and deliverables will evolve iteratively.

For Agile projects, the charter may describe the working agreements, communication plans, and tools to be used rather than fixed deliverables or schedules.

In adaptive environments, the charter is less about rigid scope and more about guiding intent. It provides high-level direction and context rather than locking the project into specific deliverables that may evolve over time. This flexibility aligns with the Agile values of responding to change over following a pre-defined plan.

## Using dynamic tools and techniques to engage dynamic stakeholders

In the adaptive environment, several tools and techniques are used to engage stakeholders effectively. These tools and techniques, including user personas, user stories, sprint reviews, and information radiators, are utilized for stakeholder engagement.

- **Personas** are fictional representations of different types of end users or stakeholders involved in a project. They are created based on research and insights gathered from real users. Personas help Agile teams empathize with stakeholders, understand their needs, and design solutions that address their specific requirements. By referring to personas, teams can align their decisions and priorities with the goals and preferences of different stakeholder groups, fostering stakeholder engagement throughout the project.

- **User stories** are concise, user-focused descriptions of functionality or features expressed from the perspective of the end user or stakeholder. User stories capture the *who*, *what*, and *why* of a requirement and serve as a means of communication and collaboration between stakeholders and the Agile team. Refer to Chapter 21 for more information about user stories.

- **Sprint (iteration) reviews** are events that occur at the end of each sprint in Agile projects. During a sprint review, the team presents the work completed during the sprint to stakeholders, including the product owner and end users. The review provides an opportunity for stakeholders to see the progress made, offer feedback, and validate whether the delivered work meets their expectations. By actively involving stakeholders in sprint reviews, the team can gather valuable insights, adjust priorities, and ensure alignment with stakeholder needs, fostering ongoing engagement.

>> **Information radiators** are visual displays of project information that are placed in prominent locations that are accessible to the team and stakeholders. Examples include task boards, burndown charts, and release calendars. Information radiators provide transparency and promote shared understanding among stakeholders. By making project information visible and easily accessible, information radiators facilitate stakeholder engagement by enabling them to track progress, identify bottlenecks, and participate in discussions around project status and decision-making.

TIP

If an exam question presents multiple terms from the Agile environment within the same scenario, it's likely testing your understanding of Agile principles. In such cases, focus on identifying an answer option that aligns with Agile practices or methodologies.

By leveraging these tools and techniques in the adaptive environment, Agile teams actively engage stakeholders throughout the duration of the project. Personas and user stories enable a deep understanding of stakeholder needs, while sprint reviews and information radiators foster regular communication, feedback, and collaboration. Together, these tools and techniques contribute to stakeholder satisfaction and alignment.

# Answer Keys

**Benefit Measurement Methods**

1. Net Present Value — Project A
2. Internal Rate of Return — Project B
3. Payback Period — Project A
4. Benefit-Cost Ratio — Project A

Overall: Choose Project A.

**Mapping Stakeholder Engagement**

Marketing Manager

>> **Current engagement:** Supportive (expressing interest but hesitant due to workload concerns).

>> **Desired engagement:** Leading (actively championing the project and rallying their team to support it).

IT Specialist

- **Current engagement:** Resistant (focusing on risks and challenges rather than solutions).
- **Desired engagement:** Supportive (actively collaborating to address technical concerns and ensure successful implementation).

CEO

- **Current engagement:** Leading (enthusiastic and driving the project forward).
- **Desired engagement:** Leading (continuing to leverage influence to eliminate barriers and secure resources).

External Consultant

- **Current engagement:** Neutral (fulfilling basic responsibilities without deeper involvement).
- **Desired engagement:** Supportive (proactively offering insights and recommendations to align with project goals).

**IN THIS CHAPTER**

» Reviewing the activities involved in the Planning Process Group

» Introducing the Project Management Plan

» Planning for predictive versus adaptive projects

» Exploring the triple constraints of scope, schedule, and cost

» Reviewing scope management processes

» Outlining schedule management processes

» Going over cost management processes

# Chapter 13
# Planning Your Project Roadmap

Many PMP aspirants feel overwhelmed by the sheer scope of planning, but this critical activity is what compels project managers to pause, evaluate, and strategically map out the steps needed to achieve the project's goals. Without a strong project plan, the chances of project success diminish significantly.

A well-designed plan serves as a cornerstone for setting clear expectations with both the team and stakeholders, while also establishing a framework for accountability and performance measurement.

Initiating the project provides the foundation, ensuring project agreements and acceptance are in place. Building on this groundwork, the planning activities transform those initial concepts into a structured and actionable roadmap, paving the way for a successful and controlled delivery of the project objectives.

# Getting Familiar with the Planning Process Group

The Planning Process Group serves as the roadmap for successful project execution and closure. This process group emphasizes defining the *how* of the project — how objectives will be achieved, resources allocated, risks managed, and quality ensured. It creates a detailed and comprehensive blueprint that guides all project activities; this includes determining resource allocation, managing risks, ensuring quality, and establishing clear workflows. Through collaboration among the project team and stakeholders, this process group sets a well-defined path forward, minimizing uncertainty and enhancing control.

By ensuring that every aspect of the project is thoughtfully planned and documented, the Planning Process Group reduces uncertainty and enhances control. Key outputs of this process group include the Project Management Plan, which integrates subsidiary plans for scope, schedule, cost, risk, resources, quality, communication, procurement, and stakeholder engagement.

The specific processes that fall under this process group include the following:

- **Develop project management plan**
- **Plan scope management**
- **Collect requirements**
- **Define scope**
- **Create WBS**
- **Plan schedule management**
- **Define activities**
- **Sequence activities**
- **Estimate activity durations**
- **Develop schedule**

- **Plan cost management**
- **Estimate costs**
- **Determine budget**
- Plan quality management
- Plan resource management
- Estimate activity resources
- Plan communications management
- Plan risk management
- Identify risks
- Perform qualitative risk analysis
- Perform quantitative risk analysis
- Plan risk responses
- Plan procurement management
- Plan stakeholder engagement

The **bold text** in the preceding list indicates those processes that are covered in detail within this chapter, while the remaining planning processes are addressed in the next chapter. Collectively, this process group ensures that projects are thoroughly prepared, systematically organized, and positioned to achieve their objectives.

TIP

With 24 processes, the Planning Process Group represents nearly 50 percent of the total project management processes. PMP aspirants should develop a solid understanding of the activities within this process group to achieve success on the PMP Exam.

The focus of the Planning Process Group is to align efforts, mitigate risks, and set realistic expectations, ensuring that the project remains focused and efficient throughout its life cycle.

REMEMBER

In adaptive environments, planning is often iterative, with the plan evolving as the team gains more information and feedback.

# Develop Project Management Plan

Following the charter, the Project Management Plan becomes the central guide that details the methodology, timeline, resources, and budget. In the predictive environment, the Project Management Plan is meticulously developed to manage the various elements that contribute to the project success, from risk assessments to communication strategies. Despite popular belief, an effective project plan is not a schedule of tasks or simply a Gantt chart. It's a dynamic document that evolves and adapts to the project's needs. Key inputs to develop the Project Management Plan process include the following:

- **Project charter:** The charter provides the initial direction for developing the Project Management Plan by defining the *what* and *why* of the project. It ensures that all planning efforts are grounded in the agreed-upon purpose and scope.

- **Organizational process assets (OPAs):** These include the internal processes, templates, policies, and historical data that organizations use to guide project planning and execution. OPAs streamline planning by providing proven frameworks and lessons learned from past projects. They offer templates for plans, guidelines for tailoring processes, and access to historical data that can inform realistic planning decisions.

- **Enterprise environmental factors (EEFs):** These include the external and internal factors that influence the project, such as organizational culture, market conditions, regulatory requirements, and available technology. EEFs ensure that the Project Management Plan is realistic and adaptable to the environment in which the project operates. For instance, understanding resource availability, compliance needs, or industry standards helps create a plan that aligns with external constraints.

- **Outputs from other processes:** These include deliverables and plans generated from other project management processes, such as a Risk Management Plan, stakeholder analysis results, and scope baseline documents. These outputs provide critical details that are incorporated into the Project Management Plan. For example, the scope baseline informs how the scope will be managed, while the Risk Management Plan guides risk management strategies. They ensure that the plan integrates all project elements cohesively.

By leveraging these inputs, project managers create a robust and comprehensive Project Management Plan that provides a clear roadmap for execution and also ensures alignment with organizational objectives, stakeholder expectations, and environmental conditions.

TIP

In many instances, these inputs are also utilized across various other planning processes, which are discussed later in this chapter.

The Project Management Plan includes methodologies, procedures, and documentation for managing changes and controlling the project. The plan establishes baselines for scope, schedule, and costs. These baselines are used for measuring project performance and applied in earned value management analysis, a key concept in the PMP Exam. The plan details how stakeholders will be engaged and how communication will be managed throughout the project life cycle. This includes identifying stakeholders, determining their requirements and expectations, and defining strategies for engaging them effectively.

At the early stages of developing the project plan, the project manager relies on techniques such as progressive elaboration and tailoring to create a plan that aligns with the specific needs of the project. Here is a quick recap:

- » **Progressive elaboration:** Think of this concept as planning in layers. The project starts with high-level information, and as more details emerge, the plan evolves with greater detail. It's about refining as you go, not wasting time perfecting the unknown up front.
- » **Tailoring:** This is where the project manager customizes tools, processes, and techniques to fit the unique needs of the project. Rather than applying a one-size-fits-all approach, the project manager develops a plan designed for the size, complexity, and goals of the work at hand.

By applying these methods, the project manager creates a plan that's flexible, focused, and equipped to handle any challenges the project may encounter.

TIP

Given the fact that the Project Management Plan is a central component of the PMI body of knowledge and frequent topic on the PMP Exam, PMP aspirants should ensure they have a strong grasp of the structure, function, and importance of this integrated plan.

By providing a detailed framework, the Project Management Plan ensures that all project activities are aligned with the project goals and that stakeholders have a clear understanding of the project's direction and progress.

In Chapter 15, you can read about how all of this comes together to create a complete, comprehensive Project Management Plan that incorporates all facets of the project needs.

## Differentiating between predictive and adaptive projects

A major takeaway for the PMP Exam is that planning in predictive projects differs significantly from planning in adaptive projects. Table 13-1 provides a breakdown of the distinction between predictive projects and adaptive projects.

TABLE 13-1 **Predictive Projects versus Adaptive Projects**

|  | Predictive Projects | Adaptive Projects |
| --- | --- | --- |
| Planning | Clear, detailed planning up front. | Continuous feedback loops and incremental delivery. |
| Scope | Fixed scope and sequential phases. | Flexible scope and iterative phases. |
| Best suited for | Projects with well-defined requirements (for example, construction, manufacturing). | Dynamic environments or software development. |

REMEMBER

Hybrid projects combine predictive and adaptive approaches.

## Triple constraints planning: scope, schedule, and cost

Every project operates within three primary and interdependent constraints known as the *triple constraints of project management*: scope, schedule, and cost. See Figure 13-1 for an illustration of the triple constraints.

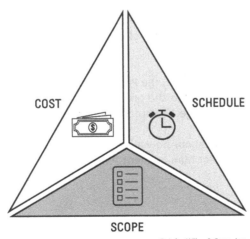

FIGURE 13-1: The triple constraints.

© John Wiley & Sons, Inc.

- **Scope:** This is what the project will deliver — its goals, features, and boundaries. Think of it as the *what* of the project.
- **Schedule:** This is the timeline for completing the project. It answers the *when* by breaking the work down into tasks, setting deadlines, and identifying milestones.
- **Cost:** This is the budget needed to complete the project. It represents the *how much*, including expenses for materials, labor, and any other resources.

These constraints form a critical framework that guides the successful delivery of any project. Managing them requires careful balance, as changes to one constraint often have significant ripple effects on the others, ultimately influencing the project's overall quality and success. For instance, if you increase the scope (adding features to the project), you will undoubtedly increase the costs and extend the timeline.

# Plan Scope Management

Scope management defines the parameters of what the project will (and just as importantly, will not) include. Effective scope management is critical in maintaining the project's integrity against scope creep, ensuring that the objectives are met without unnecessary expansion or complexity.

## Understanding project scope and product scope

There are two main types of scope: project scope and product scope.

- **Project scope** refers to the work that needs to be accomplished to deliver a product, service, or result with the specified features and functions. Its focus encompasses all the activities, tasks, and work involved in the creation of the project deliverables.
- **Product scope** is more narrowly focused and refers to the features and functions that characterize a product, service, or result. Its focus is on the end result of the project, what the product is, and how it is expected to perform.

Let's say you are implementing a new electronic medical records (EMR) system for a hospital. The tasks include conducting stakeholder interviews, selecting the software vendor, customizing the system to the hospital's needs, training staff, and going live with the system. All of the work to implement the EMR is the scope of this project, or project scope.

The product scope refers to the features and functions of the actual product or deliverable. This entails the features of the EMR such as patient data storage, appointment scheduling, integration with lab results, prescription management, and compliance with HIPAA regulations.

REMEMBER

The following summary should help you remember these concepts:

» **Project scope:** The activities required to implement the EMR system.

» **Product scope:** The functionality and specifications of the EMR system being implemented.

Balancing these two scopes effectively is key to the successful delivery of the EMR system.

## Planning the scope of work

Scope planning involves the creation of two plans. One of those plans is the *Scope Management Plan*, an output of the *plan scope management process*. The Scope Management Plan is designed to guide how the project scope will be defined, developed, monitored, controlled, and verified. It addresses several key questions to ensure that the project scope is effectively managed throughout the project life cycle:

» **How will the project scope be defined and documented?**

» **What is the process for scope validation and approval?**

» **How will scope changes be managed and controlled?**

By answering these questions and many more, the Scope Management Plan provides a comprehensive framework for ensuring that the project scope is accurately defined, communicated, and maintained throughout the project.

The additional output of the plan scope management process is the *Requirements Management Plan*, which addresses several critical questions related to the identification, documentation, and management of project requirements:

» **How will requirements be identified and documented?**

» **How will requirements be prioritized and organized?**

» **How will requirements be traced and monitored throughout the project?**

» **How will requirements be communicated to stakeholders?**

By answering these questions, the Requirements Management Plan provides a clear, structured approach to managing project requirements and ensures that all requirements are appropriately defined, understood, and met, aligning the project's output with stakeholder expectations and project goals. Keep in mind that both of these plans are components of the Project Management Plan.

## Collecting requirements

A *requirement* is defined as a condition or capability needed by a user to solve a problem or achieve an objective. It can also be a condition or capability that must be met or possessed by a system or system component to satisfy a business need. Refer to Figure 13-2 for a list of the common requirements of a project. An example from the healthcare EMR system has been incorporated to provide context.

|  | Description | EMR System Example |
|---|---|---|
| Functional | Related to the specific behavior or functions of a project. | Enable doctors to create, update, and retrieve electronic patient records, including demographics, medical history, prescriptions, and treatment plans. |
| Non-Functional | Pertains to attributes such as reliability, efficiency, and usability. | Maintain a response time of less than 2 seconds for 90% of user queries, even during peak usage with 500 concurrent users. |
| Technical | Specify the technical aspects that must be considered to successfully implement a project. | Support integration with lab systems using HL7 standards and provide APIs for interoperability with other healthcare applications, such as billing and pharmacy systems. |
| Business | High level needs defined by stakeholders, often focusing on the outcomes or benefits that a project is expected to deliver. | Streamline patient record management to reduce administrative workload by 20% and improve patient satisfaction scores by 15% within the first year. |
| Legal & Compliance | Result of applicable laws, regulations, or standards. | Comply with HIPAA regulations to ensure the confidentiality, integrity, and availability of protected health information (PHI) and meet data retention requirements for seven years. |
| Readiness | Outline the conditions that must be met before project deliverables are deployed. | All hospital staff, including doctors, nurses, and administrative personnel, must complete a mandatory 20-hour training program on the EMR system before the system goes live. |
| Transition | Steps needed to change from the current state to the desired future state at the end of the project | Migrate all existing patient data from the legacy system into the new database, ensuring 100% data accuracy and accessibility during the transition period. |

**FIGURE 13-2:** Common project requirements.

© John Wiley & Sons, Inc.

Incorporating these very types of requirements ensures that the EMR implementation project is well rounded, addressing all aspects of implementation and also preparing the hospital staff for a smooth transition to the new system. This thorough planning helps in managing potential disruptions and enhances the overall satisfaction with the completed project.

TIP

Yes, be familiar with the various types of requirements. One way the exam may test you is to describe one of them and then ask you, "What type of requirement is being described in this scenario?"

All of those requirements are captured as a result of the *collect requirements process* that focuses on documenting them; these requirements often reflect the needs and expectations of your stakeholders. This process involves engaging with your stakeholders through various techniques such as interviews, surveys, focus groups, and workshops to gather detailed information about their requirements. The goal is to ensure that all stakeholder needs are captured and clearly defined, providing a solid foundation for developing the project scope and ensuring that the final deliverables meet their expectations. The major tools and techniques used in the collect requirements process include the following:

- **Interviews:** Conducting one-on-one or group interviews with stakeholders to gather detailed information about their requirements, expectations, and preferences for the project's deliverables.

- **Focus groups:** Bringing together prequalified stakeholders and subject matter experts to learn about their expectations and attitudes regarding the project's product, service, or result.

- **Facilitated workshops:** Organizing interactive sessions that bring together key stakeholders to define product requirements. These workshops are often used to quickly achieve consensus on project scope and requirements.

- **Group creativity techniques:** Techniques such as brainstorming, nominal group technique, the Delphi technique, idea/mind mapping, and affinity diagrams. These are all used to generate and organize a wide array of ideas and requirements.

- **Group decision-making techniques:** Approaches such as unanimity, majority, plurality, and authoritarian, which are employed to reach a decision when various alternatives are available and a group consensus is needed.

- **Questionnaires and surveys:** Distributing questionnaires and surveys to a large group of people when statistical data is required or when it's not feasible to bring everyone together for interviews or workshops.

- **Observations (job shadowing):** Observing people in their environment to see how they perform their jobs or tasks and how a product or system is used, which can lead to more accurate requirements. This is often used when requirements are difficult to uncover.

» **Prototypes:** Developing a working model of the expected product or specific features to help stakeholders better understand the requirements and provide more accurate feedback, often used in the Agile environment. Variations of this approach may include storyboarding for video production or learning and development projects.

» **Benchmarking:** Comparing actual or planned project practices to those of comparable projects to identify best practices, generate ideas for improvement, and provide a basis for measuring performance.

» **Context diagrams:** Creating visual representations of the scope of a project showing a business system (process, equipment, computer system, and so on) and how people and other systems (actors) interact with it.

» **Document analysis:** Reviewing and assessing documentation from previously completed projects to gather requirements for the current project.

TIP

You guessed it. This is another list of terms you should know for the exam. PMP aspirants should be prepared for potential exam questions that describe one of these tools and techniques of the collect requirements process. The scenario will describe the term, and potentially ask you to identify which tool or technique is being described.

The use of these tools and techniques can be effective in accurately gathering and documenting the requirements from stakeholders, which in turn helps to achieve the successful completion of the project by delivering a product or service that meets needs and expectations.

Once requirements are collected, they're meticulously documented in requirements documentation, and organized within the requirements traceability matrix. The *requirements traceability matrix* is a tool that links each requirement to its origin and tracks its fulfillment throughout the project life cycle. The requirements traceability matrix typically includes columns for requirement IDs, descriptions, sources, associated project goals, current status, and verification methods. See Figure 13-3 for an example of a traceability matrix.

By maintaining this level of detail, project managers can trace each requirement from its initial identification through to its final implementation and testing. This ensures that stakeholders' needs are consistently met and helps manage changes to requirements effectively.

CHAPTER 13 **Planning Your Project Roadmap** 181

| ID | Description | Source/Requestor | Business Justification/Need | Status | Comments |
|---|---|---|---|---|---|
| 181 | Enable doctors to create, update, and retrieve electronic patient records. | Clinical Team | Improve patient care and efficiency. | Pending | Awaiting approval from stakeholders. |
| 182 | System must maintain a response time of less than 2 seconds for 90% of queries. | IT Department | Ensure system usability and performance. | In Progress | Performance tests are ongoing. |
| 184 | Streamline patient record management to reduce administrative workload by 20%. | Operations Manager | Increase operational efficiency and patient satisfaction. | Pending | Awaiting management sign-off. |
| 185 | Comply with HIPAA regulations for PHI confidentiality, integrity, and availability. | Compliance Officer | Meet regulatory compliance and avoid legal penalties. | Pending | Pending legal review for compliance. |
| 186 | Mandatory 20-hour training program for all hospital staff before system go-live. | Training Coordinator | Ensure user readiness and smooth adoption. | Pending | Training materials are being finalized. |
| 187 | Migrate all existing patient data from the legacy system with 100% accuracy. | Data Migration Specialist | Ensure uninterrupted operations during system transition. | Not Started | Data validation in progress. |
| 188 | Allow nurses to update patient vitals in real-time during care. | Clinical Team | Enhance real-time documentation and patient monitoring. | In Progress | Field testing scheduled next month. |
| 190 | Implement secure user authentication with multi-factor authentication (MFA). | Security Lead | Enhance security for sensitive patient data. | Pending | Security framework being implemented. |

**FIGURE 13-3:** A traceability matrix.

© John Wiley & Sons, Inc.

## Defining scope

The *define scope process* leads to the creation of the *project scope statement*. This document ensures that everyone involved in the project understands the project's boundaries, objectives, and deliverables. The project scope statement has detailed information about the scope of work. It includes details about the following:

>> Product scope description

>> Deliverables

>> Acceptance criteria

>> Project exclusions

**TIP**

For the exam, remember that the project scope statement differs from the project charter in terms of the level of detail. The project charter is a high-level document including general scope information, and it serves as the formal document that authorizes the project. The project scope statement provides the details of the scope, deliverables, and acceptance criteria, as well as what's in scope and what's out of scope. The project scope statement is developed only after the project has been officially authorized through the project charter.

# Creating a work breakdown structure

After defining the scope and creating the project scope statement, a key step is to break down the project into manageable components. You achieve this through the *create WBS process*, which drives the creation of a work breakdown structure (WBS). The WBS provides a hierarchical decomposition of the total scope of work, ensuring that all deliverables are identified and organized systematically. The WBS provides a visual representation of the project's scope, showing the relationship between various deliverables.

The WBS breaks down the project into smaller, manageable components, making it easier to plan, execute, and control the work. Here are the key steps to create the WBS.

1. **Clearly define the overall scope of the project.** This includes outlining the project objectives, deliverables, and final outcome expected from the project.

2. **Identify the major deliverables or components that need to be completed to fulfill the project scope.** These are typically high-level categories of work.

3. **Decompose WBS elements into smaller components.** This involves breaking down each major deliverable into smaller, more manageable components. The smallest components at this stage are called *work packages*. These are specific items of work that can be assigned and managed independently.

4. **Assign a unique identifier to each element in the WBS.** This helps in tracking and managing the project more efficiently.

5. **Review the WBS with project stakeholders and team members to ensure that nothing has been overlooked and that all components are realistic and achievable.**

There are some key definitions to point out here within the WBS:

- **The work package** represents the lowest level in the work breakdown structure, and is the point at which the project is monitored and controlled.

- **The planning package** is a WBS component below the control account and above the work package. It includes future work that is not yet detailed at the work package level.

- **A control account** is a management control point where scope, budget, resource plans, actual costs, and schedule are integrated and compared to performance as it relates to earned value management. Control accounts matter if you are performing earned value analysis.

» **A code of accounts** is a numbering system used to uniquely identify each element of the work breakdown structure. This helps in the organization, tracking, and reporting of work. As you see in Figure 13-4 of a home renovation project, each component of the WBS has an assigned number such as 1.1, 1.1.1, 1.1.2, and so on.

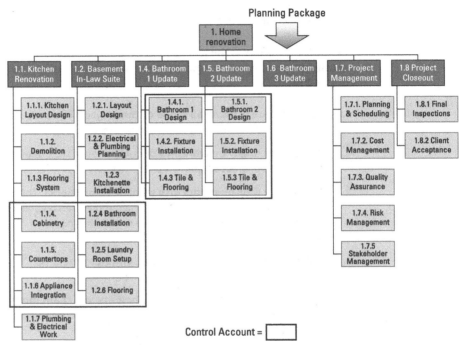

FIGURE 13-4:
A WBS for a home renovation project.

TIP

The WBS is a powerful tool for project management as it provides a clear and organized breakdown of the project scope. It aids in resource allocation, cost estimation, scheduling, and risk management. By breaking the project into smaller components, it becomes easier to manage and track progress, ensuring that the project stays on course to meet project objectives.

## Adding details in the WBS dictionary

The WBS dictionary accompanies the WBS and provides detailed information about each WBS component, including descriptions of work, deliverables, responsible parties (that is, who is completing the work), milestones, and any associated resources or costs. This documentation ensures that every aspect of the project is clearly defined and understood, facilitating better planning and execution. It may be helpful to think of the WBS dictionary as the decoder ring to the WBS.

### Defining the work in the scope baseline

The culmination of defining scope, creating the WBS, and detailing each component in the WBS dictionary leads to the creation of the *scope baseline*. The scope baseline components include the following:

» **Approved project scope statement.** Defines the project scope, including objectives, deliverables, and boundaries of the project.

» **WBS.** Breaks down the project scope into manageable components, ensuring all work is identified and organized. Within the WBS, it incorporates the work packages, planning packages, control account, and code of accounts.

» **WBS dictionary.** Provides detailed information about each WBS component.

PMP aspirants must remember the three components of the scope baseline, as they are often tested on the exam. Be prepared to recall them when needed.

The scope baseline, a component of the Project Management Plan, defines what the project will deliver and establishes boundaries for what is and is not included. It facilitates effective scope management by providing a reference for tracking performance, managing changes, and minimizing scope creep. A well-defined scope supports efforts in budgeting, resource allocation, and scheduling by enabling accurate estimates and preventing unnecessary expenditures.

Along with establishing the scope baseline, the create WBS process also results in updates to project documents such as the assumption log and the requirements documentation.

Scope is the foundation of a project. It not only defines the work to be done, but also impacts every aspect of project management, including time, cost, quality, resources, and risk.

## Managing scope in the adaptive environment

Adaptive projects are typically characterized by evolving requirements, high risk, or significant uncertainty, where the scope is either not fully understood at the start or significant changes are expected throughout the project. Consequently,

Agile projects spend less time defining scope up front and instead focus on ongoing discovery and refinement. Key aspects of scope management in adaptive projects include the following:

- Deliverables are developed incrementally over multiple iterations.
- Detailed scope is defined and approved at the start of each iteration.
- Backlogs are used to reflect current priorities and evolving needs.
- At the beginning of an iteration, the team determines how many high-priority items can be completed.

Agile projects employ a variety of prioritization techniques during planning sessions to ensure teams focus on the right work at the right time.

Prioritization in Agile is all about clarity and value. These techniques empower teams to make thoughtful, collaborative decisions, ensuring the most important work gets done first while keeping stakeholders aligned and invested. These methods, covered in the following sections, help determine what needs to be done and how to prioritize the work effectively.

## Kano analysis

Kano analysis is best for understanding customer needs and aligning features with value. It is a technique used to categorize customer requirements or features into four distinct groups to understand how customer needs relate to customer satisfaction.

- **Delighters/exciters:** Features that exceed expectations and thrill users.
- **Satisfiers:** Features that users expect and directly value.
- **Dissatisfiers:** Features that, if missing, cause frustration.
- **Indifferent:** Features that have no impact on satisfaction.

## Paired comparison

This is a technique that ranks alternatives by directly comparing them against each other, one pair at a time (that is, if you had four requirements, A, B, C, D, you would compare A to B, A to C, A to D, B to C, B to D, and C to D).

This technique is ideal for evaluating a small set of subjective requirements where clear priorities are needed.

### 100-point method

Stakeholders are given 100 points to allocate across a list of requirements based on their perceived importance. They can distribute points however they choose — concentrated on a single item or spread across several.

Effective for any group size, this method forces stakeholders to prioritize thoughtfully, encouraging deeper consideration of what truly matters.

### MoSCoW technique

This technique enables stakeholders to reach a shared understanding of requirement priorities by classifying them as follows:

- M: Must have
- S: Should have
- C: Could have
- W: Won't have (for now)

This works well for reconciling diverse perspectives and can be paired with timeboxing to focus on top priorities within limited timeframes.

## Staying within the boundaries of scope

Maintaining project control depends on staying within the defined scope boundaries. Watch out for these issues:

- **Scope creep** refers to the uncontrolled expansion of a project's scope without adjusting time, cost, or resources, which can jeopardize project success.

- **Gold plating**, which is equally problematic, occurs when team members add extra features or enhancements that were not part of the original requirements. While it might seem helpful, this practice wastes time, inflates costs, and risks delivering something the client didn't ask for. Keeping scope in check ensures the project stays on track and aligned with its objectives.

TIP

Can scope creep happen on Agile projects? Absolutely! While Agile embraces change, it's not immune to scope creep. Without clear priorities, disciplined backlog management, and strong communication, projects can spiral out of control. For instance, a product owner might add new features to the current sprint without reprioritizing the backlog, thus overloading the team. Similarly, stakeholders might request enhancements to a user story mid-sprint, increasing work without adjusting timelines. Agile's flexibility requires intentional planning and focus to avoid these pitfalls.

In predictive projects, adhering to the defined scope is a key factor in delivering business value. Effective scope management ensures the project delivers what was promised within the agreed-upon time and budget constraints. In contrast, adaptive projects embrace flexibility, treating scope as an evolving target shaped by ongoing discovery and refinement. In Chapter 17, I explore how continuous scope monitoring keeps projects on track, ensuring that the agreed-upon features and functions are delivered within the defined boundaries.

# Plan Schedule Management

The *plan schedule management process* puts focus on creating a project timeline that is both robust and flexible. This involves understanding task dependencies, estimating durations, and developing a schedule that can adapt to changes without compromising the project's objectives. Schedule management is an indispensable aspect of project management, working closely with scope and costs within the triple constraint framework. Effective schedule management is about developing the timeline of the project, setting realistic milestones, and ensuring timely delivery of project deliverables. Changes in the project timeline can impact cost and scope.

## Developing the Schedule Management Plan

The *Schedule Management Plan*, a component of the Project Management Plan, provides guidelines on how the project schedule will be managed throughout the project life cycle. It answers several key questions that aid in effective schedule development, control, and management:

- » How will the project schedule be developed?
- » What scheduling method will be used?
- » Who's responsible for schedule development and maintenance?
- » How will schedule variances be managed?
- » What tools and software will be used for schedule management?

The Schedule Management Plan ensures that there is a clear, consistent approach to managing the project schedule, facilitating better decision-making, communication, and stakeholder alignment throughout the project life cycle.

## Defining activities

The *define activities process* involves identifying and documenting the specific actions to be performed to produce the project deliverables. The starting point is the work packages from the WBS. Remember the WBS? Those work packages that were created as a result of creating the WBS will be further decomposed into activities. From here, the specific tasks to create the deliverables will be defined.

TIP

The distinction between work packages versus activities is the use of a noun versus a verb. Work packages are indicated as a noun. Activities are indicated with the use of a verb. Also take note that the terms *activity* and *task* are used interchangeably.

The define activities process creates three major project documents:

>> The **activity list** is a comprehensive list that includes all the scheduled activities that need to be performed to complete the project work. Each activity in the list is described in sufficient detail to ensure the project team members understand what tasks are required. The activity list is derived from the WBS and serves as a foundation for further schedule development, including sequencing activities, estimating durations, and assigning resources. See Figure 13-5 for an illustration of how activities are derived from the WBS.

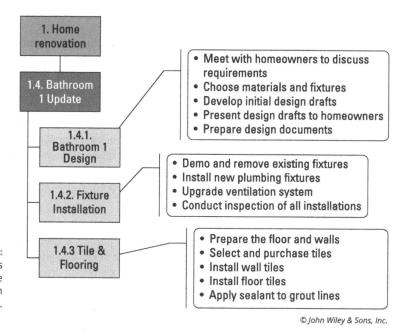

FIGURE 13-5: The activities of a home renovation project.

- » The **milestone list** identifies the project milestones that indicate significant points or events within the project timeline. Milestones typically represent a major achievement or critical decision point in the project such as the completion of a key phase, approval points, or external deliveries. Milestones are used to monitor project progress and are often used in communication with stakeholders to signify important achievements or changes in the project status. Unlike regular activities, milestones typically have no duration (meaning they have zero duration), but are pivotal for tracking and ensuring alignment with project objectives.

- » The **activities attributes** provide a description of each activity by including details that help in planning, executing, and monitoring the project work. These activity attributes often include the activity identifiers, specific resources that are required, and the location where you perform that activity, as well as any imposed dates, constraints, assumptions, leads, lags, predecessor, and successor — terms you'll find out about later in the chapter. The activities attributes provide a deeper level of detail that supports effective schedule management, resource allocation, and risk identification.

Together, these outputs of the define activities process contribute to a detailed understanding and management of the project schedule.

## Identifying activity dependencies

Activity dependencies define the precedence relationship among project activities, which will help in determining the sequence in which those tasks will be performed. The key types of activity dependencies used in schedule management include the following:

- » **Mandatory dependency** (hard logic or hard dependencies) is inherent in the nature of the work being performed. They are legally or contractually required or are necessary based on the physical limitations of the work. In the EMR example, the hardware infrastructure (such as servers and network equipment) must be installed and operational before the EMR software can be configured.

- » **Discretionary dependency** (preferred logic, preferential logic, or soft logic) is established based on best practices within a particular domain or project-specific requirements. It involves a degree of flexibility and is often determined by the project team's expertise and judgment. For example, the order of software feature development is based on priority.

- » **External dependency** involves a relationship between project activities and factors outside the project's control, such as third-party deliverables or regulatory approvals. Although these are outside of the team's control, they must be accounted for in the schedule. For instance, the EMR system must meet HIPAA requirements before it can go live.

» **Internal dependency** is internal to the project or the organization. It is typically established by the project team and is within their control to manage.

As you probably figured out, these dependencies do coexist. For example, you could have a mandatory-external dependency or discretionary-external dependency. These dependencies would be documented within the activity attributes project document.

REMEMBER

Understanding these dependencies is essential for creating a realistic and efficient project schedule. They enable the identification of the critical path, highlight where there may be some leverage to delay activities without delaying the schedule, and help anticipate the effects of any changes to the project timeline.

## Determining the sequence of activities

Once you have defined your activities and identified their dependencies, the next step is to arrange them in a logical order, which you achieve through the *sequence activities process*. Specifically, the *precedence diagramming method (PDM)* is a technique used to sequence activities by identifying those dependencies and arranging them in a logical order. PDM helps in visualizing the project schedule, understanding the flow of activities, and ensuring that all dependencies are accounted for. Here are the four types of precedence relationships:

» **Finish to start (FS).** The most common type of precedence relationship where the predecessor activity must finish before the successor activity can start. For example, the foundation must be completed (predecessor activity) before building the walls (successor activity).

» **Start to start (SS).** The predecessor activity must start before the successor activity can start. For example, once requirements gathering starts, then the design work can start.

» **Finish to finish (FF).** The predecessor activity must finish in order for the successor activity to finish. For example, when the development is completed, then testing can finish.

» **Start to finish (SF).** This is rarely used, where the successor activity cannot finish until the predecessor activity starts. For example, the new server must be operational (predecessor) before decommissioning the old server (successor), ensuring no disruption in system availability.

Sequencing activities helps project managers visualize the logical order of tasks, identify the critical path, and ensure efficient project execution.

**REMEMBER**

The predecessor is a task that must be started or completed before another task (the successor) can begin or finish. The predecessor task sets the stage for the successor task and often establishes the dependencies in the schedule.

## Accounting for leads and lags

Leads and lags are critical concepts that aid project managers in effectively sequencing activities. A *lead* allows an *acceleration* of a successor activity. For example, in a finish to start relationship, a lead can enable the successor task to start before the predecessor task is entirely finished. This is often represented as a negative value. For instance, if the interior decorating of an office space can begin two weeks before the construction is complete, this two-week period is considered a lead.

A *lag*, conversely, is a *delay* in the start or finish of a successor activity with respect to its predecessor. It introduces a waiting period after the predecessor activity completes and before the successor starts. For example, paving the walkway cannot start until three days after the landscaping has reached a certain point. This three-day wait is the lag time. See Figure 13-6 for an illustration of a lead and a lag.

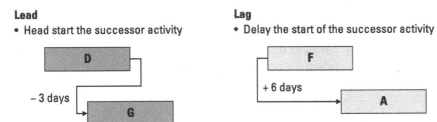

**FIGURE 13-6:** Leads and lags.

Putting it all together, the output will be a project schedule network diagram, as shown in Figure 13-7.

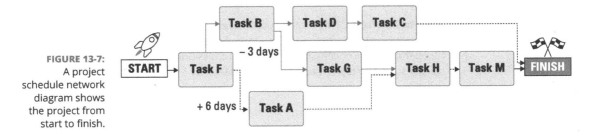

**FIGURE 13-7:** A project schedule network diagram shows the project from start to finish.

You will be making adjustments to the project schedule network diagram as necessary and continuously updating it to reflect changes in the project plan or the scope of work throughout the project's duration. Project managers should reference the Schedule Management Plan on the procedures for making any adjustments.

REMEMBER

PMP aspirants need to understand the "order" in creating a schedule. It begins with referencing the activity list and sequencing activities into a logical order. Next, you determine the type of dependency between each pair of activities. Then you use the precedence diagramming method to connect activities and illustrate their PDM relationships. Be sure to incorporate any potential leads and lags, and lastly, develop a project schedule network diagram to accurately represent the logical flow of activities. By understanding this order, you can successfully handle a potential exam question that asks, "What should you do next?"

## Estimating activity durations

Once activities have been identified and properly sequenced, the *estimate activity durations process* determines how long it takes to complete each task based on the resources available to do the work. Here are the four major types of estimating techniques:

- » **Analogous estimating** uses historical data from similar past projects as a basis for estimating durations for your projects. Analogous estimating, sometimes referred to as *top-down estimating*, considers a high-level estimation method and is generally less accurate. This technique is quick to do and can be cost-effective, especially when detailed information about the current project is unavailable. It relies heavily on expert judgment and the similarity of the current project to past projects.

- » **Parametric estimating** uses a statistical relationship between historical data and other variables such as square footage in construction to estimate the project durations. For example, if it took you five hours to build one desk, then it will take you 25 hours to build 5 desks. It's more accurate compared to analogous estimating if the underlying statistical model reflects the current project's conditions (all things being equal). A quick recall I provide to students is parametric is analogous (historical data) with math (employing a calculation).

- » **Three-point estimating** incorporates uncertainty and risk by making three estimates for each activity: the best-case (optimistic), most likely, and worst-case (pessimistic) estimates. The final estimate is calculated using the simple average or weighted average of these three estimates. A significant reason for utilizing three-point estimating is that historical information is unavailable, and you need to rely on the people who are doing the work to give you estimates. See the sidebar for more information on this estimating technique.

>> **Bottom-up estimating** involves estimating individual work packages or activities in detail and then aggregating these estimates to get the total project estimate. This method is considered the most accurate, especially when detailed information about the project is available. However, it is also considered the most time-consuming and resource-intensive as it requires detailed information about every aspect of the project. This method is useful for complex projects where precise control over costs and timelines is necessary.

Each of these estimating techniques offer different advantages and levels of accuracy, and the choice of method depends on the project-specific requirements, the availability of the data, and the project phase.

## THREE-POINT ESTIMATING IS STILL BETTER THAN GUESSING

*Three-point estimating*, often referred to as a risk-based estimate, is a method used to improve the accuracy of activity durations by considering uncertainty and risk. It involves calculating three different estimates: optimistic, pessimistic, and most likely. This technique helps to account for potential variability in project estimates, providing a more realistic and comprehensive view of the possible outcomes.

Three-point estimating is used when there's no historical data to rely on, forcing you to depend on the expertise of the people actually doing the work to provide accurate estimates — and there's probably a lot of variability in those estimates.

The optimistic estimate is the best-case scenario where everything goes better than expected. This represents the shortest duration possible. The pessimistic estimate is the worst-case scenario where everything goes wrong. This represents the longest duration possible. And the most likely estimate is the most realistic scenario, based on typical conditions. This represents the most likely duration (or cost) considering all factors.

One calculation using these three parameters is to find a simple average. This method calculates the average of the three, optimistic plus most likely plus the pessimistic divided by three.

$E = (O + M + P) / 3$

Example:

Optimistic = 5 days
Most Likely = 8 days

Pessimistic = 15 days
(5 + 8 + 15) / 3 = 9.33 days

This provides a straightforward estimate by giving equal weight to all three scenarios.

A variation to that formula is to take a weighted average, called the Beta Distribution or PERT technique. PERT stands for Program Evaluation and Review Technique—you will likely encounter the term PERT on the PMP Exam. The formula for the PERT estimate is

$$E = (O + 4M + P) / 6$$

Optimistic = 5 days
Weighted Most Likely = (4) * 8 days
Pessimistic = 15 days
(5 + (4)8 + 15) / 6 = 8.67 days

The PERT estimate calculates a weighted average, placing greater emphasis on the most likely estimate by a factor of 4. This method is widely used because it balances potential extremes with the most likely scenario, providing a more reliable and realistic estimate.

*Tip:* The PERT (Beta Distribution) calculation is your default method unless otherwise specified.

## Conducting reserve analysis

While you have done your very best to come up with duration estimates that are realistic and plausible, there still remains some level of uncertainty in the estimates. *Reserve analysis* addresses this by determining the contingency and management reserves needed for the project.

- » **Contingency reserves:** Allocated within the schedule baseline for identified risks (known-unknowns). These reserves, defined and documented, may be expressed as a percentage of the activity duration or as a fixed number of work periods.

- » **Management reserves:** Set aside in the project budget for unforeseen risks (unknown-unknowns). Unlike contingency reserves, management reserves are not included in the schedule or budget baseline and are reserved for unexpected risks impacting the project.

TIP

Contingency reserves are a part of the baselines (schedule and cost) and therefore under the control of the project manager. Management reserves are not a part of the baselines and are controlled by management (that is, senior leadership and/or the sponsor).

By the way, having reserves is not the same thing as padding your estimates. In fact, padding is not a word in the PMI lexicon. Padding suggests haphazard additions to the schedule (or budget) without documentation. Just don't do it or use the term.

# Develop Schedule

At this point, you have confidently defined and sequenced your activities as well as estimated activity durations. You are now in a position to develop a project schedule that's inclusive of analyzing those activity sequences, analyzing the durations, looking at your resource requirements, and analyzing the schedule constraints to create a project schedule model which outlines the plan start and finish dates of your project activities. This is where project managers can use a variety of tools and techniques as a part of the *develop schedule process.*

## Schedule network analysis

The *schedule network analysis* technique is a catch-all for various methods used to build the project schedule model. It leverages analytical tools such as the critical path method, what-if analysis, and resource optimization to calculate the earliest and latest start and finish dates for incomplete tasks. Schedule network analysis isn't a one-and-done process; it's iterative and refined repeatedly until you have a schedule that's both realistic and actionable.

The following sections details different schedule network analysis techniques.

## Using the critical path method

The *critical path method (CPM)* is a key project management tool used to create an efficient and realistic project schedule. Key points about the critical path method and your determination of the critical path are as follows:

>> It determines the longest duration path through a network diagram.

>> It determines the shortest time to complete the project. In other words, if you've determined that your critical path is 30 days, then the earliest (shortest) time that your entire project will be completed is 30 days.

>> It identifies all paths through the schedule network diagram and adds the activity durations along each path. The path with the longest duration is your critical path.

>> The path that has the least amount of float, typically zero float, is your critical path.

TIP

If the PMP Exam question asks you, "What is the earliest the entire project can be completed?" the answer lies with the critical path. Even though it is the longest sequence of activities, it dictates the shortest time in which the project can be completed because any shorter path would not account for all the necessary dependencies and would leave gaps in the project execution. PMP aspirants often struggle with this concept because it seems counterintuitive that the longest path represents the shortest time. The key is understanding that the critical path accounts for all necessary dependencies and constraints, and any other path either runs in parallel or has built-in float.

## FLOAT: THE SAFETY NET YOU WANT ON YOUR SCHEDULE

Float (that is, slack) is an amazing asset to have on your schedule. It represents the amount of time you can delay activities without delaying the entire project schedule — it is an indication of schedule flexibility. Understanding float helps you manage the project schedule effectively and ensures that potential delays do not derail the project timeline.

There are three types of float that you should know for the exam, and quite honestly, this is good knowledge to have for your real-world projects.

- **Total float** (also known as total slack) is the amount of time that an activity can be delayed without delaying the entire project's overall completion date. For example, if a task has a total float of five days, that means the task can be delayed by up to five days without affecting the project's finish date.

- **Free float** is the amount of time an activity can be delayed without impacting the early start date of its immediate successor. This concept is particularly valuable for managing dependencies and preventing delays in one activity from cascading into

*(continued)*

CHAPTER 13 **Planning Your Project Roadmap** 197

*(continued)*

others. For example, if a task has a free float of three days, it can be delayed by up to three days without affecting the start of the next task. However, if the same task has a total float of four days, you could theoretically delay it by four days without jeopardizing the overall project completion date. But here's the catch: delaying beyond the free float (three days, in this case) would push back the earliest successor activity, potentially causing issues further down the line. Managing free float effectively helps ensure smooth transitions between activities.

- **Project float** is the amount of time a project can be delayed without missing its externally imposed finish date, which might be set by a client or other external constraint. Understanding project float is essential for evaluating overall schedule flexibility and managing expectations around potential delays. For example, if a project has a client-mandated deadline of 45 days, the project float represents the time available for delays without exceeding that deadline. If the critical path is 40 days, you have five days of project float (yippie!). However, if the critical path is 50 days, you have negative five days of project float. Negative float indicates that the project is not on track to meet the external deadline. Notably, project float is the only type of float that can be negative, highlighting the urgency to address schedule issues.

Activities on the critical path typically have *zero float*. Delayed critical path activities often result in negative float, otherwise known as *negative* project float. That means you're not meeting that externally imposed deadline. Again, float can also be referred to as slack.

## Addressing resource overallocation: Resource optimization techniques

Developing the project schedule can sometimes lead to resource overallocation. In other words, your schedule has resources working beyond their capacity — they're stretched too thin! Resource optimization techniques help address this by balancing what's needed with the available resources. The two main resource optimization techniques are resource smoothing and resource leveling.

- **Resource smoothing (time-constrained optimization):** This technique adjusts activities within their available float or slack to help avoid exceeding resource limits while maintaining the project's end date. It ensures that resources are used efficiently without changing the critical path. For example, if a resource is over-allocated on a specific day, tasks may be shifted to less busy days, provided this doesn't affect the project's completion date.

- **Resource leveling:** This technique redistributes tasks to resolve resource constraints, even if it means adjusting the project timeline. This may involve extending task durations or the overall schedule to ensure resources are not overburdened. For example, if a resource is overbooked, tasks may be rescheduled to later dates when that resource becomes available.

The key difference: Resource smoothing *does not* alter the project's timeline, while resource leveling *may result in schedule delays*.

## Reducing the timeline: Schedule compression techniques

Sometimes, you'll need to shorten a project schedule, often because the critical path isn't meeting an external deadline (negative project float) or leadership simply wants the project completed faster. Schedule compression techniques can help reduce the timeline without altering the project scope. Two key techniques are fast tracking and crashing.

- **Fast tracking:** This technique involves overlapping tasks that were originally planned to occur one after the other. While it speeds up the timeline, it also heightens risk, as parallel execution can lead to missteps or rework if not carefully managed. For instance, in a product launch, marketing materials are prepared while the product prototype is still being finalized, increasing the risk of rework if design changes occur late in development.

- **Crashing:** This technique reduces the schedule by adding extra resources to critical-path tasks, such as additional manpower, extended work hours, or better technology. Crashing is used when time is more important than cost, as it typically increases expenses. For instance, in a software development project, you might bring on more developers or use faster hardware to accelerate coding and testing while still maintaining the project scope and quality — but it's going to cost you.

The key difference: The primary downside to fast tracking is increased risk by overlapping tasks, while crashing primarily increases the cost by adding resources. Both techniques require careful consideration to achieve a shorter schedule without sacrificing quality or scope.

## Evaluating the alternatives: What-if scenario analysis

What if the deadline changed? What if the scope was reduced? What if more skilled resources became available?

What-if scenario analysis addresses these questions by exploring how adjustments to key project factors can impact the ability to meet objectives. It answers the question:

> What happens if scenario X occurs?

The results of this analysis help evaluate the feasibility of the project schedule under different conditions and assist in planning for reserves to address unexpected changes that may affect the timeline.

## Looking at the probability: Simulations

Simulation evaluates the combined impact of individual project risks and uncertainties on project objectives. The most common simulation technique is *Monte Carlo analysis,* which uses identified risks and uncertainties to predict potential schedule outcomes for the entire project. The results provide a probability distribution, offering insights into the likelihood of completing the project within a given timeline (for example, a 12 percent probability that the project will finish on or before the target date of December 13).

## Using a project management information system

Depending on the project's needs and budget, some projects may use a robust *project management information system (PMIS)* with scheduling capabilities to streamline the creation of a schedule model. This allows tasks such as sequencing activities, estimating durations, and applying the critical path method to be efficiently managed within the system. Yes, please.

TIP

The Project Management Institute (PMI) does not endorse or rely on any specific PMIS software for managing projects. While you may encounter a specific PMIS being mentioned by its marketplace name on PMI materials or on the PMP Exam, these references are solely for context and to provide examples, not as endorsements or requirements.

The primary outputs of the develop schedule process is the *schedule baseline and project schedule.* The schedule baseline is the approved version of the project schedule model and serves as a reference for tracking progress and is a part of the Project Management Plan. Changes to the baseline must go through a formal change control process to ensure proper review, approval, and documentation. The baseline allows project managers to compare actual progress with the plan, identify variances, assess performance, and make necessary adjustments. By integrating with other elements such as the scope and cost baselines, it helps determine if the project is on track, ahead, or behind schedule. The project schedule is the detailed and dynamic project document that includes real-time updates and reflects current progress or adjustments. The project schedule can be presented in Gantt charts, bar charts, network diagrams, or a simple list format. Additional outputs of this process include schedule data (supporting data for the schedule), project calendars (outlining working days and shifts), change requests, Project Management Plan updates, and project document updates.

REMEMBER

The schedule baseline is static (changes only through change control procedures), while the project schedule is dynamic (updates as the project progresses).

## Managing a schedule in the adaptive environment

Instead of developing a detailed schedule, Agile teams use *Agile release planning*, which creates a high-level timeline for delivering product updates, usually over three to six months, based on the *product roadmap* and vision. It helps the team and product owner decide how many iterations or sprints are needed and how much work can be completed in each cycle to produce a releasable product at the end of each iteration.

In Agile projects, teams work in short cycles (that is, iterations or sprints) to complete tasks, review results, and adapt based on feedback. This approach uses two main scheduling methods:

» **Iterative scheduling with a backlog.** Work is planned using a prioritized list of requirements (user stories) that are refined before development. Teams work in timeboxed periods to deliver incremental value to the customer. For example, a new product feature might be developed and released during a two-week sprint.

» **On-demand scheduling.** Often used with Kanban systems, this method pulls work from a queue or backlog as resources become available, limiting the amount of work in progress. This balances demand with the team's capacity, ensuring steady delivery without overloading the team.

Adaptive schedule planning creates an initial plan while recognizing that priorities may shift once work starts. The plan is adjusted as needed to align with these changes. This flexibility is key to responding effectively to evolving requirements and feedback.

# Plan Cost Management

Effective cost management is about estimating, budgeting, and controlling project costs to ensure the project is completed within the approved budget. The *plan cost management process* provides guidance around defining, monitoring, and adjusting project expenses to keep the project on financial track, ensuring that resources are used efficiently and cost overruns are minimized. The *Cost Management Plan* is a document that outlines how project costs will be estimated, budgeted, monitored and controlled, and reported throughout the project life cycle. It provides a framework for ensuring that costs are managed effectively to align with the project's objectives and constraints. The Cost Management Plan is a component of the Project Management Plan. Within the Cost Management Plan, it addresses several key questions to effectively manage costs throughout project execution:

» How will the project cost be estimated, and what techniques and tools will be used?

» How will the project budget be developed, documented, and controlled?

» Who's responsible for managing costs?

» What are the cost control measures?

» How will cost performance be measured, and what metrics, key performance indicators (KPIs), or measures will be used?

» What potential risks could impact project costs, and how will they be identified, assessed, and managed?

By addressing these questions in the Cost Management Plan, project managers can establish a structured approach to managing costs effectively and efficiently throughout the project life cycle.

## Estimating costs

*The estimate costs process* involves approximating the resources required to complete project work. To ensure estimates are accurate, complete, and aligned with project objectives, several key factors must be considered, including the following:

» Direct and indirect costs

» Inflation and escalation

» Currency exchange rates

- Vendor and supplier contracts
- Resource rates
- Historical data and lessons learned
- Regulatory and compliance costs
- Contingency and management reserves

By accounting for these elements, project managers can develop a realistic and comprehensive budget that supports effective project execution within defined constraints. This process is revisited as needed through the course of the project to maintain accuracy and alignment.

## Using a guesstimate range

In the early stages of planning, cost estimates are less accurate but improve as the project progresses through its life cycle. Various estimating techniques provide ranges of accuracy that increase as more details become available.

- **Rough order of magnitude (ROM):** This is typically used during project initiation and is based on high-level historical data, expert judgment, or costing models. Accuracy range: –25 percent to +75 percent.
- **Budget estimate:** This offers a narrower range than ROM and is refined as the budget is iterated. Accuracy range: –10 percent to +25 percent.
- **Definitive estimate:** This is developed later in planning using detailed project information. Costs are estimated at the work package level within the WBS. Accuracy range: –5 percent to +10 percent.
- **Phased estimate:** This combines levels of detail, using less-accurate estimates (for example, ROM) for later phases while applying more-accurate methods (for example, definitive estimates) for earlier work in the project life cycle.

Using these techniques ensures that cost estimates evolve with the project, providing greater accuracy and supporting more informed decision-making as work progresses.

The result of estimating costs will create the outputs of cost estimates and basis of estimates (an explanation of how estimates were derived). It will also update project documents such as the risk register, assumption log, and lessons learned register.

## Estimating costs with familiar tools and techniques

Similar to the techniques previously discussed regarding schedule management, the same techniques can be utilized to estimate your costs; refer to the section on estimating activity durations process for the details:

- » **Analogous estimating** (also known as top-down estimating) involves using the cost of previous similar projects as a basis for estimating the cost of the current project.
- » **Parametric estimating** uses statistical relationships between historical data and other variables to calculate an estimate.
- » **Three-point estimating** involves calculating three estimates for each activity: the optimistic, pessimistic, and most likely.
- » **Bottom-up estimating** involves estimating the cost of individual task or work packages and then summing these estimates to get a total project cost. To determine your overall project budget, you may use a technique called *cost aggregation*, where you aggregate your costs from the bottom up.

## Determining the budget

The *determine budget process* uses several key tools and techniques to develop the project budget. *Expert judgment* can leverage the insights and expertise of the finance team to guide cost decisions, while *cost aggregation* involves summing activity and work package costs to establish an overall budget. *Data analysis*, such as reserve analysis, identifies contingencies for risks, and a *historical information review* helps refine estimates based on past project information. *Funding limit reconciliation* ensures the budget aligns with financial constraints, and *financing* addresses external funding needs, such as loans or grants, to support the project objectives.

Funding limit reconciliation compares the planned project expenditures with the funding limits imposed by the organization or sponsor. The purpose is to ensure that project spending does not exceed available funds at any given time. Identified discrepancies may require replanning the work or making adjustments to scope, time or resource allocation.

The primary output of the *determine budget process* is the *cost baseline*, which is the approved project budget, excluding management reserves and including contingency reserves. A key component of the Project Management Plan, it represents the planned expenditure over time and is used to monitor and measure actual project performance. Typically time-phased, it allocates costs across specific periods (for example, weeks or months). Changes to the cost baseline require formal approval through the change control process to maintain integrity.

Additional outputs of the determine budget process include project funding requirements (receiving the funds in monthly or quarterly increments) and updates to project documents.

TIP

The way to understand funding requirements is to recognize that not all the funds for the project will be released at one time. You may receive funding in monthly or quarterly increments. Organizations put this in place to ensure you are not exhausting all the funds and to keep track of the dollars.

## Managing costs in adaptive projects

In Agile projects where scope is a moving target, lightweight estimation methods are the go-to approach for providing quick, high-level forecasts of labor costs. These methods allow for flexibility, making it easier to adjust as project needs change. Detailed estimates are intentionally deferred until just-in-time planning, ensuring they are both relevant and accurate when applied.

### MEMORY SPRINT

Rapidly recall and jot down key PMP concepts, terms, and ideas using prompts to jog your memory. Set a timer for 15 minutes. When you're done, review your work to highlight areas where you feel confident, and circle concepts you need to revisit. Use the following prompts to guide your thinking and see what else you can recall:

- Difference between the project charter vs. project scope statement? (Hint: it's about the details. . .)
- What is tailoring?
- What is progressive elaboration?
- What are the three (3) baselines?
- What are the three (3) core elements of the scope baseline?
- What is the lowest level of the WBS?

*(continued)*

*(continued)*

- When the customer adds to the scope, it is called _____ _____
- When the team adds to the scope, it is called _____ _____
- What are the three (3) critical path rules?
- What are the three (3) different types of float?
- Name the two (2) resource optimization techniques.
- Name the two (2) schedule compression techniques.
- What are the four (4) PDM relationships (think about most common, rarely used)?
- What are the two (2) types of reserves?
- What is the most accurate estimating technique (also most time-consuming and most expensive)?
- What is the least accurate estimating technique (also quick to do)?

### IN THIS CHAPTER

» Revisiting the purpose of the Planning Process Group

» Outlining the processes of quality management

» Describing key aspects of communications management planning

» Reviewing the robust activities of risk management

» Going over the essential elements of external procurement planning

» Reflecting on resource management and stakeholder engagement processes

# Chapter 14
# Elevating Your Project Roadmap

This chapter delves into additional considerations that you may factor into the development of a comprehensive project plan. While every project must balance the core constraints of scope, schedule, and cost, certain projects require attention to other critical parameters to achieve successful outcomes.

You will examine the importance of planning for quality, developing strategies to manage risk, establishing effective communication strategies, and addressing procurement needs. The chapter also explores how these considerations are adapted in Agile environments, enabling teams to remain flexible and responsive.

# Planning Process Group

The Planning Process Group lays the foundation for successful project execution and closure by defining how project objectives will be achieved. This process group focuses on creating a comprehensive roadmap that minimizes uncertainty and enhances control, ensuring all aspects of the project are thoughtfully planned and documented.

Key outputs of this process group include the Project Management Plan and other planning deliverables, which collectively guide project activities. The specific processes within this group are as follows:

- Develop project management plan
- Plan scope management
- Collect requirements
- Define scope
- Create WBS
- Plan schedule management
- Define activities
- Sequence activities
- Estimate activity durations
- Develop schedule
- Plan cost management
- Estimate costs
- Determine budget
- **Plan quality management**
- **Plan resource management**
- **Estimate activity resources**
- **Plan communications management**
- **Plan risk management**
- Identify risks
- Perform qualitative risk analysis

- Perform quantitative risk analysis
- Plan risk responses
- **Plan procurement management**
- **Plan stakeholder engagement**

Processes in **bold** are covered in detail within this chapter. (See Chapter 13 for details on the other planning processes.) Collectively, these planning activities ensure that projects are thoroughly prepared, systematically organized, and positioned for success. By revisiting this process group, you reinforce the integral role it plays in setting the stage for effective project management.

# Plan Quality Management

Quality management encompasses all activities of the overall management function that determine the quality policy, objectives, and responsibilities, and implements them by means such as quality planning, quality assurance, quality control, and quality improvement.

To really understand everything that is involved with quality management, let's define a few key terms:

- **Quality** refers to the degree to which a set of inherent characteristics of a product, service, or result fulfills requirements. In simpler terms, quality is about meeting or exceeding customer expectations. It's about ensuring that a product or service meets specifications and about ensuring that it satisfies the needs and expectations of stakeholders.

- **Grade** refers to a category or a rank assigned to products or services having the same functional use, but different technical characteristics. Grade is about categorizing or classifying products or services based on their intended purpose or level of performance. For example, in construction, you might have different grades of materials such as steel or concrete, each with varying levels of strength and durability.

- **Quality management** involves the processes and activities used to ensure that a project satisfies the quality requirements defined for it.

You may encounter these terms on the PMP Exam — make sure you understand them.

Quality management aims to ensure that the project delivers the desired level of quality within the constraints of scope, time, and cost. The project manager and project team are responsible for ensuring that the project delivers the desired level of quality and meets stakeholders' expectations.

## Examining the three processes of quality management

In order to understand the benefits of quality planning, you need to understand quality management overall and the interrelationships of its three processes.

### Establishing guidelines: Plan quality management

The *plan quality management process* involves developing a quality management roadmap, the Quality Management Plan, which outlines how quality will be managed throughout the project. It includes establishing quality objectives, deciding on the metrics to measure quality, and defining how these metrics will be used to ensure quality standards are met. Key activities include developing quality policies that align with organizational standards, determining quality metrics and how they will be measured, and identifying quality roles and responsibilities.

### Focusing on the work: Manage quality

The *manage quality process* is centered on the operational aspects of implementing the Quality Management Plan. Manage quality involves utilizing organizational process assets (OPAs) and templates and translating the quality requirements identified during quality planning into practical, executable quality activities. *Manage quality is process-oriented and focuses on the work activities.* Key activities include conducting quality assurance activities to ensure the project will satisfy the relevant quality standards, utilizing quality audits to evaluate performance and ensure compliance with project and organizational standards, and implementing process improvement procedures and techniques to enhance overall quality. See Chapter 16 for more details on the manage quality process.

### Focusing on the deliverables: Control quality

The *control quality process* is concerned with monitoring the project results against the established quality metrics. This process is focused on identifying, analyzing, and correcting any variances from the project's quality requirements. *Control quality is product-oriented and focuses on the deliverables and outputs.* Key activities include inspecting deliverables to ensure they meet the acceptance criteria set out in the Project Management Plan; identifying the causes of poor product quality; and recommending, and taking, corrective actions. It also involves verifying that project deliverables conform to the specifications and that they fulfill customer expectations. See Chapter 17 for more details on the control quality process.

Each of these quality processes ensure that project deliverables meet or exceed the requirements and expectations set by the stakeholders. Projects can achieve higher satisfaction levels, enhance stakeholder engagement, and improve project outcomes by effectively planning, managing, and controlling quality. Each process builds on each other, creating a comprehensive approach to quality management that anticipates problems while also dynamically addressing them as the project progresses.

## Looking at the Quality Management Plan

With a focus on planning, let's direct your attention to the Quality Management Plan, which is an integral component of the Project Management Plan. The Quality Management Plan answers several key questions related to ensuring and maintaining the quality of deliverables and processes throughout the project life cycle. Here are some key questions the Quality Management Plan addresses:

- » What are the quality objectives?
- » What are the quality standards and criteria?
- » What are the roles and responsibilities?
- » What are the quality processes and procedures?
- » How is quality planned?
- » What are the quality metrics for evaluation and testing?

A well-structured Quality Management Plan integrates quality into every phase of the project, addressing the key questions above and providing clear guidance on key quality attributes. It defines what quality means for the project, outlines standard practices, identifies who will lead the quality effort, and clarifies their responsibilities. The plan specifies the processes to be followed, the meetings, reports, and metrics to be used, and also what will be measured and at what intervals. Additionally, it lays out strategies for analyzing and improving processes and procedures. With this clarity, project managers and teams can stay laser-focused on quality, proactively prevent issues, and consistently deliver high-caliber outcomes that meet or exceed stakeholder expectations.

### Knowing that quality is not free: Cost of quality

Quality is not free; you pay for it either up front or at the back-end of the project life cycle. The cost of quality (CoQ) refers to the total cost incurred to ensure that a project meets its defined quality standards. These costs are associated with preventing, detecting, and correcting defects or issues, aiming to ensure customer satisfaction and minimize waste.

TIP

PMP aspirants need to understand the cost of quality concept, as it emphasizes the importance of quality in project outcomes and highlights how proactive quality management strategies can reduce project costs in the long term.

The "upfront" costs of quality are called *cost of conformance*. This refers to costs spent during the project to *prevent failures*. Under cost of conformance are two subcategories:

- **Prevention costs** include expenses related to implementing the Quality Management Plan, training team members, reviewing designs, and establishing proper processes and standards. Examples include costs of training employees on quality standards and new technologies, and costs related to investing in software that enhances design accuracy.
- **Appraisal costs** are associated with activities that ensure products and services meet the quality standards and are defect-free before they are delivered to the customer. These costs involve testing, inspections, and audits. Examples include costs related to conducting and managing interim product reviews, in-process and final inspections, and testing of materials.

The "back-end" costs of quality fall under the category of *cost of non-conformance*, which refers to dollars spent during and after the project *because of failures*. There are two subcategories of cost of non-conformance:

- **Internal failure costs** consist of scrap, rework, or process failures that occur during production. Examples include the cost of reworking a software application after internal testing reveals functional bugs, and costs related to scrapping flawed manufactured components before they are shipped.
- **External failure costs** occur after the product has been delivered to the customer, and defects are then identified. External failure costs include warranties, replacements, liability claims, and loss of reputation or customer satisfaction. Examples include costs associated with handling customer complaints, product returns, warranty claims, and legal issues stemming from failed products.

REMEMBER

External failure costs are typically the most damaging, both to an organization's reputation and to its financial resources.

Understanding the cost of quality for the PMP Exam helps candidates grasp how quality management directly impacts both the operational efficiency and financial outcomes of a project. It highlights the fundamental principle that investing in prevention and appraisal is often far more cost-effective than addressing defects or failures after they occur. This knowledge equips project managers to make strategic decisions about quality investments and evaluate their impact on the project as a whole.

Simply put, when planning for quality, project managers must carefully evaluate the trade-offs between proactive quality measures and reactive solutions. As Benjamin Franklin wisely noted, *"An ounce of prevention is worth a pound of cure."*

TIP

When faced with questions about quality challenges, channel your inner Ben Franklin: prioritize prevention over recovery. The best answer is often the one that avoids failure in the first place.

## Establishing quality metrics

Quality planning efforts should include the establishment of quality metrics. These metrics provide measurable data on performance and the quality of outcomes, enabling objective evaluation. By defining metrics in advance, you can determine acceptable ranges of variation and set clear expectations. Here are some examples of quality metrics.

- Percentage of defective products in a production batch (manufacturing).
- Percentage of patients readmitted within 30 days of discharge (healthcare).
- Average time taken to resolve reported issues (software).
- Percentage of milestones or deliverables completed on schedule (construction).
- Percentage of orders delivered correctly to customers (retail).
- Average cleanliness rating from guest feedback surveys (hospitality).
- Percentage of calls dropped due to network issues (customer service).
- Number of change requests (project management).

From these examples, it's clear that quality metrics can be tailored to various industries and different facets of your project, providing valuable insights to ensure standards are met.

## Satisfying stakeholder requirements

Quality is also about *satisfying stakeholder requirements*; this means ensuring that the project is meeting the specific needs, expectations, and criteria outlined by stakeholders for a deliverable, process, or outcome. It starts with a deep understanding of stakeholder expectations and priorities and translating them into clear, actionable requirements. These requirements define the features, functions, and qualities the deliverables and outcomes must have to hit the mark.

TIP

When you see a reference to the term *satisfy requirements*, this is about delivering exactly what stakeholders need — no more, no less. Project managers must fully understand these needs and expectations to ensure alignment with stakeholder priorities; this should have occurred during the collect requirements process in predictive projects or prioritization of the product backlog in the Agile environment.

## Defining standards and regulations

Standards and regulations define the playing field for quality and compliance, setting the bar for consistency, safety, and performance in projects. *Standards* are guidelines or specifications established by industry bodies to ensure uniformity and quality. Let's say you have a home renovation project; the ANSI A108 series is the American National Standards Institute for ceramic tile installation. Using this series of standards guarantees high-quality results in your kitchen floor update.

Not all standards are created equal. Some emerge from practice, while others are enforced by law. The following is a review of this topic related to de facto standards, de jure standards, and regulations:

- » **De facto standards** aren't officially mandated but have become widely accepted through practice. For example, following appliance or fixture manufacturers' installation guidelines might not be legally required, but these informal standards are trusted across the industry because they work.

- » **De jure standards** are mandated and enforced by authoritative bodies. For instance, in your renovation, the National Electrical Code (NEC) ensures that every wire and connection meets the safety standards for electrical design, installation, and inspection. These are the law of the land when it comes to safety.

- » **Regulations** go a step further. These are government-enforced rules designed to protect public health, safety, and welfare. For your project, you comply with OSHA regulations to keep workers safe. For example, that means proper use of personal protective equipment (PPE) and following strict safety protocols on the construction site.

The pursuit of quality isn't a one-and-done task — it's woven into every stage of the project life cycle. The strategies and frameworks covered here give you a solid foundation for embedding quality into your processes, deliverables, and team dynamics. With a well-executed Quality Management Plan, the team can proactively meet quality standards as a part of the project work.

## Applying quality management in adaptive projects

To manage the high degree of change inherent in Agile projects, frequent quality checks are integrated into Agile practices throughout the project life cycle. These practices include the following:

- **Retrospectives:** These regularly evaluate the effectiveness of processes and team dynamics, fostering continuous improvement.
- **Daily stand-ups:** These address quality concerns, blockers, and roadblocks on a daily basis, ensuring issues are promptly identified and resolved.
- **Small batch system:** Work is delivered in small increments to uncover inconsistencies and quality issues early in the project life cycle. This approach helps keep down the overall cost of changes.
- **Iterative development:** This incorporates feedback loops and promotes continuous improvement, ensuring that quality evolves alongside project deliverables.

These practices collectively enable Agile teams to maintain high-quality standards while adapting to change.

# Plan Communications Management

Communication is more than another item on the project manager's to-do list. The *PMBOK Guide* emphasizes that project managers spend around 90 percent of their time communicating in some form. (Some would argue that number should be 100 percent!) That statistic alone drives home just how important mastering communication is to effectively lead project efforts.

Consider the wide range of communication tasks project managers juggle to keep the information flowing smoothly across the project life cycle:

- Status updates
- Stakeholder briefings
- Team meetings
- Vendor communication
- Risk discussions
- Project change notifications
- Client updates
- Performance reviews
- Gathering client feedback

That's a lot of communicating! These tasks highlight the multifaceted nature of communication in project management. Communication management involves systematically planning, executing, monitoring, and controlling the flow of information to ensure it reaches the right people, at the right time, in the right format.

Communication management is recognizing that stakeholders have varying levels of interest and influence in the project. Tools like the Power Interest Grid and the Salience Model (discussed in Chapter 12) help categorize stakeholders to best fine-tune communication strategies. These methods enable project managers to prioritize efforts and adapt messages to resonate with different audiences.

## Communications tools and techniques

Planning for communications taps into a variety of tools and techniques to ensure the right stakeholders are getting the right information, at the right time.

### Using expert judgment

Without a doubt, you will leverage the expertise of your knowledge and insight about stakeholders but also consider the expertise from individuals and stakeholder groups who have insight on topics such as the following:

- Politics and power dynamics
- Organizational culture

>> Available communication technologies

>> Historical information

>> Organizational policies and procedures

>> Insight about other stakeholders, to include knowledge, skills, abilities, and attitudes

## Analyzing communication requirements

Effective communication also relies on *communication requirements analysis*, a tool and technique used to identify, analyze, and understand the specific communication needs of each stakeholder group. This process involves determining the following:

>> What information needs to be shared

>> Who needs to receive it

>> How frequently it should be communicated

>> Which channels are most appropriate

By targeting communication efforts to align with stakeholder expectations and preferences, project managers ensure relevance and clarity. Communication requirements analysis creates a clear picture of how to engage and inform stakeholders throughout every stage of the project.

## Selecting the right communication technology

When distributing project information, project managers must carefully select communication technologies that align with their team's needs and the project's requirements. This choice is influenced by several factors, including urgency, the project environment, the sensitivity of the information, and the availability and reliability of technology.

For virtual teams, leveraging tools such as shared portals, video or audio conferencing, and instant messaging platforms can foster collaboration and keep everyone on the same page.

The Resource Management Plan should specify how specific technologies will be used to meet *team communication needs* effectively. Options range from face-to-face meetings and phone calls to email, chat, and the use of project management software.

To determine the optimal technology for a situation, project managers should ask the following questions:

- Would this information be better communicated in person or virtually?
- How quickly does this information need to be shared?
- Are there security or confidentiality concerns to address?

Selecting the right tools and technologies allows a better flow of information and increased ability for collaboration.

## Communication models

The *communication model* visually represents the communication process, providing a framework for planning and decision-making around both the methods and the message. It helps you understand how information flows and where potential issues may arise.

- **Basic model:** Focuses on the sender and receiver, where the priority is simply delivering the message. Understanding by the receiver isn't guaranteed — just getting the message out is the goal.
- **Interactive model:** Introduces feedback, emphasizing the importance of ensuring the message is understood. This model acknowledges that communication is a two-way process.
- **Complex model:** Takes into account the human element of communication, recognizing the potential for miscommunication. Factors such as the sender's emotional state, knowledge, background, personality, and biases can influence how the message is transmitted. Similarly, the receiver's emotional state, knowledge, background, personality, and biases shape how the message is interpreted.

Refer to Figure 14-1 for an example of a complex communication model.

The illustration shown in Figure 14-1 of the complex model highlights how communication can break down due to *noise* (interferences or barriers that disrupt understanding). Noise might include distractions, the receiver's perceptions, cultural differences, language barriers, or even a lack of interest or relevant knowledge. These variables remind you that communication is not just about sending a message, but also ensuring that it's received and interpreted as intended.

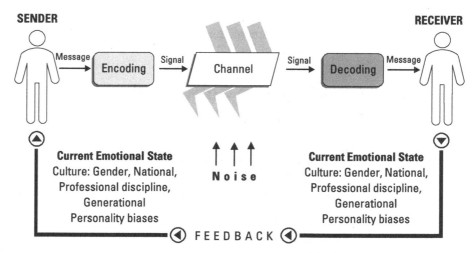

FIGURE 14-1:
A complex communication model.

Noise: Any interference or barriers that might compromise the understanding of the message.

© John Wiley & Sons, Inc.

TIP

If you come across a PMP Exam scenario that uses communication model terms like sender, receiver, encode, decode, feedback, or noise, chances are the question is testing your understanding of the communication model. In that case, focus on answer options related to the model.

## Communication methods

Project management thrives on three key communication methods: push, pull, and interactive. Each serves a specific purpose: keeping stakeholders informed and engaged.

- » **Push communication:** This involves the sender actively delivering information to recipients without expecting immediate feedback. Think of it as broadcasting updates to a broader audience. Common examples include email notifications, newsletters, memos, and status reports.

- » **Pull communication:** This shifts the responsibility to recipients, allowing them to access information when needed. This method typically involves making resources like project repositories, shared drives, or knowledge bases available for on-demand access. It promotes efficiency by letting stakeholders access what they need, when they need it, without unnecessary interruptions.

- » **Interactive communication:** This is a real-time, two-way exchange that involves meetings, calls, or workshops where ideas and feedback flow freely. It encourages collaboration, resolves issues quickly, and builds stronger team relationships, making it indispensable for brainstorming and decision-making.

Each communication method brings unique strengths to the table, making them suited for different contexts within a project.

## Creating the Communications Management Plan

The plan communications management process creates the *Communications Management Plan* that outlines the *who*, *what*, *when*, *why*, and *how* of project communication. The plan identifies key stakeholders, their communication preferences, the types of information to be shared, and the communication channels to be used. A well-crafted Communications Management Plan outlines how project information will be communicated, including the timing, frequency, and content of communications. It identifies the stakeholders who need to be kept informed, and it establishes guidelines for effective communication. Key questions answered by the Communications Management Plan include the following:

- » What information needs to be communicated?
- » Who needs to receive the information?
- » When do they need to receive the information?
- » How will the information be communicated?
- » Who is responsible for delivering the information?
- » How should information be documented and stored?
- » How is sensitive information handled?

The Communications Management Plan ensures the project information is communicated clearly and consistently to stakeholders. The plan includes strategies for engaging stakeholders through communication channels, thus fostering their involvement in active participation. It facilitates two-way communication, which encourages stakeholder feedback and ensures that their voices are heard.

REMEMBER

The Communications Management Plan goes hand in hand with the Stakeholder Engagement Plan.

### Communication matrix: A supplement to the Communications Management Plan

A communication matrix is a useful tool that maps out all of the identified stakeholders along with their communication needs, preferred channels, and desired frequencies. This document serves as a reference guide for implementing the communication plan. Figure 14-2 provides an illustration of a communication matrix.

**FIGURE 14-2:** A communication matrix for a website project.

| PROJECT NAME: New Traditions Website | | | | PROJECT MANAGER: Bobby Green, PMP | | |
|---|---|---|---|---|---|---|
| Who | | What | When | Why | Where/How | Other |
| Owner | Audience | Topic | Timing | Intent | Delivery | Comments |
| Bobby Green | Team and Stakeholders with access to secure project info area | Team Briefing | Daily at 9:00 | Team collaboration | Restricted Intranet | Refer to team charter |
| Bobby Green | Team, Sponsor, Senior Management | Weekly Web Bulletin | Weekly | Status update | Internal Intranet | Prep 2 days prior |
| Ricky Tower | Webmaster, IT Department | Technical Incident Report | Immediately after Incident | Report issues | Email | Prep 1 week prior |
| Ralph Urban | Sponsor, Senior Management | Budget and Schedule Detail | Bi-Weekly | Report on costs | Spreadsheets and detailed Gantt Chart | Check with finance team |
| Johnny Boulder | All Internal Stakeholders | Accomplishments and Setbacks | Bi-Weekly | Status update | Email and Intranet | Prep 1 day prior |
| Ronnie Belafonte | All Internal Stakeholders | Schedule Milestone | Bi-Weekly | Status update on schedule | Email and Intranet | Prep 1 day prior |
| Mike Hammer | All Internal Stakeholders | Current top 5 Risks | Weekly | Report on risks | Email and Intranet | Check with team |

© John Wiley & Sons, Inc.

Every project has its own set of challenges, needs, and nuances, making it essential to tailor communication strategies to fit the specific requirements. In a predictive project management environment, effective communication planning relies on thoughtful analysis, strategic decision-making, and a clear understanding of stakeholder dynamics to keep your stakeholders well informed.

## Additional communication concepts

Project management lives and dies by communication, and nailing it means understanding two key concepts: communication types and the 5Cs of written communication. It's all about choosing the right format for the message (whether it should be a quick chat, a formal report, or a detailed email) and making sure your written communications are clear, concise, and darn near impossible to misinterpret. Keep reading to find out about communication types and the 5Cs of written communication.

## Communication types

Communication can take on different forms, depending on the situation and audience:

- **Verbal communication**
  - **Formal:** Structured interactions such as presentations, meetings, or briefings that follow a planned agenda.
  - **Informal:** Casual conversations or spontaneous discussions that encourage quick collaboration and rapport-building. Think, water-cooler conversations.
- **Written communication**
  - **Formal:** Official documents such as contracts, reports, or project charters designed for record-keeping and accountability. These documents are typically stored in a formal archive or repository.
  - **Informal:** Quick emails, texts, or chat messages that serve to share updates or solve immediate issues without formality.

Choosing the right communication type ensures the message is effective and suits the context, whether it's delivering important updates or fostering teamwork.

## The 5Cs of written communication

The 5Cs of communication are a trusted framework for ensuring that written communication is effective and impactful. Here's the breakdown:

1. **Correct:** Ensure accuracy in grammar and spelling to prevent misunderstandings and preserve professionalism.
2. **Concise:** Say what matters and leave out the fluff. Time is limited, so get to the point quickly.
3. **Clear:** Avoid ambiguity — your message should be straightforward and easily understood.
4. **Coherent:** Structure your ideas logically so they flow seamlessly. A well-organized message ensures recipients grasp the intent without confusion.
5. **Controlled:** Manage who gets what information and when. Structured distribution avoids information overload and ensures stakeholders stay focused on what's relevant.

Applying the 5Cs minimizes the risk of miscommunication and keeps projects on track, proving that how you communicate is just as important as what you communicate.

Communication types help you choose the right format for the message, while the 5Cs ensure your written communication hits hard on clarity, brevity, and comprehension. By mastering these concepts, project managers will have the tools they need to keep stakeholders informed, engaged, and on the same page, no matter how complex the project gets.

TIP

In previous years, PMP aspirants were required to understand the communication channels formula — a simple yet powerful tool for assessing the complexity of communication in a project. While this calculation is unlikely to appear on the exam today, it remains highly useful for real-world project management. The formula for determining the number of communication channels is $n(n-1) \div 2$, where $n$ represents the number of stakeholders or team members involved.

## Managing communications in adaptive projects

Unlike traditional methods with detailed communication plans, Agile thrives on open channels for transparent information exchange, frequent interactions among cross-functional teams, and adaptable strategies that evolve with the project. This approach enhances project outcomes by fostering shared understanding, enabling quick decision-making, and ensuring a swift response to change.

In an Agile setting, information flows from end users, customers, teams, and stakeholders, driving updates to the product backlog. Collaborative meetings ensure that these flows remain unblocked, addressing tasks, progress, challenges, and discussions about both the product and team processes. The tight connection between the Agile development life cycle and communication management enables collaboration, transparency, and adaptability — core principles of Agile methodologies. Clear, effective communication supports each interaction, ensuring the success of every iteration and the project as a whole.

The Agile Manifesto itself underscores the importance of communication with values and principles such as the following:

- Individuals and interactions over processes and tools.
- Customer collaboration over contract negotiation.
- Responding to change over following a plan.

>> Business people and developers working together daily.

>> The most efficient and effective method of conveying information is face-to-face conversation.

These concepts highlight that Agile projects depend on frequent communication and regular checkpoints to keep stakeholders and teams aligned.

## Agile ceremonies: Fostering transparency, accountability, and decision-making

Agile ceremonies, or events, create a framework for collaboration and communication.

>> **Sprint planning:** At the start of each sprint, the team, including the product owner, reviews prioritized backlog items and commits to what they can complete.

>> **Daily stand-ups:** These are short, focused daily meetings where the team syncs up on progress, shares updates, and addresses roadblocks.

>> **Sprint reviews:** At the end of each sprint, the team demonstrates completed work to stakeholders, gathering valuable feedback for future iterations.

>> **Sprint retrospectives:** Following each sprint, the team reflects on what went well, what didn't, and how to improve. Everyone has a voice in shaping team performance.

>> **Backlog refinement:** While not officially an Agile ceremony, this ongoing activity involves reviewing and updating the product backlog. It facilitates communication by clarifying user stories, discussing priorities, and estimating effort.

TIP

Agile ceremonies occur at specific points during an iteration, such as the start of a sprint, or daily in the case of stand-ups. These ceremonies are timeboxed, which means they have a defined duration (for example, 15 minutes for a daily stand-up). In contrast, backlog refinement meetings do not occur at a fixed time and are not timeboxed, which is why they are not considered official Agile ceremonies, despite being widely practiced.

Agile communication also goes beyond meetings and scheduled events. Some advanced concepts include the following.

>> **Osmotic communication:** This is a passive, unintentional information exchange that happens when team members work in close proximity,

absorbing insights from overheard conversations and interactions. This creates a natural flow of updates without requiring formal meetings.

- **Fishbowl window:** This is a virtual collaboration setup where a persistent video link is open throughout the workday. It encourages spontaneous engagement and reduces collaboration lag in remote teams.
- **Remote pairing:** This is where two team members use virtual tools to share screens and collaborate in real time — whether solving technical challenges, pairing on code, or mentoring one another.
- **Caves and commons:** This concept addresses the need for balance between quiet, focused workspaces ("caves") and collaborative, open spaces ("commons") where team members can share ideas and engage in group discussions. Agile teams often ensure both types of spaces are available to accommodate different work needs, fostering productivity and creativity.

Many Agile methodologies emphasize face-to-face interactions (or their virtual equivalents), transparency, and open feedback loops. These principles make communication flexible, collaborative, and responsive to change — ensuring that information flows seamlessly and supports the iterative nature of Agile projects.

# Planning for Risks

While you hope for the best, you should plan for the worst. That's where risk management comes in. Effective project managers proactively plan for uncertainties that can impact a project's trajectory. Risk planning equips you with foresight, enabling you to anticipate potential issues and prepare strategies to manage them. Risk management is a fundamental part of project management because it helps to identify, assess, and manage potential risks before they become problems, thus ensuring that a project is more likely to succeed. For instance, you could have risks around not meeting quality standards, missing deadlines, or not addressing cost overruns. The goal is to minimize the impact of negative events and capitalize on opportunities that may arise. Effective risk management requires collaboration and communication among stakeholders, including project managers, team members, and external partners, and vendors.

## Ensuring robust risk planning happens

With traditional project management, risk management is robust and incorporates the development of a *Risk Management Plan*. The Risk Management Plan, an output of the *plan risk management process* and a component of the Project Management Plan, addresses key questions related to identifying, assessing, and managing risk from initiation to closure. Key questions answered by the Risk Management Plan:

- **What are the roles and responsibilities?**
- **What is the risk management framework?**
- **How are risks categorized and prioritized?**
- **What is the organization's risk appetite and threshold?**

A well-crafted Risk Management Plan provides a structured approach to identifying, assessing, and mitigating risk, which will ultimately help the project team minimize potential threats and seize opportunities. It ensures that risks are proactively managed to achieve project objectives successfully.

A key understanding about risks is that they introduce uncertainties, that if they happen, they could have a positive impact or a negative impact on the project objectives. Risks that have negative impacts to the project success are called *threats*. Threats are risks that you try to avoid or at least minimize. These range from potential project delays to budget overruns, equipment failure, legal issues, and stakeholder conflicts. Positive risks are referred to as *opportunities*. These are events or circumstances that could have a positive impact on the project's success. They are the risks that you want to make certain occur. This could include a discovery of a new technology, positive changes in regulations, unexpected availability of resources, and increased stakeholder support.

Effective risk management is all-encompassing: you want to minimize threats, as well as recognize and leverage opportunities. This balanced approach encourages not only defensive strategies, but also proactive efforts to enhance project outcomes.

Risks can arise from virtually any source, encompassing a wide range of factors both internal and external to the project. Risks can be

- **Schedule-related.** Experiencing schedule overruns (threat) or opportunities to compress the schedule.
- **Cost-related.** Being over budget or unanticipated expenditures.
- **Scope-related.** Scope creep (threat), poorly defined scope, or scope reduction (opportunity).

- **Stakeholder-related.** Poor communication (threat) or positive and timely communication (opportunities).

- **Resource-related.** Overallocated resources (threat) or a team member who is suddenly available (opportunity).

- **Compliance-related.** Noncompliance with environmental approvals (threat).

- **Environmental-related.** Bad weather resulting in rework, or weather delays in a project.

The ever-present potential for risk drives home the need for laser-focused, comprehensive strategies to identify and manage it effectively.

The concept of risk management is so important that it begins at the very inception of the project, with high-level risks documented during the development of the project charter.

Guided by the Risk Management Plan, the *identify risk process* focuses on identifying potential risks that could affect the project. This can involve brainstorming with the team, reviewing historical data, consulting experts, or using risk identification tools and checklists.

Common tools and checklists for identifying and categorizing risks include the following:

- **Risk Breakdown Structure (RBS).** A hierarchical framework used to categorize potential risks associated with the project. The RBS organizes risks into detailed levels, making it easier to identify and address them systematically. Refer to Figure 14-3 for an example of an RBS.

- **Prompt lists.** Structured lists that serve as reminders for potential risk areas, tailored to specific contexts. Examples include the following:

  - **PESTEL.** Political, Economic, Social, Technological, Environmental, and Legal.
  
  - **TECOP.** Technological, Environmental, Commercial, Operational, and Political.
  
  - **VUCA.** Volatility, Uncertainty, Complexity, and Ambiguity.

These tools help ensure a thorough and organized approach to risk identification, providing a foundation for more effective risk management.

**FIGURE 14-3:** An example risk breakdown structure (RBS) for a home renovation project.

| Level 1 Category | Level 2 Subcategory | Level 3 Specific Risks |
|---|---|---|
| Technical Risks | Structural Integrity | Risk of foundational damage during renovations |
| | Electrical Systems | Risk of outdated wiring requiring complete overhaul |
| | Plumbing Systems | Risk of discovering old, non-compliant plumbing |
| Operational Risks | Scheduling Delays | Risk of delays due to back-ordered materials |
| | Contractor Availability | Risk of key contractors double-booking or canceling |
| | Safety Incidents | Risk of accidents due to non-adherence to safety protocols |
| Financial Risks | Budget Overruns | Risk of exceeding budget due to change orders |
| | Unexpected Costs | Risk of additional costs from hidden issues like mold or rot |
| Regulatory Risks | Permit Acquisition Delays | Risk of project delays due to slow permit approval |
| | Compliance with Local Building Codes | Risk of failing inspections, requiring rework |
| Environmental Risks | Disposal of Hazardous Materials | Risk associated with the removal and disposal of asbestos |
| | Weather-related Delays | Risk of outdoor work being delayed by adverse weather conditions |

© John Wiley & Sons, Inc.

## Performing qualitative risk analysis

As risks are identified, the next logical step is the *perform qualitative risk analysis process*, where you evaluate their potential impact and likelihood. Qualitative risk assessment uses non-numeric, descriptive scales — such as high, moderate, and low — to gauge each risk's probability and potential impact. This approach focuses on understanding risks and their possible effects on project objectives, rather than getting fixated on crunching numbers (for now). The focus is on pinpointing risks and understanding how they could disrupt your project objectives.

The development of a solid Risk Management Plan should include clearly defined criteria in order to enable you to perform this assessment. These criteria set the guidelines for how the team and stakeholders will analyze and prioritize risks, ensuring everyone is on the same page. Crafting these criteria often involves subjective judgment, drawing on the expertise and instincts of the project team and stakeholders. See Figure 14-4 for an example of risk criteria applicable to a project.

With these examples, you see the criteria defined for this project just to give you parameters on understanding which risks need more immediate attention and resources, thereby facilitating better risk management planning. Keep in mind that this is an example, and that your application of parameters may look totally different in the case of your project.

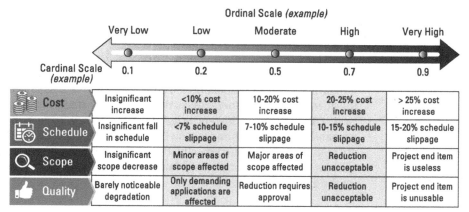

FIGURE 14-4:
A sample risk criteria for a given project.

## Probability and impact matrix

Qualitative risk analysis also involves prioritizing your risks based on their impact and probability, focusing on risks that could have the most significant impact on the project. The *probability and impact matrix* helps project managers assess and prioritize risks based on their potential impact on the project objectives and the likelihood of their occurrence.

The matrix typically features two axes: impact and probability. Each axis is divided into levels such as low, medium, and high. Risks are plotted on the matrix based on their assessed impact and probability derived from your prior analysis and expert judgment. Figure 14-5 illustrates an example of a probability and impact matrix.

| | Impact | | | | |
|---|---|---|---|---|---|
| | Insignificant | Minor | Moderate | Major | Catastrophic |
| Probability | 0.1 | 0.2 | 0.5 | 0.7 | 0.9 |
| 5 - Almost Certain | 0.5 | 1.0 | 2.5 | 3.5 | 4.5 |
| 4 - Likely | 0.4 | 0.8 | 2.0 | 2.8 | 3.6 |
| 3 - Possible | 0.3 | 0.6 | 1.5 | 2.1 | 2.7 |
| 2 - Unlikely | 0.2 | 0.4 | 1.0 | 1.4 | 1.8 |
| 1 - Rare | 0.1 | 0.2 | 0.5 | 0.7 | 0.9 |

| Extreme Risk | High Risk | Moderate Risk | Low Risk |
|---|---|---|---|
| Immediate action where senior management gets involved | Management responsibility should be specified | Managed by specific responsible person | Managed by routine process — placed on a watch list |

FIGURE 14-5:
An example of a probability and impact matrix.

© John Wiley & Sons, Inc.

As you can see in Figure 14-5, any risks that identify as high priority, such as in the category of major or catastrophic, are risks that are critical and need to be prioritized for immediate action. They will be prioritized at the top of the risk register. Medium-priority risks, or moderate risks, are those risks that have medium impact and probability. These risks receive a balanced approach, ensuring adequate preparedness. Risks that are in the categories of minor and insignificant are considered low-priority risks, and they have a low impact or low probability in terms of impacts on the project. They usually don't require immediate resource allocation. Typically, these risks in this quadrant are placed on what's called a *watch list*. All other risks (such as high priority or medium priority) remain on the risk register.

### Risk register

A *risk register* is a key document in project management primarily used for identifying, assessing, and managing risks throughout the project life cycle. It serves as a comprehensive tool for recording information about identified risks, including their nature, impact, and the actions taken to manage them. The risk register is continuously managed and updated. Each specific risk on the risk register has a risk owner assigned to it. In project management, a *risk owner* is an individual who's responsible for managing a specific risk. This person is responsible for implementing risk responses and for monitoring the risk over the life of the project.

### Risk report

The *risk report* is your go-to document for presenting the big picture of your project's overall risk exposure. It summarizes key details such as the number of identified threats and opportunities, how risks are spread across categories, and metrics or trends to watch. Think of it as the executive summary tailored for senior leadership — not the detailed spreadsheet of every project risk but rather the high-level insights they need to make informed decisions.

## Performing quantitative risk analysis

Quantitative risk analysis focuses on evaluating the potential impacts of risks in measurable terms, such as cost or time. The *perform quantitative risk analysis process* provides valuable insights for establishing contingency and management reserves and supports the development of effective risk response plans. However, it is not required for every project. Robust analysis depends on high-quality data, specialized risk software, and expertise in building and interpreting risk models. It can also be time-intensive and expensive, making it more suitable for large or complex projects, strategically important initiatives, or situations where it is contractually required.

Coupled with expert judgment and team collaboration, quantifying risks involves leveraging powerful tools and techniques to analyze uncertainties and their potential impacts. Here's a breakdown of the key methods:

- **Representations of uncertainty.** These visual or numerical models illustrate potential variability in project outcomes. They help identify how uncertainties in inputs, such as costs or timelines, can ripple through to affect project objectives.

- **Simulations (Monte Carlo).** Monte Carlo simulations involve running thousands of scenarios to model how uncertainties in inputs, such as costs or durations, affect project outcomes. For example, they can estimate the probability of completing a project within budget or on time, giving a probability distribution of potential results.

- **Sensitivity analysis.** This method identifies which variables have the greatest impact on project outcomes. By tweaking one variable at a time (such as material costs or labor hours) and observing the effects, project managers can pinpoint the most significant risks to address. Results of this analysis are displayed on a tornado diagram.

- **Decision tree analysis.** This technique is commonly used with Expected Monetary Value (EMV) to support decision-making by comparing alternative strategies. A *decision tree* visually maps out the decisions you need to make, along with the potential probabilities and impacts of each option. The process begins with identifying the decision point, followed by branching out to represent possible choices. Each branch considers the likelihood of different outcomes (probabilities) and their associated impacts, such as costs, benefits, or risks.

- **Influence diagrams.** These graphical tools show the relationships between variables and risks, offering a high-level view of how different factors interact. Often used in quality management decisions, influence diagrams are helpful when decision trees are too complex.

Together, these tools equip project managers to tackle risk analysis with precision, providing data-driven insights for smarter decision-making and stronger project outcomes. Refer to Chapter 16 for further review of EMV.

TIP

Here's a helpful tip for distinguishing between *qualitative* and *quantitative* risk analysis: focus on the "L" in qualitative to remember it's about creating a *list* of risks, and the "N" in quantitative to associate it with *numbers*, as in quantifying the impact of risks. Qualitative risk analysis should be performed for every identified risk, while quantitative risk analysis is optional. Only perform quantitative analysis if you have both the time and budget to conduct it effectively.

The result of performing the qualitative and quantitative risk analysis processes would be an update to the risk report providing an assessment of overall project risk exposure and an update to the risk register indicating a prioritized list of project risks and recommended risk responses.

## Planning risk responses

A good practice is to develop a risk response for each identified risk — or at the very least, for your highest-priority risks. Risk responses or strategies can be tailored to address negative risks (threats) or positive risks (opportunities), each requiring a specific set of approaches to effectively mitigate or capitalize on the situation.

Here are risk strategies for threats:

- **Avoid.** Eliminate the cause of the risk. Strategies might include changing the project plan to bypass a risky activity, delaying the project to avoid a timing-related risk, or scaling back deliverables to reduce complexity.
- **Transfer.** Shift the impact or responsibility of the threat to a third party. This is often indicated by paying a premium, getting insurance, or outsourcing to a vendor.
- **Mitigate.** Reduce the likelihood or impact of the threat. Strategies might involve implementing additional quality checks, adopting simpler technology, or increasing training for the project team to address skill gaps that could lead to delays.
- **Accept.** Acknowledge the risk and choose to deal with the consequences if it occurs. This strategy is typically used when no cost-effective, proactive response is available, or the effort to address the risk outweighs the potential impact. For example, a project manager might accept the possibility of minor shipping delays instead of paying extra for expedited delivery.

REMEMBER

Transferring a risk doesn't eliminate it; it simply shifts the responsibility for managing it to another party.

Here are risk strategies for opportunities:

- **Exploit.** Ensure the opportunity is realized by using resources specifically to make it happen. For instance, if completing a project two months early could open up new business opportunities, you might assign your top talent to critical tasks to ensure early delivery.

>> **Share.** Partner with other entities to maximize the opportunity's potential. This is typically indicated through joint ventures, partnerships, and teaming arrangements. For example, partnering with another company could give your project team access to specialized resources or expand your market reach.

>> **Enhance.** Increase the likelihood or positive impacts of that opportunity. For example, adding extra staff to a task could accelerate delivery or improve quality, increasing the benefits gained.

>> **Accept.** Be willing to accept the impacts of the opportunity should it occur. You're recognizing the opportunity but not pursuing it actively, often due to resource constraints. For instance, you may recognize a chance to implement advanced features in a product but choose to focus on delivering the original scope within the current timeline and budget.

TIP

There are two types of acceptance strategies for both threats and opportunities: passive acceptance and active acceptance. *Passive acceptance* is essentially a "wait and see" approach — acknowledging the risk but deciding to deal with it if it occurs. On the other hand, *active acceptance* involves planning ahead. For example, on the PMP Exam, if the scenario mentions tapping into contingency reserves or implementing a contingency plan, that's active acceptance in action, proactively preparing for the risk if it materializes.

Risks that require escalation are generally outside the boundaries of the project or beyond the authority of the project manager. Think of it as above your pay grade. *Escalation* is a strategy applied to both threats and opportunities.

In addition to creating risk responses for individual project risks, you'll also need to develop and implement strategies to address overall project risks. You can apply the same approaches used for individual risks to manage the broader risks that affect the entire project.

Understanding and planning for risk is about protecting against negative outcomes *and* proactively leveraging opportunities to enhance your project's resilience and success. Risk management involves systematically identifying risks, analyzing their potential impact, and prioritizing them for action. Furthermore, effective risk management goes a step further by crafting response plans that aim to minimize threats as well as safeguard the integrity of your project's goals, turning potential setbacks into opportunities for growth and achievement.

### Applying risk management in adaptive projects

Agile projects naturally come with more risks due to evolving scope and the need to be responsive to change. This is why frequent reviews of incremental work are critical to catching issues early. Regular backlog refinement helps identify emerging risks, while tools such as risk-adjusted backlogs and risk logs (similar to traditional risk registers) keep everything organized. In Agile, risk management is a part of the strategy to keep the project moving forward and responsive in the face of uncertainty.

## Plan Procurement Management

Planning for procurements is all about determining what project resources will be sourced externally. Effective procurement planning involves aligning purchasing decisions with project timelines, budgets, and quality standards. Project managers need to know how to identify procurement requirements and work with your procurement team to select qualified vendors to secure the best resources and services while ensuring compliance and fostering strong vendor relationships.

### Mastering the plan procurement management process

Have you encountered a situation during project planning or execution where you realized you lacked the necessary resources to complete the job? This scenario is common on many projects, highlighting the importance of procurement. The need to procure services often kicks in when assessing resource needs. When it's clear you don't have the resources to get the job done, it's time to loop in your procurement team ASAP.

Enter the *plan procurement management process*, which sets the stage for preparing procurement documents and engaging with your procurement specialists within the organization.

Effective procurement strategies can help control expenditures and mitigate potential risks associated with vendors or contracts. Additionally, procurement influences deliverable quality by ensuring that vendors meet established standards and specifications. Lastly, successful procurement requires effective stakeholder management as it involves interactions with various parties such as vendors, suppliers, internal stakeholders, and project team members.

## Understanding procurement essential terms

When dealing with procurement, you may encounter the following terms:

- » **Buyer.** The entity or individual who acquires goods, services, or resources from another party in exchange for payment. The buyer is typically the organization or individual that initiates a procurement process to fulfill project needs. The buyer may also be referred to as the purchaser or client, depending on the context of the transaction.

- » **Seller.** The entity or individual who provides the goods, services, or resources to the buyer in exchange for payment. Sellers are often external parties contracted to deliver specific products or services that are required for project completion. Sellers may also be known as vendors, suppliers, or contractors, reflecting their role in providing goods or services to meet project requirements.

- » **Procurement department.** The organizational unit responsible for acquiring goods, services, or resources that are needed to support the organization's operations or projects. The procurement department oversees the process of obtaining necessary resources, including vendor selection, contract negotiation, and supplier management. The procurement department may also be referred to as the procurement team, purchasing team or supply chain management, and individuals within the department may be referred to as procurement specialists.

These terms are key to understanding project procurement processes, contract management, and stakeholder interactions for the PMP Exam. Many organizations act as a buyer in one procurement and a seller in another.

TIP

For procurement-related PMP Exam questions, assume you're answering from the buyer's perspective, unless the question explicitly states otherwise.

## Deciding to make or buy

The *make or buy analysis* is a tool and technique used to decide whether to produce a product, service, or component internally (make) or purchase from an external source (buy). This analysis helps determine the most cost-effective and efficient approach to obtaining necessary resources or deliverables for the project. Factors considered in this analysis typically include cost, resource availability, expertise, time, constraints, and risks. The *make or buy decision* refers to the conclusion reached through the make or buy analysis. The decision directly influences your project procurement strategy and may impact project timelines, costs, and risks.

# Creating a Procurement Management Plan

A project *Procurement Management Plan* addresses key questions related to acquiring goods and services from external sources to support the project. Some of these key questions include the following:

- What are the roles and responsibilities for procurement?
- What is the procurement strategy?
- What is the procurement process?
- How are suppliers and vendors selected?
- What are the contract types that you'll use during the course of this project or at different phases of the project?
- What is the change control process for procurement, and what is the vendor management strategy?

A solid Procurement Management Plan steers the project team in acquiring external goods and services efficiently while staying compliant with legal regulations and internal procurement policies. Leverage the expertise of your procurement department to tap into their expert judgment when developing this plan, which ultimately becomes part of your overall Project Management Plan.

## Getting ready to procure

Once the Procurement Management Plan is in place, the project team can proceed in defining their procurement strategy and creating the statement of work. The *procurement strategy* outlines the approach and methods for acquiring goods and services or resources needed to support project objectives. It involves determining how procurement activities will be conducted, including vendor selection criteria, contract types, negotiation strategies, and risk management approaches. The *procurement statement of work* (SOW) is a document that specifies the requirements, deliverables, and expectations for procurement contracts. It outlines the scope of work to be performed by the vendor or supplier, including technical specifications, quality standards, timelines, and acceptance criteria. The statement of work serves as a key communication tool between the buyer and seller, ensuring mutual understanding and agreement on project deliverables and responsibilities.

TIP

Some organizations use the term *statement of work* to describe internal projects. However, in "Planet PMI," the work of internal projects is described in the project scope statement. For the purposes of the PMP Exam, when you encounter the term *statement of work*, it typically refers to a procurement statement of work — a document outlining the deliverables, requirements, and scope for goods or services being procured.

With the procurement strategy, procurement statement of work, and Procurement Management Plan in place, the focus shifts to bid documents. Bid documents are prepared by the organization (the buyer) and serve as the formal invitations to bidders that translate procurement needs into actionable opportunities for potential sellers. These documents provide a comprehensive overview of the project scope, objectives, specifications, and deliverables, ensuring potential vendors have the clarity needed to prepare accurate proposals. By inviting competitive bids, bid documents foster a fair, transparent procurement process, with the goal of driving better pricing, quality, and value while promoting equal opportunities for all bidders.

Typical bid documents include the following:

- » **Request for Proposal (RFP).** This is a comprehensive document that outlines the project requirements, objectives, scope of work, evaluation criteria, and terms and conditions. It invites potential vendors to submit proposals detailing how they will meet the project requirements and deliverables. RFPs are commonly used for procurements where the requirements are complex and the emphasis is on evaluating vendors based on their technical capabilities, experience, and proposed solutions in addition to price.

- » **Invitation for Bid (IFB) or Request for Quotation (RFQ).** These are used for procurement of goods and services with clearly defined specifications and requirements. They typically include information on the goods or services to be procured, delivery or performance requirements, and pricing terms and conditions. IFBs and RFQs are typically *focused primarily on pricing*. These procurement documents are structured to obtain competitive bids from potential vendors or suppliers based on specified criteria, with the significant emphasis on obtaining the best value or lowest price for the goods or services being procured.

- » **Request for Information (RFI).** This is used to gather information from potential vendors or suppliers about their capabilities, products, services, or solutions. Unlike a Request for Proposal or an Invitation for Bid, an RFI does not solicit bids or proposals. Instead, its primary purpose is to collect information and gain a better understanding of the market landscape, potential suppliers, and available solutions before initiating a formal procurement process.

TIP

Some organizations have internal policies (OPAs) that mandate or restrict the type of bid document that can be used. However, on the PMP Exam, you may encounter scenarios where you'll need to determine which type of bid document is most appropriate for the given situation. Planet PMI assumes that you have a procurement team to consult on the appropriate documents. Let's hope you have such a department in the real world, too!

# Interpreting contract types

When considering prospective sellers, organizations may use *source selection criteria* to evaluate vendors and identify *preferred vendors* who offer the best combination of capabilities, pricing, performance, and alignment with project objectives. By leveraging preferred vendors and applying rigorous source selection criteria, organizations can enhance the likelihood of successful project outcomes and foster productive supplier relationships. Circling back to the procurement strategy, this is where the type of contract used has been determined. For the exam, there are three major contract types and their subcategories to be aware of.

## Fixed-price contracts

This type of contract sets a predetermined price for a clearly defined product, service, or result. It is ideal for projects with a clearly defined scope of work where significant changes are minimized. Variations of fixed-price contracts include the following:

>> **Firm Fixed Price (FFP).** The price is set and does not change, regardless of the actual cost incurred. This type of contract *places the risk on the seller* as they are responsible for completing the project within the agreed-upon price. As an example, a hospital contracts a construction company to build a new wing at a fixed price of $2 million. Regardless of the construction company's actual cost, the hospital will pay only the agreed amount.

>> **Fixed Price Plus Incentive Fee (FPIF).** This contract type is similar to FFP, but includes a provision for performance-based incentive. The seller receives additional compensation for meeting or exceeding certain performance criteria. Going back to the hospital example, the hospital enters into a contract with a software developer to create a new patient management system. The contract is for $500,000 with an incentive fee of $50,000 if the system is delivered three months early and meets specified performance standards.

>> **Fixed Price with Economic Price Adjustment (FPEPA).** This allows for adjustments to the contract price due to specific economic conditions such as inflation or cost changes for specific materials. For example, a hospital may contract a supplier for a five-year supply of specialized radiology equipment. Given the long-term nature of the contract and potential market fluctuations, the agreement includes an economic price adjustment clause. This clause allows for a price adjustment based on changes in specific economic factors such as the cost of rare materials used in the equipment or changes in currency exchange rates. This ensures that the supplier is not adversely affected by unforeseen economic conditions over the long term of the contract.

Overall, fixed-price contracts shift the risk onto the seller. Fixed-price contracts are typically the preferred contract type of the buyer.

## Cost-reimbursable contract types

With cost-reimbursable contract types, the buyer reimburses the seller for all allowable costs incurred for the completed work, along with an additional fee that represents the seller's profit.

- **Cost Plus Fixed Fee (CPFF).** The seller is reimbursed for all allowed expenses to a set limit plus an additional payment; this payment is a fixed fee that is calculated as a percentage of the initial estimated project costs. With the hospital example, the hospital contracts an IT firm to upgrade its network infrastructure. The hospital agrees to pay all project costs plus a fixed fee of 10 percent of the project's estimated costs.

- **Cost Plus Incentive Fee (CPIF).** This contract type provides the seller with an additional incentive fee for meeting or exceeding agreed-upon performance or cost targets. For example, a hospital contracts with a developer to create a new electronic health record system under a CPIF agreement. If the developer completes the project under budget, the hospital shares the cost savings with the developer as a bonus. This incentive motivates the seller to control costs and deliver value efficiently. And what if they are over budget? The additional costs are typically shared between the buyer and seller based on a pre-established formula. In the hospital example, both the hospital and the developer may share the overrun costs, reducing the seller's incentive fee or eliminating it entirely. The flip side of this contract type encourages the seller to stay within budget to avoid financial penalties and maintain profitability.

- **Cost Plus Award Fee (CPAF).** This combines payment for allowable costs with an additional award fee based on the seller meeting broad, performance-based criteria. What sets CPAF apart is that the award fee is entirely subjective, determined solely based on the buyer's evaluation of the seller's performance. In the hospital example, the hospital contracts a consulting firm to improve operational efficiency under a CPAF agreement. The firm is eligible for an award fee if patient throughput increases by a percentage that the hospital deems acceptable (though not explicitly specified in the contract). Whether or not the seller receives the award fee depends on the hospital's subjective assessment of performance, with no set formula to determine success. Additionally, decisions regarding the award fee are typically final and not subject to appeals.

Generally speaking, cost-reimbursable contract types shift the risk onto the buyer.

### Time and Materials contracts

The third type of contract is Time and Materials (T&M), also known as Time and Means. Under this arrangement, the seller is compensated for the time spent performing the work and reimbursed for the cost of materials used. T&M contracts are appropriate when the project scope or duration is uncertain, making it difficult to define a precise statement of work up front.

This type of contract is commonly used for staff augmentation, hiring specialized experts, or securing external support for tasks where exact requirements aren't immediately clear. For example, in the hospital example, the hospital might hire a team of electricians under a T&M contract to handle maintenance and repair work. The electricians are paid an hourly rate, and the hospital reimburses the cost of materials they use. T&M contracts offer flexibility but require close oversight to ensure time and costs stay within reasonable limits. A defining feature of T&M contracts is the inclusion of a not-to-exceed (NTE) clause, which sets a maximum cost limit.

With time and materials, the risk is shared between the buyer and the seller.

### Choosing the right type of contract

The choice of contract type depends on the project scope complexity and the level of risk the buyer is willing to accept. Hopefully, the hospital setting examples clarified the application of each contract type, demonstrating how they can be utilized in real-world scenarios.

TIP

In practice, organizations may blend multiple contract types within a single procurement. However, expect to identify a single contract type as the correct answer on the PMP Exam. It's unlikely you'll encounter an option like "A and B" (for example, both Fixed Price and Cost-Reimbursable). Stay focused on the specific characteristics of each type.

## Ensuring procurement integration

An important step with procurement management is ensuring that you integrate your procurement activities with other planning areas and that your procurement decisions align with the overall objectives of the project. Here are some key considerations:

- » Align your procurement activities with the project timeline, including milestones and critical path.
- » Understand how risk related to vendors, contractual obligations, and supply chain and cost fluctuations can impact your project plans.

- » Ensure that procured items meet the project's quality standards and requirements.
- » Integrate the procurement costs into the overall project budget, as you will need to have an understanding and adherence to contractual terms and conditions.

Procurement planning isn't a simple task; it's a complex process that often requires close coordination with a dedicated procurement department. A thorough planning of procurement needs results in potential change requests, project document updates, and OPA updates. The unique key project artifacts created from the procurement planning efforts include the following:

- » **Procurement Management Plan:** Outlines the procurement activities and is a component of the Project Management Plan.
- » **Procurement strategy:** Establishes the project delivery method, type of contracts to be used, and outlines the steps for navigating the procurement process.
- » **Bid documents:** Tools used to request proposals from potential sellers.
- » **Procurement statement of work:** Specifies the portion of the project scope that will be included in the associated contract.
- » **Source selection criteria:** Results of the source selection analysis that details the evaluation criteria to select one or more successful bidders.
- » **Make-or-buy decisions:** Documents whether work will be completed internally or outsourced based on a make-or-buy analysis.
- » **Independent cost estimates:** Provides a benchmark on evaluating proposed costs; can be prepared internally or sourced externally, often used for large procurements.

## Looking at procurement management in adaptive projects

Procurement management success in the adaptive environment requires an Agile mindset from buyers and sellers, where adaptability and partnership are key. In the case of procuring services, sellers often act as extensions of the team, integrating their expertise to meet the project goals. As for contracts, they are dynamic agreements designed to accommodate the evolving scope of work, with built-in provisions for change that preserve the overall agreement. The buyer and seller must collaborate to navigate shifts in requirements and uncertainties, ensuring the contract stays aligned with the project's objectives while fostering a collaborative approach. Same team. Same dream.

# Addressing the People Factor in Planning

Two other planning efforts that address the people side of things in your projects include plan resource management and plan stakeholder engagement processes. In Chapters 11 and 12, each process and its corresponding activities and plans are described in detail. However, it's worth looking at those areas here to bring everything together.

TIP

Take note of how the term *engagement* is used in the context of stakeholders. In earlier iterations of the PMP Exam content, the focus was on "stakeholder management." But let's be real: you can't manage stakeholders. What you can do is observe their level of engagement and find ways to influence it effectively. If you see "stakeholder management" as an answer option on the exam, consider it a potential trap designed to throw you off.

## Planning for the project resource needs

The *plan resource management process* encompasses all of the activities to acquire the necessary resources (people and physical resources), develop and manage the project team, and come up with a plan that aligns the human talent, skills, and supporting resources with the project needs. The output of this process, the Resource Management Plan, serves as a comprehensive guide that outlines how resources will be identified, acquired, utilized, and managed throughout the project's life cycle. The purpose is to ensure that the right resources are available at the right time, in the right quantities, and with the necessary skill sets and expertise to successfully execute the project. Here are some key questions the Resource Management Plan answers:

- » What resources are required?
- » What quantity of each type of resource is needed?
- » When and how long will each resource be needed?
- » How will the resources be acquired?
- » Are the resources available internally or will the procurement department need to be involved?
- » What will be the cost of the resources?
- » Is there a limited time during which the resources will be available?
- » How will resources be managed?

During resource management planning, the project manager (perhaps with the help of the project management team) conducts the *estimate activity resources process* to determine the team resources as well as the types and quantities of materials, equipment, and supplies needed to complete the project work. Effective resource planning is instrumental to the efficient execution of a project.

## Aligning stakeholder expectations

The *plan stakeholder engagement* process focuses on aligning stakeholder needs and expectations with the project's progress and deliverables. Stakeholders are the linchpin of project management. It is, after all, stakeholders who identify the need for the project. It is the expectations of stakeholders that you need to document and to ensure they are met and satisfied.

Effective project management begins with a thorough stakeholder identification and analysis, utilizing tools such as stakeholder matrices and Power Interest Grids, enabling project managers to assess the influence and interest levels of each stakeholder and plan accordingly. Stakeholder engagement is a systematic process that leverages technical tools and frameworks to maintain clear communication, manage expectations, and foster stakeholder support, which is important for achieving your project goals. A comprehensive Stakeholder Engagement Plan provides a guide for how stakeholder engagement will be monitored and influenced throughout the project, ensuring that stakeholder needs are met and their impact on the project is as beneficial as possible. The Stakeholder Engagement Plan outlines how stakeholders will be engaged from start to finish and answers the following key questions:

>> What are the interests and expectations of each stakeholder?

>> What is the potential impact or influence of each stakeholder on the project?

>> What's the level of impact of each stakeholder, both good and bad?

>> What is the planned approach for stakeholder engagement?

>> What methods of communication will be used?

The Stakeholder Engagement Plan helps project managers establish a systematic approach to engage stakeholders, leading to better communication alignment and collaboration. The plan enables project managers to identify different stakeholder groups and develop tailored and customized engagement strategies based on their needs, interests, and influence. It ensures that engagement efforts are targeted and effective.

**TIP** Stakeholder engagement ensures that stakeholders are actively involved and supportive while communication management ensures that stakeholders are informed and aligned with the project objectives.

**REMEMBER** Tools, techniques, and processes are important, but at the end of the day, the success of any project comes down to the people involved and how well they work together. According to the *PMBOK Guide* Seventh Edition: Projects are performed by people and for people.

The preceding statement captures the human side of project management, reminding you that no matter how technical or procedural things get, the success and even the start of any project depends on the people involved.

## MEMORY SPRINT

Rapidly recall and jot down key PMP concepts, terms, and ideas using prompts to jog your memory. Set a timer for 15 minutes. When you're done, review your work to highlight areas where you feel confident, and circle concepts you need to revisit. Use the following prompts to guide your thinking and see what else you can recall:

- What's the difference between plan quality management, manage quality, and control quality?
- Describe the categories of the cost of quality (CoQ) and the subcategories.
- What are the three communication methods?
- Write down key words that comprise the elements of the communication model.
- What are the four communication types?
- What are the 5Cs of written communication?
- What are the risk response strategies to deal with threats (negative risks)?
- What are the risk response strategies to deal with opportunities (positive risks)?
- A list of individual risks and the risk responses are captured on a _____ _____.
- Risks that score low on probability and impact are placed on a _____ _____.
- What are the three major contract types?
- Why would you use one contract type over another? (Hint: It's about shifting risk. . .)
- The result of the make or buy analysis is the make or buy _____.
- What is the document called that lists all the project stakeholders?

## IN THIS CHAPTER

» Explaining the concept of project integration management

» Exploring the responsibilities of the project manager in project integration

» Developing a Change Control Plan, Configuration Management Plan, and change log

» Differentiating between Change Control and Configuration Management Plans

» Reviewing the components of a comprehensive Project Management Plan

» Analyzing the approach to planning in an Agile environment

Chapter **15**

# Integration of Plans and Processes

At the heart of every successful project lies the integrated Project Management Plan, a comprehensive document primarily used in the predictive environment that combines the various planning elements into a unified whole. Within this chapter, you will find out how all of the plans coalesce into this comprehensive master plan. The creation of all the various plans lays the groundwork for understanding the goals and direction of the project. These plans serve as detailed guides for balancing scope, schedule, and costs, engaging your stakeholders, managing communications, appropriately allocating resources, and more, thus providing a framework for anticipating and addressing challenges.

However, the effectiveness of these plans is contingent upon their integration into a cohesive whole. That is where project integration comes to the forefront.

The project manager is central to the creation and maintenance of the Project Management Plan.

## Planning: The Final Steps

The activities of the Planning Process Group concludes with the creation of a comprehensive Project Management Plan, integrating all processes, steps, and project artifacts. This plan serves as the definitive guide, outlining the course of action necessary to achieve the project or phase objectives. Once approved, the Project Management Plan becomes the *baseline*, a reference point for tracking and managing performance over the course of the project.

During the Monitoring and Controlling Process Group, the project team evaluates project performance against the baseline. Deviations are analyzed, and corrective actions are implemented to stay aligned with project objectives.

The term *baseline* indicates the approval of a plan. Think of it as a line in the sand. Any changes to the baseline require going through the change control process. Interestingly, *baseline* can also be used as a verb: to "baseline" something means to approve it.

Integrating all subsidiary plans into the Project Management Plan truly signifies the completion of the Planning Process Group and sets the foundation for successful project execution.

## Integrating Project Management Activities

*Project integration management* encompasses the processes and activities needed to identify, define, combine, unify, and coordinate the various processes and project management activities.

It involves making choices about resource allocation, balancing project constraints, and ensuring that all project elements are coordinated and work together effectively. The focus is on tying everything together.

Project integration ensures that the project progresses smoothly without any discrepancies between its various components. Integration management is important to minimize silos, align project outcomes with strategic goals, and ensure a cohesive project execution.

The intersection of project integration and the Planning Process Group is the development of the Project Management Plan that will eventually be baselined. This means that all key stakeholders will review and approve the plan as the path forward to achieving project success. Any changes to the plan would require a change request.

Why? If you agree to the plan as the path to success, then you had better make sure everyone is on the same page about the change in direction to meet the project goals.

# The Project Manager: The Expert Project Integrator

As you may have guessed, project integration is the project manager's responsibility and should not be delegated. The project manager is tasked with managing interdependencies between processes, balancing competing objectives, and making trade-offs to achieve project goals.

The key responsibilities of the project manager include the following:

>> Acting as the central coordinator for all project components.

>> Maintaining alignment between the project plan and stakeholder expectations.

>> Overseeing updates and integration of all subsidiary plans.

>> Making decisions on prioritizing changes and resolving conflicts.

The project manager is ultimately accountable for achieving the project objectives. To succeed, project managers must possess the competencies outlined in the PMI Talent Triangle:

>> **Power Skills.** Effectively managing people and fostering collaboration.

>> **Ways of Working.** Utilizing project management methodologies, tools, and techniques to guide execution.

>> **Business Acumen.** Understanding the business environment to align the project with organizational goals.

By leveraging these skills, the project manager ensures effective coordination of the project's moving parts and guides the team toward successful outcomes.

# Changes are Possible: Creating a Change Control Plan

As the Project Management Plan is being developed, two very important subsidiary plans are created and become elements of it: the Change Control Plan and the Configuration Management Plan. Specifically, the Change Control Plan outlines the process for managing changes to the project. This includes changes to scope, schedule, costs, or any aspect that could impact the project deliverables.

A *Change Control Plan* provides a structured approach for addressing changes, ensuring that the project remains aligned with the objectives and can adapt. While tight controls are put in place to minimize unruly changes, having a Change Control Plan enables the project to adapt to changes, maintaining project viability even as external or internal conditions evolve (think, new leadership wants to make a change in direction, new legislation requires specifications that were not planned, or the client requests a scope change).

TIP

You may see the term *Change Management Plan* being used interchangeably with *Change Control Plan*. The term *Change Control Plan* was introduced in the *PMBOK Guide* Seventh Edition to differentiate it from the broader concept of organizational change management, which emphasizes the organization's ability to adapt to and embrace changes in outcomes. In some cases, organizations develop a dedicated Change Management Plan specifically to address their strategies for adapting to change.

By proactively managing changes, you can effectively address stakeholder expectations, resulting in improved satisfaction and support for the project. The Change Control Plan also supports risk management by identifying and addressing risks related to changes, ensuring the project's risk profile remains within acceptable limits. Key elements of the Change Control Plan include the following:

>> **Change control board:** Decision-making authority for proposed changes.

>> **Documentation:** Process for logging and tracking changes.

>> **Evaluation:** Criteria for approving, rejecting, or deferring changes.

**REMEMBER** A key project artifact for documenting changes is the *change log*. It provides a detailed record of changes, decisions, and adjustments made during the project, which is vital for accountability, knowledge sharing, and future planning.

# Maintaining Control with the Configuration Management Plan

The other important subsidiary plan to the Project Management Plan is the *Configuration Management Plan*, which outlines the processes and procedures for maintaining control over project artifacts, including documents, software, hardware, and other assets.

The value behind the Configuration Management Plan is that it ensures that these items are identified, documented, managed, and tracked continuously. The plan helps you manage product features and functionality, ensuring consistency and maintaining the integrity and traceability of configuration items.

In layman's terms, the Configuration Management Plan is similar in nature to "version control" for your project's important items, such as documents, designs, or products. It ensures that everyone is working with the latest version and helps keep everything organized. Think of it as making sure there's a clear system for labeling, saving, and updating files so no one accidentally uses an old or incorrect version.

## Comparing change control and configuration management

While both plans deal with managing changes within a project, they focus on different aspects. The Change Control Plan aims to ensure that changes are systematically managed, whereas the Configuration Management Plan focuses on managing project outputs and components to ensure they remain in a known state and are correctly aligned with project needs.

The Change Control Plan addresses the following question:

*If a client requests a scope change mid-project, how do we assess its impact on cost, time, and quality?*

The Configuration Management Plan addresses the following question:

*What if a team member uses an outdated version of a website design file during development?*

Here is the difference in simple terms.

- **Change Control Plan:** Decides how to handle change requests and documents the impact on the project.
- **Configuration Management Plan:** Keeps things organized and up to date (version control).

Both plans work together — one to manage changes (Change Control Plan) and the other to ensure project deliverables and processes remain consistent with approved specifications (Configuration Management Plan).

### Test your knowledge: Change Control or Configuration Management?

Instructions: Match each statement to the correct plan: Change Control Plan or Configuration Management Plan. See the end of the chapter for the answers.

1. Keeps a record of approved iterations of documents, designs, or deliverables.
2. Ensures team members are working with the most up-to-date project materials.
3. Ensures all project stakeholders are informed about approved changes.
4. Tracks the impact of changes on scope, schedule, and budget.
5. Identifies items that require version control and outlines how updates will be managed.

## Developing a Comprehensive Project Management Plan

A key project artifact in predictive projects, the *Project Management Plan* is a comprehensive document that integrates and aligns all aspects of the project. It integrates all subsidiary plans and acts as a roadmap, guiding the project team through execution and ensuring all stakeholders are aligned on the project's goals, processes, and expectations.

The plan is composed of two main types of components: baselines and management plans. Together, these elements provide a structured framework for monitoring and controlling the project's progress, addressing risks, and managing changes.

» **Baselines** establish reference points for scope, schedule, and cost, forming the performance measurement baseline that helps assess project performance.

» **Management plans** provide detailed guidelines on how various aspects of the project will be managed, such as scope, schedule, cost, quality, resources, risks, and stakeholder engagement.

TIP

Management plans focus on the *how* by providing guidance on processes and methodologies. They generally do not detail the *what* because specific information, such as activity cost estimates or risks, is recorded separately in project documents.

Each plan component offers a clear approach for executing and monitoring project activities while maintaining alignment with organizational objectives.

There are three baselines in project management:

» **Scope baseline.** Includes the approved version of the project scope statement, work breakdown structure (WBS), and the WBS dictionary.

» **Schedule baseline.** Represents the approved project schedule, excluding management reserves.

» **Cost baseline.** Represents the time-phased project budget, excluding management reserves.

The integration of these baselines forms the *performance measurement baseline*, which is used to assess project performance.

Management plan components of the Project Management Plan include the following:

» **Scope Management Plan:** Outlines the processes for planning, defining, validating, and controlling the project scope.

» **Requirements Management Plan:** Describes how requirements will be collected, managed, and controlled, including handling changes to requirements.

CHAPTER 15 **Integration of Plans and Processes** 251

- **Schedule Management Plan:** Defines the methods and tools for planning, managing, and controlling the project schedule.
- **Cost Management Plan:** Defines the procedures for estimating, budgeting, and controlling project costs.
- **Quality Management Plan:** Explains how the Quality Policy will be executed and how quality assurance and quality control processes will be carried out.
- **Resource Management Plan:** Details roles and responsibilities, the project organization chart, and the staffing plan.
- **Communications Management Plan:** Identifies stakeholder communication requirements, communication methods, and technologies to be used.
- **Risk Management Plan:** Describes the approach to risk management, including methodology, budget, roles, risk categories, tracking systems, and probability/impact assessment.
- **Procurement Management Plan:** Describes the procedures for procuring goods and services, including conducting, managing, and closing procurements.
- **Stakeholder Engagement Plan:** Outlines strategies for ensuring stakeholder involvement and engagement throughout the project.
- **Change Control Plan (also known as a Change Management Plan):** Focuses on identifying, documenting, and controlling changes to the project and its baselines.
- **Configuration Management Plan:** Defines how configuration management will be conducted, including identifying configurable items, applying formal change control, and managing version control.
- **Project life cycle description:** Defines the series of phases the project will progress through.
- **Development approach:** Describes the methodology for delivering the product, service, or result, such as predictive, incremental, iterative, or adaptive (Agile).
- **Management reviews:** Identify key points for reviewing project progress with stakeholders to determine if performance aligns with expectations or if corrective actions are needed.

This comprehensive set of components ensures that all aspects of the project are planned, managed, and aligned with the overall objectives.

The Project Management Plan provides holistic oversight, which is essential to maintaining coherence and ensuring every element of the project remains in sync.

Keep in mind, this master plan is regularly reviewed and updated by the project manager (contingent upon approved change requests) throughout the project's life cycle to help address changes and sustain alignment with the project's goals.

Significant changes to any component of the Project Management Plan require submitting a change request and following the change control process outlined in the Change Control Plan.

## Approving the Project Management Plan

Formal approval, complete with signatures from management, the sponsor, the project team, and key stakeholders, signals the green light for the project. This approval of the plan is usually accompanied by a kickoff meeting where expectations are aligned, a shared understanding is established, and commitment is secured before execution begins. The kickoff sets the tone for the project or phase, ensuring everyone is ready to move forward. In Agile projects, this meeting is called *Sprint 0*, laying the foundation for the first sprint and gearing the team up to hit the ground running.

For multiphase projects, a kickoff meeting is usually held at the start of each phase.

## Using project documents to stay on track

In predictive projects — particularly large-scale ones — the planning process often results in the creation of numerous project documents that support the project manager in monitoring and managing project performance. These are the working documents of the project and typically do not require a change request for updates.

While you will not be expected to memorize all of the documents, it may be helpful to familiarize yourself with the list of major project documents that may appear on the exam. The following list represents the key project documents that are created during initiation and planning; updated all the way through execution, to monitoring and controlling; and archived at the point of project or phase completion.

- » **Activity attributes:** Detailed information about each activity in the project.
- » **Activity list:** A list of all project activities.
- » **Assumption log:** A record of all project assumptions and constraints.
- » **Basis of estimates:** Additional details explaining how estimates were developed.

- **Change log:** A record of all requested changes in the project and their disposition (that is, approved, rejected, or deferred).
- **Cost estimates:** Estimated costs associated with project activities.
- **Cost forecasts:** Predictions of future costs required to complete the project.
- **Duration estimates:** Estimated time required to complete project activities.
- **Issue log:** A record of ongoing and resolved project issues, including their resolutions.
- **Lessons learned register:** Documentation of lessons gained throughout the project life cycle.
- **Milestone list:** A list of key project milestones, which are significant points with zero duration.
- **Project calendars:** Documents showing the project team's working days, dates, and times.
- **Project communications:** Information distributed to stakeholders during the project.
- **Project schedule:** The start and end dates, as well as milestones required to keep the project on track.
- **Project schedule network diagram:** Visual representation of the sequence of activities in the project.
- **Project scope statement:** A detailed description of the work required to complete the project, including exclusions (work that will not be done).
- **Project team assignments:** Information about project team members and their roles.
- **Quality control measurements:** Data collected from inspections of deliverables.
- **Quality metrics:** Descriptions of the attributes the product or project must meet.
- **Quality report:** A summary of quality issues, recommended improvements, and corrective actions.
- **Requirements documentation:** A detailed account of all project requirements, showing how they meet business needs.
- **Requirements traceability matrix:** A tool that links product requirements to deliverables that fulfill them.

- **Resource breakdown structure:** A hierarchical breakdown of resources organized by categories and types.
- **Resource calendar:** Documentation of the working days, dates, and times for each resource (such as team members and equipment).
- **Resource requirements:** The types, quantities, and skills needed for project resources.
- **Responsibility assignment matrix (RAM):** A grid showing assigned resources to project work packages or activities. A RACI chart is a common type of RAM that uses responsible, accountable, consult, and inform categories to define stakeholder involvement in project activities.
- **Risk breakdown structure (RBS):** A hierarchical categorization of potential sources of risk.
- **Risk register:** A record of all identified project risks.
- **Risk report:** A summary of risks, opportunities, current actions, and trends.
- **Schedule data:** All schedule-specific details for the project.
- **Schedule forecasts:** Projections of future schedule adjustments based on current information.
- **Stakeholder engagement assessment matrix (SEAM):** A grid that compares the current and desired stakeholder engagement levels.
- **Stakeholder register:** A list of all project stakeholders and their relevant details.
- **Team charter:** A document outlining team direction, ground rules, and shared expectations.

This list is not exhaustive, and you won't need to memorize all the project documents. However, it's important to familiarize yourself with the terms and to bookmark this page for easy reference.

TIP

Here are some quick recall tips:

- Any document that is a *matrix* is tying back to something or making a link.
- A *register, list,* or *log* is a laundry list of that information — think of the information as being listed in a spreadsheet.
- A *report* provides a summary of that information.
- A *breakdown structure* is a hierarchical breakdown of that information.

# Developing an Agile Project Management Plan

Planning in the adaptive environment is more high-level compared to the detailed planning that occurs in the predictive project environment. As such, a Project Management Plan is typically not a project artifact developed for Agile teams.

If you come across a PMP Exam question describing the use of Agile tools and techniques alongside a Project Management Plan, it likely represents a hybrid approach in action.

Many adaptive projects rely on a product roadmap rather than a traditional Project Management Plan. A *product roadmap* is a high-level planning tool that visually outlines the anticipated sequence of deliverables over time. It depicts product releases and the components included in each release. This flexible plan is confirmed or adjusted as needed for each release, making it an effective communication tool for keeping stakeholders informed and aligned.

## Iteration planning

While Agile projects don't involve creating detailed, upfront plans as with predictive approaches, planning is very much a part of the process. Iteration planning (sprint planning) focuses on real-time, collaborative decision-making, enabling Agile teams to prioritize and prepare for the upcoming iteration. During this time, teams discuss backlog items with the product owner, use tools like planning poker (see Chapter 16 for more information on planning poker), and align on the work ahead.

Two critical discussions frame this practice:

>> **Definition of Done (DoD):** The Agile team's checklist of criteria that must be met for a deliverable to be considered ready for customer use. Often referenced during the iteration review (sprint review), the DoD ensures that deliverables meet the agreed-upon acceptance criteria. Think of it as the Agile counterpart to acceptance criteria in predictive projects.

>> **Definition of Ready (DoR):** The Agile team's checklist for ensuring a requirement is ready to start. This user-focused list ensures that the team has all necessary information before beginning work.

Iteration planning ensures that Agile teams have a clear focus and shared understanding of priorities for the upcoming iteration. It's a purposeful exercise that sets the stage for meaningful work, enabling teams to align on objectives, reduce ambiguity, and deliver value incrementally. Planning happens in Agile — it just happens differently.

## Addressing Agile project changes

In Agile projects, embracing change is a core principle, seamlessly integrated into the workflow. However, this doesn't mean changes are made haphazardly. Instead, changes are carefully managed, with the product owner serving as the gatekeeper for what gets added to the product backlog. This ensures that new ideas and adjustments align with the project's overall goals and priorities.

It's equally important to note that while the product backlog evolves to "respond to change," no changes are made during an active iteration. This approach protects the team's focus and ensures that commitments made for the iteration are delivered without disruption.

### MEMORY SPRINT

Rapidly recall and jot down key PMP concepts, terms, and ideas using prompts to jog your memory. Set a timer for 15 minutes. When you're done, review your work to highlight areas where you feel confident, and circle concepts you need to revisit. Use the following prompts to guide your thinking and see what else you can recall:

- What are the five Process Groups?
- What is the difference between change control and configuration management?
- Recall all of the components of the Project Management Plan. (Hint: there are 13 plans and 3 baselines, including 3 additional elements of the plan.)
- The Agile "plan" is called a _____ roadmap.
- What is the Agile kickoff meeting called?
- Who is responsible for maintaining the product backlog?
- Combining predictive and Agile is what kind of life cycle?

# Answer Key: Change Control or Configuration Management?

1. Configuration Management Plan
2. Configuration Management Plan
3. Change Control Plan
4. Change Control Plan
5. Configuration Management Plan

**IN THIS CHAPTER**

» Exploring the role and significance of the Execution Process Group in project management

» Reviewing the Direct and Manage Project Work process and its components

» Leveraging explicit and tacit knowledge on projects

» Exploring the concepts of managing quality

» Describing strategies for managing procurements and vendor relationships

» Evaluating decision-making processes within Agile teams

Chapter **16**

# Turning Your Plan into Action

This chapter delves into the activities and concepts required to execute a project successfully. You'll explore key activities related to directing and managing the project work, managing issues, and implementing approved change requests. Additionally, I'll unpack the nuances of work performance data, information, and reports — distinctions that drive effective decision-making and clear communication in any project.

Effective project execution is more than just following the Project Management Plan. The project manager must demonstrate ongoing oversight, adaptability, and decisive leadership. The Project Management Plan lays the foundation, but it's the project manager's ability to lead, coordinate, and make critical decisions that drives progress toward objectives.

Knowledge management is another focal area of this chapter, emphasizing the distinction between explicit and tacit knowledge and exploring best practices for leveraging these insights.

You'll also review project artifacts and their role in capturing and sharing valuable information.

Quality management concepts, such as quality audits, and the fundamentals of risk management, including quantifying risks and addressing risks in Agile projects, are addressed to ensure comprehensive execution strategies. Additionally, this chapter covers key practices for managing procurements and vendor relationships, highlighting strategies to streamline collaboration with external stakeholders.

To further support Agile project teams, you'll explore the tools and techniques for effective decision-making, including information radiator tools that enhance transparency and communication.

As you read this chapter, take time to reflect on how each concept integrates with the larger framework of project management and how it is applied in real-world scenarios.

# Executing Process Group

Orchestrating a project effectively requires navigating the complexities of execution with finesse and precision. At the heart of this endeavor lies the *Executing Process Group*, a critical point in your project where plans are put into action, resources are mobilized, and deliverables are produced. Execution is where the carefully crafted plans from your planning activities are transformed into tangible outcomes, setting the stage for achievement.

During project execution, the project manager is the driving force that keeps the project aligned and moving forward. The project manager provides leadership and direction, communication and coordination, and oversight, ensuring that the project progresses smoothly toward the objectives despite challenges and uncertainties. Among other tasks, the project manager is responsible for resource management, risk management, quality assurance, conflict management, ensuring that the project and the team members are adaptable and flexible.

The specific processes that fall under this process group include the following:

- Direct and manage project work
- Manage project knowledge
- Manage quality
- Acquire resources
- Develop team
- Manage team
- Manage communications
- Implement risk responses
- Conduct procurements
- Manage stakeholder engagement

These processes are the foundation of effective project execution, transforming plans into action. As you progress through the following sections, you'll build on this foundation, gaining deeper insights into how these processes work.

# Directing and Managing Project Work

An important process within execution is the *Direct and Manage Project Work process*, which involves overseeing and performing the work defined in the Project Management Plan. With this process, the project manager mobilizes resources, assigns tasks, and ensures that project activities are executed according to plan.

## Tracking and resolving issues

A key responsibility of the project manager is to manage and resolve issues, ensuring they don't derail the project progress. An *issue* is a current condition or situation impacting the project objectives. Issues in project management refer to any problematic events, obstacles, or deviations from the project plan that can adversely impact the project objectives, timelines, or deliverables. These can range from minor setbacks to significant challenges that require immediate attention and resolution. Issues are documented on an *issue log*. The issue log can be used to communicate new issues as well as the resolution of current issues. It facilitates the assessment of causes and impact of issues and makes recommendations for corrective actions. The issue log also lets stakeholders know their concerns are being addressed.

Figure 16-1 provides an illustration of an issue log from an Electronic Medical Records (EMR) case study.

| Issue ID | Description | Impact | Priority | Issue Owner | Status | Resolution Deadline |
|---|---|---|---|---|---|---|
| 001 | Delayed delivery of server hardware from the vendor. | Server delay may postpone software configuration, affecting overall timeline. | High | Ronnie | Open | 12/5/2024 |
| 002 | Integration API documentation from the third-party lab system is incomplete. | Incomplete API documentation is delaying integration testing. | High | Bobby | Open | 12/3/2024 |
| 003 | User training sessions are behind schedule due to resource availability. | Training delay may impact user readiness for system go-live. | Medium | Ricky | In Progress | 12/10/2024 |
| 004 | Data migration encountered compatibility issues with legacy system formats. | Compatibility issues may require rework, extending data migration timeline. | High | Mike | Open | 12/7/2024 |
| 005 | Compliance audit findings require additional updates to meet HIPAA standards. | Non-compliance could delay go-live and lead to regulatory penalties. | Critical | Ralph | Open | 12/1/2024 |

FIGURE 16-1: An issue log from an EMR case study.

© John Wiley & Sons, Inc.

Each issue has an assigned *issue owner* who is responsible for addressing a specific issue and communicating with the project manager about the effectiveness of resolution strategies.

In Agile projects, issues are tracked using an impediments board, which is prominently displayed for the entire team to see. The *impediments board* is a highly visible tool that fosters transparency and quick resolution. It keeps the team focused on removing blockers and maintaining momentum, making it an action-oriented resource to address issues in real time.

TIP

Risks and issues are two distinct concepts, although they are closely related. A *risk* is an uncertain event or condition whose occurrence could have a positive or negative impact on the project's objectives. Risks are documented on the risk register. Issues are current situations. They will always have a negative impact on the project. You document your issues in the issue log.

## Implementing approved changes

In predictive projects, the project manager takes the lead to ensure approved change requests are implemented (emphasis on *approved*). These approved change requests have gone through formal change control procedures, where the impacts on scope, schedule, budget, and resources have been evaluated and the project manager has updated plans accordingly. Implementation of approved change requests also means the project manager will monitor progress, keep an eye on risks, resolve issues, and communicate with stakeholders to keep them in the loop.

In Agile projects, teams handle changes dynamically, incorporating them directly into the iterative cycles of work without needing separate approval steps (that is, change requests are not a part of the mix). This flexibility allows teams to adjust quickly and to continuously deliver value.

## Generating work performance insights

During execution, the project manager collects work performance data to analyze and compare it against the project plans. This data forms the foundation for deeper insights into project progress and performance through the creation of work performance information and reports.

Let's break down each concept to understand how they contribute to effective project management.

- **Work performance data:** The raw numbers — metrics, measurements, and observations — collected during project execution. This unprocessed data captures the nitty-gritty details of activities, resources, schedules, costs, and quality, forming the foundation for tracking and assessing performance.

- **Work performance information:** The story behind the data. Analyzed and synthesized, it reveals trends, patterns, and actionable insights. This is where raw numbers become meaningful, guiding project managers in identifying issues, spotting opportunities, and keeping the project on course. At a minimum, it ensures stakeholders stay in the loop.

- **Work performance reports:** The polished package. These formal documents take insights from work performance information and deliver them to stakeholders with purpose. Think key metrics, status updates, variance analysis, forecasts, and recommendations — all designed to inform, engage, and align everyone with the project's goals.

Work performance data, information, and reports are integral components of project management that provide valuable insights into the project's progress, performance, and health. Work performance information and reports are typically produced as a part of monitoring and controlling activities.

A helpful mnemonic to recall the order of work performance summary is **Details Inspire Results**. *Data* provides the details, *information* inspires understanding, and *reports* deliver results. I hope this helps!

# Managing Project Knowledge

Throughout a project, the project manager and team convert information into knowledge through understanding, applying, and reflecting. At the same time, you are converting knowledge back into information by documenting, summarizing, communicating, and cataloging. It's a dynamic cycle that enhances project outcomes and contributes to organizational learning.

Information is the raw input that serves as the foundation for knowledge. Knowledge is the result of processing and understanding that information, transforming it into actionable insights and understanding. Communication facilitates the exchange of information, which, when processed and understood, becomes knowledge. This knowledge, when captured and managed effectively, becomes an invaluable resource for future projects, promoting continuous improvement.

## Differentiating levels of knowledge

Projects play an important role in building an organization's knowledge base by uncovering new processes and sharing of successes. This growth happens on three distinct levels.

- **Individual level:** Each team member needs to know how to perform their work under each assigned activity's scope, schedule, and cost, all while maintaining an acceptable level of quality. If a person does not possess the required knowledge for a particular task, they should acquire it by one of three methods: researching the topic to find out what they do not know, examining the project's or organization's knowledge repository, or collaborating with other team members to fill the knowledge gap.

- **Project level:** The focus is on achieving the goals of the current project. The project manager may solicit knowledge from project managers or project leaders involved with other projects, and their experience can be applied to the current project. The Project Management Office, (PMO), is also an excellent source of knowledge, as it exists to define and maintain standards for project management within an organization.

>> **Organizational level:** This level of knowledge concerns managing programs or portfolios. The program manager or portfolio manager can seek information from peers who manage other programs or portfolios to adapt this knowledge to their specific needs.

During execution, the project manager is responsible for managing project knowledge. One of the most important parts of managing knowledge is making sure you learn from past experiences and share those lessons with others. This helps you to avoid repeating mistakes, improves how things are done, and makes future projects more successful. Lessons learned document what went right, what went wrong, and what you should change the next time.

Lessons learned, gathered *throughout* the project life cycle and finalized during closure, are invaluable for refining processes, improving outcomes, and strengthening the organization.

When shared effectively, lessons learned benefit the organization. Of course, this only works in a culture of trust and collaboration. Teams must feel safe sharing knowledge without fear of judgment, and organizations must actively support this with tools such as discussion forums and interactive platforms that foster collaboration.

Assume a best-case scenario: your lessons learned, recommendations, and successes are encouraged, welcomed, and celebrated as drivers of progress. You are a rockstar within the organization.

## Differentiating between explicit and tacit knowledge

Project teams share and manage two types of knowledge. *Explicit knowledge* is information that can be easily articulated, codified, and transferred formally. It is tangible, structured, and can be communicated through various mediums such as documents, manuals, databases, and even verbal communication. This type of knowledge is often objective and can be shared more readily among individuals. Examples of explicit knowledge in project management could include project plans, documentation, templates, process guidelines, and established best practices.

Here's a real-world project management example: Say you're managing a software development project. You have explicit knowledge in the form of a detailed project plan that outlines the tasks, timelines, and responsibilities of each team member. This plan is accessible to all team members and serves as a common reference point throughout the project.

*Tacit knowledge* is subjective and personal. It's the type of knowledge that is deeply rooted in an individual's experience, insights, and intuition. Tacit knowledge is often difficult to articulate, codify, or transfer explicitly because it relies on personal judgment, skills, and context. It is gained through practical experience and is often unspoken or inferred. Tacit knowledge is challenging to formalize and share because it involves the know-how and understanding that comes with doing the work.

For example, consider an experienced project manager who has successfully navigated several complex projects. Their tacit knowledge includes insights on handling team dynamics, anticipating risks, and making quick decisions under pressure. This knowledge isn't easily captured in a document, but it is valuable in guiding the manager's actions and decisions based on their accumulated experience.

Be prepared for a question or two testing your understanding of the concepts of explicit and tacit knowledge.

## Using knowledge-sharing tools and techniques

Project teams are not limited to just one way of sharing knowledge with each other or with the project stakeholders. There are several ways and uses of tools to share knowledge that can benefit the team and the project overall:

- **Mentoring and coaching** occurs when experienced project managers mentor and coach inexperienced or new team members, sharing their tacit knowledge and providing guidance on real-world situations. Refer to Chapter 11 for details about mentoring and coaching.
- **Communities of practice** provide the platform for project managers to interact, discuss challenges, and share their experiences, insights, and best practices.
- **Lessons learned sessions** are conducted regularly where project teams discuss what went well and what could have been improved in completed projects, allowing for the sharing of both successes and failures.
- **Job rotation** encourages team members to rotate roles periodically. This helps to share knowledge and cross-train team members.
- **Pair programming,** often observed on Agile projects, is where project managers or team members pair up on tasks, which can lead to the exchange of different approaches and insights, enhancing the collective knowledge.

- **Networking and storytelling** encourage team members to share anecdotes and stories about their experiences in project management. This can make knowledge more relatable and memorable.
- **Webinars** are hosted virtual sessions where experienced project managers and team members can conduct webinars, workshops, or training sessions to share their expertise with a wider audience.
- **Private social media groups** are dedicated to project management discussions and knowledge-sharing among professionals. This is where teams might set up a "channel" on a collaboration and communication platform.

The effectiveness of these techniques and tools largely depends on the culture of knowledge-sharing within an organization and the willingness of individuals to participate. A combination of both formal and informal methods (lunch-and-learn session, anyone?) can create a rich knowledge-sharing environment that benefits all project team members and stakeholders involved.

## Managing project artifacts

*Project artifacts* are documents, files, or any tangible byproducts produced during a project. They serve as documentation or evidence of the project's progress and are used to communicate, execute, and manage the project through its life cycle. In *predictive projects*, the most common project artifacts produced include the following:

- Project charter
- Project Management Plan (PMP)
- Work breakdown structure (WBS)
- Gantt chart or project schedule
- Risk register
- Change log
- Issue log
- Lessons learned register
- Status reports

Conversely, adaptive projects generate far fewer artifacts compared to traditional projects. However, artifacts are produced (dispelling the myth that Agile means no documentation). Common project artifacts created in adaptive projects include the following:

- Product backlog
- Sprint backlog
- User stories
- Burn charts
- Kanban board
- Incremental deliverables

Managing project artifacts is more than storing and organizing project documents. It's about ensuring artifacts remain accurate, secure, and accessible for team members and key stakeholders. Here are some best-practice tips on how to keep your artifacts in check:

- **Keep them accurate and current:** Regularly review and update artifacts to reflect project progress.
- **Centralize storage:** Use a repository that ensures easy access for authorized stakeholders.
- **Use version control:** Track changes over time to avoid confusion and maintain a clear history.
- **Organize with purpose:** Establish naming conventions and file structures for clarity.
- **Share strategically:** Provide stakeholders with access to relevant artifacts when needed.
- **Secure sensitive data:** Protect confidentiality and ensure compliance with security standards.
- **Archive properly:** Follow project closure procedures for storing artifacts long term.
- **Follow the rules:** Adhere to organizational policies and standards for artifact management.

Artifacts are the project's memory bank, documenting decisions, actions, and expenditures. They're vital for keeping the project on track, supporting audits, ensuring compliance, and serving as a resource for future initiatives.

**TIP** Savvy project managers also tap into organizational process assets (OPAs) — a treasure trove of historical information, lessons learned, policies, procedures, and artifacts from past and current projects. Leveraging OPAs is good practice and a power move that fosters learning, drives innovation, and benefits the project in delivering value.

# Managing Quality

The *manage quality process* involves implementing the Quality Management Plan and ensuring project deliverables meet the specified quality requirements. The focus is on how work is done, ensuring that the team follows policies, standards, and processes. This step evaluates the need for improvements in the quality plan or processes. There are numerous tools to aid in managing quality.

The manage quality process involves conducting quality audits. A *quality audit* is a structured and independent review of the process and project workflows. Here are some key points about the quality audit:

» It is used to verify that project processes are being performed according to defined standards and requirements, ensuring that project deliverables meet quality expectations and stakeholder needs.

» It contributes to the project's continuous improvement efforts.

» It is independent of the project manager, project team, and even the sponsor. The quality audit should be performed by an individual or group who is not involved in the project to remove bias.

*Continuous improvement* is an important aspect of quality management, emphasizing the iterative process of enhancing processes, products, and services over time. Continuous improvement encourages innovation and creativity, empowering project teams to explore new approaches, technologies, and best practices. Examples of continuous improvement frameworks include Six Sigma, Plan-Do-Check-Act cycle (PDCA cycle), and Kaizen, as well as the application of Agile methodologies such as Scrum, Crystal, Kanban, Scrumban, and many other Agile practices.

**TIP** *Kaizen* is a Japanese term that embodies the philosophy of continuous improvement. The word combines *kai*, meaning "change" or "alter," and *zen*, meaning "good" or "better." Together, Kaizen translates to "change for the better" and emphasizes incremental, ongoing progress toward excellence.

Failing to prioritize quality management can lead to problems on your project, such as increased costs, reduced customer satisfaction, project failures, compliance issues, and damage to organizational culture. To minimize these outcomes, project managers must make quality management a central focus at every stage of the project life cycle.

# Managing Risks

Let's set the record straight: Risk management isn't about documenting risks in a risk register and then ignoring it as if the job is done. It's a dynamic, ever-evolving process that demands vigilance, proactive thinking, and adaptability at every stage of the project. Yet, too often, project managers fall into the trap of documenting risks and then leaving things to chance, hoping for the best. Spoiler alert: risks don't magically resolve themselves. Ignoring them won't make them go away — it just gives them more time to wreak havoc on your project.

Implementing robust risk management practices fosters project resilience, enabling teams to anticipate, adapt to, and recover from disruptions while maintaining progress toward project objectives. Engaging in active due diligence involves regularly monitoring the project environment for new risks, changes to existing ones, and emerging trends, allowing for timely risk assessment and effective mitigation. Additionally, initiating contingency plans involves promptly implementing predefined strategies and actions to address identified risks when they materialize.

There are some key terms that PMP aspirants need to know as they relate to risk management, and especially as they relate to managing and monitoring project risks:

- **Residual risk** refers to the risk that remains even after the Risk Response Plan has been implemented. It's sometimes called "leftover risk."
- A **contingency plan** outlines actions if a specific opportunity or threat materializes.
- A **fallback plan** details the steps to follow if the contingency plan proves ineffective.
- A **risk owner** is the individual assigned to take responsibility for implementing the risk response or managing the actual risk.

- » **Secondary risks**, also known as "spin-off risks," are new risks that arise as a direct result of executing risk response strategies.
- » **Risk triggers** are the early warning signs that signal a risk is about to occur or has already occurred.
- » A **contract** may be issued as part of a strategy to manage certain risks.
- » **Contingency reserves** can account for both time and cost, providing a buffer for addressing risks.
- » **Reserve analysis** is a tool and technique used to evaluate the contingency reserves, which are the pre-allocated amounts set aside for contingency and fallback plans to address "known-unknowns" and accepted opportunities or threats.

## RISK MANAGEMENT IN THE REAL WORLD

Hannah, a project manager, is overseeing the development of a new web application for a retail client who wants to launch in time for the holiday shopping season. During planning, Hannah identifies a risk that the development team might fall behind due to the complexity of integrating payment gateways and inventory management systems. She documents this risk in the risk register and assigns herself as the *risk owner*.

To address the risk, Hannah develops a *contingency plan:* if the team falls behind, they will hire an experienced consultant to assist with the integrations. She also prepares a *fallback plan* in case the consultant option doesn't work out — such as implementing a simplified version of the payment system that can be expanded after launch.

Midway through the project, the risk materializes when the payment gateway integration runs into unexpected technical issues. Hannah activates the contingency plan and hires the consultant. However, this creates a *secondary risk* (or "spin-off risk"): the consultant may need additional time to become familiar with the client's infrastructure, potentially causing further delays. Hannah updates the schedule and ensures the new risk is documented.

To stay ahead of the situation, Hannah monitors *risk triggers,* such as delays in resolving support tickets with the payment gateway provider or bottlenecks in testing environments. These early warning signs help her take action quickly to minimize disruptions.

*(continued)*

*(continued)*

> Fortunately, Hannah had allocated a *contingency reserve* for both time and cost, covering the consultant's fees and any delays related to onboarding. She uses *reserve analysis* to monitor these reserves and ensure there's enough budget left for unforeseen risks later in the project.
>
> As the deadline approaches, Hannah reassesses the situation and identifies some *residual risk* (or "leftover risk"): even with the consultant's help, the inventory management system integration might not be fully optimized by launch. Hannah communicates this to the client and agrees on a phased rollout plan to prioritize critical functionality.
>
> Finally, as part of her risk management strategy, Hannah had included a clause in the consultant's *contract* specifying penalties if milestones were not met, ensuring accountability and mitigating further risk.

## Quantifying risks

*Expected Monetary Value (EMV)* is a quantitative risk analysis technique used to evaluate the potential financial impact of risks by considering both their probability of occurrence and the potential outcomes. This technique is the math nerd's way of saying, "Let's put a price tag on our worries — and our wins." By assigning a monetary value to each risk — whether positive (opportunity) or negative (threat) — and weighing it against its likelihood, project managers can calculate the overall expected impact. EMV provides a data-driven approach to prioritizing risks, helping project teams allocate resources effectively and make informed decisions to address risks.

Expected Monetary Value (EMV) boils down to a simple formula:

$$EMV = Probability\ (P) \times Impact\ (I)$$

Here's how it works: you take the likelihood of a risk happening (P) and multiply it by the monetary impact it would have (I). This gives you a clear, dollar-based way to evaluate the potential impact of each risk — whether it's a threat or an opportunity.

For example, in Hannah's web application project (see the sidebar, "Risk Management in the Real World"), she identified the risk of delays in integrating the payment gateway. Let's say there's a 40-percent chance (P = 0.4) that this delay could cost an additional $10,000 (I = 10,000). The EMV for this risk would be

$$EMV = 0.4 \times 10{,}000 = (\$4{,}000)$$

On the flip side, Hannah also sees an opportunity to complete the inventory integration early, which has a 20-percent chance (P = 0.2) of saving $5,000 (I = 5,000). The EMV for this opportunity is

EMV = 0.2 × 5,000 = $1,000

To get a clear picture of the project's overall risk impact, Hannah adds the total EMV of the opportunities to the total EMV of the threats. In this case,

Total EMV = ($4,000) + $1,000 = ($3,000) net threat impact

By using EMV, Hannah can quantify risks in monetary terms, helping her prioritize which risks need immediate attention and which opportunities are worth pursuing.

TIP

When calculating EMV, a better practice is to represent *threats as negative numbers* (since they involve potential costs or losses) and *opportunities as positive numbers* (since they offer potential gains). By doing this, when you sum up the EMVs of all risks, you'll get a *net result* — either positive or negative — that shows the overall financial impact of risks on the project.

## Additional risk management considerations

Reserve analysis isn't just about spreadsheets and forecasts; it's about preparing for the curveballs that your project will inevitably throw at you. This includes evaluating *management reserves*, which cover the *unknown-unknowns* — those risks no one saw coming. These are the "surprise guests" of the risk world, and having a plan (and a budget) is to your benefit. Projects typically account for two types of reserves: *contingency reserves* for risks you've identified and *management reserves* for the ones you haven't. Both are non-negotiable if you want to avoid scrambling when the unexpected happens.

As you implement and monitor risks, prepare to make some updates to major project documents, including the following:

» The **risk register**— your list of identified risks and proposed responses — there's always the possibility that the risks evolve when you're not paying attention.

» The **risk report**, which provides the big-picture view of how risk exposure is shifting and what's being done about it. Think of it as your project's "weather forecast" for risk. Senior leadership tends to appreciate this project document.

>> The **lessons learned register**, which captures successful and unsuccessful risk response outcomes, contributing to future projects' risk management strategies. It's best to continuously update the lessons learned register so you can proactively note the "well, we won't do that again" moments.

Risk management is not a "set it and forget it" activity. It requires proactive engagement, constant vigilance, and a willingness to adapt when things go sideways. Done right, risk management doesn't just protect your project — it makes it stronger. It allows for early identification of potential threats, smarter response planning, optimized resource allocation, and better decision-making. Plus, it builds a culture of continuous improvement that can save your team (and your sanity) down the line.

Embedding risk management practices into project processes strengthens a project's resilience, which helps organizations to navigate uncertainties and continuously meet expectations.

## Managing risks in the adaptive environment

When uncertainty and risk are high, many projects find significant advantages in adopting adaptive approaches. Adaptive methodologies leverage frequent reviews of incremental work products, enabling teams to identify and address risks early and often. Cross-functional teams play a key role in ensuring that risks are actively managed and well understood throughout the project life cycle.

In Agile, risk management is integrated into iterative development. For example, teams consider risks when selecting backlog items for each iteration. By doing so, this deliberate prioritization helps teams proactively stay ahead of potential issues. Risks are also a natural topic of discussion during *daily stand-ups*, where teams can quickly identify and analyze emerging concerns in real time.

A particularly effective Agile technique for researching and managing risks is the use of *spikes*. A *risk-based spike* is a short, timeboxed effort dedicated to exploring or resolving a specific risk. This focused investigation allows the team to uncover unknowns, test assumptions, or experiment with solutions without overcommitting resources. By encouraging *fast failure*, spikes help teams fail quickly and early, minimizing the potential impact on the project while gaining valuable insights.

# Managing Procurements and Vendor Relationships

During planning, the *Plan Procurement Management process* assesses how to address resource shortages to meet the needs of the project. This includes conducting a *make or buy analysis* to evaluate whether the work should be performed in-house or outsourced to external resources. The outcome of this assessment is the creation of a comprehensive *Procurement Management Plan* and a well-defined *procurement strategy* to guide your procurement activities. As part of this process, you also referenced a list of *preferred vendors*, chosen based on their past performance and alignment with the project's objectives.

For certain projects, the decision was made to procure services by partnering with vendors to provide the goods, services, materials, or equipment needed to meet project requirements. Consequently, the logical next step is to establish a formal agreement with one or more vendors: the *conduct procurements process*. This process involves three important steps to select qualified vendors and establish a legal agreement between the buyer and seller.

1. **Obtain seller responses:** Solicit proposals or bids from vendors by issuing *Requests for Proposals (RFPs)* or *Requests for Quotations (RFQs)*. Clearly outline project requirements, evaluation criteria, and terms and conditions to ensure comprehensive and relevant responses from sellers.

2. **Select a seller:** Evaluate seller responses carefully, considering factors such as technical expertise, pricing, competitiveness, past performance, and compliance with project requirements. Through a systematic review, identify the vendor that best aligns with project objectives and offers the greatest overall value.

3. **Award a contract:** Formalize the agreement by finalizing contractual terms, negotiating revisions if necessary, and executing the contract documents. This solidifies the partnership between the organization and the selected vendor(s).

These steps require close collaboration with the procurement department to ensure a thorough and compliant process.

## Selecting the vendor

The vendor selection process is all about finding the right partner — one that can deliver the goods (literally and figuratively) while aligning with your project objectives. This requires a thoughtful evaluation of key factors like technical expertise, pricing, past performance, and overall fit. A key tool and technique in this process is the *bidder conference*, which lays it all out for potential vendors, clarifying expectations, and answering any questions. These conferences promote open communication, ensuring vendors have a clear and shared understanding of the project requirements before submitting proposals.

*Seller proposals*, also called vendor proposals or bids, are formal documents in which vendors outline how they intend to fulfill the requirements specified in the solicitation. These proposals detail the goods, services, or solutions they will provide to meet project needs.

To keep things fair and above board, the tool and technique of *independent cost estimates* may be conducted to validate the reasonableness of vendor pricing. These estimates serve as objective benchmarks to compare against vendor proposals, helping to identify discrepancies or outliers that may warrant further review.

Another tool and technique, *proposal evaluation*, involves systematically reviewing vendor proposals against established criteria, such as technical merit, pricing, competitiveness, and overall fit for the project. This technique may include scoring or ranking submissions, with the procurement department working closely with the project manager and other key stakeholders to ensure all perspectives are considered.

Once a vendor is selected, *negotiations* are conducted to finalize the contract terms. These discussions cover pricing, scope of work, deliverables, timelines, and other contractual provisions. The goal is simple: strike a deal that meets both parties' needs, minimizes risks, and maximizes value. Done right, the result is a solid contract and a vendor prepared to hit the ground running.

TIP

For the PMP Exam, your procurement department takes the lead in negotiations, with the project manager serving as the subject matter expert. In real life, you'll want this arrangement, too — trust me on this.

Negotiations conclude with the signing of the contract, formalizing the agreement. For a contract to be legally binding, it must include the following.

>> **An offer:** A clear and definite proposal made by one party to another, expressing intention to enter into a contract on specified terms.

>> **Acceptance:** When the other party agrees to the terms to that offer without modification.

>> **Consideration:** Something of value exchanged between the parties to the contract, such as money, goods, services, or promises.

>> **Legal purpose:** What the contract must have to be enforceable. This means that the agreement must not involve illegal activities or violate public policy.

>> **Legal capacity:** What the parties entering into the contract must have in order to have a legally binding agreement. This means that they must be of legal age, mentally competent, and not under duress or undue influence.

When the procurement department negotiates and creates the contract for the vendor, typical elements include the following:

>> Description of work

>> Delivery dates and schedule information

>> Identification of authority, where applicable

>> Responsibilities of both parties

>> Management of technical and business aspects

>> Price and payment terms

>> Provisions for termination

>> Guarantees and warranties

>> Intellectual property and security considerations

>> Confidentiality and data privacy provisions

While many of these elements may already exist in templates or be managed by specific organizational departments, it's valuable for project managers to understand the components of contracts. These elements directly relate to the project management function and can impact successful project execution.

REMEMBER

Other names for contracts include Memorandum of Understanding (MOU), Memorandum of Agreement (MOA), Service Level Agreement (SLA), and Letter of Intent (LOI).

## Integrating the vendor

As the vendor selection process wraps up, the project manager is responsible for seamlessly integrating the chosen vendor into the project framework. This involves revisiting and updating project plans and documents to reflect the newly established partnership and their deliverables. Key priorities include aligning vendor timelines with the overall project schedule, allocating resources to support vendor activities, and ensuring the project budget accounts for anticipated vendor costs. Sometimes a vendor may increase the budget (change request, anyone?).

Stringent adherence to quality requirements is non-negotiable — project standards and objectives depend on it. Equally important is proactively identifying potential risks associated with vendor engagement and implementing solid risk management strategies.

With the vendor now onboard as a key stakeholder, their role becomes increasingly central as the project evolves. This highlights the importance of ongoing collaboration and open communication to keep the partnership on track and aligned with project goals.

It's also worth noting that procurements can happen at any stage of the project life cycle. Successfully navigating the *conduct procurements process* requires mastering key steps, from soliciting and evaluating proposals to negotiating contracts and managing vendor relationships.

Selecting a vendor marks the start of a collaborative partnership aimed at achieving project objectives. But let's be clear: the process doesn't end with signing the contract. Managing the vendor relationship is an ongoing effort, one that demands attention and care until the contract period concludes.

# Managing People Performance and Expectations

People are the heart of every project, driving its outcomes and impacting success — positively and negatively. During project execution, the project manager must rely on the team to carry out the work and stakeholders to provide crucial feedback. Success in these areas requires tapping into power skills — such as leadership, communication, and influence — to effectively manage team performance and stakeholder expectations. Many of the tools and techniques discussed in this chapter overlap across these efforts, emphasizing the importance of managing both people and processes.

Building and managing the project team is a dynamic, ongoing responsibility — and hard work! The *develop team process* involves creating an environment where trust and cooperation thrive, empowering members to achieve high performance and project objectives. This includes providing training, supporting individual growth, and recognizing contributions. The *manage team process* involves day-to-day tasks such as tracking performance, mentoring team members, resolving conflicts, and using tools such as an issue log to address challenges and keep the team aligned. These are all responsibilities of the project manager.

TIP

On larger projects, the project manager may have a project management team to share the load of day-to-day tasks related to developing and managing the team — thankfully. However, the ultimate accountability for completing these tasks rests squarely with the project manager.

Effective communication is another important component of project execution. The *manage communications process* is focused on implementing the communication plan by disseminating information, conducting meetings, and engaging stakeholders according to established strategies. Communication management also involves meeting stakeholder needs, overcoming constraints, and tailoring messages to ensure clarity and impact. Leveraging the right technologies, models, and methods ensures that communications are received, understood, and acted upon.

The *manage stakeholder engagement process* requires proactive effort throughout project execution. The project manager must address stakeholder needs, resolve their concerns, and maintain their interest and involvement. This involves reviewing project documents such as the Stakeholder Register and issue log to identify and mitigate any issues affecting engagement. Following the communication plan ensures stakeholders remain informed, aligned, and supportive of the project's objectives.

Ultimately, the tools and techniques discussed in this chapter reinforce a fundamental truth: managing people — team members and stakeholders alike — is the key to driving project outcomes. By developing strong teams, fostering clear communication, and maintaining active stakeholder engagement, project managers create the momentum needed to deliver results that matter.

TIP

Stakeholder engagement emphasizes *why*, as in why stakeholders need information and how that information will help manage their involvement and "excitement" about the project. Communications management emphasizes the *what*, *when*, and *how*; its focus is on the technology and methods that are used to distribute information to stakeholders.

# Project Execution in the Adaptive Environment

Agile project management has become a hallmark of flexibility, efficiency, and delivery of value at lightning speed. Its true power lies in a diverse arsenal of tools and techniques that keep projects laser-focused on stakeholder needs and organizational goals throughout the iterative development life cycle.

During each iteration, Agile teams stay locked in on delivering the iteration's objectives. To cut down on administrative overhead, Agile prioritizes *self-reporting* through visual task management tools like Scrum boards, kanban boards, and burndown charts. These tools go beyond tracking tasks: they also drive transparency, continuous value delivery, and quick pivots when changes arise. The goal is to eliminate the traditional burden of weekly progress reports while keeping everyone on the same page.

Agile practices such as *iterative development*, *frequent feedback loops*, and *daily stand-ups* keep teams delivering high-value features, incorporating real-time feedback, and continuously improving workflows. By leveraging these tools and practices, project managers can ensure tangible, meaningful benefits throughout the Agile development life cycle. Let's break down some of the most commonly used Agile tools and techniques.

- **Product backlog and product roadmap:** The *product backlog* is a detailed list of the known scope of work, while the *product roadmap* provides a high-level vision of intended releases. These tools align the team with the project's overarching goals.
- **User stories and epics:** These are the building blocks for managing the known scope of work. They define functionality from the user's perspective and are grouped into *epics* for larger initiatives.
- **Sprint planning and burn charts:** Used to estimate effort and track progress, these tools ensure teams are working toward realistic goals while maintaining visibility of project progress.
- **Quality assurance:** Agile emphasizes *built-in quality* through practices like frequent testing, integration, and validation. Tools such as *daily stand-ups*, *retrospectives*, and delivering in *small batches* foster continuous improvement.
- **Risk management:** Identifying and managing risks is baked into the iterative planning and delivery process. Tools like the *risk-adjusted backlog* or *risk burndown charts* help teams proactively address risks while maintaining momentum.
- **Cost and value management:** Agile supports continuous cost estimation and monitoring with tools like *story points* and techniques like *planning poker*, helping teams focus on delivering high-value features within budget constraints.

Agile is about delivering results, adapting to change, and keeping value front and center. By mastering these tools and techniques, project managers can maintain control, stay agile, and consistently exceed expectations.

Transparency and communication are the core of Agile practices, ensuring everyone involved in a project is on the same page. Enter *information radiators*, visual tools that turn complex project data into easily digestible insights. These tools, ranging from task boards to burndown charts, help teams track progress, spot bottlenecks, and make informed decisions in real time, all while promoting collaboration and accountability.

One powerful example of an information radiator is the Big Visible Chart (BVC), a large, prominent display of key project information, such as progress and goals. Positioned in a shared workspace, BVCs eliminate guesswork, foster transparency, and make issues or delays immediately visible — no lengthy status updates required.

## READY FOR PLANNING POKER?

Let's take a moment to spotlight *planning poker*, a collaborative estimation technique used during sprint planning. It's simple but effective: team members discuss and assign effort estimates to tasks, using diverse perspectives to ensure accuracy. This ensures alignment, accountability, and realistic workload distribution.

Here's how planning poker works: A task or user story is presented to the team for estimation. Each team member, using numbered cards (typically a modified Fibonacci sequence), secretly selects the card representing their estimate of the effort required. Once everyone's ready, the cards are revealed simultaneously. If the estimates vary widely, the team discusses their reasoning to ensure a shared understanding of the task. After the discussion, the team may re-estimate until they reach consensus.

Planning poker fosters team collaboration, minimizes bias, and leads to more accurate estimates.

A quick detour on the Fibonacci sequence: this mathematical series, introduced in the 13th century, is based on adding the two previous numbers to generate the next (0, 1, 1, 2, 3, 5, 8, 13, 21, and so on). In Agile, the sequence has been simplified and modified for estimation, typically using 1, 2, 3, 5, 8, 13, 20, 40, and 100.

While you won't need to demonstrate planning poker on the PMP Exam, it's helpful to understand the details for context. You might encounter a scenario describing elements of this Agile practice, where identifying it as the correct answer could be required.

## Visualizing the flow of work through kanban boards

A kanban board provides a clear, visual representation of the workflow, typically divided into columns such as *To Do*, *Doing*, and *Done*. Each task or user story is represented by a card that moves across the board as work progresses. The beauty of a kanban board lies in its simplicity and transparency — it shows at a glance what's being worked on, who's doing it, and where potential bottlenecks are forming. By limiting tasks in the *Doing* column, teams can maintain focus, complete work efficiently, and deliver value incrementally. See Figure 16-2 for a visual example of a kanban board.

**FIGURE 16-2:** A kanban board.

© John Wiley & Sons, Inc.

## Tracking progress with burn charts

Burn charts — both burndown and burnup — are utilized to track progress in Agile projects. A burndown chart shows the remaining work over time, with a downward slope indicating progress toward completion. It's a great way to see if the team is on track to meet deadlines, identify delays early, and adjust as needed.

On the flip side, a burnup chart highlights work completed over time, showing both the total scope and progress toward it. This dual view is especially useful for managing scope creep and making scope changes visible to all stakeholders.

The burn charts can be likened to reading pages of a book (which reminds me I'm behind in my book club reading). Imagine you're in a book club with a goal to finish a 300-page book by the end of the month.

**Burndown chart:** Shows how many pages you still have left to read. As you work through the book, the number of unread pages decreases, and the line slopes downward toward zero.

Now think about tracking how many pages you've already read.

**Burnup chart:** Shows your progress climbing up as you turn pages. If the book club decides to add an extra chapter (scope increase), the total page count rises, but your completed pages continue to stack up.

Here's a quick memory recall on the difference between the two charts.

- **Burndown:** Focus on what's *left* to do.
- **Burnup:** Focus on what's *already* done.

## Assessing team capacity with velocity charts

*Velocity charts* measure how much work a team completes in each iteration, typically in story points or tasks. Over time, this data helps teams predict future performance and plan iterations more effectively. A steady or increasing velocity can indicate improving efficiency, while a drop might flag issues like technical debt or overcommitment. It often takes 4 to 8 sprints to achieve a stable velocity, and it's important to note that velocity is team-specific and should never be compared across teams. That would be like comparing apples to golf balls.

Here's an example of how to calculate velocity: If a team completes 20 story points in sprint 1, 25 in sprint 2, and 22 in sprint 3, the velocity is

(20 + 25 + 22) / 3 = 22.33 story points per sprint

This metric helps teams predict future capacity and plan upcoming sprints more effectively.

Refer to Figure 16-3 for an example of a velocity chart. Also test yourself: can you calculate the velocity?

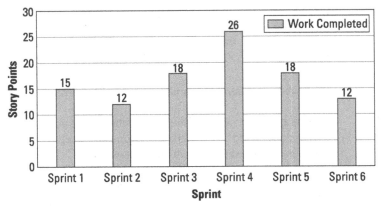

FIGURE 16-3:
A velocity chart.

© John Wiley & Sons, Inc.

## Identifying bottlenecks with cumulative flow diagrams

A *cumulative flow diagram* (CFD) offers a snapshot of how tasks move through various workflow stages over time. Using colored bands to represent stages like *To Do*, *In Progress*, and *Done*, a CFD can reveal bottlenecks or inefficiencies. For instance, a widening *Work In Progress (WIP)* band may indicate work piling up, while a steady growth in the *Done* band shows consistent task completion. CFDs are particularly valuable for larger teams or scaled projects, helping identify workflow issues and optimize efficiency. Figure 16-4 shows an example of a CFD.

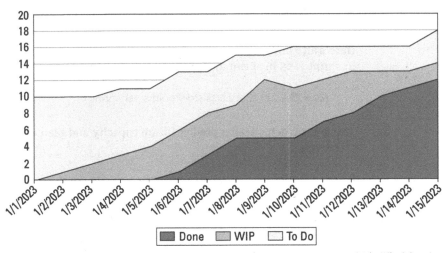

FIGURE 16-4:
A cumulative flow diagram.

© John Wiley & Sons, Inc.

TIP

Be familiar with the Agile tools discussed here, as you may need to recognize their descriptions in a scenario and correctly identify the specific tool if asked.

Information radiators are key tools in the Agile environment, transforming raw data into clear, actionable insights that drive value delivery. Whether it's through a kanban board that visualizes workflow, burn charts that track progress, velocity charts that measure team capacity, or cumulative flow diagrams that identify bottlenecks, these tools provide teams with the information they need to stay aligned with their goals. And conducting retrospectives is key to refining the use of these tools, enabling teams to reflect on what works, identify areas for improvement, and ensure that tools and processes evolve to meet project needs and goals.

## Decision-making in Agile teams

Agile thrives on the power of *self-organizing, cross-functional teams* working collaboratively to deliver value in iterative cycles. Unlike traditional hierarchies, Agile teams operate with autonomy, taking ownership of decisions, managing workloads, and adapting continuously. This approach fosters innovation, efficiency, and rapid decision-making, enabling teams to stay flexible and aligned with project goals.

Agile teams use quick, inclusive decision-making methods like the following:

- **Roman voting:** Thumbs up (agree), thumbs down (disagree), or sideways (neutral).
- **Dot voting:** Members distribute dots among options to prioritize ideas.
- **Fist of Five:** Hand signals, from a fist (strong opposition) to displaying five fingers (full support). Those below three fingers share concerns, and voting continues until the team reaches consensus.

And what of the project manager when it comes to decision-making? Agile leadership is about serving the team — servant leadership — by removing obstacles, supporting growth, and aligning efforts with the project goals. This leadership style fosters collaboration, boosts morale, and empowers teams to deliver value through adaptability and shared ownership. It truly is about "when the team works, the dream works." Too cheesy?

# MEMORY SPRINT

Rapidly recall and jot down key PMP concepts, terms, and ideas using prompts to jog your memory. Set a timer for 15 minutes. When you're done, review your work to highlight areas where you feel confident, and circle concepts you need to revisit. Use the following prompts to guide your thinking and see what else you can recall:

- What is the difference between a risk and an issue?
- In predictive projects, issues are captured on an issue log; on Agile projects, issues are referred to as impediments and are captured on an _____ _____.
- Summarize the three types of work performance (Hint: Details Inspire Results).
- What are the three levels of knowledge?
- What is the difference between explicit and tacit knowledge?
- What is and who performs a quality audit?
- What are some additional key terms of risk management?
- What is the Expected Monetary Value (EMV) formula?
- What are three key tasks of the conduct procurements process?
- What is the purpose of a bidders' conference? (Common and shared...)
- What are the elements of a legally binding contract?
- List the common tools and techniques used in the Agile environment.
- A kanban board, burnup chart, burndown chart, task board, and story maps are examples of _____ _____ in Agile projects. (Hint: They radiate.)
- What are three voting techniques used among Agile teams?

**IN THIS CHAPTER**

» Identifying the processes in the Monitoring and Controlling Process Group

» Explaining the Integrated Change Control process

» Interpreting the outputs of monitoring and controlling processes

» Applying earned value management techniques to assess project performance data

» Demonstrating the use of quality control techniques in a project context

» Evaluating the role of the Control Procurements process

» Keeping tabs on stakeholder engagement

# Chapter 17
# Keeping Your Project on Track

In this chapter, I dive into the details of monitoring and controlling your project. You'll explore how to measure and track performance, compare it against your Project Management Plan and baselines, understand what the data is telling you, and convert that data into information. This chapter will provide you with a walkthrough of each monitoring and controlling process (I'll distinguish between monitoring and controlling later on) to enhance your understanding of this concept. I'll also walk you through the integrated change control process, breaking down the steps needed to manage changes and keep everything on track effectively.

I've taken the extra step to highlight the outputs of all of the monitoring and controlling processes — something I did not do in previous chapters. These outputs provide valuable context, showing how your planning efforts and execution activities come together. While the goal isn't to memorize every output, this chapter is designed to help you connect the dots, giving you a clearer picture of how these processes support your project as it evolves.

# Getting Familiar with the Monitoring and Controlling Process Group

The Monitoring and Controlling Process Group is where the rubber truly meets the road (sticking with the roadmap theme). This is the process group where you track, review, and regulate the project's progress and performance while pinpointing areas that may require changes to the plan.

*Monitoring* focuses on gathering project performance data, producing performance measures, and reporting or sharing that information. *Controlling* involves comparing actual performance against the plan, analyzing variances, spotting trends, and recommending corrective actions when necessary.

When done right, this process group ensures that project performance is regularly measured and analyzed or addressed promptly when exceptions arise to identify and correct any deviations from the Project Management Plan.

The specific processes that fall under this process group include the following:

- Monitor and control project work
- Perform integrated change control
- Validate scope
- Control scope
- Control schedule
- Control costs
- Control quality
- Control resources
- Monitor communications
- Monitor risks

- » Control procurements
- » Monitor stakeholder engagement

These processes are performed from start to finish of the project.

# Monitor and Control Project Work

The *monitor and control project work process* is where the project manager takes center stage. This process demands the project manager's full attention and should not be delegated. It spans the entire project life cycle, from initiating to closing, and focuses on comparing actual and forecasted performance against the Project Management Plan. By taking a holistic view of the project's progress, the project manager can identify issues early and take appropriate actions to keep things on track.

This process provides stakeholders with a clear picture of the project's current status and offers visibility into its future with cost and schedule forecasts. Work performance information from other controlling processes feeds into this process, resulting in outputs such as *work performance reports*, change requests, and updates to the Project Management Plan as needed. It's the heartbeat of ensuring the project stays aligned with its goals.

Continue to the next section to find out more about change control procedures and best practices for handling change requests effectively.

# Perform Integrated Change Control

Ah, changes. They happen. As the saying goes, the only constant in projects is change (or something close to that). All kidding aside, no matter how detailed your plans may be, changes are inevitable. This is especially true when they stem from regulatory requirements or shifting stakeholder needs. Much like risks, changes can arise for all sorts of reasons, such as the following:

- » Shifting stakeholder priorities or new stakeholder involvement.
- » Regulatory or compliance updates that impact the project.
- » Budget constraints or unexpected funding changes.
- » Resource availability issues, such as team members leaving or joining.

- » Technological advancements or updates impacting project deliverables.
- » Market or environmental changes that require the project to pivot.
- » Errors or omissions in the original project plan or scope.
- » Unforeseen risks that materialize during the project life cycle.

That's where the *perform integrated change control process* steps in. This process encompasses many of the concepts touched on in previous chapters:

- » Following the *Change Control Plan*, which outline the processes and procedures for managing changes within a project.
- » Defining roles and responsibilities, change control procedures, and gathering the documentation required for requesting, reviewing, approving, and implementing changes.
- » Referencing the *Configuration Management Plan*, which details the procedures for maintaining control over project artifacts.
- » Updating the *change log*, a comprehensive list of submitted change requests. This project artifact documents all change requests received to date and their disposition. The change log includes information as to whether change requests have been approved, delayed, or rejected.

There are other key concepts in the realm of change control:

- » **Change control system:** A set of procedures that describes how modifications to the project deliverables and documentation are managed and controlled. The change control system documents the formal procedures, the documentation updates, how you'll track changes, what it means for project deliverables if those changes have been approved, and the configuration steps around that.
- » **Change control board (CCB):** Detailed in the Change Control Plan (or the Change Management Plan), the CCB includes the group of people responsible for reviewing, evaluating, and deciding to approve, delay, or reject change requests.

TIP

While the names for the change control board may differ (change advisory board is one example), the default term you should remember for the PMP Exam is change control board (or CCB). For some changes, the project manager may have the authority to approve, reject, or delay changes per the specifics of the Change Control Plan.

# Detailing the different types of change requests

A change request is routed to the project manager, upper management, or the CCB for its evaluation and approval. There are four types of change requests to be aware of:

- **Corrective action** involves rectifying errors or deviations from project requirements or objectives. For example, the project manager for a home renovation project may realize that the original labor schedule didn't account for sufficient time to complete the electrical wiring, requiring adjustments to the schedule to avoid delays. *Corrective action means you are off track and need to get back on track.*

- **Preventive action** is a proactive measure taken to prevent potential issues or risks from occurring. For example, on a home renovation project, to mitigate the risk of labor shortages, the project manager may decide to hire additional subcontractors in advance to ensure adequate manpower is available throughout the renovation process. *Preventive actions ensure that you stay on track.*

- A **defect repair** modifies a non-conforming product or project. For example, during the installation of plumbing fixtures in the home renovation project, the owners may discover that a pipe joint was improperly sealed, leading to a small leak. Additional labor is needed to repair the joint and prevent further water damage.

- **Updates** are where you modify a formally controlled document or a project baseline. In the home renovation project example, the homeowner may decide to incorporate smart home features into the in-law suite, requiring additional labor to install smart lighting, thermostats, and security systems according to updated specifications.

Approved change requests are a key output of the perform integrated change control process. Once approved, these requests are routed to the direct and manage project work process, where they are implemented and their impacts to the project are evaluated (see Chapter 16). Approved change requests can lead to new or revised cost and schedule estimates, adjustments to activity sequences, changes to resource requirements, and an evaluation of risk response options. Most importantly, these requests may require rebaselining the Project Management Plan and updating project documents — configuration management helps with version control of key documents. As a result, additional outputs of this process include Project Management Plan updates and project document updates, namely updates to the change log.

WARNING

Rebaselining the Project Management Plan is a perfectly acceptable practice, but it's important to remember that rebaselining is forward-looking only. In other words, you should not go back and change what has already happened just to make the project — or yourself — look better. That historical data is valuable and plays a key role in capturing lessons learned.

## Outlining the workflow of the change control process

Whenever a change request impacts any aspect of the project baselines, a formal change control process is required. PMI has established a workflow to effectively handle project changes. PMP aspirants are encouraged to memorize this sequence in preparation for the all-too-popular PMP Exam question, "What happens next?"

The workflow is outlined in the following steps:

1. **Initiate a change request;** note that changes may be initiated verbally.
2. **Address the root cause of the change.** In some cases, the change request may resolve itself, eliminating the need to take additional action. In other instances, it may need to go through a review or approval filter before progressing further in the process.
3. **Document the change request** in writing and enter the change information in the change control or configuration management system.
4. **Evaluate the impact of the change.** An impact analysis may include information on schedule or cost impacts, risk impacts, or any other project parameters. The key benefit of an impact analysis is that it provides information for the CCB to make an informed decision.
5. **Submit the evaluated change request to the CCB.**
6. **Receive a decision from the CCB and document the decision** in the change log.
7. **Update any other relevant project documents,** potentially rebaselining formally controlled project artifacts.
8. **Implement approved change requests** as a part of the direct and manage project work process.

## Keeping key project documents current and consistent

*Version control* is a subset of configuration management, focused on tracking and documenting revisions, updates, and modifications. It helps maintain consistency, integrity, and traceability of project components, especially in collaborative environments where multiple stakeholders contribute to or depend on project documentation. Best practices involve including a version number, date and time stamp, and the name of the user who made the updates. This ensures that the entire project team and all stakeholders have access to the most current and accurate information at all times.

Project managers will encounter the inevitable shifts that occur during the project life cycle. Effective change control helps maintain stability and keeps the project aligned with its goals, even in changing conditions. Adopting a systematic approach to evaluating, approving, and implementing changes can ensure each adjustment is thoughtfully assessed for its impact on the project's scope, schedule, and resources.

## WHEN VERSION CONTROL GOES WRONG

To drive home the concept of version control, review the following scenario of a business process improvement project:

> A retail company launched a business process improvement project to streamline its order fulfillment process. The project team included operations, IT, and customer service members, all collaborating on updating workflows and process documentation. Multiple versions of the "Order Fulfillment Workflow" document were created throughout the project as updates were made based on team feedback.
>
> However, due to the lack of proper version control, an outdated version of the workflow, which included incorrect shipping timeframes, was mistakenly shared with the IT department. Based on this version, they updated the system logic, causing delays and incorrect delivery time estimates for customers. By the time the error was identified, the team had to roll back the changes and redo the coding, resulting in increased project costs and missed deadlines.

What can you take away from this example? Proper version control would have ensured all team members were working with the latest, most accurate document. Also, a system for labeling files with version numbers, timestamps, and editor details would have helped to avoid confusion. Finally, storing project files in a central repository with clear access controls could have prevented outdated documents from circulating. This example highlights the importance of implementing version control practices in business process improvement projects to avoid costly errors and delays.

# Validate Scope

The two processes that assess the progress of scope are validate scope and control scope. The *validate scope process* encompasses reviews with the customer or sponsor to gain acceptance of deliverables during monitoring and controlling. This process is conducted at the end of each project, phase, or other points throughout the project, and results in the formal acceptance of deliverables by the customer. The outputs of the validate scope process include accepted deliverables, work performance information, and change requests.

When you encounter terms like *validate*, *validation*, or *validating deliverables*, they all point to the same concept: obtaining formal acceptance from the customer for the deliverables. Always focus on the customer during this process. And the customer refers to the internal stakeholder within the organization who has requested or is funding the project. Refer to Chapter 10 for clarity on this role.

# Control Scope

The *control scope process* starts with having a clear definition of the scope outlined in the scope baseline and some completed project work to measure against. This is where you evaluate work performance data, compare it to the scope baseline, analyze variances, and submit change requests if necessary. Controlling scope is a proactive process aimed at ensuring the team stays focused on completing only the work within the project boundaries. Controlling scope helps to minimize scope creep and gold plating (see Chapter 13 for additional insight).

The outputs of the control scope process include the following:

- **Work performance information:** This provides context on how the project and product scope are performing compared to the scope baseline. It may include details such as the number of scope variations and their causes.
- **Change requests:** If the analysis of project performance shows the need for adjustments, a change request may be submitted to update the scope baseline — or even other baselines.
- **Project Management Plan updates:** Any changes impacting the scope or related areas are reflected in updates to the Project Management Plan.
- **Project document updates:** Supporting documents, such as the requirements documentation, is updated with the latest information.

## "INNOCENTLY" EXPANDING THE SCOPE OF WORK

Sometimes, scope creep can happen very innocently. Perhaps a stakeholder approaches the project team with the following requests:

"Hey, can you add this to the product?"

"Can you add these features? It would be a game-changer for our customers!"

Sound all too familiar?

Scope creep occurs when requests are made without considering time, budget, or resource constraints. Typically, the requests want you to bypass formal change control procedures.

The same applies to *gold plating*. Team members may add extra features, thinking, "This will be great for the customer!" or "I want to impress them." However, this can lead to issues when the team loses focus and spends time on work that wasn't part of the plan. It would be an uncomfortable conversation explaining to the customer that the project was behind schedule because unauthorized work was taking priority. Awwwkwaaaaard. Even if you have extra time or the project is under budget, gold plating should always be avoided.

# Control Schedule

The *control schedule process* is where you compare the schedule baseline to actual schedule performance to date. Here are some key concepts to revisit.

- **Critical path method:** Assess the critical path to determine if it has changed or if a new critical path has emerged. You'll also check whether there is any float remaining.
- **Resource optimization techniques:** If resources are overallocated, you may need to use these techniques, namely resource smoothing or leveling, to resolve the issue.
- **Schedule compression techniques:** If the schedule needs to be shortened, you could consider fast tracking, which increases risk, or crashing, which increases costs.

For projects using a project management information system (PMIS), these tools can help you evaluate the situation accurately, decide whether to use these techniques, and adjust leads and lags where necessary.

The outputs of the control schedule process include the following:

- **Work performance information:** This highlights how the project is performing compared to the schedule baseline, offering insights into progress and any deviations.
- **Schedule forecasts:** These are predictions about when tasks or milestones are likely to be completed based on the project's current progress.
- **Change requests:** If the analysis shows the need for adjustments, a change request may be made to update the schedule baseline or other related baselines.
- **Project Management Plan updates:** Any changes to the schedule or related strategies are reflected in updates to the overall plan.
- **Project document updates:** Supporting documents, such as the project schedule or risk register, are updated with the latest information.

# Control Costs

During project execution, project managers regularly monitor actual costs incurred against the cost baseline to identify discrepancies and deviations from the planned budget. As a part of the control costs process, project managers are also responsible for managing reserves effectively, including monitoring their usage, updating reserve amounts as risks are mitigated or new risks emerge, and obtaining approval for tapping management reserves as needed, a tool and technique called *reserve analysis*. Contingency reserves explicitly address planned known risks, while management reserves serve as more of a general buffer, for unexpected events. This involves using project progress data to assess whether the project is on track and taking corrective action as needed. Additional assessments of cost performance may include the following:

- **Percent complete:** While often used, percent complete can be an unreliable metric for assessing progress due to its subjective nature.
- **Work package completion:** A more dependable approach is to measure the actual completion of deliverables at the work package level, comparing it to cost and schedule estimates. This ensures progress is tied to tangible outcomes.

» **Earned value management (EVM):** This is a technique for evaluating project performance by integrating scope, schedule, and cost (*performance measurement baseline*). EVM provides key metrics such as cost variance (CV), schedule variance (SV), the schedule performance index (SPI), and the cost performance index (CPI). You can find more information about EVM in the following section.

## Assessing project performance: Earned value management

Earned value management (EVM — not to be confused with EMV, Expected Monetary Value) is a data analysis technique used to measure project performance in terms of cost, schedule, and resources. EVM starts with four key measurements:

» **Earned value (EV):** The earned value of work completed — the work that *is* completed to date.

» **Planned value (PV):** The planned value of work — what *should* be completed to date.

» **Actual costs (AC):** The actual costs incurred to date.

» **Budget at completion (BAC):** The total budget for the project — the cost baseline.

You need these four measurements to proceed with the EVM analysis. These measurements also represent work performance data. For instance, if you said that $60,000 worth of work was completed at month four for a home renovation project without context, the homeowners would have no idea if that was good or bad.

The EVM analysis compares what was completed to what was planned to be completed to derive work performance information — context to inform stakeholders on project performance.

REMEMBER

The terms *earned value management* (EVM) and *earned value analysis* (EVA) are used interchangeably.

### Assessing schedule performance

When evaluating a project's schedule health, two key metrics come into play: *schedule variance* (SV) and *schedule performance index* (SPI). These metrics provide valuable insights into whether the project is adhering to its planned schedule and how efficiently time is being used.

CHAPTER 17 **Keeping Your Project on Track** 297

For many project managers, maintaining effective schedule oversight is just as important as managing costs. The schedule performance metrics of SV and SPI provide a clear picture of where the project stands in relation to its timeline. By tracking these measures, project managers can proactively address delays, reallocate resources, and make informed decisions to keep the project moving forward. Let's break these down.

### SCHEDULE VARIANCE

If you're asking, "Are we ahead of or behind schedule?" the answer lies in *schedule variance* (SV). The formula is

$SV = EV - PV$, where

- **EV** is earned value, representing the value of the work completed.
- **PV** is planned value, the value of the work that should have been completed by now.
- **If SV is negative:** You're behind schedule.
- **If SV is positive:** You're ahead of schedule.
- **If SV equals zero:** You're right on schedule.

For example, in a home renovation project, if by month four the planned value (PV) is $75,000 and the earned value (EV) is $60,000, your SV = $60,000 − $75,000 = −$15,000, indicating you're behind schedule.

### SCHEDULE PERFORMANCE INDEX

If you're assessing how efficiently time is being used, *schedule performance index* (SPI) is the metric to use. The formula is

$SPI = EV \div PV$, where

- **If SPI is less than 1:** You're behind schedule.
- **If SPI is greater than 1:** You're ahead of schedule.
- **If SPI equals 1:** You're exactly on schedule.

Using the same renovation example, SPI = $60,000 ÷ $75,000 = 0.8, meaning the project is using time less efficiently than planned and is behind schedule.

The way to think about this situation is that the project is progressing at 80 percent of the planned schedule.

Understanding and applying SV and SPI helps project managers identify potential delays or opportunities for improvement early in the project life cycle. This allows for timely adjustments and better allocation of resources, helping the project stay as close to the planned timeline as possible.

## Cost performance

When evaluating a project's cost efficiency or variance, two metrics are at work: *cost variance* (CV) and *cost performance index* (CPI). These metrics provide insight into how well a project is managing its budget compared to the work that is actually performed. By analyzing CV and CPI, project managers can identify financial discrepancies early, allowing them to take proactive steps to address budget overruns or reallocate funds more effectively. Let's break these down.

### COST VARIANCE

If you're asking, "Are we under or over budget?" the answer lies in *cost variance* (CV). The formula is straightforward:

**CV = EV − AC,** where

- **EV** is earned value, the monetary worth of the completed work.
- **AC** is actual cost, the total cost incurred for that work.
- **If CV is negative:** You're over budget.
- **If CV is positive:** You're under budget.
- **If CV is zero:** You're right on budget.

For example, in a home renovation project, if by month four you've completed $60,000 worth of work (EV) and spent $70,000 to achieve it (AC), your CV is $60,000 − $70,000 = −$10,000, indicating you're over budget.

### COST PERFORMANCE INDEX

If you're looking at how efficiently resources are being used, CPI is your go-to metric. Its formula is

**CPI = EV ÷ AC,** where

- **If CPI is less than 1:** You're over budget.
- **If CPI is greater than 1:** You're under budget.
- **If CPI equals 1:** You're exactly on budget.

Using the same renovation example, CPI = $60,000 ÷ $70,000 = 0.86, meaning you're over budget and using resources inefficiently.

A great way to interpret this result is to say that for every dollar you spend, you're only achieving 86 cents worth of work. Ouch.

CV and CPI are examples of *work performance information* — metrics that give context to raw data and tell a story.

TIP

For all of the calculations, notice that EV is always the first variable in these formulas — a hallmark of earned value management. Remembering this can help you feel confident with the formulas and concepts.

## Forecasting overall project financial health

To assess the overall financial health of a project, you can calculate three additional metrics.

- » **Estimate at completion (EAC):**

    Forecasts the total cost of the project at completion.

    Formula for PMP Exam preparation: **EAC = BAC ÷ CPI**, where BAC is the budget at completion.

    Answers, "What will the project likely cost?"

- » **Variance at completion (VAC):**

    Measures the difference between the budget at completion (BAC) and the estimate at completion (EAC).

    Formula: **VAC = BAC – EAC**.

    Answers, "Will we be over or under budget?"

- » **Estimate to complete (ETC):**

    Predicts the additional cost needed to complete the project.

    Formula: **ETC = EAC – AC**.

    Answers, "What will the remaining work cost?"

TIP

There are four formulas for calculating estimate at completion (EAC), but the default and most commonly used formula is EAC = BAC ÷ CPI. This formula is preferred because it assumes that the current spending performance will continue unchanged throughout the remainder of the project.

Let's return to the home renovation example:

- **BAC** is the total budget, say $150,000.
- **EAC** reflects the adjusted estimate based on current performance, calculated as $150,000 ÷ 0.86 = $174,418, showing a potential overrun.
- **VAC** tells you by how much you're over or under budget: $150,000 − $174,418 = −$24,418, indicating an overrun of $24,418.
- **ETC** calculates the cost to complete: $174,418 − $70,000 = $104,418, meaning an additional $104,418 is needed to finish (versus only needing to spend an additional $80,000 to complete the project if we were on budget).

From this analysis, the project manager will need to determine if contingency reserves are available to address this overage or if a change request needs to be submitted to tap management reserves.

The outputs of the control costs process include the following.

- **Work performance information:** This is information on how the project work is performing compared to the cost baseline.
- **Cost forecasts:** The calculated EAC value or a new estimate developed from the ground up (that is, bottom-up EAC value) is recorded and shared with stakeholders.
- **Change requests:** If the analysis of project performance reveals the need for adjustments, a change request may be submitted to update the cost baseline or other related baselines.
- **Project Management Plan updates:** Any changes to cost management strategies or baselines are reflected in updates to the overall plan.
- **Project document updates:** Supporting documents, such as the cost estimates or risk register, are updated to capture the latest information.

TIP

A common question from PMP aspirants is, "How many math questions will be on the exam?!" No need to stress. You're more likely to be asked to interpret numbers rather than perform detailed calculations. That said, it's still a good idea to study the formulas and practice questions, especially for EVM and other math concepts, to boost your confidence.

# Test Your Knowledge: What's the Situation at Week 7?

Instructions: Review Figure 17-1 and determine the following:

1. EV: _____
2. PV: _____
3. AC: _____
4. BAC: _____ *(Hint: represented by the end point of the PV line)*
5. CV: _____
6. CPI: _____
7. SV: _____
8. SPI: _____
9. EAC: _____
10. ETC: _____

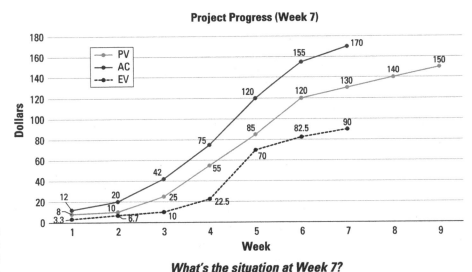

**FIGURE 17-1:** Earned value management example.

# Control Quality

*Control quality* is the process that ensures project deliverables meet agreed-upon quality standards. It involves monitoring and recording results from quality activities along with evaluating performance and recommending necessary changes. This ensures that deliverables align with requirements, contributing to customer satisfaction and the overall value of the project. Control quality is not just about completing tasks, but also about achieving the level of quality that meets or exceeds stakeholder expectations, making it a core part of project execution.

Many PMP aspirants confuse manage quality with control quality. The *manage quality process* focuses on reviewing processes and performing audits to ensure tasks are done correctly and to prevent problems. Control quality, on the other hand, ensures the deliverables themselves are correct by identifying and addressing actual issues.

Project managers have several tools to ensure quality and identify problems of the project deliverables. Let's review the most common ones frequently seen on the PMP Exam:

- **Check sheets:** Provide an organized way to collect and analyze data, such as defect frequency or trends. For example, in a home renovation project, a check sheet could track the types and frequencies of installation defects over time.

- **Statistical sampling:** Instead of inspecting every item, a representative sample is selected. This reduces costs and saves time while maintaining a reasonable level of confidence in the results. For instance, inspecting 10 percent of installed cabinets instead of all of them can indicate overall quality without unnecessary expense.

- **Performance reviews:** Compare project performance against the plan in order to assess if outputs meet performance requirements. These reviews evaluate cost, schedule, technical performance, and deliverables to identify areas needing corrective action.

- **Root cause analysis:** A problem-solving method that identifies the fundamental reasons for defects or issues. By addressing root causes, teams prevent recurring problems instead of just managing symptoms. For example, analyzing why cabinet installation delays occur may reveal training gaps or material delivery issues.

- **Inspections:** Walkthroughs and verifications that ensure deliverables meet requirements and that approved changes are implemented correctly. For example, inspecting a completed kitchen installation ensures it aligns with the design and client expectations.

- **Control charts:** Monitor process stability by plotting data points over time against control limits. Control charts can reveal trends and variations, allowing project managers to take corrective action before issues impact quality. The control chart contains control limits and specification limits that are set by the customer or industry standards. An unstable process is illustrated by the following:

  - A data point falls outside the control limits, indicating that the process may be out of control.
  - Rule of Seven: If seven *consecutive* data points fall on one side of the mean, even within limits, it signals a potential issue.

  See Figure 17-2 for an example of a control chart.

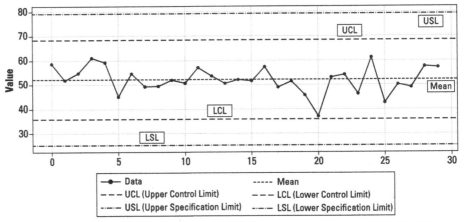

FIGURE 17-2: An example control chart.

© John Wiley & Sons, Inc.

- **Cause-and-effect diagrams:** Also known as Ishikawa or fishbone diagrams. This tool helps teams to identify potential factors contributing to quality deviations or defects. By identifying the root causes of quality issues, project teams can develop targeted strategies to eliminate these causes and improve the quality of the project's outputs. For example, in a renovation project with delays, causes could include the following:

  - **People:** Skill shortages or communication breakdowns.
  - **Management:** Poor oversight or unclear stakeholder communication.

  Refer to Figure 17-3 for an example of a cause-and-effect diagram for the home renovation project.

FIGURE 17-3: An example cause-and-effect diagram.

» **Histograms and Pareto charts:** *Histograms* show data distribution, helping identify patterns or anomalies, such as common defects. *Pareto charts*, a type of histogram, reorder the data to prioritize issues by frequency, following the 80/20 rule (80 percent of problems stem from 20 percent of causes). For example, a Pareto chart may reveal that poor measurements account for most renovation delays. See Figure 17-4 for an example of a Pareto chart for the home renovation project.

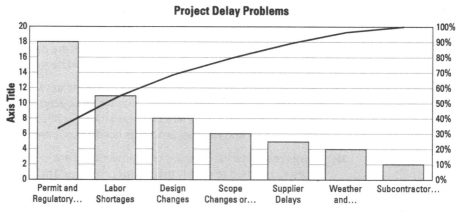

FIGURE 17-4: An example Pareto chart.

» **Scatter diagrams:** A *scatter diagram*, also known as a scatter plot, is a graphical representation used to show the relationship between two variables. Scatter diagrams are useful in identifying the type of relationship between variables, such as whether they are positively related (as one increases, the other tends to increase), negatively related (as one increases, the other tends to decrease), or not related at all. The scatter diagram allows you to visually and quickly get a sense of any correlations or trends present in the data. See Figure 17-5 for some examples of scatter diagrams.

**Scatter Diagrams**
- Track **two variables** to determine their relationship
- Trend lines show correlation of variables
- Can be used for estimating and forecasting

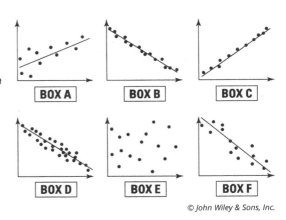

FIGURE 17-5: Example scatter diagrams.

The outputs of the control quality process include the following:

- **Quality control measurements:** These are the documented results of the quality control activities, formatted as outlined in the Quality Management Plan.
- **Verified deliverables:** The main goal of control quality is to ensure deliverables are correct. Once verified, these deliverables are passed along to the validate scope process for formal acceptance (validate = customer).
- **Work performance information:** This includes details such as how well project requirements are being met, reasons for rejections, any rework needed, recommendations for corrective actions, verified deliverables, quality metric statuses, and whether processes need adjustments.
- **Change requests:** When issues or improvements are identified, these requests are raised to modify the plan or processes. This is especially important if improvements were not a part of the original scope of work.
- **Project Management Plan updates:** Any necessary changes to the overall plan based on quality findings are captured here.
- **Project document updates:** Supporting documents, such as quality reports or the risk register, are updated to reflect the latest quality control results.

Quality control is key to delivering great results. By using tools like control charts, root cause analysis, and Pareto charts, project managers can uphold quality standards, tackle issues before they escalate, and ensure deliverables hit the mark — or even go beyond expectations. Plus, getting familiar with these tools not only helps on the job, but also gives you an edge when facing PMP Exam questions.

## Control Resources

The *control resources process* is about managing physical resources — the equipment, supplies, materials — not the people. This process involves ensuring that the resources assigned to the project are available when they are needed and used efficiently. It includes monitoring the amount, cost, and quality of these resources to make sure they align with the project plan. If discrepancies arise, corrective action is taken to address any issues and keep the project on track. By staying on top of physical resources, project managers can ensure that the necessary tools, materials, and equipment are in place to support project activities effectively.

REMEMBER

What about controlling *human* resources? The management of team members was addressed in the develop team and manage team processes. Refer to Chapter 11 for more insight.

Outputs of the control resources process include the following:

- **Work performance information:** This is information on how the project is progressing and is gathered by comparing resource requirements and allocation with actual resource utilization. It helps to identify any gaps in resource availability that may need attention.
- **Change requests:** If issues arise, such as resource shortages or inefficiencies, change requests are submitted to adjust the plan or processes.
- **Project Management Plan updates:** Updates are made to reflect any changes needed to keep the plan aligned with the project's resource needs.
- **Project document updates:** Supporting documents, such as the resource breakdown structure (RBS) or the risk register, are updated to capture the latest resource-related information.

## Monitor Communications

The *monitor communications process* is about ensuring that information flows as planned, delivered in the right way, to the right people, and at the right time. It involves measuring the effectiveness and efficiency of communications based on the Communications Management Plan. This includes encouraging stakeholders to share whether the communication methods and content are meeting their needs. If gaps or issues are identified, adjustments should be made to maintain clarity and momentum.

REMEMBER

Why is it called monitor communications and not control communications? As you may recall from the description of the Monitoring and Controlling Process Group, controlling involves comparing actual performance against the plan, analyzing variances, identifying trends, and recommending corrective actions when needed. However, there isn't a predefined "set" of communications to distribute in a strict sense. Communications simply exist and evolve as part of the project's ongoing dynamics.

The monitor communications process produces the following outputs:

- » **Work performance information:** This shows how well project communications are performing and includes feedback, including survey results, on how effective the communication has been.
- » **Change requests:** If issues are identified, such as gaps in communication or ineffective methods, change requests are submitted to adjust the approach. Perhaps you need to invest in a new communications tool or PMIS that will impact the budget.
- » **Project Management Plan updates:** Any changes needed to improve communication strategies are reflected in updates to the plan.
- » **Project document updates:** Supporting documents, such as the stakeholder register or communication matrix, are updated to capture the latest findings and adjustments.

# Monitor Risks

The *monitor risks process* is a dynamic and proactive process that identifies, analyzes, and plans for potential risks from initiation to closure. This process helps project managers to anticipate unforeseen issues and develop strategies to minimize their impact. Several activities and efforts are part of monitoring risks.

- » **Reserve analysis:** Evaluation of contingency reserves for time and cost to address identified risks effectively.
- » **Risk reviews:** Regular evaluations to monitor identified risks, residual risks, and any new risks that arise.

» **Technical performance analysis:** Assessments of technical achievements compared to planned performance measures.

Risk monitoring often involves *risk audits*, where teams assess how well risk management processes are functioning for the project as a whole.

The primary document updated during the monitor risks process is the *risk register*, which includes the following:

» Results of risk reassessments and audits.

» Outcomes of implemented risk responses.

» Updates to earlier stages of risk management.

» Closure of risks that are no longer relevant.

» Documentation of lessons learned.

Regular updates to the risk register, clear communication with stakeholders, and responsive action plans are key aspects of effective risk monitoring.

TIP

The process is called monitor risks (not control risks) because risks aren't fixed or entirely controllable. They're dynamic, often unpredictable, and can change throughout the project. Monitoring risks is about keeping an eye on them, tracking their progress, and responding when needed to make sure your risk responses stay effective and aligned with the project's needs.

The monitor risks process produces the following outputs:

» **Work performance information:** This includes insights into how well risk management is performing. Information can reveal how effective the response planning and implementation have been.

» **Change requests:** If adjustments are needed to improve risk management or address new risks, change requests are created.

» **Project Management Plan updates:** Any changes to strategies or approaches for managing risks are reflected in updates to the overall plan.

» **Project document updates:** Supporting documents such as the risk register and risk report are updated with the latest information.

» **Organizational process assets updates:** These may include updated templates for the Risk Management Plan, risk register, and risk report, as well as potential revisions to tools like the risk breakdown structure or the probability and impact matrix for future use.

# Control Procurements

The *control procurements process* ensures that procurements meet project requirements in terms of quality, quantity, delivery timelines, and cost. The process is also about managing procurement relationships, monitoring contract performance, and implementing changes as needed during all phases of the project. The goal is to ensure that the procurement requirements are being met, as defined in the contract. This process also involves ensuring all work is completed and accepted, final payments are made, and lessons learned are documented for future reference.

The control procurements process has distinct focuses for the buyer and the seller.

- **Buyer:** Measures the seller's performance against the contract and procurement plans.
- **Seller:** Focuses on completing the work as agreed.

Key activities of the buyer include conducting inspections, performing a structured review of the seller's work, performing earned value and trend analyses, interpreting contract terms and conditions, and managing claims.

REMEMBER

*Claims administration* is all about handling contested changes, or *claims*, and finding the best way to resolve them. The preferred method to handle contract disputes is *negotiation*. The procurement specialist should be the lead negotiator.

## Types of contract changes

During the project, procurement contracts may need to be updated to reflect changing circumstances. The main types of contract changes include the following:

- **Administrative changes:** Minor, non-material updates, such as changing the contractor's address due to an office move.
- **Contract modifications:** Significant changes to terms and conditions, such as adding skylight installation to the home renovation contract, which requires a budget increase and timeline extension.
- **Supplemental agreements:** Additional agreements negotiated separately, such as upgrading kitchen finishes with a separate cost agreement.
- **Constructive changes:** Informal or implied changes not formally documented, such as a homeowner requesting a wall color change on-site, which the contractor implements without a signed change order.

>> **Termination of contract:** Contract termination due to breach or for the buyer's convenience, such as deciding to sell the property and halting the renovation.

Contract changes are handled through the contract management system, which includes the *contract change control system*. Specifically, the contract change control system is used to collect, track, review, and communicate any changes to the contract. It ensures that contract changes are properly evaluated for impacts on things like scope, schedule, cost, and quality. This process keeps everyone — buyers and sellers — on the same page and makes managing contract changes clear and straightforward.

## Closing procurements

The control procurements process also includes closing out contracts. Procurement closure involves finalizing contractual obligations, resolving disputes, documenting performance and lessons learned, and ensuring financial closure. Closing out contracts may occur as procurements are completed or terminated. A contract can be terminated if the seller breaches its terms or if the buyer no longer needs the work (termination for convenience). When extensive changes are needed, it may be best to terminate the existing contract and negotiate a new one with the current seller or perhaps find another vendor who can meet the needs of the contract.

TIP

A common trap is assuming that a contract can be terminated at the convenience of the seller. (You may even see this as an answer option on the PMP Exam.) Think about it: would you, as the buyer, sign a contract knowing the seller could cancel it whenever they wanted? Probably not. That's why this wouldn't be a valid answer option.

Upon contract completion, project managers perform *procurement audits* to ensure the process was fair, transparent, and effective. These audits help maintain quality and integrity over the life cycle of the project.

REMEMBER

Did you notice the three types of audits mentioned in the content? Quality audits, risk audits, and procurement audits. Be sure to understand the differences between them for the PMP Exam.

The outputs of the control procurement process include the following:

>> **Closed procurements:** This is typically finalized through formal written notice, ensuring that all deliverables have been approved by the project management team before closure.

- **Work performance information:** This provides insights into the seller's performance by comparing received deliverables, achieved technical performance, and incurred costs against the statement of work (SOW) budget for the work completed.

- **Procurement documentation updates:** These include revisions to contracts, agreements, or any relevant procurement records based on vendor progress.

- **Change requests:** If adjustments to the procurement process or agreements are needed, change requests are created. An example would be replacing a vendor, which may add to costs and time.

- **Project Management Plan updates:** Any changes affecting procurement strategies or timelines are reflected in updates to the overall plan.

- **Project document updates:** Supporting documents, such as the risk register or lessons learned, are updated with the latest procurement information.

- **Organizational process assets updates:** Updates may include improvements to templates, processes, or other assets related to procurement for future projects.

# Monitor Stakeholder Engagement

Monitoring stakeholder engagement is all about maintaining strong relationships and staying attuned to how stakeholders perceive the project's progress. The *monitor stakeholder engagement process* involves collecting and analyzing work performance data to measure stakeholder engagement levels and identify any discrepancies. The key project artifacts to support this process can include the issue log, lessons learned register, risk register, and stakeholder engagement assessment matrix, to name a few. Additionally, monitoring the engagement of your project stakeholders requires a subjective approach to understanding their needs by using communication and interpersonal skills such as active listening and emotional intelligence (and a lot of patience). As the project evolves, updates to engagement strategies may be necessary to keep everyone aligned and informed.

Why is it called monitor stakeholder engagement (can't we control stakeholder engagement)? Stakeholder engagement is not something you can rigidly control. Engagement evolves as relationships, priorities, and project dynamics shift. Monitoring stakeholder engagement focuses on observing and assessing how effectively stakeholders are involved, ensuring that their needs are addressed, and that their engagement remains aligned with the project's objectives.

The outputs of the monitor stakeholder engagement process include the following.

- **Work performance information:** This gives insights into how stakeholders are currently engaged, compared to the desired levels outlined in tools such as the stakeholder engagement assessment matrix.
- **Change requests:** If adjustments are needed to improve engagement or address gaps, change requests for corrective action or preventive action are submitted.
- **Project Management Plan updates:** Any changes to strategies or approaches for stakeholder engagement are reflected in updates to the plan.
- **Project document updates:** Supporting documents, such as the stakeholder register or issue log, are updated with the latest information.

# Monitoring and Controlling in the Adaptive Environment

In the adaptive environment, monitoring and controlling the project work is dynamic and iterative, aligning with the principles of flexibility and continuous feedback. Instead of rigid plans, the focus is on adjusting to change, ensuring value delivery, and making sure the team and stakeholders remain on the same page. Key aspects include the following:

- **Maintaining a backlog:** Tracking, reviewing, and regulating progress and performance is achieved through maintaining a prioritized backlog.
- **Frequent check-ins:** Monitoring happens at regular intervals, often at the end of each iteration or sprint. Tools like daily stand-ups, retrospectives, and sprint reviews provide real-time feedback on progress and roadblocks.
- **Continuous stakeholder engagement:** Adaptive teams maintain close collaboration with stakeholders to ensure evolving requirements are understood and addressed promptly.
- **Emphasis on value delivery:** Metrics focus on delivering incremental value rather than adhering strictly to initial scope or timeline.
- **Dynamic risk management:** Risks are assessed continuously, with team members identifying, analyzing, and addressing them as they arise rather than relying on upfront planning alone.

Monitoring and controlling in this environment is about staying flexible, responsive, and aligned with current priorities rather than sticking rigidly to a predefined plan.

In adaptive projects, change is expected and embraced rather than overburdened by a rigid change control process. Change control in the Agile environment is designed to accommodate shifts in priorities and requirements without derailing the team's momentum. Key activities to ensure Agile teams are responsive to change include the following:

- **Backlog management:** The product backlog serves as the primary tool for managing changes. New requests are added to the backlog and prioritized during backlog refinement sessions. This ensures that only the most valuable changes are addressed.
- **Iterative decision-making:** Changes are evaluated at the start of each iteration, enabling the team to assess impact and determine feasibility without interrupting ongoing work.
- **Team autonomy:** Decisions about small-scale changes are often made within the team, while larger changes may require input from stakeholders or the product owner.
- **Time-boxed responses:** Instead of endless deliberation, changes are reviewed within set timeframes to maintain focus and ensure rapid decisions.

Adaptive change control activities prioritize agility while ensuring that changes add value and align with the project's evolving goals. By embracing change as an integral part of the process, teams can deliver outcomes that meet stakeholder needs without unnecessary delays or complexity.

## MEMORY SPRINT

Rapidly recall and jot down key PMP concepts, terms, and ideas using prompts to jog your memory. Set a timer for 15 minutes. When you're done, review your work to highlight areas where you feel confident, and circle concepts you need to revisit. Use the following prompts to guide your thinking and see what else you can recall:

- What are the four different types of change requests?
- What is the distinction between Validate Scope and Control Scope?

- What are the four key measurements you must have in order to perform earned value management analysis? (Hint: what you did, what you planned, what you spent, total budget)
- What are other names for the cause-and-effect diagram?
- A scatter diagram shows the relationship between _____ variables.
- The Control Resources process focuses on _____ resources; the Develop Team and Manage Team processes focus on _____ resources.
- Name the three types of audits described in the material.
- What is the preferred method of handling contract disputes?

# Answer Key: What's the Situation at Week 7?

1. EV: 90; what was completed by week 7.
2. PV: 130; what was planned to be completed by week 7.
3. AC: 170; costs incurred through week 7.
4. BAC: 150; the total planned budget, the sum of all PVs.
5. CV: –80; you are over budget.
6. CPI: 0.53; for every dollar spent, you only get 53 cents worth of work from the team (resources).
7. SV: –40; you are behind schedule.
8. SPI: 0.69; you are progressing at 69 percent of the planned schedule.
9. EAC: 283; this is what you will likely spend for the entire project given today's cost performance.
10. ETC: 113; this is how much more you need to spend from now until the end to complete the project based on the projected overall budget on the project.

**IN THIS CHAPTER**

» Identifying why projects end

» Prioritizing the essential tasks for effective project closure

» Comparing project closure in predictive and Agile environments

» Creating an effective final project report

» Differentiating between a lessons learned register and a lessons learned repository

» Supporting ongoing success after project completion

Chapter **18**

# Closing the Project or Phase

Closure represents the formal completion of a project or phase, ensuring that all tasks are finalized, objectives are met, and the project's output is either delivered to the client or transitioned into ongoing operations. However, project and phase closure is often the most overlooked step in the project life cycle.

Many project teams are simply relieved to reach the end after enduring setbacks, communication hurdles, fractured relationships, and the general wear and tear of project demands. As a result, a thorough evaluation of project outcomes and lessons learned often falls by the wayside.

Yet, when project teams bypass this critical step, they miss a valuable opportunity to refine their processes, enhance team dynamics, and strengthen stakeholder relationships.

This chapter focuses on best practices for project and phase closure, ensuring teams are recognized for their efforts, confirming client satisfaction, delivering outputs to the organization, and validating the achievement of intended outcomes.

Additionally, I discuss the change management process and strategies for sustaining project outcomes and ensuring the benefits are realized long after the project has been completed.

## The Closing Process Group

The *Closing Process Group* is where the project or phase formally concludes. This process group ensures that all planned activities are completed and verified as finished. It also handles scenarios where projects are abandoned, perhaps due to a lack of resources, or canceled as a result of senior leadership intentionally deciding to terminate the project or phase. The Closing Process Group ensures that no loose ends remain, regardless of how the project concludes.

There's just one specific process that falls under this process group: Close Project or Phase.

REMEMBER

While this process group has only one process, it involves a comprehensive list of activities such as verifying project deliverables, obtaining stakeholder acceptance, archiving project documents, and evaluating lessons learned to ensure the organization benefits from the project experience.

## Uncovering Why Projects End

When it comes to wrapping up projects, it's more complex than just putting a full stop and calling it a day. The end of a project often depends on various factors, and not all of them are about crossing the finish line with flying colors. Let's bring this concept to life with another hospital case study. Imagine you're managing a project to implement a new electronic health record (EHR) system in a hospital. When exactly would you consider your mission accomplished and the project ended?

## Realizing the project's objectives have been achieved

This is the ultimate goal of project management: the project is complete and the objectives have been met. In the case of the hospital project, the new EHR system is fully functional, and all staff members are trained and comfortable using it. Your objective to digitize patient records and streamline department communication has been realized. You've crossed the finish line! This is also called *extinction*. It's super weird, I know.

## Seeing that the objectives will not or cannot be met

Sometimes, despite the best plans, things don't go as expected. If, for instance, the new EHR system continually malfunctions, causing more trouble than it's worth, the project objectives cannot be met. At this point, the project may be considered finished (although not successfully). This is also an example of project extinction.

## Cutting the project funds

There are times when a project runs out of funding, making it impossible to move forward. Going back to the hospital example, implementing the EHR system has proven to be expensive. If the hospital runs out of allocated funds before completion, the project will have to end, ready or not. This concept is also called *starvation*.

## Discovering that the project is not needed

Organizations have been known to simply change direction with existing projects. Perhaps a project is no longer a strategic fit with the organization's vision. Or, the new CEO has other plans and would prefer to divert time and resources to other initiatives. For instance, if a more effective and efficient EHR system is discovered midway through implementation that requires minimal setup, the original project might be rendered redundant, marking its end. It happens.

## Identifying that the human or physical resources are no longer available

If key project team members leave or there's a shortage of necessary equipment, the project may need to end, as the resources required to complete it aren't available. In the case of the EHR project, perhaps the key vendor team contract has ended without extension and the organizational staff do not have the capacity to work on the project; thus, the project comes to an end.

## Terminating the project for legal cause or convenience

Projects can sometimes be terminated due to legal requirements or simply for convenience. For example, new legislation might render the chosen EHR system non-compliant, or the hospital may decide it's more convenient to stick with the current system for now. In such cases, the project may be terminated.

Be familiar with the reasons for project closure beyond completion, such as funding cuts or changes in strategic alignment, as this may come up in situational questions.

As you can see, there are many reasons for project or phase closure. Some reasons are because the goals and objectives were achieved. Other reasons are due to lack of resources, funding, or interest in the project moving forward. Regardless of the reason, you should follow structured project closure steps to ensure that all aspects of the project are concluded satisfactorily and set the stage for lessons learned and future success. The conclusion of a project can be complex and sometimes political. Recognizing these end points is important for project managers, as it can help them to understand when to move resources to new initiatives and when to evaluate the success or shortcomings of the completed project.

# Addressing Project Closure: Close Project or Phase Process

The specific project management process to address project closure is the *Close Project or Phase process*. This process occurs when the project team finalizes all activities of the project, phase, or contract. During this process, all project or phase documentation is archived, the planned work is completed, and project team resources are released. While you might think closure activities occur only once, these activities can actually occur at certain predetermined points of a project, such as at the end of a phase.

When closing the project, the project manager reviews the Project Management Plan to ensure that all project work is completed and that the project objectives have been achieved. This is often referred to as *administrative closure*, which is distinct from contract closure.

Focus on the importance of administrative closure tasks versus contract closure. The PMP Exam frequently tests this distinction, so be clear on the steps in each circumstance. You can refer to Chapter 17 for details on contract closure.

## Tackling essential tasks for smooth project closure

The Project Management Institute outlines a structured set of steps to project closure, ensuring all aspects of the project are systematically concluded. These steps are as follows:

- **Confirm work is complete.** Verify that all project tasks have been completed according to the project plan and that all deliverables meet the agreed-upon standards and criteria for acceptance.

- **Obtain formal acceptance.** Secure formal acceptance of the final project deliverables from the client or key stakeholders, confirming that all project requirements have been satisfied.

- **Conclude the procurement activities with final transactions and settlements.** This is the process of finalizing all procurement-related activities, ensuring that all contractual obligations are met and vendors are paid.

- **Settle all project accounts and ensure financial obligations are fulfilled.** Confirm that all financial transactions related to the project are completed, including making payments to suppliers and closing out project accounts.

- **Hand over project documentation.** Compile and hand over all project documentation to the appropriate entities, ensuring that all necessary information is accessible for future reference or operational use. This includes project plans, project documents, and key project artifacts.

- **Compile and submit a final report.** This entails creating a final project report that summarizes the team's performance and captures the project's scope, schedule, cost, and quality metrics.

- **Archive project information.** Securely archive all project information, including documentation, correspondence, and data, in a designated repository for future access.

- **Consolidate lessons learned into the organizational knowledge repository.** This step is about capturing the lessons learned during the project and updating the organization's knowledge base to improve future project processes.

>> **Release project resources.** Systematically release project resources, including team members, equipment, and materials. Ensure that team members are recognized for their contributions and are transitioned to new roles or projects as appropriate.

Following these steps ensures a thorough and effective project closure, allowing for a smooth transition to post-project activities and establishing a strong foundation for future initiatives.

The steps can generally occur in any order — except for one. Can you guess which one? Releasing project resources, especially your team members, should be the final step before officially closing the project or phase.

Here's why: First, your team members are invaluable in helping wrap up the remaining closure tasks. Second, if any last-minute issues arise, having the team available saves you from the hassle of tracking them down. Imagine the administrative and negotiation efforts required to reassemble team members after they've moved on to other projects. Keeping them involved until the end avoids unnecessary delays and ensures a smoother, more efficient closure process.

The PMP Exam may ask you for the "correct" order of project closure. Any answer option that lists releasing the team resources last is the correct answer. You're welcome.

## STAKEHOLDER SATISFACTION AS A MEASURE OF SUCCESS

Contrary to the popular belief that project success is solely defined by meeting time, budget, and scope requirements, stakeholder satisfaction is equally important. If a project meets its time, scope, and budget goals but does so at the cost of strained relationships, it's unlikely you'll be invited back to manage the next one. Would that really be considered a success? Probably not.

This is why stakeholder engagement is essential in traditional projects — and why, in adaptive and Agile environments, it's considered the pinnacle of project success. For the PMP Exam, stakeholder satisfaction is more than just about delivering results; it's about building and maintaining relationships. Expect questions on assessing and improving stakeholder satisfaction, which often requires the application of power skills like conflict management, negotiation, communication, and emotional intelligence, to name a few.

## Supporting project closure efforts with project artifacts

Talk about a full-circle moment! You might have thought all the project artifacts discussed in previous chapters were just extra work. Yet, these very documents become invaluable resources during project closure activities. Here's a quick rundown of key documents and how they support closure.

- » **Project charter:** Check if the project met its exit criteria.
- » **Business case:** Validate that the original objectives have been fulfilled.
- » **Deliverables:** Ensure all deliverables are complete and accepted by stakeholders.
- » **Lessons learned register:** Archive insights in the lessons learned repository to benefit future projects.
- » **Risk register and risk report:** Review data on risk occurrence, evaluate strategies that worked, and confirm that all risks were successfully managed.
- » **Change log:** Assess the impact of any changes made to the project scope, timeline, or budget.
- » **Agreements:** Confirm all contracts and agreements are formally closed.

By revisiting these documents, project managers can conduct a thorough and organized process to close the project or phase. Leveraging these artifacts helps validate that objectives were met and ensures that valuable insights and information are preserved for future projects.

REMEMBER

Closing a project with this level of diligence strengthens your credibility and builds a foundation of knowledge that will support ongoing improvement across the organization.

## Supporting project closure with key meetings

Let's not overlook the importance of meetings in the project closure process. While some meetings may feel like they could have been emails, a project closure meeting plays a crucial role in ensuring all aspects of the project have been thoroughly addressed. Closure meetings help confirm that deliverables are accepted, validate that the exit criteria have been met, formalize contract completion, assess stakeholder satisfaction, capture lessons learned, transfer knowledge, and, importantly, celebrate project successes. Types of closure meetings include the following.

- **Close-out reporting meetings:** Review project outcomes and performance.
- **Customer wrap-up meetings:** Engage with customers to confirm satisfaction and gather feedback.
- **Lessons learned meetings:** Document insights and improvements for future projects.
- **Celebration meetings:** Recognize achievements and foster team morale.

Attendees can include project team members, key stakeholders, and any individuals affected by the project outcomes.

Regarding celebration meetings, remember how I discussed that releasing your team should be the final step in project closure? One key benefit of this approach is that it allows you to celebrate successes with the team. By taking this time to recognize and honor the project's achievements with both the team and stakeholders, you acknowledge everyone's hard work and boost morale. This shared celebration reinforces team cohesion and sets a positive tone for future projects.

At the end of a project phase, a *phase gate review* (also known as a stage gate review) may occur. While it may not always be labeled as a formal meeting, this review assesses whether the project should progress to the next phase, continue with adjustments, or conclude entirely. Of course, it's safe to assume a meeting is involved — decisions like these aren't made through telepathy!

## Bringing projects to a close in the Agile environment

Agile projects typically don't follow a formal project close-out process like traditional project management. Instead, with value delivered incrementally and regular reviews conducted with stakeholders, closure can occur at any point once the project objectives are met and the customer is satisfied with the product. This flexibility allows the project to conclude naturally whenever its goals are achieved.

In some organizations, an Agile team might conduct a final retrospective, while in a predictive project environment, the project manager holds a final "all-hands" meeting for the team. These are similar ceremonies for closing a project or phase.

# Reflecting on Project Achievements: Documenting the Journey

Compiling and submitting a final project report is a key task for a smooth project closure. Here are some key benefits of the final report:

- **Provides project overview:** The final report offers a comprehensive overview of the project, summarizing its objectives, deliverables, performance metrics, and whether it met its goals.
- **Documents lessons learned:** The report captures valuable lessons learned during the project duration, providing a resource for continuous improvement in future projects.
- **Facilitates knowledge transfer:** The report serves as a knowledge transfer document, allowing team members, stakeholders, and other organizational projects to benefit from the project's experiences.
- **Supports stakeholder communication:** The report communicates the project's outcomes to stakeholders, offering transparency and a basis for evaluating the project's success.
- **Serves as a closure document:** The final report acts as an official closure document, signifying the end of the project. It includes recommendations for future projects and any follow-up actions needed.

Key elements of the final report include the following.

- **Description:** Includes the summary-level description of the project or phase.
- **Scope objectives:** Includes the criteria used to evaluate the scope and evidence that the completion criteria were met.
- **Cost objectives:** Includes the acceptable cost range, actual costs, and reasons for any variances.
- **Schedule objectives:** Verifies that project objectives were completed on time, and reports on any variances and schedule impacts.
- **Quality objectives:** Includes a description of evaluation criteria for project and product quality. The report verifies that objectives are met, and gives actual milestone delivery dates and reasons for any variances.
- **Validation information:** Includes required approvals for the final product, service, or result, such as user satisfaction survey results.

- » **Benefits realization:** Includes how the final product, service, or result achieved the business needs and expected benefits; if these needs are not met at the project's close, the report indicates the degree to which they were achieved and estimates when the business needs will be met.

- » **Risks or issues encountered:** Includes a summary of any risks or issues encountered on the project and how they were resolved.

In addition to reporting metrics, the final project report summarizes overall project performance, alignment with objectives, and lessons learned for future projects. Be ready to identify its key components on the exam. The final report is generally a document created in the predictive environment.

Of course, the specific requirements for this report for any given project will be guided by the organizational process assets (OPAs). Remember OPAs? They provide the standards and templates for how project documents, including the final report, should be prepared.

# Capturing Insights: Lessons Learned

As covered in Chapter 17, you capture lessons learned through every stage of the project in the lessons learned register. These lessons encompass what was done right and wrong and what would be done differently if the project were to be done again. During project closure, you finalize lessons learned as part of the Close Project or Phase process.

The lessons learned register is updated over the course of the project, not just at the end. Be prepared to answer questions about iterative updates of the lessons learned register.

Key lessons that may be documented in the lessons learned register include the following:

- » Accuracy of the business case
- » Risk and issue management
- » Project and development life cycles
- » Stakeholder engagement

- Effective requirements collection techniques
- Challenges encountered
- Approaches that worked well for validating deliverables
- Scope control efforts
- Accuracy of duration and cost estimates
- Vendor relationships

At the end of the project or phase, the information and knowledge gained from the lessons learned are transferred to an OPA called a *lessons learned repository*. The repository centralizes knowledge, and organizations use it to improve future projects, aligning with continuous improvement — a key concept in the PMP Exam.

For the PMP Exam, know the difference between a lessons learned *register* and a lessons learned *repository*. The register is project-specific, while the repository is an organization-wide resource.

# Referencing the Business Case and Benefits Management Plan

I want to briefly discuss the business case and the Benefits Management Plan. The *business case* provides the rationale for the project, outlining the expected benefits and why the project is worth the investment. It serves as the foundation for project approval, helping stakeholders understand the project's value proposition.

To ensure these benefits are fully realized, organizations develop a Benefits Management Plan, which acts as a roadmap for identifying, managing, and tracking benefits over the course of the project. Key components of a Benefits Management Plan include target benefits, benefit metrics, a benefits realization timeline, benefit owner, risk assessment, and methods for monitoring and reporting. This plan defines the processes for creating, maximizing, and sustaining the benefits provided by a project or program, ensuring that the project delivers the anticipated value to both the organization and its stakeholders.

The business case and Benefits Management Plan are developed with the benefits owner before initiating the project. Both documents are also referenced during the Close Project or Phase process.

## THE BENEFITS OWNER: AN IMPORTANT ROLE FOR PROJECT SUSTAINMENT

The benefits owner plays a key role in ensuring a smooth transition of benefits and setting up the monitoring systems needed to assess whether the benefits are being realized. The benefits owner is the accountable person or group that monitors, records, and reports realized benefits throughout the timeframe established in the Benefits Management Plan. This responsibility begins as soon as the benefits are delivered and often extends well beyond the project's conclusion, sometimes lasting several years.

In traditional projects, the benefits owner may be a business analyst, sponsor, or operations manager, but they are typically not the project manager. The benefits owner ensures that the promised benefits are delivered upon completion. The role is more static, with clear expectations and a linear path toward realizing benefits.

In the adaptive environment, the product owner is typically responsible for ensuring that the prioritized features deliver the highest value to the customer. The role is more dynamic, as benefits realization is ongoing throughout the project's iterative cycles. The benefits owner works closely with the Agile team to ensure that each iteration moves the project closer to achieving its intended benefits, continuously refining and adapting the project to maximize value.

Reviewing these documents at closure confirms that the project has met its intended objectives and delivered the expected value. By revisiting the business case, you verify that the project fulfilled its original purpose, and by assessing the Benefits Management Plan, you ensure that processes are in place for continued benefit realization beyond project closure. This final review allows the organization to validate success and secure long-term value, providing essential insights for future projects.

TIP

Be ready to recall details from the Benefits Management Plan, especially its role in monitoring benefits after project completion — a common PMP Exam question.

# Test Your Knowledge: Closing the Project

**Instructions:** Read each of the following statements and determine whether it is true or false based on your understanding of project closure steps. After answering, check the answer key to see if you were correct. Use the explanations provided to deepen your understanding of key project closure concepts. The answers are at the end of the chapter.

1. **True or False:** The final project report should only focus on metrics and quantitative outcomes.
2. **True or False:** Lessons learned should be documented only at the end of the project to ensure a complete overview.
3. **True or False:** Contract closure and administrative closure are the same thing and can be handled together without distinction.
4. **True or False:** The Benefits Management Plan helps ensure that the project's intended value is realized even after the project has officially closed.
5. **True or False:** Stakeholder satisfaction is only important at the start of the project and doesn't need to be revisited during project closure.

# Sustaining Project Outcomes

Even though the project has ended, the organization needs to have plans for long-term viability beyond project completion. That is where transition planning and change management efforts come into play, bridging the gap between project completion and sustained success.

Transition planning can include discussions on building a team within the receiving organization to support and evolve the product over its life cycle.

Although it is not an official component of the Project Management Plan in predictive projects, you may encounter the term *transition plan*, which outlines the activities to properly hand over project deliverables to the organization. In hybrid projects, post-implementation support may be referred to as *DevOps* or *hypercare*.

Successful transition also requires careful attention to the human side of change, as people within the organization adapt to new processes, tools, or responsibilities.

## Applying change management as a strategy

While change management is about managing the logistics of change, it also involves guiding people, teams, and the organization through the transition of the new product, service, or result.

Change management is a structured approach to transitioning individuals, teams, and organizations from their current state to a desired future state. It entails preparing, supporting, and enabling employees to adopt change, ensuring that changes are implemented smoothly and achieve the intended outcomes.

Change management includes the following:

- Communicating strategies, engaging stakeholders, providing training and development, and providing support mechanisms.
- Emphasizing the importance of addressing the human aspect of change, and recognizing that people's acceptance and adaptation are essential to the success of any project.
- Understanding and managing resistance, fostering a positive attitude, and building commitment.

Effective change management can minimize resistance, reduce the impact of change on productivity, and increase the likelihood that changes will be adopted and sustained over time. When done well, change management can turn potential disruption into an opportunity for growth and innovation.

## Using change management frameworks

To support the smooth transition from the current state to the desired future state, various change management models are available to help project managers proactively and effectively navigate change initiatives. Each of these models offers unique insights and strategies for managing change, making them valuable tools for project managers and leaders who want to guide their teams and organizations through periods of transition and ensure sustainability of the project outcomes.

Five widely recognized change management models used in the business world include the following: the Prosci ADKAR Model, John Kotter's 8-Step Model, Virginia Satir's Change Model, William Bridges' Transition Model, and Kurt Lewin's Change Management Model. Each of these models offers valuable insights and strategies for managing change, whether you're leading a small team or steering an entire organization through a significant transformation.

### Prosci ADKAR Model

ADKAR stands for Awareness, Desire, Knowledge, Ability, and Reinforcement, representing the five outcomes an individual needs to achieve for change to be successful.

- **Awareness** involves helping individuals understand why the change is necessary.
- **Desire** addresses the motivation and willingness of individuals to support and participate in the change.
- **Knowledge** provides the information and training required for individuals to know how to change.
- **Ability** focuses on the practical skills and behaviors needed to implement the change.
- **Reinforcement** ensures that the change is sustained over time by reinforcing behaviors and providing ongoing support.

The ADKAR model is particularly effective for understanding and addressing the human side of change, ensuring that individuals are fully prepared to adopt new behaviors and processes.

## John Kotter's 8-Step Model

John Kotter's 8-Step Model is a comprehensive framework designed to guide organizations through the process of change. It emphasizes the importance of leadership and urgency in driving change initiatives. This model involves eight steps:

1. Create a sense of urgency.
2. Form a powerful coalition.
3. Create a vision for change.
4. Communicate the vision.
5. Remove obstacles.
6. Create short-term wins.
7. Build on the change.
8. Anchor new approaches in the culture.

Kotter's model emphasizes the importance of each step to ensure successful change. In addition, Kotter's model is widely used for large-scale organizational change and is known for emphasizing the emotional and motivational aspects of change.

## Virginia Satir Change Model

The Virginia Satir Change Model provides a psychological perspective on how individuals experience and cope with change. The model outlines the emotional journey people typically experience during change and emphasizes the importance of understanding these emotions to manage change effectively. The stages include the following.

- **Late status quo:** The initial state where everything is familiar and stable. People are comfortable with the existing situation, "business as usual."
- **Foreign element:** The period when an event or new information disrupts the status quo, introducing uncertainty and discomfort.
- **Chaos:** The period of confusion and distress as people struggle to adjust to the change. Productivity and morale may decrease temporarily.
- **Transforming idea:** The point in time where people come up with an idea that helps them make sense of the situation. Work performance begins to improve.
- **Practice and integration:** The period when people start to make sense of the change, experimenting with new ways of doing things, and beginning to regain stability. This leads to improved performance, and performance is often at a higher level.
- **New status quo:** The period when change is fully integrated, and a new, stable state is achieved, often with improved processes or understanding.

This model highlights that change can be challenging but ultimately leads to growth and a new level of functioning.

## William Bridges' Transition Model

William Bridges' Transition Model focuses on the internal psychological transition that individuals undergo during change rather than the actual external change. The Bridges model distinguishes between change, which is situational, and transition, which is psychological and involves the process of adaptation.

The model has three stages.

1. **Ending, losing, and letting go:** This is a period when individuals begin by acknowledging what they are losing due to the change. This stage involves feelings of grief, fear, and uncertainty.
2. **The neutral zone:** This is a period of ambiguity and confusion, where old behaviors are no longer valid, but the new ways are not yet established. It's a

critical phase during which individuals are in a state of flux and working through the change.

3. **The new beginning:** This is the period when individuals accept the change, embrace the new ways, and begin to build new behaviors and attitudes.

The Bridges model highlights change's emotional and psychological aspects, emphasizing that successful change requires carefully managing these transitions.

### Kurt Lewin's Change Management Model

Kurt Lewin's Change Management Model is one of the earliest and best-known change models. It provides a simple yet powerful framework for understanding and managing change within organizations. Lewin's model is based on three key stages.

1. **Unfreezing:** This initial stage involves preparing the organization to accept that change is necessary. It involves breaking down the existing status quo and challenging current beliefs, behaviors, and processes. The goal is to create a sense of awareness and readiness for change.

2. **Changing:** In this stage, once the organization is "unfrozen," the change is implemented. This is the phase where new processes, behaviors, and ways of thinking are introduced. It's a dynamic stage where learning, experimentation, and adjustment take place.

3. **Refreezing:** In the final stage, the new behaviors and processes are solidified or "refrozen" to ensure that they are embedded in the organization. This phase involves reinforcing the change, ensuring stability, and preventing a return to old ways.

Lewin's model is particularly useful for understanding the importance of preparing for change and ensuring that new practices are firmly established.

## Applying change management models

While each model takes a different approach, they all emphasize the importance of understanding and managing the human side of change. These models are not one-size-fits-all solutions but rather tools that can be adapted to fit your organization's specific needs and context. By applying these models, you can effectively guide your teams through change.

TIP

For the PMP Exam, you may be provided with a description of one of these change models and asked to indicate which one is being described in the scenario.

As for real-world application, consider how these change management models can be integrated into your projects and organizational strategies to ensure sustained outcomes. Managing organizational change effectively is crucial for embedding project results and realizing long-term benefits. It all starts by clearly articulating the vision for change. You need to communicate the purpose, expected outcomes, and lasting advantages to all stakeholders, underscoring how the change will support the project's goals. By ensuring everyone understands the value behind the change, you foster alignment and build a foundation for sustained support beyond project closure.

Effective change management is about engaging and involving key stakeholders throughout the process. Project managers should actively seek their input, address their concerns, and ensure they feel heard and valued. This collaborative approach increases buy-in and reduces resistance, making it more likely that the organization will embrace and maintain the changes necessary for long-term success.

TIP

Finally, you need to develop a comprehensive Change Management Plan (not to be confused with a Change Control Plan) that outlines each step of the transition, complete with a timeline, necessary resources, and ongoing support. Such a plan should incorporate strategies for communication, training, and reinforcement to help integrate the changes into the organization's daily operations. By providing a structured roadmap, the plan facilitates a smooth transition, ensuring that project outcomes are not only achieved but also sustained, thus enabling the organization to fully realize the intended benefits well into the future.

# Delivering Value

As I cover in Chapter 7, the ultimate goal of any project is to deliver value to the organization and end users. Delivering value is at the core of everything you do as a project team. Projects create value by addressing stakeholder needs, solving pressing issues, and supporting the organization's strategic objectives. However, value is not a one-size-fits-all concept; it varies based on the unique goals and priorities of each project's stakeholders. For one project, value might come from introducing cutting-edge innovation, while for another, it might be achieved through increased operational efficiency or ensuring compliance with regulatory standards.

By understanding the specific ways in which your project can deliver value, you can align your actions with what matters most to your stakeholders. This alignment ensures that the project outcomes are successfully implemented and are meaningful and impactful to those who benefit from them. Ultimately, your role as project manager extends beyond completing tasks: you are instrumental in leading the efforts to create lasting value that supports the organizational strategic goals and meets the evolving needs of its stakeholders.

# Answer Key: Closing the Project

1. **False.** The final report should include both quantitative and qualitative insights, such as project alignment with objectives, challenges faced, and lessons learned.
2. **False.** Lessons learned should be documented throughout the project life cycle to capture insights in real time.
3. **False.** Contract closure involves completing all contractual obligations, while administrative closure focuses on formalizing project completion and archiving records.
4. **True.** The Benefits Management Plan outlines how value will be tracked and maintained post-project.
5. **False.** Stakeholder satisfaction is crucial throughout the project, including at closure, as it reflects the project's success in meeting expectations.

# Agile and Hybrid Approaches

**IN THIS PART . . .**

Explore core principles and fundamentals of Agile project management.

Examine the characteristics that drive high-performing Agile teams.

Get an overview of Agile ceremonies and artifacts.

Learn about the dynamics of hybrid project management.

IN THIS CHAPTER

» Reviewing the history of Agile and its evolution

» Getting familiar with the Agile Manifesto

» Identifying the common Agile frameworks

» Gaining insight on the Agile Inverted Triangle of Constraints

Chapter **19**

# The Fundamentals of Agile Project Management

This chapter is solely focused on providing you with the basics of Agile. For some of you, Agile may seem like a new project management approach that is taking the project management world by storm. But did you know that Agile was born in response to a group of frustrated software developers tired of long, drawn-out, and rigid project management processes? These "rebels" wanted to deliver quality software products to their customers faster, and they were tired of being bogged down by the slow processes of traditional project management approaches. As a result, Agile was born, with its emphasis on collaboration, flexibility, and delivering value to the customer in small increments. Since its inception, Agile has been rapidly adopted by industries beyond software development, and it's been a booming methodology ever since.

In this chapter, you will discover that Agile is not a new fad that has emerged over the last few years. Agile has a rich history, providing the building blocks that will enable you to be agile on your future projects. Regardless of the name you give it or the framework you choose, Agile is about embracing the mindset and adopting good practices to create a more collaborative, flexible, and adaptive project management approach to best suit the changing needs of an organization and its customers.

# Realizing that History Matters

No, you will not be tested about the history of Agile for the PMP Exam. (You will, however, need to know this for the PMI-ACP exam.) I would be remiss in overlooking the history of this dynamic approach for your success both with the PMP Exam and in real-world projects.

Here are some quick facts about the history of Agile (sourced from *Agile Project Management For Dummies*):

- 1930s: Walter A. Shewhart conceptualizes short-cycle projects to improve quality with PDSA (Plan-Do-Study-Act).
- 1970: Dr. Winston W. Royce publishes "Managing the Development of Large Software Systems," suggesting that the waterfall method is ineffective and would need to iterate at least twice to be successful.
- 1986: H. Takeuchi and I. Nonaka publish "The New Product Development Game" in *The Harvard Business Review*.
- 1990s: Jeff Sutherland and Ken Schwaber create a timeboxed approach called Scrum.
- 2001: The Agile Manifesto is born, creating Agile methods and the Agile Alliance.
- 2004: Scrum Alliance is formed.
- 2010: U.S. Department of Defense requires Agile techniques on all IT projects (NDA Section 804).
- The present: Agile will continue evolving with new frameworks and implementing artificial intelligence.

Why go down memory lane with Agile? History provides the foundation of how Agile came to be, so that you can understand the relevance and potential implementation of Agile in your projects. Stay with me on the next topic about the Agile Manifesto as I paint a clearer picture.

# Examining the Values and Principles of the Agile Manifesto

From the previous section, you found out that Agile practices and techniques have been used for decades. However, it wasn't until 2001 that the Agile Manifesto was developed, which defined Agile values and principles, leading to the substantial growth of Agile implementation.

In 2001, multiple Agile frameworks were in operation in the software development industry. One particular meeting in February 2001 in Snowbird, Utah, brought together 17 experts in the software development industry, who saw an opportunity to find common ground among the various emerging Agile frameworks. The goal of the meeting was to also discuss ways to simplify and create a lightweight methodology that could also adapt to the fluctuating needs of projects. From that meeting, the Manifesto for Agile Software Development, lovingly called the Agile Manifesto, was born.

Key highlights of that meeting include the following:

- Base new methods on incremental and iterative development.
- Build working software quickly.
- Develop higher-quality software in shorter time frames.
- Create minimal front-end planning and documentation with an emphasis on seeking customer feedback.
- Allow requirements and solutions to evolve through collaboration and self-organizing, cross-functional teams.

The Agile Manifesto was intended to provide guiding values and principles instead of rules and constraining processes. After all, it was the rules and process-heavy limitations of traditional project management that led the 17 software developers to the meeting. The Agile Manifesto today is the basis for many Agile methodologies currently in use, such as Scrum, Extreme Programming, Lean, and Crystal Methods.

REMEMBER

It's been over 20 years since the Agile Manifesto was created, and some have argued that perhaps it's time for an update, especially since Agile has expanded its reach beyond software development. As it stands, the Agile Manifesto has not changed and remains a guide that can be applied in many different industries. Despite the suggested iterations of the Agile Manifesto, PMP aspirants will be expected to be familiar with the original guidance that was created in 2001.

## The four values

The Agile Manifesto authors stated the following about the four paired values:

- Individuals and interactions over processes and tools
- Working software over comprehensive documentation
- Customer collaboration over contract negotiation
- Responding to change over following a plan

That is, while there is value in the items on the right, we value the items on the left more.

## The Twelve Principles

The Agile Manifesto did not stop with creating the four Agile values. The authors also created twelve guiding principles for Agile methods. Here's a review of the Twelve Principles of the Agile Manifesto.

1. **Our highest priority is to satisfy the customer through early and continuous delivery of valuable software.**

    The focus is to deliver value to the customer through continuous delivery. When faced with a potential Agile situation on the exam, the highest priority is to deliver value.

2. **Welcome changing requirements, even late in development. Agile processes harness change for the customer's competitive advantage.**

    Changes are welcomed, even late in the game. You may encounter an exam scenario where project requirements need to change in the Agile environment. You welcome changes!

3. **Deliver working software frequently, from a couple of weeks to a couple of months, with a preference for the shorter timescale.**

    Unlike predictive projects, where deliverables are created at the project's end, Agile focuses on delivering products and value frequently in shorter timeframes.

4. **Business people and developers must work together daily throughout the project.**

    In Agile, developers and business people are working together to deliver value.

5. **Build projects around motivated individuals. Give them the environment and support they need, and trust them to get the job done.**

    This focuses on creating a work environment where the team is motivated to problem-solve, collaborate, and deliver results.

6. **The most efficient and effective method of conveying information to and within a development team is face-to-face conversation.**

    Communication is a significant part of Agile, and teams are ideally co-located. In the Agile environment, Agile teams aim to follow this principle whenever possible.

7. **Working software is the primary measure of progress.**

    The real measure of progress is working software, rather than numerous meetings and comprehensive documentation updates.

8. **Agile processes promote sustainable development. The sponsors, developers, and users should be able to maintain a constant pace indefinitely.**

    You may encounter a scenario on the exam where the Agile team is working overtime and putting in a lot of long hours. This situation goes against this principle. Agile methods recognize a manageable work environment that allows for work-life balance.

9. **Continuous attention to technical excellence and good design enhances agility.**

    Paying attention to good design creates value for the customer. When the team keeps the design clean and efficient, this actually helps them to better understand and update the design easily when changes arise — thus speeding up the team's progress.

10. **Simplicity — the art of maximizing the amount of work not done — is essential.**

    When teams focus on prioritized requirements and don't create more than what's needed, this strategy mitigates risks and boosts stakeholder confidence.

11. **The best architectures, requirements, and designs emerge from self-organizing teams.**

    Same team, same dream. Agile teams are self-organizing and self-governing, leading to better solutions and better outcomes.

**12.** **At regular intervals, the team reflects on how to become more effective, then tunes and adjusts its behavior accordingly.**

Teams need to pause and reflect. That includes openly communicating about what did and did not work well and making adjustments as necessary. If you encounter scenarios in the exam where Agile teams are not pausing to fine-tune and adjust their work, you should recognize that something is amiss.

TIP

It's not necessary to memorize the Agile Manifesto per se. However, having a general understanding of it will help you select the *most* correct PMI answer for Agile questions.

The value behind providing the details of the Agile Manifesto is to help you have the right Agile mindset in preparation for the exam. When you have an Agile mindset, you will be in the best position to correctly answer the Agile questions.

## Exercise: Agile Manifesto principles scenario matching

Following are ten scenarios that describe common project management situations. Match each scenario with a principle.

1. Review the Twelve Principles of the Agile Manifesto from the previous section.
2. Read each scenario and write the number of the Agile principle it best applies.
3. Once you have completed the exercise, check your answers with the answer key at the end of this chapter.

Here are the scenarios.

1. During a project, the team frequently seeks feedback from the customer after each iteration to ensure the product aligns with their needs and expectations.
2. A project team encounters a sudden change in market conditions. Instead of sticking rigidly to the original plan, they quickly adapt their approach to respond to the new requirements.
3. At the end of every sprint, the team holds a retrospective meeting to discuss what went well, what didn't, and how they can improve their processes for the next sprint.
4. The development team works closely with the product owner daily to ensure a mutual understanding of the product requirements and immediate clarification of any uncertainties.

5. A project is progressing, but the team decides to simplify the process by removing unnecessary documentation that does not contribute directly to the delivery of the product.

6. A team member suggests a new tool that could streamline the development process. The team discusses and decides to implement this tool as an experiment for one sprint.

7. The project manager prioritizes fostering a collaborative environment where each team member feels comfortable sharing ideas and taking ownership of tasks.

8. The team decides to deliver a simple, working version of the software quickly to gather user feedback, instead of waiting until all features are developed.

9. The team ensures the technical excellence and good design of the product throughout the project to enhance agility and ease future modifications.

10. Every team member is encouraged to work at a sustainable pace, avoiding overtime to maintain high quality and productivity over the long term.

# Delivering Value: The Agile Development Life Cycle

*Agile development* is a method of managing projects in small, incremental portions of work that can be easily assigned, easily managed, and completed within a short period of time. A good place to start is to walk through an illustration of the Agile development life cycle.

## EMBRACE THE AGILE MINDSET

Project professionals who are new to Agile often get fixated on *doing* Agile rather than *being agile*. Agile is not about a framework or the use of tools; rather, it is a mindset that is defined by values, guided by principles, and manifested through many different practices, such as Scrum or Kanban. As an Agile practitioner, you will decide on the best practice to use that meets the needs of the project. For PMP Exam aspirants, you will be tested on general Agile tools and techniques, but most importantly, on your ability to demonstrate the Agile mindset to best answer the exam questions.

In the following description, this life cycle is specific to the Scrum framework, and thus Scrum terminology is used. While specific to Scrum, it is a good representation of what an Agile life cycle looks like, as you can see in Figure 19-1.

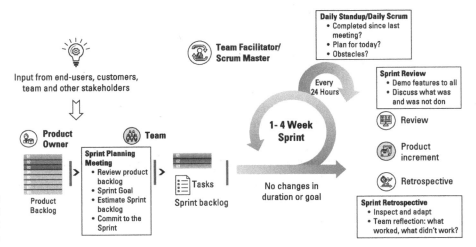

FIGURE 19-1: An Agile development life cycle.

Let's break down the life cycle.

>> At the beginning of the model, the product owner works with the customer and other stakeholders to get input into the features that should go into the product. In Agile, a *sprint* is a timeboxed period of work during which a development team completes a set of pre-planned and prioritized tasks. The sprint typically lasts between one and four weeks and is a critical part of the Agile framework.

>> During a **sprint planning meeting**, the development team estimates the time needed to implement each feature and determines which features they will focus on delivering for the next sprint (or iteration). The tasks to complete the work are housed in a *sprint backlog*.

>> During the sprint, the development team works together to achieve the goals documented in the sprint backlog. No changes are added during the sprint. The team gathers daily in a short meeting, known as the **daily stand-up** or **daily Scrum**, to discuss their progress and any challenges faced, and to plan their work for the next 24 hours. The daily Scrum allows each of the developers to quickly communicate to the team what was done yesterday, what is the planned work for today, and what, if any, impediments are holding them up.

» At the end of each sprint, the team delivers a potentially shippable product increment that provides real value to stakeholders. This product increment should be working and fully tested, even if it doesn't include all the features planned for the final product.

» At the end of each sprint, the team also shows the work that has been completed and asks the customer to accept the work as done. This is called the **sprint review meeting**. At this point, an increment of software is delivered to the system as a whole.

» A **sprint retrospective** then occurs, which allows the team to reflect on the most recent sprint and what can be improved with respect to the process.

To reduce the need for unnecessary meetings, Scrum prescribes these four meetings and declares a *timebox* for each one to keep the meetings focused. The timebox concept involves using time as a restraint, where each event is completed over a maximum duration.

The Agile development framework is a popular approach to software development that emphasizes collaboration, flexibility, and continuous improvement. By embracing Agile, project managers can create a more responsive, customer-focused, and collaborative development process that delivers value quickly and adapts to changing circumstances.

# Implementing Common Agile Frameworks

Several Agile frameworks have emerged over the years, each with its own set of principles, practices, and guidelines for implementing Agile project management. This section explores some of the most common Agile frameworks, including Scrum, Kanban, Extreme Programming (XP), and Dynamic Systems Development Method (DSDM). While the review of these frameworks will be brief, you may encounter these frameworks as a part of your PMP Exam experience.

You'll only need to know the fundamentals of the following Agile frameworks. There's no need to get overwhelmed by the details or to do additional research. More than likely, if any of these frameworks are mentioned, it is a hint that the scenario is describing an Agile project and thus, you should have the Agile mindset when answering the question.

## Scrum framework

The Scrum framework is one of the most widely used Agile frameworks because it provides a simple and effective way to manage complex projects while promoting collaboration, transparency, and continuous improvement. Key characteristics of Scrum include the following:

- Uses a single team process framework
- Consists of roles, events, artifacts, and rules
- Uses an iterative approach to deliver a working product
- Runs on timeboxes of one month or less, called *sprints*
- A Scrum team consists of a product owner, development team, and Scrum Master.

Scrum is based on three pillars: transparency, inspection, and adaptation. In addition to the three pillars, Scrum also recognizes five fundamental values: focus, courage, openness, commitment, and respect.

Because of the wide popularity of Scrum, don't be surprised if you encounter Scrum terminology in the description of an Agile scenario.

## Extreme Programming

*Extreme Programming*, commonly referred to as XP, is a software development method based on frequent cycles, or iterations, that typically last for two weeks on a typical project. Key characteristics of this methodology include the following:

- Focuses on software development best practices
- Delivers large amounts of software within the shortest time
- Is based on frequent cycles
- Has the core values of simplicity, communication, feedback, courage, and respect
- Uses metaphors to explain designs and create a shared technical vision

You may encounter the term *XP metaphor* when preparing for the exam. Metaphors are used to explain concepts in a relatable way through the use of an example that is relative to the individual's experience; for example, "I've streamlined the system so that it should feel like you're hitting the 'easy' button."

## Kanban Method

The Kanban Method, pronounced "con bon," is derived from the Lean production system developed at Toyota. *Kanban* is a Japanese word meaning "signboard." The key characteristics of the Kanban Method include the following:

- Derived from Lean thinking principles
- Enables and promotes the visualization and flow of work
- Does not prescribe timebox iterations

Kanban uses a "pull system" to move work through the process. Teams use a kanban board (discussed in Chapter 16) to visualize their work and to show the work items in each stage. When the team completes an item, they can pull the item to the next stage.

## But wait, there's more: Additional Agile methods

As previously mentioned, numerous Agile methodologies are in practice today. While it is not necessary to get into the weeds about these methodologies, including the ones mentioned in this chapter, it's good to have an awareness of them, in case you encounter an experimental question that asks about them. Some additional notable Agile methodologies are listed here.

- **Scrumban:** Scrum is used as a framework where work is organized into small "sprints" and leverages the use of kanban boards to visualize and monitor the work.
- **Dynamic Systems Development Method (DSDM):** This is a delivery framework designed to add more rigor to existing iterative methods that were popular in the 1990s. It is known for its emphasis on constraint-driven delivery.
- **Agile Unified Process (Agile UP):** This is a simplistic and understandable approach to developing business application software using Agile techniques and concepts. Agile UP is a simplified version of the Rational Unified Process (RUP).

Additionally, scaling frameworks have appeared in industry to account for large-scale Agile implementation, allowing organizations to apply Agile across multiple teams. Some of these frameworks include Scaled Agile Framework (SAFe), Large Scale Scrum (LeSS), and Disciplined Agile (DA).

### Deciding which framework to use

Each Agile framework has its strengths and weaknesses, so it's important to choose the one best suited to your organization's specific needs and goals. There's more to it than saying, "Let's implement Agile!" You need to know which Agile will fit your organization's and end users' changing needs.

You may still be asking the question, "So, which framework?" The answer is, "It depends." Key considerations in your choice of Agile framework include the following:

- Frameworks can be used as is or combined
- The frameworks adapt to what works best for the situation and environment
- Some approaches are centered on a single project activity (Scrum)
- Other approaches need to extend across multiple teams in large organizations (such as SAFe).

REMEMBER

As long as you adhere to the mindset, values, and principles of the Agile Manifesto, you have the flexibility to tailor the methods and techniques that meet the needs of your project.

## Comparing the Triangle of Constraints in Predictive and Agile Projects

The triple constraints of project management — scope, schedule, and cost — form an essential framework that governs the successful delivery of any project. This concept is sometimes referred to as the iron triangle because it stresses that the constraints are "iron," and that you cannot change one constraint without impacting the others.

In the traditional project management triangle, scope is fixed and costs and time are variable. The original iron triangle project management concept was proposed by Dr. Martin Barnes in 1969.

The Agile environment uses the Agile Inverted Triangle of Constraints. This triangle is inverted so that time and resources are fixed, and the scope is variable. Figure 19-2 shows how the traditional and Agile triangles differ.

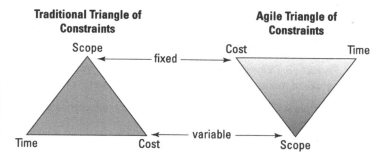

FIGURE 19-2: Comparing the traditional triangle of constraints to the Agile triangle.

In Agile development, the scope of the project is the most important aspect, as it defines the value that will be delivered to the customer. Time and resources are then managed around the scope, with the goal of delivering the most valuable features to the customer in the shortest amount of time and at the lowest cost possible. By understanding and balancing the three key constraints of time, cost, and scope, project managers can ensure they deliver value to the customer while staying within the project's limitations. This allows for a more flexible, collaborative, and adaptive development process that can quickly respond to changing requirements and deliver value.

REMEMBER

Managing these constraints is a balancing act, regardless of your project's environment. Changes to one constraint can significantly impact the others, affecting overall project quality. However, being aware of the project environment compels you to be more intentional about your choices.

# Answer Key: Agile Manifesto Principles

1. Principle 1. The highest priority is to satisfy the customer through early and continuous delivery of valuable software.

2. Principle 2. Welcome changing requirements, even late in development. Agile processes harness change for the customer's competitive advantage.

3. Principle 12. At regular intervals, the team reflects on how to become more effective, then tunes and adjusts its behavior accordingly.

4. Principle 4. Business people and developers must work together daily throughout the project.

5. Principle 10. Simplicity — the art of maximizing the amount of work not done — is essential.

6. Principle 11. The best architectures, requirements, and designs emerge from self-organizing teams.

7. Principle 5: Build projects around motivated individuals. Give them the environment and support they need, and trust them to get the job done.

8. Principle 3. Deliver working software frequently, from a couple of weeks to a couple of months, with a preference for the shorter timescale.

9. Principle 9. Continuous attention to technical excellence and good design enhances agility.

10. Principle 8. Agile processes promote sustainable development. The sponsors, developers, and users should be able to maintain a constant pace indefinitely.

> **IN THIS CHAPTER**
> » Identifying attributes of successful Agile teams
> » Analyzing the distinct roles of the cross-functional team, product owner, and team facilitator
> » Exploring the difference between I-shaped and T-shaped people
> » Describing the role of the Agile coach

Chapter **20**

# Agile Teams: Key Roles and Responsibilities

In the Agile environment, we value "individuals and interactions over process and tools." Agile places value on "we" rather than "me," encompassing a cross-functional team that coordinates their own work, a team facilitator who coaches and guides the team, and a business representative who collaborates with the team to guide the direction of the product.

This chapter expands upon these roles and provides a foundational understanding of the key attributes that make up successful Agile teams.

If you practice specific Agile frameworks such as Scrum or Scaled Agile Framework (SAFe), which are covered in Chapter 19, you may encounter roles that are called something different in your world. Bear in mind that the names referenced in this chapter are based on the terminology from the *Agile Practice Guide*, which is one of the key references of the PMP Exam Content Outline.

# Getting an Overview of Agile Teams

The *Agile Practice Guide*, published in collaboration with the Project Management Institute and the Agile Alliance, succinctly describes the key characteristics of Agile teams:

- Agile teams focus on rapid product development.
- In practice, Agile team sizes are less than ten people, where the most effective teams tend to range in size from three to nine team members.
- Ideally, Agile teams are co-located in a team space.
- Team members are 100 percent dedicated to the team.
- Agile encourages self-managing teams, where they decide how they perform the work.
- Agile teams thrive with servant leadership.
- The leaders support the teams' ways of working.

Most importantly, cross-functional teams consistently deliver functional product increments. By collectively owning the work and possessing all the necessary skills, they ensure the successful completion of functional work.

The following list outlines the key attributes of a successful Agile team. This list illustrates how Agile teams encourage collaboration, boost productivity, and facilitate innovation and problem-solving.

- Dedicated people who are focused and productive.
- Cross-functional team members who integrate all the work activities to deliver finished value.
- The ability to manage any location challenges through communication skills and knowledge sharing.
- A composition of both generalists who offer adaptability and specialists who bring expertise.
- A stable work environment with an agreed-upon way of working.

# Building Better Products with Cross-Functional Team Members

As previously mentioned, cross-functional teams are valued in the Agile environment. These types of teams have all the necessary skills to collectively produce a working product. Cross-functional teams can fulfill more than one role necessary to complete the work, which is different from the typical specialized team member that can only fulfill one role in traditional projects. Because of their diverse skills, they are more self-sufficient, allowing the team to make significant and fast progress in producing a working product at the end of every sprint.

In the Scrum framework, the cross-functional team members are referred to as *developers*.

Cross-functional teams are comprised of members with diverse skills and expertise, enabling them to handle various aspects of the project without relying on external resources. Agile teams function better when they have a mix of I-shaped and T-shaped team members.

» **An I-shaped person** has deep expertise in one particular area (represented by the vertical line of the "I"). This type of team member has deep specialization in one domain and rarely contributes outside of that domain. This singular specialization may create a bottleneck for the rest of the team. Imagine if this person were called off the team because they were the *only* person in the company with this skill set, or they were on vacation and the team had to wait for their return to complete the work product.

» **A T-shaped person,** on the other hand, has expertise in one area but also possesses a broader range of skills and can collaborate across different domains (represented by the horizontal line of the "T"). I like to think of the "T" as standing for "team player." As a team player, this type of person is more collaborative; there's less of the "that's not my job" mentality, and this type of team member reduces the need for relying on one person to do the job.

In Agile teams, having a mix of I-shaped and T-shaped individuals promotes a balance between specialized expertise and flexibility in handling different tasks. However, many successful Agile teams are made up of generalizing specialists, or "T-shaped" people.

Other names that are used interchangeably with cross-functional teams include developers, development team, and Scrum team. You may encounter these terms in the exam.

CHAPTER 20 Agile Teams: Key Roles and Responsibilities    355

There is no hero on the cross-functional team, as the entire team has a single accountability to deliver the increment at the end of the iteration (or sprint if you're working with the Scrum framework). Same team, same dream.

# Representing the Voice of the Customer: Product Owner

The product owner is responsible for prioritizing the product backlog and deciding which items are most important for the development team to work on in the next sprint. Key highlights of the product owner's responsibilities include the following:

- Ensures work items in the product backlog are up to date and accurately prioritized
- Ensures that the business and the cross-functional team have a clear and shared understanding of the project vision
- Works with stakeholders, customers, and teams to define product direction

While the product owner is responsible for prioritizing the product backlog, they can delegate or seek assistance from the team facilitator and/or cross-functional team members. See Chapter 21 for additional information about the product backlog.

REMEMBER

A key success factor for Agile teams is strong product ownership. If the product owner does not maintain the backlog, Agile teams risk creating features and work products that are not valuable to the stakeholders. What a waste of time!

Typically, the product owner has a business background and has deep subject matter expertise that they can apply to decision-making efforts. Ideally, the organization has empowered the product owner to make decisions and serve as the "voice of the customer" or "voice of the sponsor."

# Using Skilled Facilitation via the Team Facilitator

The team facilitator role is a dramatic shift from the command and control that embodies the project manager role in predictive projects. In the traditional project environment, project managers take on the responsibility to lead, direct, and delegate the work. They are the focal point of projects, and if decisions need to be made, rest assured that the project manager will make those decisions.

That is not the case in the Agile environment. Here, the team facilitator's role is that of a servant leader. As a servant leader, the team facilitator's focus is to do the following:

- Coach team members on embracing Agile values
- Ensure Agile methodologies are understood and used effectively
- Lead with influence and empathy
- Remove roadblocks that impede the team's progress
- Assist the product owner with managing the backlog and communicating the product/project vision

The team facilitator sets up the environment to encourage and empower the team to self-organize and self-manage. In addition, the team facilitator makes sure that good Agile practices are being followed and coaches the team throughout.

**TIP** The team facilitator may also be called a project manager, Scrum Master, project team lead, or team coach. For instance, you may encounter an exam question that says, "You are the project manager on an Agile project...". If that is the case, you need to approach the question with a servant leadership mindset.

# Focusing on Servant Leadership

Servant leadership is a leadership approach that focuses on understanding and addressing the needs and development of project team members. Servant leaders share power, put the needs of the team first, and allow teams to self-organize. As a servant leader, the team facilitator is more focused on removing obstacles, shielding the team from distractions (please don't pull them into a meeting that could have been an email), and providing guidance and support to help team members succeed.

In Agile, servant leaders serve their teams and ensure that the team's goals are aligned with the project's objectives, empowering them to make decisions and take ownership of their work. This leadership style fosters a positive and collaborative team environment, leading to higher team morale and productivity.

Servant leadership complements the Agile principles of collaboration, customer focus, and continuous improvement, leading to successful project deliveries and higher stakeholder satisfaction. This leadership style empowers team members to excel and take ownership of their work.

While Agile promotes servant leadership, this approach is also embraced in predictive projects. Should you encounter an exam question that says, "You are a servant leader..." yet you notice the project environment is traditional, you should focus on the fact that the project manager has chosen to use this coaching and guiding approach in the context of the predictive project environment.

# Benefitting from an Agile Coach

Some organizations may decide to bring on an Agile coach (also referred to as a mentor) to help the team embrace the Agile methodologies and mindset, particularly when Agile is new to them. Agile coaches are not a required role on Agile projects, yet they can serve as a resource as the organization is working toward developing the internal resources they need to fully and comfortably serve in the team facilitator role. Here are some key points regarding the advantages and disadvantages of an external and internal Agile coach:

» **An external Agile coach** has the advantage of breadth and depth of experience, having worked with various organizations and Agile projects. The downside is that they may have weak relationships with the client organization.

» **An internal Agile coach** has strong relationships with organizational stakeholders but may lack a breadth of experience.

**IN THIS CHAPTER**

» Exploring Agile ceremonies

» Highlighting the purpose of each Agile ceremony

» Getting an overview of key Agile artifacts

» Discovering the purpose of the minimum viable product

Chapter **21**

# Key Agile Practices

This chapter describes the purpose of the key Agile ceremonies conducted and artifacts created to ensure team and stakeholder collaboration and to support continuous improvement. While many people fall into the trap of thinking there are no meetings or documentation in the Agile environment (you won't fall for that trap), the fact is that Agile has streamlined meetings and documentation to serve a specific purpose.

The four ceremonies of the Agile development model (iteration planning, daily stand-up, iteration review, and iteration retrospective) provide structure and guidance to the development process, while three key artifacts (product backlog, sprint backlog, and product increment) ensure that everyone on the team is aligned and working toward the same goals. Together, the ceremonies and development of project artifacts foster collaboration and put focus on delivering value.

# Facilitating Agile Ceremonies

Meetings do occur in the Agile environment, but the meetings (or events) that occur are designed to drive collaboration and continuous improvement within Agile teams. These events are pivotal in fostering transparency, accountability, and effective decision-making. Here are some key benefits of Agile ceremonies:

- Allowing teams and stakeholders to interact on a regular basis
- Sharing progress
- Addressing challenges
- Obtaining feedback from stakeholders and among the team

Agile events help ensure that the project team, stakeholders, and clients maintain a shared understanding and effectively work together toward meeting the project and product goals.

REMEMBER

You'll see the words *ceremonies* and *events* used interchangeably to describe the key meetings of Agile.

## Planning dynamically: Iteration planning

Iteration planning occurs at the beginning of each iteration and involves the entire Agile team, including the product owner. During this meeting, the team reviews the prioritized backlog items and collectively decides which items they can commit to completing in the upcoming iteration. This meeting includes everyone: the team facilitator (Scrum Master), the product owner, and the cross-functional team. The purpose of the meeting is to establish an iteration goal (sprint goal) and select the user stories that the team will address during the iteration. Furthermore, the team will spend time during this meeting discussing how to break down the user stories into individual tasks.

> ### SPRINT VERSUS ITERATION
>
> Agile projects work in iterations, which are smaller segments of the project work. Sprints are small segments of work in the Scrum framework. The term *sprint* is specific to the Scrum practice of Agile. Given that many Agile practitioners use the Scrum framework, teams often default to using the term *sprint* — that is, sprint review, sprint retrospective, sprint planning, and so on. PMI and the Agile Alliance are not framework specific, so you may encounter the term *iteration* in place of sprint. In either case, iteration and sprint may be used interchangeably on the exam.

Iteration planning results in the creation of the iteration backlog (also known as sprint backlog). I discuss this artifact later in this chapter. After iteration planning, the cross-functional team can immediately start working on the tasks to create the product.

In the Scrum framework, iteration planning is called sprint planning.

## Gathering the team for insight: The daily stand-up

*The daily stand-up* is a short, daily gathering that brings the team together to synchronize their activities, share progress, and identify any potential roadblocks. As a servant leader, the team facilitator encourages open communication during this event, ensuring that team members feel supported and able to voice any challenges they may face. The daily stand-up is typically timeboxed to no more than 15 minutes where team members answer three questions:

>> What did I complete since the last stand-up?

>> What am I planning to complete between now and the next stand-up?

>> What are my impediments (or risks or problems)?

The team has the opportunity to coordinate their efforts and plan what each team member will be working on during the day to achieve the iteration goal. During this meeting, the team facilitator can note completed items and identify impediments or roadblocks. By actively removing impediments, the team facilitator empowers the team to work efficiently and focus on their goals.

In the Scrum framework, the daily stand-up is referred to as the daily Scrum.

General practice is that the team members with assigned tasks need to answer the three questions. Typically, the team facilitator is present at the daily stand-up to ensure the meeting happens and to listen for any roadblocks.

## Engaging the stakeholders: Iteration review

The iteration review occurs at the end of each iteration (sprint). It is a collaborative space for showcasing completed work and for gathering feedback. Stakeholders and product owners can inspect the increment, ask questions, and provide insights. This open dialogue helps the team understand if the product is moving in the right direction or if any adjustments are necessary for future iterations. These reviews foster transparency, collaboration, and stakeholder engagement, ensuring that the project remains on track and meets stakeholders' needs.

CHAPTER 21 **Key Agile Practices** 361

In the Scrum framework, the iteration review is called the sprint review or demonstration (demo).

During the review, the product owner assesses whether the work meets the *definition of done,* ensuring that it meets all criteria for completeness. This is an opportunity for the team and stakeholders to evaluate the increment and confirm that it aligns with the agreed-upon requirements. The definition of done acts as a checklist of all the required criteria and any other acceptance criteria specific to the deliverable.

## Reflecting on the outcomes: Iteration retrospective

The *iteration retrospective,* held after each iteration, is where the team reflects on their performance, processes, and interactions. The team facilitator ensures that all team members have a voice in discussing what went well and what could be improved. All team members are encouraged to actively participate in this reflective process, with the goal that the team members take ownership in their actions and drive toward continuous improvement in their work practices.

In the Scrum framework, the iteration retrospective is called the sprint retrospective. Some teams simply shorten the term to retrospective or simply, retro.

## Refining the backlog: An unofficial Agile event

There has been some debate about whether *backlog refinement* is an actual Agile event. Product backlog refinement involves the product owner and the cross-functional team collaborating to add details, estimates, order, and decomposition to the product backlog. The primary goal of this meeting is to enhance the clarity of the backlog items to a level where the team comprehends the backlog content and relative complexity.

Product backlog refinement is more of an activity than it is a timeboxed meeting that should happen at a set point during Agile development (unlike iteration planning, which occurs at the start of the iteration, the retrospective, which occurs at the end, and so on). Nor is there a timebox for how long the meeting should run (as with 15-minute daily stand-up meetings). This activity can occur daily, weekly, or once per iteration. The important takeaway about backlog refinement is that it *should* happen to ensure the product backlog is updated and accurately prioritized. Without a properly maintained backlog, Agile teams risk working on items that aren't relevant to stakeholders or the overall product vision. The product owner can informally delegate this task to the cross-functional team.

For PMP aspirants, you need to be prepared for questions about the purpose and benefits of backlog refinement. The purpose is to ensure an accurately prioritized backlog and that the product owner is ultimately accountable for it, even when they delegate some tasks.

You may encounter the term *backlog grooming* as a part of your studies and when taking practice exams. The term *grooming* has negative connotations in other parts of the world, so Agile professionals have transitioned to *backlog refinement*.

Backlog refinement is an iterative process that aids in improving the overall understanding of the work to be done. Additionally, backlog refinement serves as an avenue for the product owner to introduce new backlog items to the team while providing an opportunity for the team to discuss potential challenges or issues with the product backlog items.

# Using Agile Artifacts

In the Agile environment, project artifacts serve as helpful tools for facilitating transparency and collaboration among teams. Unlike traditional project management where documentation tends to be comprehensive, Agile emphasizes lightweight and flexible artifacts that evolve throughout the project duration. These artifacts provide the right amount of structure for teams to plan, execute, and track progress without becoming overwhelming or burdensome. Moreover, these artifacts are designed to foster shared understanding and allow for quick adaptation as priorities change, ensuring the development process remains aligned with the customer's needs and the product vision. Let's take a look at the major artifacts that are produced in the Agile environment.

## Envisioning the Agile journey: The product roadmap

The *product roadmap* is a holistic view of the high-level functionality required to achieve the product vision. It provides the "big picture" view that teams need to focus on, as it visually depicts the product releases and the main components that will be included in each release. Moreover, the product roadmap serves as a powerful communication and high-level planning tool to share with stakeholders.

## AGILE CHARTERS DO EXIST!

Agile projects also have project charters. Just as in predictive projects, an Agile project charter should be one of the first documents the team produces, outlining the project's goals, purpose, composition, and approach. Charters in the Agile environment can be lightweight documents acknowledging that scope may change and that initially some aspects of the project are unknown. Here are some key highlights of what a team may include in the Agile charter:

- Processes and approaches used by the team
- Iteration lengths
- Acceptance criteria used to verify the project outcomes

Agile charters focus on the goals envisioned for the project, but the level of detail and assumptions are different than what you would expect in a project charter for a traditional project.

For the purposes of the PMP Exam, assume every project, whether it is a predictive project or adaptive (Agile) project, will have a project charter.

## Maintaining a master list of requirements: The product backlog

The product backlog is a prioritized list of user stories, desired features, enhancements, and bug fixes to achieve the product vision (remember the product roadmap from earlier?). The product backlog provides more detail than the product roadmap, where the stakeholders, including customers, users, and other relevant parties, contribute by identifying and prioritizing items based on their requirements and preferences. The product backlog is a central tool for stakeholder engagement, guiding the development team's work and facilitating ongoing collaboration. The product owner is responsible for maintaining and continuously prioritizing backlog items.

The product backlog is the primary source for items that a team works on. That means they only work on items on the product backlog. Conversely, the presence of a backlog item on a product backlog does not guarantee that it will be delivered. A backlog item represents an option for the team in order to deliver a specific outcome rather than making a commitment that *everything* on the product backlog be delivered.

Typically, the product backlog items are user stories, and the order of these items changes as the team gains a better understanding of the outcome and the identified solution. This reordering of existing product backlog items, the ongoing addition and removal of items, and the continuous refinement of items is what makes the product backlog so dynamic.

The product owner is the primary person responsible for maintaining the product backlog.

TIP

PMP aspirants should expect quite a few questions on the concept of the product backlog, especially in terms of how it differs from the product roadmap and the sprint backlog and who is responsible for maintaining the product backlog.

The product backlog can be represented in physical form using index cards or sticky notes, or it may be represented in electronic forms such as a text file, spreadsheet, or one of the many cloud-based backlog management tools that exist. Remote teams often rely on electronic boards. Co-located teams may rely on physical boards, which offer the advantage of making the product backlog continuously visible and concrete during discussions around the product backlog.

## USER STORIES PROVIDE INSIGHT ON STAKEHOLDER VALUES

*User stories* are concise, user-focused descriptions of functionality or features expressed from the perspective of the end user or stakeholder. User stories capture the *who*, *what*, and *why* of a requirement and serve as a means of communication and collaboration between stakeholders and the Agile team. User stories follow a pattern:

Role — As a (name of role)

Goal — I want to (do something)

Benefit — So that I (get a result I want)

The user story approach focuses on the stakeholder, the need, and the desired outcome. Framing the user's desire as a story enables the team to focus on the user and what they value.

## Planning the team's list of to-dos: The iteration backlog

Also known as a sprint backlog, an iteration backlog is a subset of the product backlog. Iteration backlog items are usually pulled from the product backlog during the iteration planning session. The result of iteration planning is the creation of the iteration backlog.

A clear iteration backlog prevents scope creep by clarifying exactly what the team will be doing — and not doing — during each iteration. The purpose of an iteration backlog is to define work items to tackle within the iteration. This keeps information in one shared space to streamline communication and create one central source of information.

Teams generally track the iteration backlog on an information radiator to provide a visual of their progress and indicate the scope of the current iteration. Teams may also track their progress on a task board, such as a kanban board.

Agile teams often "walk the board" that represents their iteration backlog. Because teams generally place the board in a section of the room where they walk over and gather around to discuss their progress, they are typically standing around the board — hence, the daily stand-up.

Most backlog items included on the iteration backlog are user stories that are described according to the team's definition of ready. Other backlog items could represent bugs the team needs to address, research they need to do (typically in the form of spikes), or changes they need to make to the architecture or infrastructure of the product.

The iteration backlog only lasts for the duration of the iteration. Each new iteration starts with a new iteration backlog. However, the team may choose to add items from the previous iteration backlog to the new iteration backlog if those items contribute to completing the new iteration goal — or if the team did not complete them in the last iteration.

The Agile team collaborates to create and maintain the iteration backlog. Typically, only the development team makes any modifications to the iteration backlog, which reflects the day-to-day progress of the team.

## Bringing the vision to life: The product increment

The *product increment*, also known as the potentially shippable product increment, is the fully developed, functioning feature set that the team delivers at the end of each iteration. While the product owner does not have to release every increment to the customer immediately, they can be confident that each increment is market-ready for release when sufficient value has been aggregated. Each product increment should be fully functional and demonstrate proper operation. An Agile project is considered complete once it delivers enough shippable functionality to satisfy the customer's business requirements.

## Gaining a competitive advantage with an MVP

A *minimum viable product* (MVP) is a package of functionality that is complete enough to be useful to the market yet small enough that it doesn't represent the entire product. In Lean methodologies, it can be referred to as *bare-bones* or *no-frills* functionality. An MVP allows Agile teams to see how the product increment appeals to the customer and how the customer uses the product. A tangible output allows for targeted conversations, which generate feedback and ideas. An MVP is not a minimal product; it is a strategy and process for making and selling a product. It is an iterative process of idea generation, prototyping, presentation, data collection, analysis, and learning. Here are some key points about MVPs:

- » **Early validation:** MVPs allow teams to test assumptions early in the development process.

- » **Speed to market:** By focusing on the essential features, Agile teams can deliver products faster, gaining a competitive advantage.

- » **Customer-centric approach:** Engaging with early adopters and iterating based on their feedback ensures that the product evolves in a way that aligns with customer needs and preferences.

Agile teams deliver business value often, and delivering an MVP is a way to achieve that goal.

REMEMBER

Some Agile teams and organizations may use the terms *minimal viable product*.

Some notable real-world MVPs include the following.

- » **Dropbox:** When Dropbox started, they created a simple demo video showing how their product would work. The video was shared with potential users, generating feedback and gauging interest before any significant development. The MVP was a proof of concept to test the hypothesis that people wanted a convenient file-sharing service.

- **Airbnb:** The founders of Airbnb built a basic website; took photos of their San Francisco apartment during the time when a huge convention was held in town, and all the hotels were booked; and listed it for short-term rental. This MVP allowed them to validate their hypothesis by getting their first few customers and finding out what users wanted before building out the full platform.
- **Zappos:** Zappos, the online shoe retailer, started with an MVP where the founder took pictures of shoes at local stores and listed them online to see if people would actually buy shoes over the internet. If an order came through, he would go to the store, buy the shoes, and ship them. This allowed Zappos to test the market demand before building an entire inventory and fulfillment system.

MVPs don't have to be famous brand stories. They include the following:

- Pilot programs for new services
- Landing pages for product validation
- Internal employee feedback trials
- Pre-sales campaigns
- Pop-up shops for retail concepts
- Food trucks for future restaurants
- Webinars as a trial for new workshops

These examples show how companies of all shapes and sizes can utilize MVPs to test new ideas, reduce risk, and ensure they are aligning their offerings with customer needs before investing in significant resources. MVPs can appear in marketing, operations, product management, retail, food, customer service, and software development.

While Agile promotes flexibility and adaptability, it also incorporates practices designed to provide structure and guidance to teams. These practices are not intended to restrict teams but rather to establish a foundation for feedback, learning, and continuous improvement.

# Exercise: Convert Scenarios into User Stories

**Instructions**: Convert the following scenarios into user stories using the following format:

"As a [type of user], I want [goal] so that [benefit]."

**Scenario 1**: There is a need to have a system to log customer complaints and track their resolution status to ensure that issues are resolved promptly. This need has been requested by the customer support team.

**Scenario 2**: The marketing department requires a tool to segment their audience based on behavior so they can send personalized emails that increase engagement.

**Scenario 3**: The HR department wants an application that sends automated reminders for upcoming performance reviews to ensure all employees receive timely feedback. This application will be utilized by the specialists in the department.

# Answer Key: Convert Scenarios into User Stories

**Scenario 1:** As a customer support representative, I want a system to log customer complaints and track their resolution status so that I can ensure prompt issue resolution.

Variation: As a support agent, I need a tool to log and monitor complaints so that I can follow up and promptly resolve them within our service-level agreements.

**Scenario 2:** As a marketing team member, I want a tool to segment our audience based on behavior so that I can send personalized emails to increase engagement.

Variation: As a digital marketer, I need a platform to create behavior-based audience segments so I can target them with relevant content.

**Scenario 3:** As an HR specialist, I want an application that sends automated reminders for performance reviews so that all employees receive timely feedback.

Variation: As an HR manager, I need a system to automate performance review reminders so that no employee misses their evaluation.

# 6
# The Part of Tens

### IN THIS PART . . .

Develop a game plan that sets you up for exam success.

Decode the alphabet soup of acronyms you'll encounter on test day.

Uncover key assumptions to adopt the right exam mindset.

IN THIS CHAPTER

» Getting ready for the PMP Exam

» Creating a plan for success

Chapter **22**

# Ten Tips for PMP Exam Success

I've shared these tips with hundreds of students, with many coming from folks just like you. Time and again, successful students have come back to validate that these tips work. Consider the following tips as your playbook to PMP Exam success. You've got this!

## Pick an Exam Date

Setting a deadline gives you a sense of urgency to not make excuses. Here are some additional reasons to go ahead and pick an exam date:

- **Deadlines allow you to plan and schedule accordingly.** Setting a deadline allows you to plan out your weekends and figure out the steps you need to take toward your goal of passing the PMP Exam.
- **Deadlines keep you accountable.** If you don't set a deadline, you will never get around to it. Someday is not a day of the week.
- **Deadlines keep you motivated.** We've all been there when that looming deadline kicks us into high gear to finish the darn thing.

› **Deadlines help you prioritize.** When the deadline for a goal is near, you know what you need to do to get it done and make it a priority.

# Familiarize Yourself with the Exam Content Outline

Review the PMP Exam Content Outline provided by PMI to understand the domains and tasks covered in the exam. You can find more information about the Exam Content Outline on the PMI website: `https://www.pmi.org/certifications/project-management-pmp`.

# Create a Study Plan

Establish a study schedule that fits your lifestyle, setting aside regular, focused study time. Also be sure to break down the material into manageable sections, and set milestones to track your progress.

# Take Practice Exams

When students practice answering questions, even incorrectly, before learning the content, their future learning is enhanced. Research has shown that taking practice tests improves your test results more than spending the same amount of time studying. Here are some things to keep in mind:

› Take full-length practice exams to simulate the test environment and build your confidence.

› Analyze your practice exam results, understand the rationale behind each answer, and learn from your mistakes.

› Regularly take timed quizzes to improve your speed and accuracy.

How many practice tests, you ask? That depends on what works for you. Three practice exams should suffice, especially when you see your scores improve. What that entails is that after each practice exam, you should analyze and review your results so that you understand why you got the wrong answers.

# Adopt Good Study Habits

Experts at the Louisiana State University's Center for Academic Success suggest dedicating 30 to 50 minutes to studying new material.

Experts also suggest that you improve retention and recall with short bursts of studying rather than trying to study for hours on end. Focused study time of 30 to 50 minutes, with a 5- to 10-minute break before the start of the next session, allows you to rest your mind and do things like check your email.

REMEMBER

Brief, frequent studying sessions are much better than longer, infrequent ones. Also, put the study time on your calendar.

# Take Good Notes

Ever heard of the Cornell Method - 5 Rs of note taking? Here is a summary:

- **Record:** During the lecture, record meaningful facts and ideas.
- **Reduce:** Soon after the lecture, write a summary of the ideas and facts using key words as cues.
- **Recite:** Recite all the information in your own words without looking at your notes or the text. It may help to recite to a friend or family member.
- **Reflect:** Think about what you learned and make connections to your own ideas and understanding. Ask yourself: Which topics did I already understand well? Which topics do I need to further research? Are there examples or practice questions that can help solidify the content?
- **Review:** Before reading or studying new material, take ten minutes to quickly review your notes, going over the main ideas and details.

TIP

Take notes by hand! Recent research has shown that this can significantly improve information retention and recall by engaging more areas of the brain. This is due to the physical act of writing, which creates a deeper connection with the material compared to simply typing on a computer.

# Find the Right Testing Environment

You have options. If you are not going to take the exam at a Pearson VUE testing facility and choose the online proctored exam, consider the following options:

- A trusted friend's or family member's house with a quiet room
- A reserved room at your local library
- Your company's office space

Your company's office is my favorite option considering that many office spaces are working in hybrid work environments. There is less competition for the coveted conference space and office, given that many folks are working from home. Just be sure the conference room has four walls and a door and it's not a fishbowl scenario (windows as walls) so that you are not distracted.

# Stay Healthy and Focused

You don't want to burn yourself out while preparing for the exam. So, you can prioritize your well-being with these suggestions:

- **Take breaks.** Schedule short, regular breaks during study sessions to recharge and prevent burnout. Your brain needs time to process and retain information.
- **Embrace a healthy lifestyle.** Fuel your body and mind with a balanced diet, regular exercise, and sufficient sleep. These habits will enhance your focus, memory, and overall performance.

Right before the exam, make sure you do the following:

- **Get a full night of restful sleep** before the exam to stay sharp and energized.
- **Stay calm and confident on exam day.** Trust in your preparation and approach each question with a clear, focused mindset. Remember, success isn't just about knowing the material but also about applying it effectively.

Your well-being is non-negotiable!

## Stay Motivated with a Study Buddy or Study Groups

Engage with peers in study groups or online forums to share knowledge and stay motivated.

Research shows that having a study buddy or joining a study group can be beneficial when preparing for an exam. This is because it fosters accountability, improves motivation by making studying more engaging, and provides community and support.

## Plan for PMP Success

Have a plan in place as you prepare to study for the PMP Exam. I often encounter folks who just "wing it" and have unsuccessful outcomes.

The reason: They did not have a plan.

Here's an exercise adapted from the Agile environment, called "Remember the Future." I've facilitated this exercise many times with my students to help them develop a plan and get in the right mindset to be successful with the exam.

**INSTRUCTIONS:** Imagine it is 60 to 90 days from now and you just passed the PMP Exam. Hooray! You are basking in the glow of success but you know it could not have been possible without your proper planning and setting expectations at home and at work. Look back and describe what it will take to pass this exam within 60 to 90 days.

*What will you need to do to prepare yourself to get into the right exam mindset?*

_____

_____

_____

*What will you need to do to prepare your family and friends? Negotiate the chores schedule? Study outside of the home?*

_____

_____

_____

*What will you need to do to prepare your colleagues? Block your calendar? Take time off from work?*

_____

_____

_____

*What will you need to do to prepare your schedule? Clear your calendar? Block study time on your calendar?*

_____

_____

_____

IN THIS CHAPTER
» Decoding project management jargon
» Memorizing terms

# Chapter 23
# More Than Ten Common Acronyms

When preparing for the PMP Exam, many PMP aspirants encounter a seemingly endless array of acronyms that can feel both confusing and overwhelming. What follows is an alphabetical list of common acronyms, making it easier to reference and internalize them as you prepare for the exam. Think of this as your decoder to navigate the language of project management with confidence.

**AC:** Actual Cost

**BAC:** Budget at Completion

**CAPM:** Certified Associate in Project Management

**CCB:** Change Control Board

**CI/CD:** Continuous Integration/ Continuous Delivery

**CoQ:** Cost of Quality

**CPAF:** Cost Plus Award Fee

**CPFF:** Cost Plus Fixed Fee

**CPI:** Cost Performance Index

**CPIF:** Cost Plus Incentive Fee

**CPM:** Critical Path Method

**CR:** Change Request

**CV:** Cost Variance

**DA:** Disciplined Agile

**DSDM:** Dynamic Systems Development Method

**EAC:** Estimate at Completion

**EEFs:** Enterprise Environmental Factors

**ESG:** Environmental, Social, and Governance

**ETC:** Estimate to Complete

**EV:** Earned Value

**EVM:** Earned Value Management

**FFP:** Firm Fixed Price

**FPEPA:** Fixed Price with Economic Price Adjustment

**FPIF:** Fixed Price Incentive Fee

**IFB:** Invitation for Bid

**IRR:** Internal Rate of Return

**LOE:** Level of Effort

**MMF:** Minimal Marketable Feature

**MVP:** Minimum Viable Product

**OBS:** Organizational Breakdown Structure

**OPA:** Organizational Process Asset

**OPM:** Organizational Project Management

**PBI:** Product Backlog Item

**PDM:** Precedence Diagramming Method

**PDUs:** Professional Development Units

**PMBOK:** Project Management Body of Knowledge

**PMI:** Project Management Institute

**PMIS:** Project Management Information System

**PMO:** Project Management Office

**PMP:** Project Management Professional

**PV:** Planned Value or Present Value

**QA:** Quality Assurance

**QC:** Quality Control

**QFD:** Quality Function Deployment

**RACI:** Responsible, Accountable, Consulted, Informed

**RAM:** Responsibility Assignment Matrix

**RBS:** Resource Breakdown Structure or Risk Breakdown Structure

**RFI:** Request for Information

**RFP:** Request for Proposal

**RFQ:** Request for Quotation

**ROI:** Return on Investment

**RUP:** Rational Unified Process

**SAFe:** Scaled Agile Framework

**SME:** Subject Matter Expert

**SOW:** Statement of Work

**SPI:** Schedule Performance Index

**SV:** Schedule Variance

**SWOT:** Strengths, Weaknesses, Opportunities, Threats

**T&M:** Time and Materials

**TDD:** Test-Driven Development

**TQM:** Total Quality Management

**VAC:** Variance at Completion

**WBS:** Work Breakdown Structure

**XP:** Extreme Programming

**IN THIS CHAPTER**

» Navigating questions lacking complete information

» Developing the right mindset when on "Planet PMI"

# Chapter 24
# Ten Assumptions of the PMP Exam

Based on the PMI framework (what I lovingly call "Planet PMI"), the PMP Exam assesses your knowledge and application of project management principles. However, the questions often provide limited context, requiring you to make certain assumptions to interpret and answer them correctly. These assumptions reflect best practices and standardized methodologies in project management.

Knowing these assumptions can minimize your confusion and help you approach the exam with the right mindset. They ensure that you align your responses with how PMI envisions an ideal project environment — one that prioritizes proactive leadership, structured processes, and effective stakeholder collaboration. By internalizing these assumptions, you can confidently navigate scenarios and choose answers that reflect the PMI way of thinking, even when the questions lack complete information. And you will encounter many of these situations.

The following list outlines the top ten assumptions you should keep in mind during the exam. These assumptions act as a mental framework, guiding you to interpret each scenario with clarity and precision.

# Organizational Structure

You are in a strong-matrix organization, meaning you, as the project manager, have a high level of control over the project. You've selected your team, you have a significant amount of authority, and you can make decisions without seeking constant approval from the sponsor. This setup implies that you rarely need to ask for permission unless required for major escalations or if there are significant changes that could impact scope or stakeholder satisfaction. Your responsibilities extend to managing team performance, stakeholder relationships, and project execution independently.

# Best Practices

The organization follows project management best practices and ensures the use of proper tools and techniques. This means the following:

- You are documenting everything appropriately, from project charters to lessons learned.
- You are adhering to company policies, processes, and guidelines.
- You are anticipating problems, and solutions are proactively implemented, reducing the risk of issues snowballing.

This environment assumes that you are operating in alignment with the PMI standard processes and methodologies. No cutting corners!

# Proactive Project Managers

The PMP exam expects project managers to be proactive leaders who anticipate problems and take action swiftly. You are not passive or reactive but rather someone who does the following:

- Takes ownership of issues.
- Actively engages in resolving challenges.
- Directly addresses risks to avoid escalation.

This proactive approach ensures that the project stays on track and aligns with its objectives.

## Conflict Resolution

Conflicts within the team or with stakeholders should initially be addressed by the parties involved, without your direct intervention. Your role as the project manager is to observe and only intervene if the conflict starts to affect the project's performance or deliverables negatively. When dealing with sponsors or senior executives, collaboration and problem-solving are the preferred approaches. In these cases, focus on resolutions that prioritize their needs while maintaining the project's goals and objectives and still following sound project management practices.

## Procurement

Procurement responsibilities are centralized within a procurement department or specialist. This means you should do the following:

- Defer to procurement experts for contract-related decisions or disputes.
- Focus on managing vendor performance and contract requirements within your scope.

You are not expected to directly handle legal, financial, or compliance-related procurement issues.

## Organizational Context

You are working in a multinational organization with a diverse workforce. The exam assumes you are aware of the following:

- Cultural differences and how they can impact communication, collaboration, and decision-making.
- The importance of diversity and inclusion, fostering an environment where all team members feel valued.

- >> Challenges associated with global teams, including time zone differences, virtual communication barriers, and office politics.

## Historical Information

Your organization has documented historical project data, referred to as organizational process assets (OPAs). These assets include the following:

- >> Lessons learned from past projects.
- >> Templates, guidelines, and procedures available for reuse.
- >> Historical records that can be leveraged to improve planning, estimation, and risk management.

The availability of these assets means you are not starting from scratch and can build on previous successes — and failures.

## Absolute Statements

The PMP Exam often includes tricky wording in answer choices. Be cautious of options containing words like *always*, *never*, *only*, or *must* as they are generally not the most correct PMI answer.

- >> Watch out for these absolutes, as they often oversimplify complex project scenarios.
- >> Avoid answers that lack nuance or adaptability — the PMI framework values contextual decision-making and flexibility.
- >> Look for balanced and practical solutions and answer options that align with PMI principles.

## Change Control

For predictive (waterfall) projects, change control procedures are being followed rigorously. These include the following:

- » Ensuring all changes to the project scope, schedule, or budget are formally documented, reviewed, and approved.
- » Deferring to a Change Control Board (CCB) or similar governance body for major change decisions.
- » Maintaining strict adherence to baseline plans unless approved changes are implemented.

This ensures that the project stays aligned with its original objectives. Random scope changes are not okay.

# Agile Environment

In an Agile environment, the exam assumes you are working as a facilitator and coach, empowering the team rather than directing them. Your role includes the following responsibilities:

- » Responding to change over following a plan as new requirements or challenges emerge.
- » Encouraging collaboration, self-organization, and cross-functionality within the team.
- » Facilitating ceremonies like sprint planning, retrospectives, and daily stand-ups while maintaining focus on delivering value.

Your primary responsibility is to support the team, remove impediments, and foster continuous improvement. Think less "boss" and more "cheerleader" and reap the benefits of a self-organized team.

# Index

## A

AC (actual cost), 297, 299–300
acceptance strategies, 233
accountability, of PMs, 70–71
active acceptance, 233
active listening, 138
activity attributes, 190–191, 253
activity dependencies, 190–191
activity lists, 189, 193, 253
actual cost (AC), 297, 299–300
adaptive (Agile) project management, 339–352, 385
  adaptive *versus* Agile life cycles, 65
  Agile Inverted Triangle of Constraints, 350–351
  Agile Manifesto, 341–345
  Agile *versus* agile, 62
  ceremonies, 359–363
  Closing Process Group, 323–324
  defined, 60, 62–63
  Executing Process Group, 262, 268, 274, 279–285
  frameworks for, 347–350
  historical overview of, 340
  Initiating Process Group, 166–168
  life cycle of, 345–347
  mindset of, 345
  Monitoring and Controlling Process Group, 313–314
  overview, 61
  Planning Process Group, 176, 185–187, 201, 205, 215, 223–225, 234, 241, 256–257
  product owners, 105
  project artifacts, 363–369
  selecting, 65
  teams, 143–144, 353–358
adjourning (mourning) stage of Tuckman Ladder, 130
Agile (adaptive; change-driven) life cycles, 65
Agile Inverted Triangle of Constraints, 350–351
Agile Manifesto, 340–345
  communication, 223–224
  four paired values of, 342
  scenarios, 344–345, 351–352
  Twelve Principles of, 342–344
*Agile Practice Guide*, 353–354
Agile project management. *See* adaptive project management
Agile Unified Process (Agile UP), 349
Airbnb, 368
analogous (top-down) estimating, 193, 204
Angelou, Maya, 1
appraisal costs, 212
assumption logs, 156, 185, 203, 253
authoritative leadership style, 147
autocratic decision-making, 125
avoidance strategies, 232

## B

BAC (budget at completion), 297
backlog management, 313–314
  backlog grooming, 363
  backlog refinement, 224

backlog management *(continued)*
  iteration (sprint) backlogs, 346, 366
  iterative scheduling with a backlog, 201
  product backlogs, 280, 362–365
  risk-adjusted backlogs, 280
Barnes, Martin, 350
baselines, 246, 251
basic communication model, 218–219
basis of estimates, 253
benchmarking, 181
benefit cost ratio (BCR), 153
benefit measurement methods (comparative approach), 153–154, 168
Benefits Management Plan
  Closing Process Group, 327–328
  components of, 152
  identifying stakeholders, 157
  Initiating Process Group, 152
  project charters, 155
bid documents, 237
bidder conferences, 276
Big Five Personality Model (OCEAN), 121
Big Visible Charts (BVCs), 281
bottom-up estimating, 194, 204
brain dumps (cheat sheet notes), 30
brain writing, 157
brainstorming, 157, 180, 219, 227
breakdown structures, 119
  defined, 255
  organizational, 119
  resource, 119, 255
  risk, 227–228, 255
  work, 119, 183–185
breaks, 24–25
Bridges, William, 332–333
budget at completion (BAC), 297

budgeting, 73, 203–205
built-in quality, 280
burn charts, 280, 282–283
business cases, 151–152, 323, 327–328
Business Environment domain, 22–23
business value, 150–151
business-based measurement methods, 153
buyers
  Control Procurements process, 310
  defined, 235
BVCs (Big Visible Charts), 281

# C

capacity planning, 144
CAPM (Certified Associate in Project Management) certification, 17
cause-and-effect (Ishikawa; fishbone) diagrams, 304–305
caves and commons, 225
CCBs (change control boards), 248, 290
*CCR (Continuing Certification Requirements) Handbook*, 34–37
celebration meetings, 324
centralized management and leadership, 146
Certified Associate in Project Management (CAPM) certification, 17
CFDs (cumulative flow diagrams), 283–284
change control boards (CCBs), 248, 290
Change Control plan, 248–250
  Configuration Management Plan *versus*, 249–250, 258
  defined, 248
  integrated change control, 290
  key elements of, 248
  Project Management Plan and, 252

change logs, 249, 254, 290, 323
change management, 329–334, 384–385
  Change Control Plan, 248–250, 252, 258, 290
  change control systems, 290
  Change Management Model, 333
  Change Management Plan, 248–250, 334
  frameworks and models for, 330–334
  Perform Integrated Change Control process, 289–293
  as strategy, 329–330
change requests (CRs)
  Change Control Plan, 250
  Control Costs process, 301
  Control Procurements process, 312
  Control Quality process, 306
  Control Resources process, 307
  Control Schedule process, 296
  Control Scope process, 294
  Direct and Manage Project Work process, 263
  Monitor and Control Project Work process, 289
  Monitor Communications process, 308
  Monitor Risks process, 309
  Monitor Stakeholder Engagement process, 313
  Perform Integrated Change Control process, 290–292
  Project Management Plan, 253
change-driven (adaptive; Agile) life cycles, 65
change-driven approach. *See* adaptive project management
channel partner value, 151
cheat sheet notes (brain dumps), 30
check sheets, 303

choosing approaches, 63–65
claims administration, 310
close-out reporting meetings, 324
Closing Process Group, 317–335
  Benefits Management Plan, 327–328
  business case, 327–328
  change management, 329–334
  Close Project or Phase process, 320–324
  defined, 12, 318
  final project reports, 325–326
  lessons learned registers, 326–327
  reasons why projects end, 318–320
  transition planning, 329
  value delivery, 334–335
coaching
  Agile coaches, 358
  coaching leadership style, 146
  as interpersonal skill, 138–139
  as knowledge-sharing tool, 266
  team development through, 126–127, 147
code of accounts, 184
Collect Requirements process, 179–182
  requirements traceability matrices, 181–182
  tools and techniques used in, 180–181
communication management
  in adaptive environment, 223–225
  communication matrices, 220–221
  communication models and methods, 218–220
  communication requirements analysis, 217
  communication types, 221–223
  Communications Management Plan, 220, 252

communication management *(continued)*
  Manage Communications process, 279
  Monitor Communications process, 307–308
  Plan Communication Management process, 215–225
  responsibility of PMs, 71
  virtual co-location, 120
Communications Management Knowledge Area, 13
communities of practice, 266
comparative approach (benefit measurement methods), 153–154, 168
competitive advantage, value creation and, 66
complex communication model, 218–219
compliance-related risks, 227
Conduct Procurements process, 275–278
  awarding contracts, 275
  integrating vendors, 277–278
  obtaining seller responses, 275
  selecting sellers, 275
  selecting vendors, 275–277
Configuration Management Plan, 249–250
  Change Control Plan *versus*, 249–250, 258
  defined, 249
  integrated change control, 290
  Project Management Plan and, 252
conflict management, 140–143, 383
  in adaptive environment, 142
  approaches to, 141
  as interpersonal skill, 137
  scenario, 143, 147–148
  typical causes of conflict, 140–141
constrained optimization (mathematical model techniques), 153
construction projects, 57

context diagrams, 181
contingency plans, 270–271
contingency reserves, 195, 271–273, 296
*Continuing Certification Requirements* (*CCR*) *Handbook*, 34–37
continuous improvement, 274
contractors, as drivers of product delivery, 108
contracts
  changes to, 310–311
  Conduct Procurements process, 275
  contract change control systems, 311
  disputes, 310
  elements of, 277
  legally binding, 276–277
  negotiating, 276, 310
  risk management, 271–272
  termination of, 311
  types of, 238–240
control accounts, 183
control charts, 304
Control Costs process, 296–301
  earned value management, 297–300
  overall financial health assessment, 300–301
Control Procurements process, 310–312
Control Quality process, 303–307
  outputs of, 306
  tools for, 303–306
Control Resources process, 307
Control Schedule process, 295–296
Control Scope process, 294
controlling PMOs, 93, 95–96
CoQ (cost of quality), 211–213
Cornell Method, 375
corrective actions, 291
cost aggregation, 204

cost baselines, 204–205, 251
cost estimates, 254
cost forecasts, 254, 300
cost management
  Control Costs process, 296–301
  Cost Management Plan, 202, 252
  Estimate Costs process, 202–203
  Plan Cost Management process, 202–205
  triple constraints of project management, 176–177
Cost Management Knowledge Area, 13
cost of conformance, 212
cost of non-conformance, 212
cost of quality (CoQ), 211–213
cost performance index (CPI), 299–300
Cost Plus Award Fee (CPAF) contracts, 239
Cost Plus Fixed Fee (CPFF) contracts, 239
Cost Plus Incentive Fee (CPIF) contracts, 239
cost savings, value creation and, 66
cost variance (CV), 299–300
cost-benefit analysis, 153
cost-reimbursable contract types, 239
cost-related risks, 226
CPAF (Cost Plus Award Fee) contracts, 239
CPFF (Cost Plus Fixed Fee) contracts, 239
CPI (cost performance index), 299–300
CPIF (Cost Plus Incentive Fee) contracts, 239
CPM (critical path method), 196–197, 295
crashing, 199
Create WBS process, 183–185
critical path method (CPM), 196–197, 295
critical thinking, 136
cross-functional teams, 355–356
CRs. *See* change requests
cultural awareness, 139

cumulative flow diagrams (CFDs), 283–284
customer experience, value creation and, 67
customer representatives. *See* product owners
customer value, 151
customer wrap-up meetings, 324
customers
  defined, 106
  as drivers of product delivery, 105–106
  as drivers of value delivery, 68
CV (cost variance), 299–300

# D

DA (Disciplined Agile), 349
daily stand-ups (daily Scrums), 215, 224, 280, 346, 361
data-related responsibilities of PMs, 71
de facto standards, 214
de jure standards, 214
decision tree analysis, 231
decision-making
  in adaptive environment, 285
  groups and teams, 125, 180
  iterative, 313–314
defect repairs, 291
Define Activities process, 189–190
Define Scope process, 182
definitive estimates, 203
Determine Budget process, 204–205
Develop Schedule process, 196–201
  in adaptive environment, 201
  primary outputs of, 200–201
  project management information systems, 200–201
  schedule network analysis, 196–200
Develop Team process, 278

development approaches. *See also* adaptive project management
  choosing, 63–65
  defined, 62
  hybrid, 60, 62–63
  incremental, 61, 64
  iterative, 61, 64
  methodologies *versus*, 62–63
  predictive, 60–61, 63–64
  Project Management Plan and, 252
diagnostic information, 25
Direct and Manage Project Work process, 261–264
  implementing approved changes, 263
  issue tracking and resolution, 261–262
  work performance summaries, 263–264
Direction of Influence, 159
directive PMOs, 93, 95–96
DISC personality assessment tool, 121
Disciplined Agile (DA), 349
discretionary dependencies (soft logic; preferential/preferred logic), 190
distributed management and leadership, 146
diversity, on project teams, 127–128, 383–384
document analysis, 181
dot voting, 285
Dropbox, 367
duration estimates, 254
Dynamic Systems Development Method (DSDM), 349

# E

EAC (estimate at completion), 300
earned value analysis (EVA). *See* earned value management
earned value (EV), 297
earned value management (EVM), 297–300
  actual costs, 297
  budget at completion, 297
  earned value, 297
  overall financial health assessment, 300
  planned value, 297
  schedule performance assessment, 297–299
Education PDUs, 35–36
EEFs (enterprise environmental factors), 99–101, 174
efficiency, value creation and, 66
8-Step Model, 331
emotional intelligence, 137
employee knowledge, 151
EMV (Expected Monetary Value), 272–273
end users
  defined, 106
  as drivers of product delivery, 105–106
enhancement strategies, 233
enterprise environmental factors (EEFs), 99–101, 174
environmental-related risks, 227
epics, 280
Estimate Activity Durations process, 193–194
Estimate Activity Resources process, 243
estimate at completion (EAC), 300
Estimate Costs process, 202–203
estimate to complete (ETC), 300
estimating techniques, 203–204
EV (earned value), 297
EVA (earned value analysis). *See* earned value management
evaluation
  applying project management principles in, 73
  Change Control Plan, 248

EVM. *See* earned value management
Executing Process Group, 259–286
  in adaptive environment, 279–285
  Conduct Procurements process, 275–278
  defined, 12, 260
  Develop Team process, 278
  Direct and Manage Project Work process, 261–264
  Manage Communications process, 279
  Manage Project Knowledge process, 264–269
  Manage Quality process, 269–270
  Manage Stakeholder Engagement process, 279
  Manage Team process, 278–279
  Plan Procurement Management process, 275
  processes in, 261
  risk management, 270–274
Expected Monetary Value (EMV), 272–273
expert judgment
  budget determination through, 204
  identifying stakeholders through, 157
  Plan Communication Management process, 216–217
explicit knowledge, 265
exploitation strategies, 232
external dependencies, 190–191
external failure costs, 212
Extreme Programming (XP), 348
extrinsic motivation, 133–134

# F

facilitated workshops, 180
fallback plans, 270–271
fast tracking, 199

fees
  credential renewal, 37
  exam, 19, 21, 24
financial-based measurement methods, 153–154
financing, budget determination through, 204
finish to finish (FF) precedence relationship, 191
finish to start (FS) precedence relationship, 191
Firm Fixed Price (FFP) contracts, 238
fishbone (cause-and-effect; Ishikawa) diagrams, 304–305
fishbowl windows, 144, 225
Fist of Five, 285
5Cs of written communication, 222–223
5Rs of note taking, 375
Fixed Price Plus Incentive Fee (FPIF) contracts, 238
Fixed Price with Economic Price Adjustment (FPEPA) contracts, 238
fixed-price contracts, 238–239
flashcards, 30
float (slack), 197–198
focus groups, 180
forming stage of Tuckman Ladder, 129
formulas, 29–30
FPEPA (Fixed Price with Economic Price Adjustment) contracts, 238
FPIF (Fixed Price Plus Incentive Fee) contracts, 238
Franklin, Benjamin, 213
free float, 197–198
frequent feedback loops, 280
FS (finish to start) precedence relationship, 191

functional managers, 68, 108
functional structure, 69
funding limit reconciliation, 204

# G

Giving Back PDUs, 36–37
gold plating, 187, 295
governance
    determining how much is needed, 94–96
    as driver of value delivery, 68
    organizational governance, 91–92
    project governance, 92
government projects, 58
grade, defined, 209
ground rules, 124–125
group creativity techniques, 180
group decision-making techniques, 180
*Guide to the Project Management Body of Knowledge, A.* See PMBOK Guide

# H

hard (mandatory) dependencies (hard logic), 190
healthcare projects, 57
Herzberg, Frederick, 135
Herzberg's Two-Factor Theory, 135
histograms, 305
historical information reviews, 204, 384
human resources, 117–119
hybrid approach to project management, 60, 62–63
hygiene factors, 135

# I

Identify Risk process, 227–228
IFBs (Invitations for Bid), 237
impediments boards, 262
incremental approach to project management, 61, 64
independent cost estimates, 276
individual-level knowledge, 264
influence diagrams, 231
influencing, defined, 137
information radiators, 168, 281, 285
information technology (IT) projects, 56–57
Initiating Process Group, 12, 149–169
    Benefits Management Plan, 152
    business cases, 151–152
    defined, 12
    prioritizing projects, 153–154
    processes in, 150
    project charters, 155
    stakeholders, 155–169
innovation, value creation and, 67
in-person exams, 27
inspections, for quality control, 303
intangible benefits, 150
Integration Management Knowledge Area, 13–14
interactive communication model, 218–219
internal dependencies, 191
internal failure costs, 212
internal rate of return (IRR), 154
interpersonal skills, 136–143
    active listening, 138
    coaching, 138–139
    conflict management, 137, 140–143
    critical thinking, 136
    cultural awareness, 139
    emotional intelligence, 137
    influencing, 137
    motivation, 137

negotiating, 138
political awareness, 139
team building, 138
interviews, 180
intrinsic motivation, 132–133
intuition aspect of project management, 60
Invitations for Bid (IFBs), 237
IRR (internal rate of return), 154
I-shaped team members, 355
Ishikawa (cause-and-effect; fishbone) diagrams, 304–305
issue logs, 164, 254, 261–262
issue owners, 262
issues
  defined, 261
  risks *versus*, 262
  tracking and resolution, 261–262
IT (information technology) projects, 56–57
iterations (sprints), 79–80. *See also* sprints
  backlogs, 346, 366
  planning, 360–361
  retrospectives, 224, 347, 362
  reviews, 167, 224, 361–362
iterative approach to project management, 61, 64
iterative decision-making, 313–314
iterative development, 215, 280
iterative scheduling with a backlog, 201

## J
job rotation, 266
job shadowing, 180–181

## K
Kaizen, 269
kanban boards, 282

Kanban Method, 349
Kano analysis, 186
key stakeholders, defined, 108
kickoff meetings, 253
kill points, 83
Knowledge Areas, 13–14
Kotter, John, 331

## L
lags, 192–193
Large Scale Scrum (LeSS), 349
leadership
  approaches to, 146–147
  characteristics of, 145
  management *versus*, 122–123
  real-world demonstration of, 123
leads, 192–193
Leas, Speed B., 142
LeSS (Large Scale Scrum), 349
lessons learned
  meetings, 266, 324
  registers, 254, 274, 323, 326–327
Lewin, Kurt, 333
LinkedIn Learning, 37
lists
  activity, 189, 193, 253
  defined, 255
  milestone, 190, 254
  prompt, 227
logs
  assumption, 156, 185, 203, 253
  change, 249, 254, 290, 323
  defined, 255
  issue, 164, 254, 261–262
Louisiana State University, 375

# M

majority voting technique, 125
make-or-buy analysis, 235, 275
Manage Communications process, 279
Manage Project Knowledge process, 264–269
  explicit *versus* tacit knowledge, 265–266
  knowledge levels, 264–265
  knowledge-sharing tools and techniques, 266–267
  project artifacts, 267–269
Manage Quality process, 269–270
Manage Stakeholder Engagement process, 279
Manage Team process, 278–279
management plans, 251–252
management reserves, 195, 273, 296
management reviews, 252
mandatory (hard) dependencies (hard logic), 190
marketing projects, 57
Maslow, Abraham, 134
Maslow's Hierarchy of Needs, 134–135
massive open online courses (MOOCs), 26
mathematical model techniques (constrained optimization), 153
matrices
  communication, 220–221
  defined, 255
  matrix structure, 69
  probability and impact, 229–230
  requirements traceability, 181–182, 255
  responsibility assignment, 121–122, 255
  stakeholder engagement assessment, 162–163, 255
McClelland, David, 135
McClelland's Theory of Needs, 135
McGregor, Douglas, 135
memorization, 12, 29–31
mentoring
  Agile coaches, 358
  as knowledge-sharing tool, 266
  team development through, 126–127, 147
methodologies, defined, 62–63
milestone lists, 190, 254
minimal marketable feature (MMF), 367
minimum viable product (MVP), 367–368
mitigation strategies, 232
Monitor and Control Project Work process, 289
Monitor Communications process, 307–308
Monitor Risks process, 308–309
Monitor Stakeholder Engagement process, 312–313
monitoring, applying project management principles in, 73
Monitoring and Controlling Process Group, 287–315
  in adaptive environment, 313–314
  Control Costs process, 296–301
  Control Procurements process, 310–312
  Control Quality process, 303–307
  Control Resources process, 307
  Control Schedule process, 295–296
  Control Scope process, 294
  defined, 12, 288
  Monitor and Control Project Work process, 289
  Monitor Communications process, 307–308
  Monitor Risks process, 308–309
  Monitor Stakeholder Engagement process, 312–313

Perform Integrated Change Control process, 289–293
processes in, 288–289
Validate Scope process, 294
Monte Carlo simulations, 231
Montgomery GI Bill, 19
MOOCs (massive open online courses), 26
MoSCoW technique, 187
motivation, 132–136
　defined, 132
　extrinsic, 133–134
　as interpersonal skill, 137
　intrinsic, 132–133
　motivational theories, 134–136
　recognition, 133–134
　rewards, 133–134
mourning (adjourning) stage of Tuckman Ladder, 130
multicriteria decision analysis, 125
MVP (minimum viable product), 367–368
Myers-Briggs Type Indicators, 121

# N

needs assessments, 150
negative float, 198
negotiations
　acquiring resources, 118
　contract disputes, 310
　defined, 138
　finalizing contract terms, 276
net present value (NPV), 153
networking, as knowledge-sharing tool, 267
noise, 218
Nonaka, I., 340
norming stage of Tuckman Ladder, 129

# O

objectives, 54, 73, 319
OBSs (organizational breakdown structures), 119
OCEAN (Big Five Personality Model), 121
on-demand scheduling, 201
100-point method, 187
online exams, 27–28
OnVUE online proctoring, 27
OPAs. *See* organizational process assets
operations, projects *versus*, 54–55, 91
operations management, 90–91
operations managers, 108
OPM. *See* organizational project management
opportunity cost, 153
organizational breakdown structures (OBSs), 119
organizational governance, 91–92
Organizational Knowledge Repositories category of OPAs, 98
organizational process assets (OPAs), 98–101
　defined, 98
　EEFs *versus*, 99–100
　as knowledge-sharing tool, 269
　Organizational Knowledge Repositories, 98
　Plan Quality Management process, 210
　Processes, Policies, and Procedures, 98
　Project Management Plan, 174
　updates to, 309, 312
organizational project management (OPM), 88–93
　defined, 88
　organizational *versus* project governance, 91–92

organizational project management (OPM) *(continued)*
  portfolios, 90
  programs, 89
  Project Management Offices *versus*, 92–93
  projects, 89
  purpose of, 88
organizational structures, 68–70, 382
organizational-level knowledge, 265
osmotic communication, 224–225
Ouchi, William, 136
overall financial health assessment, 300–301

# P

pair programming, 266
paired comparison, 186
parametric estimating, 193, 204
Pareto charts, 305
passing score, 25
passive acceptance, 233
payback period, 153
PDM (precedence diagramming method), 191
PDSA (Plan-Do-Study-Act), 340
PDUs. *See* Professional Development Units
Pearson VUE testing centers, 27–28
People domain, 22
percent complete, 296
Perform Integrated Change Control process, 289–293
  causes of change, 289–290
  change requests, 291–292
  key concepts in, 290
  version control, 292–293
  workflow, 292

Perform Qualitative Risk Analysis process, 228–230
  probability and impact matrices, 229–230
  risk registers, 230
  risk reports, 230
Perform Quantitative Risk Analysis process, 230–232
performance measurement baseline, 297
performance reviews, 303
performing stage of Tuckman Ladder, 129
personas, 167
PESTEL prompt list, 227
phase entrances and exits, 83
phase gate (stage gate) reviews, 80, 83, 324
phased estimates, 203
physical resources, 116–117
Plan Communication Management process, 215–225
  in adaptive environment, 223–225
  communication matrices, 220–221
  communication methods, 219–220
  communication models, 218–219
  communication types, 222
  Communications Management Plan, 220
  5Cs of written communication, 222–223
  tools and techniques for, 216–218
Plan Cost Management process, 202–205
  in adaptive environment, 205
  Cost Management Plan, 202
  Determine Budget process, 204–205
  Estimate Costs process, 202–203
  estimating techniques, 203–204
Plan Procurement Management process, 234–241
  in adaptive environment, 241
  contract types, 238–240

make-or-buy analysis, 235
plan procurement management process, 234
procurement integration, 240–241
Procurement Management Plan, 236
procurement strategy, 236–237
terminology, 235
Plan Quality Management process, 209–215
  in adaptive environment, 215
  Control Quality process, 210–211
  defined, 209
  Manage Quality process, 210
  Quality Management Plan, 211–215
  terminology, 209
Plan Resource Management process, 242–243
Plan Risk Management process, 225–234
  in adaptive environment, 234
  Identify Risk process, 227–228
  Perform Qualitative Risk Analysis process, 228–230
  Perform Quantitative Risk Analysis process, 230–232
  Plan Risk Responses process, 232–233
  Risk Management Plan, 225–228
  types of risk, 227
Plan Risk Responses process, 232–233
Plan Schedule Management process, 188–201
  Define Activities process, 189–190
  Develop Schedule process, 196–201
  Estimate Activity Durations process, 193–194
  identifying activity dependencies, 190–191
  leads and lags, 192–193
  reserve analysis, 195–196

  Schedule Management Plan, 188
  Sequence Activities process, 191–192
Plan Scope Management process, 176–188
  in adaptive environment, 185–187
  Collect Requirements process, 179–182
  Create WBS process, 183–185
  Define Scope process, 182
  project *versus* product scope, 177–178
  Requirements Management Plan, 178–179
  Scope Management Plan, 178
  staying within boundaries, 187–188
Plan Stakeholder Engagement process, 243–244
Plan-Do-Study-Act (PDSA), 340
plan-driven approach. *See* predictive project management
planned value (PV), 297
planning, applying project management principles in, 73
planning package, 183
planning poker, 280–281
Planning Process Group, 171–205, 207–258
  defined, 12
  Estimate Activity Resources process, 243
  Plan Communication Management process, 215–225
  Plan Cost Management process, 202–205
  Plan Procurement Management process, 234–241
  Plan Quality Management process, 209–215
  Plan Resource Management process, 242–243
  Plan Risk Management process, 225–234
  Plan Schedule Management process, 188–201

Index   399

Planning Process Group *(continued)*
  Plan Scope Management process, 176–188
  Plan Stakeholder Engagement process, 243–244
  processes in, 172–173, 208–209
  project integration management, 246–255
  Project Management Plan, 174–177, 245–247
plurality voting technique, 125
*PMBOK Guide (A Guide to the Project Management Body of Knowledge)*, 23
  Agile *versus* agile, 62
  Change Control Plan *versus* Change Management Plan, 248
  defined, 23
  importance of, 23
  process domain, 22
  product management definition, 78
  project life cycle/development approach, 63
  project management definition, 60
  as source of exam content, 11
  stakeholder engagement, 156
  tailoring, 83
PMI. *See* Project Management Institute
PMI Talent Triangle, 9–11
  defined, 9
  PMP Exam domains and, 9–10
  Power Skills element, 9–10, 123, 247
  Strategic Business Acumen element, 10–11, 248
  Ways of Working element, 10, 247
PMISs (project management information systems), 200–201
PMOs. *See* Project Management Offices
PMP. *See* Project Management Professional credential; Project Management Professional Exam
PMs. *See* project managers
political awareness, 139
portfolio managers, as drivers of product delivery, 109
portfolios, 90
Post-9/11 GI Bill benefits, 19
potentially shippable product increment (product increment), 366–367
Power Interest Grid, 159
power skills, 122–123, 136–143
Power Skills element, 35, 247
preassignment, 118
precedence diagramming method (PDM), 191
precedence relationships, 191
precision aspect of project management, 60
predecessor tasks, 191–192
predictive (waterfall) project management
  defined, 60, 63
  overview, 61
  project artifacts, 267
  Project Management Plan in, 176
  selecting, 65
preferential/preferred logic (discretionary dependencies; soft logic), 190
preferred vendors, 238, 275
prevention costs, 212
preventive actions, 291
private sector projects, 58
private social media groups, 267
proactivity of PMs, 382–383
probability and impact matrices, 229–230
Process domain, 22

Process Groups, 12–13
  Closing, 12, 317–335
  defined, 12
  Executing, 12, 259–286
  Initiating, 12, 149–169
  Monitoring and Controlling, 12, 287–315
  Planning, 12, 171–205, 207–258
  project phases *versus*, 12
Processes, Policies, and Procedures category of OPAs, 98
procurement department, 235, 383
procurement management
  Conduct Procurements process, 275–278
  Control Procurements process, 310–312
  Plan Procurement Management process, 234–241
  Procurement Management Plan, 236, 252, 275
Procurement Management Knowledge Area, 13
procurement strategy, 236–237, 275
product backlogs, 280, 362–365
product increment (potentially shippable product increment), 366–367
product life cycle, 75–76, 78–79
product management, 74–80
  defined, 74
  product life cycle, 75–76, 78–79
  products, defined, 77–78
  programs, defined, 78
  project phases, 79–80
  projects, defined, 77–78
  roles of managers, 76–77
product managers, 76–77
product owners
  Agile teams, 356

  as drivers of product delivery, 105
  as drivers of value delivery, 68
product roadmaps, 280, 363
products, defined, 77–78
professional development plans, 37–39
  creating, 37–39
  lack of, 38–39
Professional Development Units (PDUs), 33–37
  defined, 35
  Education category, 35–36
  Giving Back category, 36–37
  professional development plans, 37–39
program managers, as drivers of product delivery, 108–109
programs, 78, 89
progressive elaboration, 81–82, 175
project artifacts. *See also names of specific artifacts*
  in adaptive environment, 268, 363–369
  defined, 116
  managing, 267–269
  most common, 267–268
  in procurement planning, 241
  in project closure, 323
  in stakeholder engagement, 312
project calendars, 254
project charters
  in adaptive environment, 166–167, 364
  in Close Project or Phase process, 323
  components of, 155
  in Initiating Process Group, 155
  in Project Management Plan, 174
project communications. *See* communication management
project float, 198

project governance, 92
project initiation, 149–169
project life cycle descriptions, 252
project management
  applying principles of, 72–74
  continuum of, 60–65
  defined, 60
  intuition aspect of, 60
  methodologies, 62–63
  precision aspect of, 60
  product management *versus*, 74–80
  progressive elaboration, 81–82
  project life cycle, 63
  projects, 53–58
  roles that drive project delivery, 103–110
  rolling wave planning, 82
  tailoring, 83
  value delivery, 65–70
project management information systems (PMISs), 200–201
Project Management Institute (PMI), 8–9
  *CCR Handbook*, 34–37
  Code of Ethics and Professional Conduct, 18
  continuing education credits, 33
  defined, 8
  Global Accreditation Center for Project Management Education Programs, 16
  lexicon, 13, 32
  *PMBOK Guide*, 11, 23
  PMI Talent Triangle, 9–11
  PMISs, 200
  Role Delineation Study, 22
Project Management Offices (PMOs), 92–93
  controlling, 93, 95–96
  defined, 92
  directive, 93, 95–96
  as drivers of value delivery, 68
  scenarios, 93–94
  supportive, 93, 96
Project Management Plan, 174–177, 250–255
  in adaptive environment, 256–257
  approving, 253
  baselines, 251
  key inputs for, 174
  management plans, 251–252
  predictive *versus* adaptive projects, 176
  project documents related to, 253–255
  techniques used in, 175
  triple constraints of project management, 176–177
  updates to, 294, 296, 300, 306–309, 312–313
project management processes, 11–12. *See also names of specific processes*
Project Management Professional (PMP) credential, 7–8
  earnings differences for holders of, 18
  lapsed, 39–40
  maintaining, 33–39
Project Management Professional (PMP) Exam. *See also* Process Groups
  acronyms, 379–380
  applying for, 18–21
  arriving late, 28
  assumptions to make about questions in, 381–385
  breaks, 24–25
  diagnostic information, 25
  domains of, 9–10, 21–23
  dos and don'ts of, 30
  effects of, 17–18
  ensuring continued relevance, 22

Exam Content Outline, 11, 21, 374
fee for, 19, 21, 24
Knowledge Areas, 13–14
locations, 27–28
mindset for, 29
passing score, 25
pre-assessment, 41–49
preparing for, 25–26, 30, 374
project management processes, 11–12
questions, 24–25, 31–32
results, 25
sources of content, 11
standards and requirements for, 9, 15–17, 19–20
survey following, 25
time allotted for, 24
tips for, 373–378
tutorial preceding, 25
project management teams, 107, 115
project managers (PMs), 70–74
  alternative names for, 71–72
  as drivers of product delivery, 104
  as drivers of value delivery, 68
  proactivity of, 382–383
  product managers *versus*, 76–77
  project integration responsibilities, 247
  responsibilities of, 70–71
project phases (iterations; sprints), 79–80
project schedule network diagrams, 254
project schedules, 200–201, 256. *See also* schedule management
project scope. *See* scope
project selection techniques, 151
project teams. *See* teams
project-level knowledge, 264
project-oriented (projectized) structure, 69
projects, 53–58
  defined, 54–55, 77–78
  deliverables, 54
  industries, 56–58
  objectives, 54
  operations *versus*, 54–55, 91
  in organizational project management, 89
  products, 54
  reasons for, 55–56
  results, 54
  services, 54
prompt lists, 227
proposal evaluation, 276
Prosci ADKAR model, 330–331
prototypes, 181
psychological safety, 127
pull communication, 219
punctuality, 27
push communication, 219
PV (planned value), 297

# Q

quality management
  continuous improvement, 269
  Plan Quality Management process, 209–215, 269–270
  quality, defined, 209
  quality assurance, 71, 280
  quality audits, 269
  quality control measurements, 254, 306
  quality metrics, 254
  quality reports, 254
Quality Management Knowledge Area, 13
Quality Management Plan, 211–215
  cost of quality, 211–213
  Manage Quality process, 269–270
  Project Management Plan and, 252

Quality Management Plan *(continued)*
  quality metrics, 213
  satisfying stakeholder requirements, 214
  standards and regulations, 214–215
questionnaires
  Collect Requirements process, 180
  identifying stakeholders through, 157

# R

RACI charts, 121–122, 254
RAMs (responsibility assignment matrices), 121–122, 255
Rational Unified Process (RUP), 349
RBSs
  resource breakdown structures, 119, 255
  risk breakdown structures, 227–228, 255
recognition, 133–134
registers, defined, 255
regulations, defined, 214
remote pairing, 144, 225
reports
  defined, 255
  final project, 325–326
  risk, 230, 255, 273, 323
  work performance, 289
representations of uncertainty, 231
Requests for Information (RFIs), 237
Requests for Proposal (RFPs), 237, 275
Requests for Quotation (RFQs), 237, 275
requirements
  Collect Requirements process, 179–182
  common, 179
  defined, 179
  documentation of, 254
  estimating resource requirements, 117

Requirements Management Plan, 178–179, 251
requirements traceability matrices, 181–182, 255
satisfying stakeholder requirements, 214
reserve analysis, 195–196, 204, 271–272, 296, 308
residual risk, 270, 272
resource breakdown structures (RBSs), 119, 255
resource calendars, 119, 255
resource leveling, 199
Resource Management Knowledge Area, 13
Resource Management Plan, 115–119
  acquiring resources, 117–119
  estimating resource requirements, 117
  human resources, 116
  physical resources, 116
  Project Management Plan and, 252
  releasing resources, 119
  typical resource scenario, 114–115
resource optimization techniques, 198, 295
resource requirements documents, 255
resource smoothing (time-constrained optimization), 198–199
resource-related risks, 227
resources
  Control Resources process, 307
  Estimate Activity Resources process, 243
  human, 116–119
  physical, 116–117
  Resource Management Plan, 115–119
responsibility assignment matrices (RAMs), 121–122, 255
results, 25

retail projects, 57
retrospective meetings, 132
retrospectives, 215, 280
return on investment (ROI), 154
revenue, value creation and, 66
rewards, 133–134
RFIs (Requests for Information), 237
RFPs (Requests for Proposal), 237, 275
RFQs (Requests for Quotation), 237, 275
risk breakdown structures (RBSs), 227–228, 255
risk burndown charts, 280
risk management, 270–274
  in adaptive environment, 274, 280
  evaluating risks, 73
  Identify Risk process, 227–228
  issues *versus* risks, 262
  management reserves, 273
  Monitor Risks process, 308–309
  monitoring and controlling project work, 313
  Perform Qualitative Risk Analysis process, 228–230
  Perform Quantitative Risk Analysis process, 230–232
  Plan Risk Management process, 225–234
  Plan Risk Responses process, 232
  project documents, 273–274
  quantifying risks, 272–273
  real-world example, 271–272
  Risk Management Plan, 174, 225–228, 252
  risk owners, 270–271
  risk registers, 230, 255, 273, 309, 323
  risk reports, 230, 255, 273, 323
  risk reviews, 308
  risk triggers, 271
  risk-adjusted backlogs, 280
  terminology, 270–271
  value creation and risk mitigation, 67
Risk Management Knowledge Area, 13
ROI (return on investment), 154
rolling wave planning, 82
Roman voting, 285
root cause analysis, 303
rough order of magnitude (ROM), 203
Royce, Winston W., 340
Rule of Seven, 304
RUP (Rational Unified Process), 349

# S

Salience Model, 160–161
Satir, Virginia, 332
Scaled Agile Framework (SAFe), 349
scatter diagrams, 305–306
schedule management
  Control Schedule process, 295–296
  Develop Schedule process, 196–201
  Plan Schedule Management process, 188–201
  project schedules, 200–201, 254
  schedule baselines, 200–201, 251
  schedule compression techniques, 199, 295
  schedule data documents, 255
  schedule forecasts, 255, 296
  Schedule Management Plan, 188, 252
  schedule network analysis, 196–200
  schedule network diagrams, 192–193, 197
  schedule-related risks, 226
  triple constraints of project management, 176–177

Schedule Management Knowledge Area, 13
schedule performance index (SPI), 297–299
schedule variance (SV), 297–299
Schwaber, Ken, 340
scope
　Control Scope process, 294
　Plan Scope Management process, 176–188
　project scope statements, 254
　project *versus* product scope, 177–178
　scope baselines, 251
　scope creep, 187, 295
　Scope Management Plan, 178, 251
　scope-related risks, 226
　staying within boundaries, 295
　triple constraints of project management, 176–177
　Validate Scope process, 294
Scope Management Knowledge Area, 13
Scrum Alliance, 340
Scrum framework, 348
Scrum masters, as drivers of value delivery, 68
Scrumban, 349
secondary risks (spin-off risks), 271
seller proposals (vendor proposals/bids), 276
sellers
　Conduct Procurements process, 275
　Control Procurements process, 310
　defined, 235
sensitivity analysis, 231
Sequence Activities process, 191–192
servant leadership style, 144, 147, 357–358
SF (start to finish) precedence relationship, 191

shareholder value, 151
sharing strategies, 233
Shewhart, Walter A., 340
Shu-Ha-Ri model, 131–132
simulations, 200, 231
slack (float), 197–198
small batch system, 215, 280
SMEs (subject matter experts), 68, 108
social value, value creation and, 67
soft logic (discretionary dependencies; preferential/preferred logic), 190
SOWs (statements of work), 236
SPI (schedule performance index), 297–299
spin-off risks (secondary risks), 271
sponsor representatives. *See* product owners
sponsors
　as drivers of product delivery, 104–105
　as drivers of value delivery, 68
sprints (iterations), 79–80, 346–347, 360
　backlogs, 346, 366
　planning, 224, 280
　retrospectives, 224, 347, 362
　reviews, 167, 224, 361–362
　sprint planning meetings, 346
　sprint review meetings, 347
SS (start to start) precedence relationship, 191
stage gate (phase gate) reviews, 80, 83, 324
stage gates, 83
Stakeholder Cube, 160
Stakeholder Management Knowledge Area, 13
stakeholders, 155–169
　analyzing, 158–161

business value and, 151
as drivers of product delivery, 109–110
engagement of, 156–157, 162–168, 243–244, 252, 255, 279, 312–313, 361–362
ensuring management of, 73
final project reports, 325
identifying, 157
key stakeholders, 108
prioritizing, 161–162
satisfaction as measure of success, 322
satisfying stakeholder requirements, 214
stakeholder registers, 157, 255
stakeholder-related risks, 227
understanding motivations and expectations of, 158
standards, in quality management, 214–215
start to finish (SF) precedence relationship, 191
start to start (SS) precedence relationship, 191
statements of work (SOWs), 236
statistical sampling, 303
storming stage of Tuckman Ladder, 129
story points, 280
storytelling, 267
Strategic Business Acumen element, 35, 248
subject matter experts (SMEs), 68, 108
successor tasks, 191–192
suppliers, as drivers of product delivery, 108
supportive PMOs, 93, 96
surveys
  Collect Requirements process, 180
  following exam, 25
  identifying stakeholders through, 157

sustainability, value creation and, 67
Sutherland, Jeff, 340
SV (schedule variance), 297–299
SWOT analysis, 121
systems view of value delivery, 66

# T

T&M (Time and Materials/Means) contracts, 240
tacit knowledge, 266
tailoring, 83, 175
Takeuchi, H., 340
tangible benefits, 150
teams, 113–148
  in adaptive environment, 143–144, 353–358
  assignments, 254
  autonomy, 313–314
  charters, 124–125, 255
  coaching, 126, 147
  considerations about composition of, 106
  contractors, 108
  coordination of, 73–74
  culture, 128
  culture of, 128
  decision-making dynamics, 125
  defined, 106
  development of, 128–132, 138, 278
  diverse and global, 127–128, 383–384
  as drivers of product delivery, 106–108
  as drivers of value delivery, 68
  facilitators of, 356–357
  functional managers, 108
  goal of, 147
  ground rules, 124–125
  interpersonal skills, 136–143
  leadership skills, 145–147

Index   407

teams *(continued)*
　　Manage Team process, 278–279
　　management *versus* leadership, 122–123
　　mentoring, 126, 147
　　motivating, 132–136
　　operations managers, 108
　　project management teams, 107, 115
　　Resource Management Plan, 115–119
　　roles and responsibilities, 121–122
　　skill and personality assessments, 121
　　subject matter experts, 108
　　suppliers, 108
　　training, 125–126, 147
　　vendors, 108
　　virtual, 119–120, 217
technical performance analysis, 309
TECOP prompt list, 227
Theories X, Y, and Z, 135
three-point estimating, 193–195, 204
time allotted for exam, 24
Time and Materials/Means (T&M) contracts, 240
timebox concept, 313–314, 347
time-constrained optimization (resource smoothing), 198–199
top-down (analogous) estimating, 193, 204
total float (total slack), 197
traditional approach. *See* predictive project management
training, team development through, 125–127, 147
transference strategies, 232
transition planning, 329
triple constraints of project management, 176–177, 350–351
T-shaped team members, 355

Tuckman, Bruce, 129
Tuckman Ladder, 129–131
tutorial preceding exam, 25

# U
Udemy, 37
unanimity voting technique, 125
updates, 291
urban planning projects, 57
U.S. Department of Defense, 340
U.S. military, 19
user stories, 167, 280, 365, 368–369

# V
VAC (variance at completion), 300
Validate Scope process, 294
value creation, 66–67
value delivery, 65–70, 313, 334–335
variance at completion (VAC), 300
velocity charts, 283–284
vendor proposals/bids (seller proposals), 276
vendors
　　as drivers of product delivery, 108
　　integrating, 277–278
　　preferred, 238, 275
　　selecting, 275–277
verbal communication, 222
verified deliverables, 306
version control, 292–293
Virginia Satir Change Model, 332
virtual co-location, 120
virtual teams, 119–120, 217
voting techniques, 125, 285
VUCA prompt list, 227

## W

waterfall project management. *See* predictive project management
Ways of Working element, 35, 247
webinars, 267
what-if scenario analysis, 199–200
William Bridges' Transition Model, 332–333
work breakdown structures (WBSs), 119
   Create WBS process, 183–185
   WBS dictionary, 184–185
work package, 183, 296
work performance information, 263–264, 289, 294, 296, 299–301, 306–309, 312–313
written communication, 222–223

## X

XP (Extreme Programming), 348

## Z

Zappos, 368
zero float, 198

# About the Author

**Crystal Richards** isn't your typical project management trainer. As the principal and owner of MindsparQ, she is on a mission to empower teams with the skills they need to tackle any project challenge head-on.

Crystal holds a master's degree in healthcare administration from the University of North Carolina at Chapel Hill and a bachelor's degree in economics from Georgetown University. She also earned graduate certificates in adult training and development (instructional systems design) and community college teaching from North Carolina State University.

A certified Project Management Professional (PMP), PMI Agile Certified Practitioner (PMI-ACP), and Certified Scrum Master, Crystal serves as adjunct faculty at the University of Maryland–College Park. There, she designed and launched an online PMP Exam Preparation program, which `Classcentral.com` has recognized as the Best University-Level PMP Exam Prep course.

Crystal has trained over 2,500 professionals to achieve their PMP and PMI-ACP credentials, equipping them to excel in project management and Agile methodologies. For more than 15 years, she has partnered with startups, healthcare organizations, nonprofits, and government agencies to improve project outcomes.

Crystal's mission is clear: to help teams sharpen their project management, communication, and leadership skills. She does more than teach the technical stuff; she's here to unlock your inner project management superhero, providing the tools, techniques, and mindset to consistently deliver with clarity, courage, and confidence

# Dedication

To my students, who inspire me every day. Your curiosity, enthusiasm, and relentless pursuit of knowledge have fueled my desire to be a better trainer, constantly challenging me to think deeper and push the boundaries of my comfort zone. You keep me on my toes, and for that, I am eternally grateful.

May this book inspire and challenge you as you have done for me, and serve as a guide to help you navigate the journey toward your PMP success.

To you, I dedicate this book.

# Author's Acknowledgments

This book is a heartfelt acknowledgement to the many people who have inspired, supported, and shaped my journey in more ways than I can express in words.

To my life partner and closest confidante, Steve: You have been my mentor, advisor, and steadfast battle buddy in all things big and small. This book would not exist without your unshakable faith in my capabilities, even when I doubted myself. Your guidance, encouragement, and love have held me steady through life's uncertainties and inspired me to continually grow into my best self.

To the PM Collective, an extraordinary group of bold and tenacious women: As small business owners with audacious goals, you've shown me the power of thinking beyond conventional limits.

To my DC Crew — Sameera, Arlene, Naheed, Alicia, Cornelius (Corn Bread), and Earl: Thank you for being my sounding board during our text exchanges and for always providing a safe and supportive space for over 20 years. The jokes, our collective celebrations, and your phenomenal cheerleading mean the world to me.

To the Wiley team, Elizabeth Stilwell and Tim Gallan: Elizabeth, I am eternally grateful that you saw something in me to represent the Wiley family of authors. I'm so glad I was Johnny on the Spot and responded to your emails! And Tim, thanks for your patience and flexibility, and for being a thoughtful partner giving me the creative space to pour into this book.

Finally, I would like to acknowledge my parents, Melvin and Hannah Crutcher, the foundation of my strength and values. To my father, who served our country with honor: You instilled in me the principles of discipline and resilience, inspiring me to be a leader, not a follower. I am forever grateful. And to my mother, the embodiment of sacrifice and love: Your strength inspires me, and your unwavering dedication serves as my guide.

Every word inked on these pages carries the imprint of your influence, the people who have shared in my journey, challenging me, supporting me, and inspiring me. This book is my humble tribute to the profound impact you've had on my life, a small token of the immense gratitude and respect I hold for each of you.

## Publisher's Acknowledgments

**Acquisitions Editor:** Elizabeth Stilwell
**Development Editor:** Tim Gallan
**Copy Editor:** Marylouise Wiack
**Production Editor:** Tamilmani Varadharaj
**Senior Managing Editor:** Kristie Pyles
**Cover Image:** © wee dezign/Shutterstock